Critical Systems Thinking
Directed Readings

Critical Systems Thinking
Directed Readings

Edited by
Robert L. Flood
and
Michael C. Jackson

Department of Management Systems and Sciences,
University of Hull, UK

JOHN WILEY & SONS
Chichester · New York · Brisbane · Toronto · Singapore

Other Wiley Editorial Offices

John Wiley & Sons, Inc., 605 Third Avenue,
New York, NY 10158-0012, USA

Jacaranda Wiley Ltd, G.P.O. Box, 859, Brisbane,
Queensland 4001, Australia

John Wiley & Sons (Canada) Ltd, 5353 Dundas Road West,
Fourth Floor, Etobicoke, Ontario M9B 6H8, Canada

John Wiley & Sons (SEA) Pte Ltd, 37 Jalan Pemimpin #05-04,
Block B, Union Industrial Building, Singapore 2057

Library of Congress Cataloguing-in-Publication Data:

Critical systems thinking: directed readings / edited by Robert L.
   Flood and Michael C. Jackson.
       p.   cm.
   Includes bibliographical references and index.
   ISBN 0-471-93098-9
   1. System analysis.   I. Flood, Robert L.   II. Jackson, Michael
C., 1951–
T57.6.C68   1992
658.4'032—dc20   91–18868
                                                             CIP

British Library Cataloguing in Publication Data:

A catalogue record for this book
is available from the British Library.

ISBN 0-471-93098-9

Typset in 9½/12pt Linotron Palatino
by Cambridge Composing (UK) Ltd, Cambridge
Printed and bound in Great Britain by Biddles Ltd, Guildford, Surrey

Contents

List of Contributors

RUSSELL L. ACKOFF

Current positions: Chairman of the Board of INTERACT: the Institute for Interactive Management, USA; Professor Emeritus of Management Science, The Wharton School of the University of Pennsylvania, USA; Anheuser-Busch Visiting Professor of Marketing, Olin School of Business, Washington University, St. Louis, USA; and Core Faculty, The Union Institute, Cincinnati, Ohio, USA.

Career: Ackoff received his undergraduate degree in Architecture (1941) and PhD in The Philosophy of Science (1947) from the University of Pennsylvania. Later at the same university he became Chairman of the Social Systems Sciences Department and the Busch Center, which specialised in systems planning, research and design. He was a Charter Member and President of the Operations Research Society of America, a Founding Member and Vice President of the Institute of Management Sciences, and has been President of the Society for General Systems Research. He received the Silver Medal of the British Operational Research Society and the George E. Kimball Medal of the Operations Research Society of America. In 1967, he was awarded an Honorary Doctorate of Science by the University of Lancaster. Ackoff's research, consultancy and educational activities have involved him in more than 300 corporations and 50 government agencies in the USA and elsewhere.

Main recent publications: Redesigning the Future, (1974), John Wiley, New York; *Creating the Corporate Future,* (1978), John Wiley, New York; *Revitalizing Western Economies,* (1984), John Wiley, New York (with Paul Broholm and Roberta Snow); *Management in Small Doses,* (1986), John Wiley, New York.

PETER B. CHECKLAND

Current positions: Professor of Systems at Lancaster University, UK; Visiting Professor, University of New England, Australia; and Visiting Professor, NW Technological University, Xiam, China.

Career: Checkland received First Class Honours in Chemistry at Oxford. He then worked for fifteen years as manager of a 100-strong research and development group in ICI. Since 1969, he has led a major research effort at Lancaster University, rethinking "systems thinking" and its use in tackling real-world problems. Checkland edits the learned *Journal of Applied Systems Analysis*.

Main recent publications: Systems Thinking, Systems Practice, (1981), John Wiley, Chichester; "Information systems and systems thinking: time to unite?" (2nd Rank Xerox Lecture), *International Journal of Information Management*, Volume 8, 1988; "Soft Systems Methodology" and "An Application of Soft Systems Methodology", in Jonathan Rosenhead (Ed.), *Rational Analysis for a Problematic World*, (1989), John Wiley, Chichester; *Soft Systems Methodology in Action*, (1990), John Wiley, Chichester (with Jim Scholes).

C. WEST CHURCHMAN

Current positions: Professor of Business Administration at the University of California, Berkeley; and Research Philosopher at the Centre for Research in Management Science.

Career: Churchman is one of the best known and respected scholars in the systems field. His career details are too extensive to be recounted. As his writing has evolved from early work in operations research through his studies of modes of inquiry, it has taken on a philosophical bent. In one sense, he has become the conscience of the systems movement, striving to engender a strong focus on morality and a continuing attention to the needs of people. In 1984 he was nominated for the Nobel Prize Award in the field of social systems.

Main recent publications: Challenge to Reason, (1968), McGraw-Hill, New York; *The Systems Approach*, (1968), Delacorte Press and Dell Publishing, New York; *The Design of Inquiring Systems: Basic Concepts of Systems and Organisation* (1971), Basic Books, New York; *The Systems Approach and its Enemies*, (1979), Basic Books, New York; *Thought and Wisdom*, (1981), Intersystems Publications, Seaside, California.

ROBERT L. FLOOD

Current positions: Sir Q.W. Lee Professor of Management Sciences, and Head of Department of Management Systems and Sciences, University of Hull, UK; Associate, PA Consulting Group, UK; and Chairman, Systems Intervention Ltd, UK.

Career: Flood worked for seven years in local government and business— three years for Berkshire Area Health Authority, three years management for Paramount Pictures, and one year in management for National Opinion Polls. He then studied for an undergraduate degree in Systems and Management, receiving First Class Honours (1983), and was awarded a PhD in Systems Science (quantitative modelling of fluid and electrolyte distribution in humans, 1985), both from City University, London. He then lectured in systems science at the City University for three years before taking up his current position. In

1988 he received (with Sionade A. Robinson) the Outstanding Scholarly Contribution Award at the International Conference on Systems and Cybernetics Research in West Germany. He is founding and current editor of the learned journal *Systems Practice*. He sits on the Learned Society Board of the Institute of Measurement and Control and is a Chartered Engineer. Flood champions critical systems thinking through education, training and consultancy in a diverse range of organisations.

Main recent publications: Dealing With Complexity: An Introduction to the Theory and Application of Systems Science, (1988), Plenum, New York, 2nd edition 1992 (with Ewart R. Carson); *Liberating Systems Theory*, (1990), Plenum, New York; "Entrepreneurship, intrapreneurship and innovativeness," Inaugural Lecture, Anniversary Speech of the NTU Peat–Marwick Entrepreneurship Development Centre in Singapore, *Entrepreneurship, Innovation and Change*, Volume 1, 1991; *Creative Problem Solving: Total Systems Intervention*, (1991), John Wiley, Chichester (with Michael C. Jackson).

RAMSÉS L. FUENMAYOR

Current positions: Associate Professor at the University of Los Andes, Venezeula; and Head of the postgraduate programme in Interpretive Systems Management and of the research group in Interpretive Systemology at the University of Los Andes.

Career: Fuenmayor received his undergraduate degree in Systems Engineering (1975) from the University of Los Andes in Venezuela, MSc in Control Systems (1978) from the University of Manchester in the UK and PhD in Systems Philosophy (1986) from Lancaster University in the UK. In 1975 he became lecturer at the University of Los Andes where he has been appointed member of the Faculty Council (1982–1984), Director of the School of Systems Engineering (1984–1987), and Head of the Research Centre in Systems of the School of Systems Engineering (1987–1988). He is a founder member of the research group in Interpretive Systemology, to become the Department of Interpretive Systemology. He has been awarded an honorary distinction twice for academic excellence by the University of Los Andes. He is a member of the International Advisory Committees of *Systems Practice* and *Sistemica*. Fuenmayor has played an active role in applying his research in more than 20 management related projects.

Main recent publications: "El Enfoque de Sistemas y el estudio de situaciones humanas: reflexiones de caracter metodologico y etico", *Ciencia e Ingineria*, Volume 18, 1981; "Esquema de una posicion onto-epistemologica para el Enfoque de Sistemas", *Sistemas*, Volume 2, 1983; *Resumen de una Teoria Sistemico–Interpretativa sobre Organizaciones* (1989), publications of the Faculty of Engineering of the University of Los Andes, Venezuela; "Systems thinking and critique: I. What is Critique?", *Systems Practice*, Volume 3, 1990.

MICHAEL C. JACKSON
Current positions: Professor of Management Systems at the University of Hull, UK; and Director of Systems Intervention Ltd, UK.

Career: Jackson studied at University College, Oxford, and in 1973 received a BA Honours degree in Politics, Philosophy and Economics. He spent four years in the civil service before returning to university and gaining an MA degree in Systems in Management from Lancaster University. In 1979 he was appointed Lecturer in Management Systems at Hull. Jackson teaches courses on systems approaches to management and has research interests in systems theory and systems methodology. He is at present (1991) Chair of the UK Systems Society. He has written and/or edited eight books, published over 50 academic papers and is deputy editor of the learned journal *Systems Practice*.

Main recent publications: New Directions in Management Science, (1987), Gower, Aldershot (with Paul Keys, Eds); *Operational Research and the Social Sciences*, (1989), Plenum, New York (with P. Keys, S. Cropper, Eds); *Systems Methodology for the Management Sciences*, (1991), Plenum, New York; *Creative Problem Solving: Total Systems Intervention*, (1991), John Wiley, Chichester (with Robert L. Flood).

PAUL KEYS
Current position: Senior Lecturer in Management Systems at the University of Hull, UK.

Career: Keys received an undergraduate degree in Pure and Applied Mathematics from the University of St. Andrews (1976). He worked for four years as a member of a research group exploring the behaviour of urban systems in the School of Geography at the University of Leeds. In 1980 he moved to a lectureship at the University of Hull, where he has been researching into mathematical modelling, systems methodologies and the process of operational research and has received a PhD. Keys is an active member of the Operational Research Society and the UK Systems Society.

Main recent publications: New Directions in Management Science, (1987), Gower, Aldershot (with Michael C. Jackson, Eds); *Operational Research and the Social Sciences*, (1989), Plenum, New York (with M. C. Jackson, S. Cropper, Eds); "OR as technology: some issues and implications", *Journal of the Operational Research Society*, Volume 40, 1989; *Operational Research and Systems*, (1991), Plenum, New York.

MARTIN LOCKETT
Current position: Executive Consultant with Nolan, Norton & Co., an information technology firm of KPMG Management Consulting.

Career: Lockett currently specialises in integrating IT and business strategies and in executive education for senior managers on the business exploitation of IT investments. He joined Nolan, Norton & Co., from the John Lewis partnership, a major UK retailer, where he held both business and IT management positions. Previously he worked at the Oxford Institute of Information Management (at Templeton College—Oxford Centre for Management Studies), Imperial College of London University, the Open University Systems Group and Cambridge University. He has published widely on the management of information technology, innovation, worker participation, organisation studies, research methods as well as management and economic issues in China.

Main recent publications: Organisations as Systems, (1980), Open University Press, Milton Keynes (with Roger Spear Eds); *The China Challenge*, (1986), Routledge and Kegan Paul, London.

JOHN C. OLIGA

Current position: Associate Professor at the School of Accountancy, Nanyang Technological University, Singapore.

Career: Oliga began a career in accountancy and finance as a trainee accountant in 1962. By 1970 he had become Director of Finance for East African Harbours Corporation in Tanzania. During the period 1970 to 1977 he was Financial Expert in the East African Community, negotiating terms with bilateral and multilateral agencies and foreign governments for development finance. In 1977 Oliga moved to the University of Sheffield, receiving an MA (1979) and a PhD (1982), both in Accounting and Financial Management. He then lectured at both the University of Sheffield and the University of Birmingham. Subsequently he has been Senior Lecturer at Papua New Guinea University of Technology, and Senior Lecturer at the National University of Singapore. He has the following qualifications: FCCA of the Chartered Association of Certified Accountants (UK), FCMA of the Chartered Institute of Management Accountants (UK), FCIS of the Institute of Chartered Secretaries and Administrators (UK), and CPA of the Institute of Certified Public Accountants (Singapore). Oliga has carried out many consultancies in East Africa, the UK and Singapore. He is Founding Editor of *Entrepreneurship, Innovation and Change*.

Main recent publications: "Accounting standards in developing countries", *International Journal of Accounting Education and Research*, Volume 18, 1982 (with J. M. Samuels); "Power in organisations: a contingent relational view", *Systems Practice*, Volume 3, 1990; "Conceptions of ideology: an exegesis and critique", *Systems Practice*, Volume 4, 1991; *Power, Ideology and Control* (1992), Plenum, New York.

DAVID SCHECTER

Current positions: Internal Management Consultant and Organisational Development Methods Researcher at Pacific Bell, San Ramon, USA; and Doctoral Candidate at the University of Hull, UK.

Career: Schecter received an undergraduate degree in Liberal Studies from San Francisco State University (1982) and an MA in cybernetic systems from San José State University (1990). He has worked in the field of information systems since 1983. In 1987 he became an internal organisational consultant at Pacific Bell, dealing with issues of organisational diagnosis and design, employee involvement in decision making and the social context of information systems technology.

Main recent publications: "For whom and to do what: questions for a liberating systems approach", *Proceedings of ISSS Conference*, Edinburgh, 1989; "Beer's Organisational Tensegrity and the challenge of democratic organisational structure", *Systems Practice*, Volume 4, 1991.

ALAN R. THOMAS

Current position: Senior Lecturer in Systems at the Open University, UK.

Career: Thomas has been based at the Open University for over twenty years. His more recent interests have involved him as Chair over the innovative interdisciplinary course on "Third World Studies" and in the production of a replacement course called "Third World Development." Areas of research include workers' co-operatives and not-for-profit organisations as well as organisational action research.

Main recent publications: "The survival and growth of worker cooperatives: a comparison with small businesses", *International Small Business Journal*, Volume 8, 1989 (with Chris Cornforth); *Co-ops to the Rescue*, (1989), ICOM Co-publications, London (with Jenny Thornley); "Measuring the performance of worker cooperatives", in D. Cooper and T. Hooper, (Eds), *Critical Accounts*, (1989), Macmillan, London; *Developing Successful Worker Co-operatives*, (1988), Sage, London (with Chris Cornforth, Jenny Lewis and Roger Spear).

WERNER ULRICH

Current positions: Director of the Office of Evaluation Research of the Department of Public Health and Social Services of the Canton of Berne, Switzerland; Member of Faculty of the Department of Philosophy at the University of Fribourg, Switzerland; and Honorary Senior Fellow of the Department of Management Systems and Sciences at the University of Hull, UK.

Career: Ulrich holds PhDs in Economics and Social Science from the University of Fribourg, and in the Philosophy of Social Systems Design from the University of California at Berkeley. Since 1981 he has built up and directed the Office of Evaluation Research in the Canton of Berne. He has been a faculty member of the Department of Philosophy at the University of Fribourg since 1986, where he teaches courses in social planning, evaluation research, and poverty research. Ulrich is an editorial advisor of the learned journal *Systems Practice* and is Director-at-large for publications with the International Society for the Systems Sciences.

Main recent publications: Critical Heuristics of Social Planning: A New Approach to Practical Philosophy, (1983), Haupt, Berne; "Critical heuristics of social systems design", *European Journal of Operational Research*, Volume 31, 1987; "Churchman's 'process of unfolding'—its significance for policy analysis and evaluation", *Systems Practice*, Volume 1, 1988; "Systemtheorie der Planung", in N. Szyperski (Ed.), *Handworterbuch der Planung* (1989), Poeschel, Stuttgart, Germany.

Preface

The need for a new book of readings on systems thinking arises at this time because substantial developments have taken place in the discipline over the last ten years or so. Major efforts in research and development have been undertaken, which carefully work out credible intellectual foundations for systems thinking, taking on board important debates in philosophy and social theory. A book is required that shows this to be the case. This we have achieved by bringing together key papers and critical commentaries documenting the changes that have occurred.

Readers in systems thinking have previously been published and remain extremely valuable, but fall short on the recent stages of advancement. The two-volume work *Systems Thinking* (F. Emery, Ed., Penguin, 1981; first published in a shorter volume in 1969), for example, covers the emergence of systems thinking in the 1940s, 1950s and beyond. This effectively offers a comprehensive overview of the positivist roots and main concepts of systems thinking which led to a break with mechanistic thought. Another volume worth consulting is *Systems Behaviour* (Open Systems Group, Eds., Open University Press, 1981, 3rd edition) which in one section recognises the emergence of soft systems thinking. Now, with *Directed Readings*, we bring the whole story up to date, covering shifts from hard (positivist) to soft (interpretive) to critical systems thinking (based on critical theory), concentrating on the latter stages of this evolution.

The reader of this volume should be aware, however, that although we are convinced that these changes are essential, not everyone will agree with our analysis of them nor indeed with the importance that we attach to critical systems thinking. The critical argument presents a challenge to the dominant wisdom in the systems community. We eagerly await the community's critique. *Directed Readings* thus offers a historical documentation and a challenge.

Thanks are obviously due to many people who have enabled this volume to move from conception to reality. First and foremost, we are grateful to our authors for allowing us to include and interpret their articles. Authors are identified elsewhere. We acknowledge the agreement to allow us to use and discuss the table in the "Conclusion", granted by our co-constructors Ramsés

Fuenmayor, John C. Oliga, David Schecter and Werner Ulrich. We are also grateful to the Institute of Management Sciences, the Operational Research Society, Elsevier Science Publishers B.V., Gordon & Breach Science Publishers, and Plenum Publishing Corporation, for giving us permission to reproduce articles.

We appreciate that working on large projects such as this book places extra pressure on our families. For the tolerance and patience of our families we have a special thank you. Thanks to the ladies, Mandy and Pauline; and thanks to our children, Christopher, Richard and Ross.

ROBERT L. FLOOD
MICHAEL C. JACKSON
April, 1991

Overview

INTRODUCTION

A popular way of describing the development of academic disciplines is as consisting of periods when one paradigm holds sway, interrupted when that paradigm comes under threat and eventually gives way to a new dominant paradigm. The history of systems thinking, and indeed of management science generally, can usefully be looked at in these terms. The 1950s and 1960s saw the dominance of a positivist quantitative paradigm of operational (or operations) research (OR) and "hard systems" approaches to the subject, as found with traditional OR, general system theory, management cybernetics, systems analysis and systems engineering (Stafford Beer's organisational cybernetics offered a possible alternative but remained outside the mainstream of work). During the 1970s and 1980s the limitations of OR and hard systems thinking came to be recognised and, through the work of C. West Churchman, Russell L. Ackoff and Peter B. Checkland, a new qualitative paradigm, interpretive "soft systems" thinking, began to take shape and to challenge the "harder" approaches for hegemony. Particularly in the work of Checkland, the nature of the change overtaking the subject was carefully recorded, and the soft approach argued to be capable of encapsulating the hard as a special case. The proponents of OR and hard systems thinking had been intellectually routed. But subject areas do not stand still. A new wave of thinking has been building and is now ready to break into the systems and management science field. This new wave is "critical systems thinking," and its emergence is heralded by this book.

Critical systems thinking is an important and substantial development in the management and systems sciences. It shares the soft systems thinkers' critique of the hard approaches, but is able to reflect more fully upon the circumstances in which such approaches can properly be employed. It recognises the unique contribution of organisational cybernetics, in terms of both its strengths in organisation design but limitations in handling cultural and political phenomena, and is able to incorporate cybernetics back into a

Critical Systems Thinking: Directed Readings. Edited by R. L. Flood and M. C. Jackson
© 1991 John Wiley & Sons Ltd

reformulated conception of the nature of systems work (which soft systems thinking singularly failed to do). Fundamentally, critical systems thinking locates major shortcomings in the soft systems paradigm, particularly its failure to question its own theoretical underpinnings and to be reflective about the social context in which it is employed. In seeking to establish itself as the new dominant paradigm, therefore, critical systems thinking demonstrates that earlier systems approaches are all special cases with limited domains of application. The valid and successful use of the earlier approaches for systems intervention depends upon the broader understanding of them provided by critical systems thinking.

The critical systems endeavour possesses perhaps three interrelated intentions:

1. *Complementarism*—to reveal and critique the theoretical (ontological and epistemological) and methodological bases of systems approaches, and to reflect upon the problem situations in which approaches can be properly employed and to critique their actual use.

2. *Emancipation*—to develop systems thinking and practice beyond its present conservative limitations and, in particular, to formulate new methodologies to tackle problem situations where the operation of power prevents the proper use of the newer soft systems approaches.

3. *Critical reflection*—to reflect upon the relationship between different organisational and societal interests and the dominance of different systems theories and methodologies.

The current volume provides a compilation of historical and contemporary writings addressing these topics. It is not simply a "reader" however. The themes outlined above will be traced through the book and will undergo critical reflection, making the offering a critical and a directed set of readings. A comprehensive and coherent account of critical theory in management and systems thinking will therefore be enjoyed.

The book, which brings together an international authorship, comprises articles in three portions. Proceedings start with significant "historical" chapters that focus on the shift from hard to soft approaches and progress with a review of the "critical" break with soft systems thinking, and are completed by a collection of writings about critical systems thinking as it stands today. As an introduction to the main text of the book we will now provide an overview of each section.

BEYOND OPERATIONAL RESEARCH AND HARD SYSTEMS THINKING

The first section, Part One, looks "Beyond Operational Research and Hard Systems Thinking" with key contributions from Churchman, Ackoff and Checkland.

We hardly need to mention that Churchman showed remarkable foresight in his writings. Our selection from his work expresses ideas which underpin this book as a whole and the critical movement as such.

Churchman's critical assessment of "Operations Research as a Profession" (1970) sets the philosophical scene. He drew upon Jung's idea that each human being effectively has two lives, and extended this to a search for two lives of OR. First there is the rational life, founded on the works of Locke, Berkeley and Hume. Then there is the irrational life of judgements and opposing judgements, founded on the works of Kant and Hegel. The rational OR, the dominant one, is about truth, objectivity and optimisation. But these, Churchman said, seem to have absolutely nothing to do with the societal anxieties which OR purported to deal with. Churchman therefore proposed shifting lives from traditional OR to systems thinking with a critical Kantian base, which accepted that the rationality of one person could equally well be an irrationality for others.

One of Churchman's closest colleagues during the 1950s OR era was Russell L. Ackoff. Following Churchman, Ackoff argued that "The Future of Operational Research is Past" (1979). This did not altogether represent a dead-end for Ackoff, because he too recognised systems thinking as highly relevant to the complex of interacting problems, or the "mess," which we are facing in the second half of the twentieth century. Outdated OR ideas like optimisation, prediction and control, Ackoff said, are relevant only to the kinds of problems encountered earlier this century, and should be replaced with management of systems by design and invention. Ackoff also proposed a sort of complementarity between approaches. He claimed that "mechanical" thinking underpinning OR "is a special case" of "purposeful systems" thinking.

Peter B. Checkland was also inspired by Churchman's challenging arguments. The selection we have chosen from Checkland's work, "From Optimizing to Learning: A Development of Systems Thinking" (1985), completes the powerful argument that shows the limitations of OR, and extends the criticism to include early "hard systems" thinking. Checkland does this by contrasting OR and hard systems thinking with "soft systems" thinking, explaining that they represent two different paradigms. Checkland's main contribution, present in this article, was to consolidate and clarify the main arguments capable of taking problem solving beyond hard systems thinking. This paved the way for a new soft paradigm and enabled it to emerge with relative ease. The new paradigm made the qualification that hard "is a special case" of soft, sharing Ackoff's notion of complementarity.

In summary, our first three contributors argued in their own inimitable styles for two paradigms for management science, the new soft one being dominant over the old hard one in a sort of complementary relationship.

THE BREAK WITH SOFT SYSTEMS THINKING

Although many researchers and practitioners have hung on to the hard paradigm without swaying from the old dictums or responding to the new criticisms, the struggle and rise of soft systems thinking has been a phenomenon unchecked until recently. In the 1980s, a challenge from critical systems thinking surfaced, representing the concerns of a growing number of scholars. Part Two of *Directed Readings* traces "The Break With Soft Systems Thinking" and by so doing outlines the foundations of critical systems thinking.

By the late 1970s soft systems thinking had attracted critics. Two main concerns led to two substantive lines of development, emancipatory theory and practice, and complementarism, although clarity of distinction between the two was initially missing. The first line focused on the inappropriateness of the interpretive theory underpinning soft systems thinking for understanding and acting in social situations where there are inequalities in power and economic relations. The articles brought together in force in Part Two provide evidence of a more appropriate emancipatory theory.

The second line of development we have called complementarism. The soft perspective was rejected by critical thinkers because it is isolationist in orientation, accepting only the tenets of interpretivism and hence denaturing methodologies used from other theoretical bases. Furthermore, the critical school was concerned that an isolationist position proposed a theory that assumed inherent conflict in the development of disciplines. Although this does appear to be the norm, critical systems thinkers argued that it does not have to be the case. The critical turn led to an open and conciliatory approach which emphasised the need for a set of well formulated methodologies. A qualification attached to this asked for reflective use of methodologies, ensuring that they would be employed to tackle problematic situations which their inherent assumptions about the nature of social reality dictate they are most appropriate for. This argument was initially articulated at a methodological level and took the best part of the 1980s to be couched effectively in epistemological terms.

The articles in Part Two, then, will be concerned with the break with soft systems thinking. The first two deal with the need for an emancipatory methodology, the remaining four also deal with complementarism. Let us review the six articles.

Thomas and Lockett in their paper "Marxism and Systems Research" (1979) tackle the soft systems claim that its methodologies are politically and ideologically neutral. They rejected the argument that in principle soft systems methodologies are available to any interest in society, and that they do not serve any particular group or class. Thomas and Lockett explained how, for example, power relations structure the way problems are considered. Nonemancipatory soft methodology therefore will be managerialist in orientation and reformist in character—not capable of bringing about significant change. This accusation was levelled at both Ackoff and Checkland.

Whilst Thomas and Lockett outlined the main problem area that soft systems thinkers should be aware of, Ulrich set out to develop a methodology that dealt with the political and coercive nature of social reality. This was reported at length in his major work *Critical Heuristics of Social Planning* (1983, Haupt, Berne). The article selected for this volume offers an excellent introduction to his work. In it Ulrich outlines the basis for an approach to deal with the normative implications of problem definition and system design. The key idea is that the boundary judgements inherent in any plan can and should be considered by employing a systemic and critical approach. By achieving this, critical systems heuristics became the only emancipatory methodology to be developed explicitly employing systems thinking.

Pursuing the emancipatory theme, Jackson discussed "Social Systems Theory and Practice: The Need for a Critical Approach." Jackson made out his own case to criticise hard and soft systems thinking. He argued that methods from the natural sciences cannot simply be taken over to the domain of the social sciences, and soft methods cannot be used where economic and social structures give rise to coercive constraints. He stressed the need to evaluate the suitability of methods of inquiry for use in systems science, and consequently laid the foundations of a *critically reflective* complementarity for systems thinking.

At more or less the same time, the new vision of complementarism received its first genuine expression. Jackson and Keys moved "Towards a System of Systems Methodologies" (1984). The argument was presented entirely at a methodological level and no reference was made in the paper to the epistemological concerns of Habermas to which it evidently aspired and to which both Jackson and Oliga were giving independent attention elsewhere. The system of systems methodologies is an attempt to define a critical approach to systems-based problem solving, by examining the inherent assumptions of the most important systems methodologies, the contexts of organisational and social problems and how the two can be linked to guide methodology choice. An emphasis on methodologies being appropriate for the social systems of concern is a notable addition. The further call for a coordinated research programme to deepen understanding of different problem contexts was to be answered in force by authors like Flood, Oliga and Ulrich, as we shall now see.

Oliga made an important contribution by reviewing complementarism in systems thought. He looked at "Methodological Foundations of Systems Methodologies" (1988), building into the scientific literature an epistemological dimension to the debate under way. He considered critically the nature and limits of the epistemological and ethical claims of systems approaches to problem solving. He also showed the relevance of Habermas' idea that three kinds of knowledge, the technical, practical and emancipatory, imply different methodological rules and practices. It is this idea which underpins the Jackson and Keys framework. Additionally, Oliga discussed the two versions of complementarism, one found in soft and the other in critical systems thinking. In the end he does not come down strongly on either side, but in the review he sounds some very useful warnings about a naive contingency approach.

The last paper in this section is Flood and Ulrich's "Testament to Conversations on Critical Systems Thinking Between Two Systems Practitioners" (1990). A critical analysis of positivist, interpretive and critical theories is undertaken, outlining comprehensively each one's epistemological legitimacies and limitations. Positivist theories are found to be untenable, interpretivist to be impoverished and critical to be adequate.

This does not invalidate the complementary use of methodological ideas logically derived from different epistemological positions, the co-authors conclude, as long as they are employed in reflective fashion. Flood and Ulrich's article also points out that systems thinking, when studied according to its original critical intent, inherently implies the two main lines of development being pursued by critical systems thinkers—emancipation and critique.

In summary, the break with soft systems thinking is characterised by the development of emancipatory methodologies appropriately designed to penetrate coercive political structures, and by the realisation of a critically reflective complementarist framework articulated at the methodological and epistemological levels.

CONTEMPORARY CRITICAL SYSTEMS THEORY AND PRACTICE

Achievement of the break with soft systems thinking created conditions in which a whole new area of systemic thought could be developed. This opportunity was quickly seized upon. The rate of maturation of the critical challenge was swift, with several major texts and journal coverage already available (see the Appendix). Critical systems thinking was rapid in establishing a place within the systems and management sciences, and has now branched out to assess its own tenets critically in the face of wider debates, such as that surrounding post-modernism, currently being discussed in contemporary social theory. The complementarist idea has also been pragmatised and developed by applying its propositions to a multitude of contrasting business, organisational, community and societal problems, followed by reflection and redevelopment. The contributions which make up Part Three enable us to show these continuing and crucial developments in "Contemporary Critical Systems Theory and Practice."

The first article is Schecter's "Critical Systems Thinking in the 1980s: A Connective Summary" (1991). This paper blends with the argument of *Directed Readings*, recognising three commitments, or lines of argument as we have called them, to characterise the development of critical systems thinking. These are commitments to critique, to emancipation and to pluralism (we use the term complementarism instead). Our commentary has focused on an outline argument based on a few key points, but Schecter is able to detail each commitment by reflecting on a wider selection of writings. For example, Schecter covers the critique of structuralism, as distinct from the hard approaches that we have concentrated on, he discusses critiques of the history of systems thinking, and underlines the contribution made by Community OR. In this effort, he provides a firm springboard, connecting the foundational work of critical systems thinking in the 1980s with the new challenging ideas that are currently being explored.

One of these developments is called "interpretive systemology." As Schecter points out, interpretive systemology helps to advance the interpretive theory employed in systems thinking from the less-than-comprehensive accounts given by the soft systems school. Interpretive systemology comprehensively works out the onto-epistemological basis for interpretive thought in the systems sciences. This theory poses a "counter" system of critical thought to the Habermasian line that we have concentrated on. Heidegger, Husserl and their phenomenological philosophies provide the critical underpinnings. Interpretive systemology can be used to critique Habermasian based critical systems thinking, as Fuenmayor shows in his invited contribution "Between Systems Thinking and Systems Practice." He claims that a theoretically rooted interpretive systems science is critical, in the most authentic sense of the word.

Contrasting with this, Ulrich argues that contemporary practical philosophy holds the essential foundations necessary for systems thinking to serve the cause of socially rational decision making. In his paper "Systems Thinking, Systems Practice, and Practical Philosophy: A Program of Research" (1988), he builds a bridge between the two traditions of systems thinking and practical philosophy, coming up with a three-level framework of rational systems practice. He uses this as a suggested point of departure for a programme of research.

Another area of research and development opens up debate on power, ideology and control. Oliga has been developing an interesting thesis on this subject. We have included his paper "Power–Ideology Matrix in Social Systems Control" (1990) to represent this strand. He draws attention to power, ideology and social control in sociocultural systems, recognising that preference is usually given to naturalistic accounts of systems behaviour, using either hard or soft systems models. His main line of argument is that unless an account of systems stability and change is sought in the conscious actions of humans as makers or victims of history, no valid explanation of constancy and change in sociocultural systems is likely to ensue.

Jackson then takes the argument on to the controversial terrain of the debate between modernism and post-modernism in his paper "Modernism, Post-modernism and Contemporary Systems Thinking" (1991). He first sets out the nature of this debate and then relates the different strands of modern systems thinking, hard, cybernetic, soft, and critical, to different versions of modernism. This allows a critique to be developed of the role played by systems methodologies in contemporary organisations and society. Even critical systems thinking as it developed in the 1980s is seen to be wedded to a modernist programme. It is essential therefore, if it is to be self-reflective, for systems thinking to respond to the post-modern challenge.

The next contribution by Flood represents a first serious response from critical systems thinking to a post-modern challenge. It consolidates his argument from *Liberating Systems Theory* (Plenum, New York, 1990), moving a step on from the foundational work discussed in Part Two. In "Redefining the Management and Systems Sciences" (1990), Flood introduces a post-modern critique of the work of the critical systems school to date, adding a new methodological element—we need to "liberate and critique." Liberate here refers to Foucault's work, arguing that it is simply no good expecting knowledges and their logical methodological rules to be independently awaiting our critique. There are institutional and other forces invisibly at work at a micro-political level which are suppressing many of them. We therefore need to introduce a methodological element that helps to liberate dominated knowledges and methodologies, which in turn helps to grow a diversity of approaches necessary to tackle the great variety of phenomena we face in contemporary society.

Total Systems Intervention (TSI) is a pragmatic version of critical systems thinking that is employed in consultancy. This new comprehensive approach is recorded in full in *Creative Problem Solving: Total Systems Intervention* (Robert L. Flood and Michael C. Jackson, John Wiley, Chichester, 1991). A detailed account is given by the two originators, Flood and Jackson, who review "Total Systems Intervention: A Practical Face to Critical Systems Thinking" (1991). Total Systems Intervention as a methodology has permitted the critical idea to be employed in a variety of interventions, for example, in community projects, helping local government, and extensively for consultation in businesses and firms. TSI is also seen to envelop a whole range of practical ideas, such as evaluation and quality management. This final contribution therefore realises a most important requirement that critical theory demands of itself—that in order to be valid, critical thinking must be shown to have a theory with practical relevance.

SUMMARY AND CHALLENGE

In this book we present one set of papers which portray a particular vision of the development and changes in contemporary systems thinking. First, we consider soft systems thinking, a trend that moved beyond operational research and hard systems thinking. We then trace the fundamental concerns that led to the critical systems ideas, these representing the break with soft systems thinking. In the last part of the book we are concerned to show that the subject area is not standing still, and that critical systems thinking continues to move on, now facing up to new challenges such as a reworking of interpretive systems thinking, political and ideological issues in social control, and reconsidering the main critical ideas in the face of the post-modern critique.

Of course, the last section can hardly document all the main lines of thought under way, nor can it predict all those that will emerge in the future. We do not hope and have not attempted to be comprehensive. Rather, in the three parts of this book we have tried to achieve two things only. First, to provide meaningful commentary and articles that paint a picture of how systems thinking has and continues to develop. Second, to convince you of the necessity of the changes, so that you may take up the challenge with us and contribute to Part Four of this book, which has yet to be written.

Part One

Beyond Operational Research
and Hard Systems Thinking

Commentary

The management and systems sciences came into popular use in the Second World War, when operational research (OR) developed powerful mathematical and statistical techniques to aid technical planning and decision making. Approaches were perfected to optimise efficiency of solutions to logistical problems, the operation of weaponry, and destruction in bombing raids. OR helped to create the great war machines of the 1940s. The post-war era saw a period of further development of quantitative ideas, for example, in industrial manufacturing. Later, new techniques such as systems analysis were developed for managers aiming to optimise problem solution through cost/benefit calculations. The ideas of cybernetics also influenced planning and decision making. For example, in the guise of systems engineering they contributed massively to the United States of America's space programme among other spectacular technological achievements. Model validity was assessed using the scientific method and by applying Popper's falsificationism, a critical approach aimed at achieving truth, knowledge and correct intervention. The stage was therefore set in the 1960s for the application of OR and hard systems thinking to the *apparently* simpler task of solving organisational, community and societal problems.

C. West Churchman and Russell L. Ackoff were founding figures in both OR and the goal-seeking conception of purposeful systems, but they became concerned that positivist, hard, quantitative approaches were unable to tackle the kind of issues contemporary society faced. They foresaw major difficulties emerging because researchers and educationalists were unwilling to move on from the security of the great heights already conquered. They felt that the management and systems sciences had become rock-steady and inappropriate for the diverse tasks they had originally set themselves. Our two critics felt compelled to set about their discipline with an unreserved onslaught on what had become established and cherished ideas. We start the readings in this book with two, one each, of their most notable papers which convincingly explain the need to progress "Beyond Operational Research and Hard Systems Thinking."

Critical Systems Thinking: Directed Readings. Edited by R. L. Flood and M. C. Jackson
© 1991 John Wiley & Sons Ltd

As stated in the "Overview," Churchman is a man of remarkable foresight. His paper in *Directed Readings* is a testament to this, providing the philosophical underpinnings for the book as a whole and the critical systems movement as such.

In his paper "Operations Research as a Profession" (1970), Churchman undertook a critical investigation into the profession of OR and management science. He outlined the role for OR "in the growing societal anxiety over poverty, pollution and privacy,", but found that "it plays virtually no significant role in these matters." He decided to explore this curiosity by drawing an analogy between Jung's theory of two lives of human beings—the rational and the mythical—and the possibility of two ORs—the rational and the irrational. What would a rational and an irrational OR look like (he asked)? Churchman answered this question by going back to his own philosophical groundings, using these to establish a philosophical base from which a whole new direction for management and systems science could be constructed.

The first OR, the traditional rational one, reflects a mix of rationalism (i.e. truth from first principles, by reason and with intuition—e.g. Descartes) and empiricism (i.e. learning truths by observation of natural events—externally by senses, internally by reflection). The fathers of the empiricist philosophical system of thought are Locke, Berkeley and Hume.

The second OR, the irrational one that Churchman was imagining, would have a tradition of theory and sensation. It would be characterised by integration of the systemic judgements necessary to make data meaningful. Churchman pointed out that these challenging ideas had been aired by Kant, for example in his *Critique of Pure Reason* (2nd edition published in 1787). Developing this tradition, Churchman continued, Hegel had argued that there are systemic judgements, *Weltanschauungen*, but there are also alternative systemic judgements, counter-*Weltanschauungen*. This suggests, unlike rational OR, that there can be no absolutely right knowledge or way to design systems.

Following on, the two ORs linked to their respective groundings exhibit the following attributes.

Rational OR shares the values of traditional science. Organisations can advance, it is assumed, to clear understanding through scientifically based rational thought and by employing systematic methods derived from a branch of applied mathematics called optimisation theory.

Irrational OR assumes that life is ambiguous and characterised by persistent failure to resolve basic issues. Organisations proceed to deeper misunderstanding and disaster. Problems are elusive, and seeking clarification and solution distorts the significance of issues. OR is therefore an inquiring system that can have no absolute beginning nor end.

In terms of change in ideas, one of the themes of this book, rational OR is evidently static whilst irrational OR is naturally dynamic. The dominant static OR has given rise to an explosion of clone-like publications. Meanwhile, the irrational OR has had to struggle out of Churchman's dreams. It has had to forge its place in contemporary theory and practice through persistent criticism of the dominant wisdom. This has led to a growing number of important works, some of which are provided as readings in this volume.

Churchman pointed out in his article that rational OR mostly assumes that the "future will be found in the past." Ackoff very cleverly played on this expression in his paper "The Future of Operational Research is Past" (1979), rather frustrated at seeing the future of OR in its own past.

Ackoff shared many of Churchman's sentiments, being concerned that OR had "lost its pioneering spirit, its sense of mission and innovativeness." OR was now concerned with consolidation, "survival, stability and respectability." OR had stagnated and had become increasingly irrelevant to modern day issues. Like Churchman, Ackoff chose to think of two views of OR, but replaced the philosophical bent on rationality and irrationality, pursued by Churchman, with a more worldly conception. Ackoff identified two main eras in the recent development of the human race, a "machine age" and a "systems age."

The machine age, where rational OR is placed, is about analysis and reduction. It is concerned with self-control, optimisation and objectivity. This is the paradigm of "predict and prepare."

The systems age is about wholes whose essential properties are lost when they are taken apart. It is concerned with self-control, humanisation, environmentalisation and dealing with messes. Messes are complex systems of changing problems; problems being abstractions from messes by means of analysis. Messes, Ackoff argues, need to be managed rather than optimised. This is the paradigm of "design and invent."

Ackoff's way of relating the methods of each age is the first interpretation of complementarism to be found in this volume. He argued that the machine age and all its techniques are "a special case" of the systems age and all its methods. This particular brand of complementarism arose as a natural consequence of the attempts being made to go beyond hard systems thinking. Hard had indisputably been applied successfully and had to be given a place, albeit a subordinate one. Although this conception was challenged later by the critical systems school, it was no less remarkable than the critical idea given the break that it represented at that time.

As we have seen, Ackoff saw a need for a change in management and systems science. His propositions were methodologically more concrete than Churchman's, culminating in interactive planning, a methodology for managing messes. This methodological trend is picked up in the third of our papers, selected from the works of Peter B. Checkland.

As the title of his paper makes clear, Checkland was concerned with the change "From Optimizing to Learning: A Development of Systems Thinking for the 1990s." For the third time in this volume we are presented with the idea of two paradigms, in this case one relating to optimisation and the other to learning. Checkland very carefully worked out the main differences between the two paradigms and was consequently able to provide a legitimation for his own methodological work titled soft systems methodology. He named the two paradigms "hard systems thinking" and "soft systems thinking."

Hard systems thinking incorporates OR, systems analysis, and systems engineering. It is about optimisation. OR treats small numbers of variables in this way. The hard systems approaches are concerned with engineering optimal goal-seeking strategies for complex systems. The key feature of all hard approaches is the formulation of a clear definition of ends and the optimal means of achieving those ends. Optimisation involves the use of models which are considered to be of the world, or the problem. This has the disadvantage of possibly losing touch with the messy reality of the problematic situation. Overall, the hard approach rests on a theory which is applicable to human affairs only if identifying the problem and the ends is not problematic.

Soft systems thinking is oriented to learning by using systems models to explore problematic situations. The models are not considered to be of the world, amounting to intellectual constructs which help to surface important issues arising from problem situations that may be debated, leading to accommodation between ideas and the maintenance of relationships. The soft approach therefore has a theory which is relevant to human affairs, particularly when identifying the problem to be tackled is in itself problematic. The relationship between the hard and soft paradigms is complementary, Checkland claimed. His notion of complementarity was identical to Ackoff's, even down to phraseology. He reckoned that hard "is a special case" of soft, although choice of approach must be according to judgements made concerning the systems thinking appropriate in particular situations in human affairs. As with Ackoff's notion, however, Checkland's *fundamental* idea of complementarity falls to the same argument promoted by the critical systems school, as we shall explore later in the book.

The break with hard systems thinking can be summarised in the following way.

There are two paradigms which are popularly called hard and soft (see the table). Hard is the traditional paradigm which incorporates OR and hard systems thinking. It is positivist, characterised by a search for objectivity, quantification, systematic techniques and methods, optimisation, goal-seeking and determining correct solutions to tangible problems. There have been some developments in the hard paradigm, from OR to hard systems thinking, but this represents intraparadigmatic refocusing. Hard thinking rests on a theory which is relevant to narrow areas of human affairs. Beyond hard thinking lies a second paradigm, popularly called soft. It accepts irrationality as inevitable and is characterised by subjectivity, a qualitative approach, systemic methodologies, and learning and accommodation in the face of contrasting world

Table 1 Contrasting hard and soft systems thinking

School of thought	Essential conception	Theory	Focus	Activity
Hard	Rational	Positivist	Quantitative	Optimisation
Soft	Accepts irrationality	Interpretivist	Qualitative	Management

views. Soft systems thinking is underpinned by interpretive theory which is relevant to messy human affairs.

The hard paradigm has been static in its fundamental ideas for some time, whereas the soft paradigm has enjoyed a dynamic period and has led to some necessary epistemological and methodological shifts and developments in the management and systems sciences.

With the soft paradigm came an interpretive brand of complementarity. The hard paradigm was seen as a special case of the soft and its methods could be called in to use in the perceived narrow area of goal-seeking and optimisation.

The contemporary soft thinkers have also introduced a notion of criticism which goes beyond Popper's idea of falsification. In social affairs truth cannot be established according to whether hypotheses resist falsification. Instead, people hold different viewpoints, all being regarded as equally legitimate. The critical intent of soft systems thinking is therefore to uncover these different conceptions of reality.

Unfortunately during the main period of its development the soft tendency neglected to deal with issues of moral and ethical judgement which Churchman had debated at length, and which were to be picked up again by the critical systems school.

The idea of two paradigms, complementarity and criticism, as characterised by soft systems thinking, were to undergo rigorous assessment leading to further changes. The consolidation of these criticisms has led to a break with soft systems thinking, labelled critical systems thinking, as explored in the next section.

Chapter 1

Operations Research as a Profession

C. WEST CHURCHMAN

INTRODUCTION

This paper is concerned with the profession of operations research and specifically with the preparation for the profession. On a fairly general plain, the paper expresses a concern about the future of a profession which ought to be in the lead in the growing societal anxiety over poverty, pollution and privacy, but in fact plays virtually no significant role in these matters.

In his autobiography, *Memories, Dreams, Reflections,* C. G. Jung argues for a fascinating way of telling the story of one's life. There are, he says, two stories. One story is the rational, a story of a man's struggles, frustrations and joys in seeking his life's goals. The other is the "irrational," the primitive often unexpressed mythic elements of his life. At some risk of perverting the richness of Jung's suggestion, I'd like to tell two stories of a profession, operations research, but in the end I'll not be sure which is the rational.

The reason for telling these two stories is to obtain a critical overview of the profession of operations research, primarily to assess its educational base, not just in colleges and universities, but in the overall program of learning: in meetings, journals and informal discussions.

Reprinted by permission from *Management Science,* Volume 17, 1970.
© 1970 Operations Research Society of America and the Institute of Management Sciences

THE "RATIONAL" STORY: PRECISION AND CERTAINTY

The first story is well described in the texts of the two American societies, the Operations Research Society of America (ORSA) and the Institute of Management Sciences (TIMS). First of all, ORSA: "The object of the Society shall be the advancement of the science of operations ressearch, through exchange of information, the establishment and maintenance of professional standards of competence for work known as operations research . . ."[1]

Then TIMS: "The objects of the Institute shall be to identify, extend, and unify scientific knowledge that contributes to the understanding and practice of management. To this end the Institute proposes . . . to stimulate research and promote high professional standards in the development of a unified management science; and in general, to promote the growth of management science and its practice."[2]

Of course, we should expect to find such high sounding phrases in the beginnings of fledgling societies which have yet to learn to fly. What is significant in both statements is that "science's" values are to prevail, and that professional standards are to be met. ORSA, from the outset, seemed reasonably confident that it knew the meanings of these two concepts, "science" and "professional standards," for it wrote into its constitution: "There shall be elected to Fellowship only such persons as have contributed to the advancement of operations research through original and significant work in that field . . . There shall be elected to Membership persons who have demonstrated professional competence in the field of operations research."

Later reflection caused ORSA to drop its fellows, but the membership distinction still holds, based on a fairly elaborate list of properties. TIMS from the outset was not inclined to define the profession, and its history displayed a healthy confusion about what "science" means as well as "standards" for the profession.

But every profession is vague to some degree about its standards. This vagueness does not prevent our telling a fairly straightforward story about the objectives of the profession, as well as methods of evaluating individual performance.

In the more recent edition of *Encyclopedia Americana*, L. E. Blauch sets down three conditions for the existence of a profession:

1. a body of erudite knowledge, a set of attitudes, and a technique which are applied to the service of mankind through an educated group;

---

[1] Constitution and Bylaws of the Operations Research Society of America, May, 1952.
[2] Constitution and Bylaws of the Institute of Management Sciences, December, 1953.

2. a standard of success measured by accomplishment in serving the needs of the people rather than by personal gain;

3. a system of control over the practice of the calling and the education of its practitioners.

If we tentatively accept these conditions, then it is clear that the usefulness of asking whether a service should be described as a profession lies mainly in directing attention to the proper preparation for the service; that is, its educational foundation. So our "rational" story will try as best it can to describe the educational foundation for the *practice* of operations research (OR). That is, I am concentrating attention on those who work in purely theoretical research. Now both Blauch's statement and ORSA's initial promise indicate that "preparation" for the profession means some fairly intense education in a recognized science plus some experience "doing OR." In the early 1950s, the "recognized science" might be mathematics, physics, biology, economics or engineering; "doing OR" tended to be regarded as research in some practical area. But with the advent of masters and doctoral programs in OR in the latter part of the 1950s, it appears that a definition of the preparation for the profession of OR could be given in a far more adequate manner; an individual is prepared for the profession, if he has received at least a Masters in OR from a qualified institution and has had at least two years of satisfactory internship in doing OR.[3]

Judging by the OR texts in the market today, we can tell the rational story in rather specific terms, for they display a remarkable consensus on the part of instructors in universities as to the formal educational requirement for the profession. Blauch's "body of erudite knowledge" seems to be well defined; it is a branch of applied mathematics called optimization theory. A recent text, *Principles of Operations Research* (Prentice Hall, 1970) by Harvey Wagner, goes so far as to map the structure of the field so that the mathematical body of knowledge can be stated with some real degree of precision. Of course, there are some differences among curriculum designers concerning the relative importance of economics, accounting, organization theory, and so on. But these differences are minor compared with the basic agreement, if credit hour is used as a basis.

More to the point, the OR curriculum in universities helps us tell the rational story quite well in terms of the educational objectives. The aim of the education is to develop an ability to *clarify* issues, to make the alternatives *precise*, to spell out in detail and to *measure* the utilities of the objectives, and to become as *unambiguous* as possible about the relative worth of the alternatives. What emerges is the story that a professional should, to the best of his ability, be

---

[3] Note that this is assumed to be a sufficient condition for preparation, not a necessary one; as in all professions, there are satisfactory alternative pathways of preparation.

unambiguous, and should be able to defend his recommendation in a rational or "scientific" manner. This does not mean that he is expected to avoid uncertainties, because this is an unreasonable requirement; but he should be as clear and rational about uncertainty as possible. Nor do the standards of the profession, according to the rational story, require the practitioner to be totally comprehensive, because this requirement is not feasible; but he should be clear and consistent about his assumptions.

THE "IRRATIONAL" STORY: AMBIGUITY AND INCONSISTENCY

The other story of the preparation for the profession says that we are to prepare the practitioner for a life of ambiguity and persistent failure to resolve the basic issues. He must prepare himself to appreciate that every human problem is fundamentally elusive, and the attempt to clarify its meaning and to identify a solution distorts the problem and destroys its real significance. Put otherwise, uncertainty is the key concept, but not the clear uncertainty of probability or game theory. Furthermore, uncertainty and ambiguity are the highest values, because they represent the natural condition of the civilized intellectual person.

At first sight, this does not appear to be a very attractive story. Indeed, the early history of OR could be regarded as an attempt to get away from the ambiguity and uncertainty of management practices of the military and industry. However, as we shall see, this attempted journey into clarity may be interpreted as a journey into a deeper blackness.

ON ACADEMICS

At this point, when the reader is deciding whether to read on, it may be important once more to emphasize who the audience of this confusing piece is supposed to be. The audience can best be described as "academics," those who educate others to prepare for the profession.[4] This does not imply that the concern is restricted to professors in universities, because some of the greatest teachers are outside the cloister, while many who talk endlessly inside are obviously not teachers at all. One might regard the so-called management sciences as the academic wing of OR, in which case the management sciences are the proper safeguardians of the profession of OR.

_____
[4] And not "purely academic" in the current odd and negative sense of "empty of practical import."

The discussion of the paper is also academic in the sense that it has a tradition, and specifically a philosophical tradition. Writers like Plato, Hobbes, Kant and Bentham still have much to say in the debate about the profession of OR; it is not a debate whose issues are most clearly revealed by recent citations alone. Hence in this paper I have intentionally used the voices of the past to provide suggestions and clarification.

OR—AN ACADEMIC DEFINITION

I need to define OR, with the sole purpose of providing an outline for the two stories. OR, let us say, is the *securing* of *improvement* in *social systems* by means of *scientific method*. Each of these terms will have a different meaning in each story.

The definition is academic in that it states that preparation for the profession of OR requires preparation for conducting research on social systems in order to improve them in some real manner, where the research meets the standards of scientific inquiry. Furthermore, there must be preparation for the task of transforming the research findings into real change; i.e. implementing the recommendations. But "securing" has a much deeper meaning than selling managers on OR findings. It also means observing the implementation process and controlling the change in the face of unforeseen consequences. In general, it means "learning how to do OR better the next time."[5]

SCIENTIFIC METHOD

We can begin with what appears to be the easiest of the list to explain, namely, "scientific method."

The meaning of scientific method which is commonly accepted today by most scientific communities has its origin in two great philosophical traditions, rationalism and empiricism. Rationalism emphasized the deduction of truth from first principles arrived at by reason and intuition. Its chief spokesmen were Descartes, Spinoza and Leibniz.[6] Empiricism emphasizes the process of learning truths from direct observation of natural events, either externally

---

[5] The concept of OR's dual function, to solve social problems and improve its research capability, is well expressed in Russell Ackoff's "On the Ambiguity of the Researcher and the Researched," a talk delivered at the "Symposium on the Place of Research in Social Choice," in memory of W. N. Jessop, Tavistock Institute, London, 1969.

[6] See, for example, Descartes' *Meditations on First Philosophy* (1642) and *Discourse on the Method of Rightly Conducting Reason* (1637); Spinoza's *Ethics* (1663) and (more to the point here) *Treatise on the Improvement of the Understanding* (1660); Leibniz's *Monadology* (1714) and other essays and letters—e.g., in *Philosophical Works*, translated by G. M. Duncan, New Haven (1908).

through the senses or internally through reflection. Its chief spokesmen were Locke, Berkeley and Hume.[7]

The disciplines of science have used various combinations of these philosophies as descriptions of their methods. Rationalism is characteristic of the intuitionist theory of mathematics, and of much of economic and decision theory, while empiricism describes how many sociologists and geologists behave. A rather popular combination is the "hypothetico-deductive" method, in which the scientific method is described as the generation of significant hypotheses about the natural world, and the testing of specific consequences of these hypotheses. A successful test strengthens the scientific community's belief in the hypothesis, and an unsuccessful test requires revision or even total abandonment of the hypothesis.

Most of the descriptions of scientific method tell a very rational story, which often tends to be naive and simplistic. The history of physics from Einstein to Heisenberg cannot be described accurately by the hypothetico-deductive account; for example, the Michelson–Morley experiments did not lead to immediate abandonment of the theory of the ether.[8]

When we turn to OR, the basic texts seem again to be in remarkable agreement about the rational story. We are told, or can safely infer from their contents, that "doing OR" consists of (i) observing a system, (ii) formulating a problem, (iii) generating a model which predicts how the system will work if certain changes are made, (iv) gathering the necessary data to "plug into the model," and (v) estimating from the model the change that maximizes the value of the system.

Normally, very little is said in the texts about any of these steps in detail except for (iii) and (v). The methodology of OR does not provide any systematic rules for observing a system or formulating the "best" problem to work on. This lack may be justifiable, because, as we shall see, there really are some deep mysteries in both of these areas which our present knowledge cannot clarify. These mysteries have their impact on the whole enterprise.

It is in (iv), the data collecting activity, where the two stories most obviously conflict, and where the texts can be severely criticized for failing to tell both sides. In almost every text I have examined, the discussion of data collection seems very strongly to imply that the data items are to be obtained by observation; i.e. that step (iv) is based on the classical empiricist notion that the true events of external nature are to be learned through our senses. Consider, for example, the typical treatment of inventory. The student is accurately told

---

[7] See, for example, Locke's *Essay Concerning Human Understanding* (1690), Berkeley's *Dialogues* (1713) and Hume's *Enquiry into Human Understanding* (1758) and a *Treatise on Human Nature* (1739).
[8] The history of science has frequently constrasted the rational story telling of scientists about what they do with the reality in practice. See, for example, Thomas Kuhn's *The Structure of Scientific Revolutions*, Chicago (1962).

that in doing OR on an inventory problem one needs to ascertain demand. Some texts spend considerable time on probability distributions and statistical techniques of forecasting. In all these discussions, the student is led to believe that the appropriate data base for estimating future demands is past demands. To be sure, some texts caution the student against assuming that "the future will be like the past," but few if any caution him against using past invoices or other records as his base. And yet a little reflection shows that in using past experiences one is making a very strong systemic judgment, namely, that the component which generates the demand on inventory is properly designed. To the practicing operations researcher this point is commonplace; if there are awkward seasonal variations in demand, then, *before* designing an inventory policy, *first* see if pricing or advertising can smooth out the demand. Thus the "demand data" for an inventory problem are based on estimates of how the demand-generating component ought to work, not how it will work if no change occurs in it. And if one says that the marketing department won't change no matter what is recommended, then again a very strong systemic assumption has been made about the behavioural characteristics of managers.

Though it is obviously difficult to assess the seriousness of ignoring the systemic judgment implicit in OR data, I'd estimate that it is a far more serious error than the typical errors associated with statistical analysis to which formal education does devote a great deal of its time. It is to be noted that the problem of the correct systemic judgment is not handled by statistical theory, which, in effect, presupposes that it has been solved.

The same basic idea applies to cost estimates as well. One can say that the operational definition of the cost of capital in inventory systems is "whatever the comptroller says it is," but the definition is not arbitrary because it is based on the strong systemic assumption that the comptroller can judge optimal allocations of funds in the organization. How he does this may be a mystery to the operations researcher, but somehow such a judgment must be made if the system is to be improved.

Any cost estimate made by the practicing operations researcher is based on one of the following systemic assumptions: some components of the system are operating at near maximum performance; nothing can be done about their performance; or the optimal OR strategy is to act as though the other components were operating correctly, with the intention of turning to the study of these later on. Thus if the operations researcher accepts the comptroller's estimate of the cost of capital in inventory, he either assumes that the comptroller knows how to run the financial system of the company, or that his current policies are unalterable, or that a financial study should be postponed. The point is that the "facts" about costs relative to a component like a purchasing department are based on assumptions about how the whole system should work or inevitably does work.[9]

---

[9] At times OR texts show a peculiar mixture of attitudes about data. Thus in some inventory

That OR texts fail to tell both sides of the data collection story is well illustrated by their "exercises" which are phrased as though they were real problems. In an exercise, the data are authorized by the text or teacher, so that the student never needs to raise the serious systemic issues; in effect he has only one systemic question, namely, he takes the data and fits them into the model. But in a real problem there is no obvious authorization of data, and the critical issue is to decide which systemic assumptions can legitimately be made.

Thus we see that the so-called "data" of OR are not the result of observation alone, but of observation plus strong systemic assumptions. This is no philosophical news, because there is a strong philosophical tradition which says that all data are a combination of theory and sensation.[10] The setting for this thesis was given in Hume's *Treatise*, but it was Kant in the *Critique of Pure Reason* (1781) who provided the first detailed elaboration. Kant believed that some of the systemic judgments (he called them "*a priori* synthetic") which are required to make data meaningful are necessary; i.e. no alternative judgments can sensibly be made. Later philosophers, and notably Hegel, as we shall see, suggest that there are alternative systemic judgments (*Weltanshauungen*) which can be made; Hegel's work suggests a kind of learning process in which the systemic judgments become richer and more meaningful. This Hegelian assumption is the basis for one of the systemic assumptions mentioned above, namely that one can postpone research on questionable matters for a later time. The rational story tells us that organizations, nations and even mankind can advance safely through the land of uncertainties to a deeper and clearer understanding. The irrational story tells us that there is just as much evidence for the worldview that we are proceeding towards a deeper misunderstanding and disaster.

In more contemporary language, one would say that data collection in OR involves strategic decisions, i.e. alternative choices which have to be evaluated in terms of desired outcomes. Thus OR in practice is itself a system, an "inquiring system," and susceptible to systemic analysis. Perhaps one of the deepest mysteries of doing OR is how to understand OR as a system; but if

---

models involving lead time, the student learns that he should spend time gathering information about the costs of holding inventory and ordering from the accounting department, but that the out-of-stock cost is to be obtained by asking management for the "probability of shortage."
[10] This particular philosophical thesis is still being debated among philosophers and scientists. For an elaboration of the character of the debate, see C. W. Churchman, *Theory of Experimental Inference*, Macmillan, New York (1948). Many social scientists, for example, seem to hold the metaphysical position that there are "raw data" which the scientist can know and which entail no theoretical commitments. Others, like Herbert Simon, take a strong positivist view regarding the primacy of observation. The debate becomes involved in some rather subtle problems, but for OR, the case in favor of the thesis seems rather obvious to people with practical experience.

the meaning of the scientific method of OR is based on the supposition that OR is a system, then the meaning of the last term of my definition of OR, "by means of scientific method," remains basically mysterious.

I need to emphasize that this conclusion is far from being a negative one. If the meaning of "preparing for a profession" given above is correct, then my discussion tends to show that formal education cannot teach the candidate all there is to be known about the scientific method of OR. It can certainly caution him about data, and here, as I said, the texts have been dangerously negligent.[11] Formal education can also provide some understanding of alternative scientific methods, perhaps along the historical lines of this section, and for any candidates such an exposure may be very beneficial. But at this time, our ignorance of the formal properties of OR as a system are such that the candidate will have to learn an important part of what the scientific method of OR is for him in "doing OR."

However, some fairly definite things can be said about OR's methodology in practice, but they will mean more in a broader context, once we have examined the two additional concepts of "social system" and "improvement."

SOCIAL SYSTEMS

Some OR practitioners may feel inclined to disagree that OR concerns itself with social systems, because they may feel that excellent OR studies have been made on hardware systems; for example, weapon, computer or space systems. But I have used the term "social" to indicate that in all OR studies we are concerned with a three-way relationship between people, namely, (i) the decision makers, (ii) the people who are supposed to benefit from the system, (i.e. the clients or beneficiaries), and (iii) the operations researcher.

Briefly, the decision makers can realize changes in the system; the operations researchers conceptualize and evaluate change in terms of service to the clients, and then attempt to influence the decision makers to realize those changes which benefit the appropriate client. This description, of course, applies to any profession, but in each case with a different emphasis.

In the case of OR, the problem is to identify the "whole relevant system," since OR is normally concerned with fairly large systems: corporations, transport systems, poverty-control systems, etc. The limits of a system and the decision makers of a system are correlative problems. If the operations researcher, in classical fashion, believed that God is the decision maker of all systems, then, like Leibniz in his *Monadology*, he would see that the basic

---

[11] I can say this without feeling very smug about it, because Churchman, Ackoff and Arnoff's *Introduction to Operations Research*, John Wiley, New York (1957), could be criticized on this account.

obligation of OR as a profession is to understand the purpose and structure of all reality.

It is interesting today to see how many practically minded operations researchers shun Leibniz's approach as being axiomatically unfeasible. Thus an OR team may decide to study optimal strategies for a fire department of a city. They realize, of course, that there is a larger system in which the fire department is embedded, which includes police, education, recreation, etc. They also realise that a dollar spent in fire prevention could be spent in crime prevention. But this realization, once released, pushes one on to realizing that the city is a subsystem of the region, which is a subregion of the state, which . . . With a laugh, they point out that such reasoning forces one to consider "the whole universe including God," which is taken to be a *reductio ad absurdum*. What is one age's self-evident becomes another's absurd.

The point which OR's own philosophy implies is that the determination of the bounds of the system and hence also the nature of the decision maker are again strategic problems of the OR inquiring system. Thus both Leibniz and the "practical" operations researchers may be wrong. To be simple for illustrative purposes, one might argue that the larger[12] the system the more time and cost is entailed in the OR study and implementation, but the greater the real social benefit. The strategic problem is to balance these "costs" and "benefits." It is clear that formal education provides very little help on this problem; the operations researcher needs experience to teach him where to set the system boundaries. OR in the past decade has tended to be very conservative in setting system boundaries. In an age when society is showing a great interest in distinguishing between relevant and irrelevant activities, OR runs a real risk of being on the irrelevant list. The recent "R-and-D depression" is evidence that OR is not alone among the sciences in this regard.

The reason why the nature of the decision maker and the system boundaries are correlative problems is easy to see. We say that the *environment* of a system consists of those aspects of the natural world which influence the effectiveness of a system relative to the client, but which the decision maker cannot change. The *resources*, on the other hand, also influence the effectiveness, and can be changed by the decision maker. Thus the head of a purchasing department can change inventory policy, say, but not pricing policy; the former is a resource (for him), while the latter is in the environment. We see that our earlier discussion of data fits into the present discussion of the decision maker; the systemic judgment implicit in data includes a judgment about the nature of the decision maker as well as the boundaries of the system.

---

[12] The idea that one system x is "larger" than another y if and only if y is embedded in x and x is not embedded in y is an example of the simplistic nature of this principle. I suspect that the logic of system size and the interrelationship between systems need to be far richer concepts than this version suggests.

The second problem of the decision maker might be called the problem of its anatomy. I have used the neuter "its" to emphasize that the decision maker is always a complicated structure of partially conflicting values and attitudes, even when the operations researcher concludes that the decision maker is "one" individual person.[13] It is in this regard that much of so-called decision theory tends to be confusing, because it seems to assume an integrated decision making body. One should rather say that the decision making is a resultant of many influences,[14] and that the real task of the practitioner is to guess the structure of these influences. To use a more or less obvious example, many a naive operations researcher has assumed that top management makes the decisions, especially when it says it does, only to find the enormous power of sabotage of middle and bottom management.

Since OR is concerned with system improvement, it may be less concerned with describing the anatomy of the decision maker than it is with determining what it ought to be. This brings OR into what I consider to be the major organizational problems of management and government in the coming decades: centralization versus decentralization. The problem for OR is somewhat of a paradox. The assumption implicit in OR models is that decision making should have a centralized locus, where information from all sources is digested by the model and an optimal allocation of resources is calculated. But OR practitioners realize the importance of maintaining at least the appearance of local decision making. This paradox will be discussed in more detail when we come to examine the concept of system improvement.

OR's third problem of the decision maker is an analysis of the system he controls, (i.e. his resources) into its component parts. Here, of course, formal education has much to contribute, because the available models act as guides to the analysis. Experience, too, plays a significant role: the practitioner learns to make strategic judgments about the appropriate detail and precision of the model, for example.[15]

It is a matter of serious debate whether the first two problems of the decision maker should be introduced into the formal educational curriculum. I'd be inclined to say that the first, the appropriate boundaries of the system, is a mystery of deep importance. It certainly should be discussed and illustrated in

---

[13] If one is willing to accept psychoanalytic theories, this assertion is, of course, obvious. But on a more commonplace level, it is also obvious that any person's moods and values change over time, and OR plans over considerable time spans.

[14] This is one reason why, for example, the transitivity of preference is far from obvious; the resultant of forces operating to choose A over B, and the forces that choose B over C, may be different from the forces that operate when the choice is between A and C.

[15] This issue is apt to produce some "purely academic" battles, e.g., whether program planning and budgeting, cost–benefit analysis, or "disjointed incrementalism" ("muddling through"; see Braybrooke and Lindblom, *A Strategy of Decision Policy Evaluation as a Social Process*, New York (1963)) are appropriate OR techniques. The practitioner is apt to be so desperate to find one workable approach that the purely academic battle seems largely irrelevant.

the curriculum, if only to get the student beyond the cliches.[16] The second problem, the anatomy of decision making is also a deep mystery, but one on which there is some considerable research effort. The studies include psychoanalytical analyses of individual decision making and decision theoretic models and experiments, though neither group of researchers talks to the other. The studies also include group experiments, sociological case studies, multi-decision making models, and so on. Here again the lack of communication is apparent. One example will suffice. I dare say that most practicing operations researchers assume that the law lies in the environment of the decision maker, which assumption is translated into constraint equations where the constraints cannot be relaxed. But a student of law would regard such an assumption as thoroughly naive; for one thing, laws are necessarily ambiguous, and every good lawyer (or manager) recognizes that a translation of a law into a rigid constraint may be a very poor strategy.

The other basic entity in systems is the client or beneficiary, the group of individuals the system ought to serve. This group poses a real problem relative to the profession of OR. In many other professions, one assumes that the client is the person who pays the bills for professional service, or at least it is entirely up to the bill payer to designate the client as well as the client's interests. OR in the past has tended to accept this principle, which, in a sense, is an imputed moral code of the profession. Hence OR teams, either internal or consulting, try to get the bill payer to help formulate the problem and assist in developing an appropriate measure of performance.

Now it is surely a worthwhile academic question to ask whether this strategy of the practitioner is a good one. To be specific, let us suppose that the vast majority of social systems today are serving the wrong client, not a "slightly" wrong client, but are serving one group while largely ignoring or even being detrimental to the right client.[17]

---

[16] For example, "study the system within feasible limits," which semantically says practically nothing, because "feasible" means "capable of being done." The principle therefore, says "study what you are capable of studying" The major question of system boundaries is "what are we capable of studying?" Leibniz would say "the whole universe"; a cautious incrementalist would say "only a little bit." A more subtle principle says "set the boundaries at some departmental level (e.g. one NIH institute), but present the recommendations so that the next higher level can compare these with recommendations for other departments (so that the director of NIH can make comparisons across institutes)." But this principle is based on a very dubious systemic judgment, namely, that the departmental boundaries are appropriate.

[17] There is plenty of evidence that many of our concerned young people believe this assumption. They need not be very young, either. In one of my graduate seminars consisting of students ranging from ages 23 to 40, the term reports described and analyzed a social system, a hospital, a company, a credit department, a counter-insurgency division, etc. Of the 22 papers, 21 concluded that the actual system was serving the wrong client. The hospital serves the doctors, not primarily the patients; the company serves top managers; the credit department serves the merchandising manager, not the customers; the counter-insurgency division serves the Pentagon, not the natives. Obviously the experiment was biased, but today's professors are not all that influential on mature student opinion, I think.

Then OR as a profession would have to regard itself as an arm of the Devil: it is assisting decision makers to become more rational and more adept at using social systems to serve the people who do not deserve the service. Hence, if the thesis is plausible, and I think it is, then it is clear that it should be thoroughly examined. To return to the earlier point, the examination is an academic matter—it is the concern of those who prepare people for the profession; no prescription to the practitioner to cease and desist is contemplated. But it should be pointed out that the academic concern extends to academic institutions; to say that the university *is* the faculty is to reach a conclusion about its clients, a rather questionable conclusion, to say the least.

The academician faces two tasks with respect to the thesis that most social systems are serving the wrong client; one is to determine whether the thesis can be tested, and, if so and it passes the test, what the implications are for OR as a profession, and specifically, for the preparation for service. With respect to the latter, we can return to Blauch's second condition for a profession: "serving the needs of the people rather than personal gain." I assume that the academic version of OR is based on this criterion, and hence that the professional operations researcher is concerned that the system serves the right client. He is essentially a man of good will. If he is convinced that decision makers are serving the wrong client, then his professional obligation is to change the decision making process. That is, he must try to "secure" such a change.

IMPROVEMENT

But before examining this heroic mission, we need to see whether the unpleasant thesis is testable; this discussion takes us to the second of the list of four terms in the definition of OR: "improvement." Here the mystery becomes deepest. But philosophical tradition does help to define OR's basic ethical assumptions. First of all, two very common philosophical positions need to be examined, for either one, if adopted, makes the mystery disappear, and the thesis of the wrong client becomes unimportant. The two viewpoints are *ethical relativism* and *determinism*.

Determinism is perhaps the easier to eliminate from this discussion. It states that there are no choices, since man's every action is determined by forces outside of his control. In effect, determinism shrinks the social system to its limit by regarding everything to be in the environment. Since there are no resources and no decision makers, the whole activity of planning is a farce, and the "client" is the most farcical character of all. For present purposes, it seems enough to say that a determinist does not believe in professions, and hence is *hors de combat*.

The far more serious and prevalent philosophy is ethical relativism, which is based on two very strong systemic judgments: (i) people are reasonably adept at deciding what they really want or need, or, more generally, at deciding what they really believe ought to happen; and (ii) the only basis for deciding what ought to happen is the personal belief. One can extend ethical relativism to groups of people, in which case the two conditions become: (i) there is a reasonably adequate way to decide what a group believes ought to be done (e.g. by a majority vote) and (ii) the group belief is the sole basis for such a decision.

Some adherents to relativism would like to weaken their position by admitting that people are not very good at deciding how they think things should be, especially in the face of considerable evidence that supports this viewpoint. But then they land in a rather awkward "absolute relativism," which says that there is an absolute ("objective") way of telling what people want, and the "good" is what they want. Such a position really gives up on the whole spirit of relativism, since clearly the justification for controlling people's behaviour is now in the hands of those who can decide what people really want.

Although it is not difficult to discover the serious flaws of ethical relativism, it is more important to OR as a profession to recognize why it is so appealing. Indeed, the first quarter century of OR can be described as one in which the vast majority of practitioners accepted this doctrine, almost without reflection. True, most operations researchers would hesitate to work for organized crime or a dictator, and, more seriously, there is an ongoing debate about the appropriateness of working on secret defense contracts. But I suspect that most practitioners regard their judgments on these matters to be "subjective," i.e. not susceptible to an objective test.

Since the academician explores issues as deeply as he can, in this case he must ask what the distinction is between "objective" and "subjective" judgments in OR. We are back to the issues of scientific method, and the promise to say some more about it. If we could use some combination of rationalism and empiricism as the epistomological base, then we could say that "objective" results are those which arise from clearly warranted observation and reason. But we have seen that OR results also depend on very strongly systemic judgments. Are these "objective"? They are certainly not verifiable, either by observation or clear reasoning. And yet most practitioners would reject the idea that their work is purely subjective, in the sense that some other practitioner with a different opinion about the system could legitimately reach a quite opposite opinion about the optimal decision.

To make the point clear, suppose, following Kant,[18] we make a destinction between a hypothetical and a categorical value judgment. In the simplest of

---

[18] *Critique of Practical Reason* (1788)

terms, the hypothetical judgment says "if such-and-such a state of affairs has the highest value, then do X." A categorical value judgment says "such-and-such a state of affairs is best." Most practitioners, I think, would say that OR can be reasonably objective in making some hypothetical judgments. Even Kant thought that the hypothetical judgments could be verified by observation, while the categorical required an entirely different approach. But if we accept the analysis given above of OR's scientific method, then hypothetical judgments also require strong, non-verifiable systemic judgments.

It seems clear that the rationalist–empiricist concept of objectivity has no place in OR as a profession.[19] Objectivity requires, instead, a Hegelian basis.[20] Here objectivity is attained by exposing the systemic judgments to their "deadly" opponents. The Hegelian idea is that one's "world view" (*Weltanschauung*) shapes the information one uses to reach conclusions. No data can ever fatally destroy a *Weltanschauung*, though it may produce modifications in the basic story. If you are convinced that there is a communist plot to overthrow democratic government by inciting the young and other susceptibles to demonstrate and revolt, then no amount of data will ever make you change your mind.[21] Many managers remain convinced they are in one business (e.g. railroad transportation) even though to others the far more plausible story is that they are in another (e.g. real estate).

The Hegelian exercise means confronting one's most cherished assumptions with a plausible counter assumption. It is by no means an easy exercise for one person to carry out, and often in the history of science and management the confrontations have been played out by different people. The point is less the design of the confrontation, as in really exposing oneself to the possibility of colossal error. This is the essence of the uncertainty of a profession; if one endures the heroic trail, then the result might be called "objective." To be sure, the distinction between subjective and objective now becomes social. The subjective is not derived from some one person's observations and thoughts; it rather derives from a social agreement not to examine the foundation of beliefs beyond a certain point. The more open the society is to such examination, the more "objective" its beliefs become.

The foregoing account carries with it the smug tone of superiority, as though

---

[19] I might add that this remark can be generalized to any profession; to use a trivial example, the doctor who says, "if you go home, take an aspirin and go to bed, you will maximize your chances of getting well," makes the strong systemic judgment that lying in bed will produce no adverse anxiety reactions.

[20] G. W. F. Hegel, *Phenomenology of Mind* (1807), and *Logic* (1816).

[21] Ackoff likes to tell a relevant joke. A man was persuaded to go to a psychiatrist because he was convinced he was dead. "Look here," said the therapist, "dead men don't bleed, do they?" "No," said the patient; at which the doctor took a needle and pricked the other's finger. "My God!" exclaimed the patient, "dead men *do* bleed!" A believer in the communist plot, if told by a very reliable expert that no such plot exists, would sadly conclude that his expert was no longer reliable, having probably been bought out by the enemy.

objective societies are necessarily better than subjective ones. This would be a fallacious conclusion, much like the fallacious but commonly held belief that communication is always better than non-communication. The inquiring mind is all too apt to believe that open inquiry is always superior to no inquiry. But even on its own grounds, this belief is untenable, because inquiry is a non-seperable component of the total social system. A well known disharmony of this century is the pursuit of nuclear and biological results long before man has invented a society capable of tolerating their impact. We sadly come to learn that "truth for its own sake" is a myth, because it fallaciously assumes that the inquiring subsystem of society can improve its own measure of performance independent of the rest of society and its problems.

Furthermore, the task of objectivity is not a clear one. It is all very well to say that one should examine one's own basic beliefs, but how? They do not come up at our beck and call. And even if we seek out a known opponent, how can we be sure that he is an opponent of our most sacred opinions? The court room today does not put on trial some of our most serious convictions: e.g. that criminals ought to be convicted and punished if found guilty by their "peers."

But these two caveats, that the way of objectivity may be both dangerous and uncertain, make the quest a heroic one, and therefore not to be scorned. Mythical heroes were terribly disruptive of people's lives, even of those who were relatively peaceful and benign. Also in performing their heroic tasks they tackled the wrong set of problems, and it is only late in the game that a Hercules or Psyche asks why they are undertaking such monstrous efforts. Nethertheless, heroism is a great quality of the human spirit. I should say that a profession which lacks it is degraded thereby. I don't mean that all OR practitioners should constantly be questioning the basic systemic judgments of the OR group. It's simply that as a profession we should have our share of heroes. Who knows? "OR Central" may eventually be on prime time.

Now if the objectivity of "fact" in OR results from the dangerous and uncertain enterprise of arriving at a judgment in the context of the opposition of basic world views, then what about morality and ultimate value judgments? It certainly appears as though the popular dismissal of objectivity in moral matters holds no water. It is based on the idea that people differ about moral principles, within and between cultures. But people also differ about relevant facts for decision making, within and between cultures. It begins to look as though the ethical relativists have made a thoroughly arbitrary choice. Although the same basic methodology is used to determine both facts and the ultimate values of goals, they choose to regard the former as potentially objective but not the latter. And if they argue that it is not feasible to reach group agreement on ultimate values whereas it is feasible to do so on facts, then we are back to the familiar issue of systems analysis: when is agreement a reliable criterion? Since this is still an unresolved problem of the OR inquiring system, the issue of ethical relativism is also unresolved. The heroes of OR will abandon relativism and embark on the dangerous quest.

A non-relativistic ethics for OR is not hard to find, because it is implicit in the very methods which OR uses. The principle is based on what can be called an "enabling" theory of value. Again, the basic theme goes back to Hobbes and Hume, as well as to Jeremy Bentham. The idea is that, with one exception, men differ radically in what they want; i.e. in the state of affairs they hope will occur. As E. A. Singer puts it, "With only one wish to be had, choose rather the power to get whatever you may come to want than the pleasure of having any dearest thing in the world."[22] That is, the one exception is that each man wishes the ability to attain whatever it is each wants. True, the principle so stated in its baldest form, is close to being a tautology: the meaning of "want" implies a wish for a specific ability. The real problem of an enabling philosophy is to spell out the details of how such a system of ethics would work, especially since it is all too obvious that some men wish to slit another's throat, while the other wants nothing of the kind, or some men wish to abolish all wishing, and so on.

The nineteenth century, which gave us the present of technology, also left one possible solution to the theory of enabling value: produce enough so that everyone can attain what he wants. Of course, along with this proposed solution went the idea that people need to be educated to use their affluence. Thus the fundamental ethical values are technology and practical education. What was not clear in the nineteenth century theory was how people could be taught not to misuse it. There is a kind of "how-to-keep-the-natives-quiet" mystique on the part of the enthusiastic technological elite, based on the totally unwarranted assumption that the more power a man has, the less he will tend to disturb his fellow man. At the risk of this paper sounding like a Tchaikovsky symphony, we've got again to play the inseparability theme which is one basis of OR's mystery: one cannot expect that more and more success in productivity will inevitably lead to system improvement. Nor do we understand the way in which man's cooperation with man should be designed to mesh well with man's increasing affluence and education. To mention one further example in this regard, a levelling of opportunity (i.e. the equalization of equity) which many believe to be the essence of cooperation, can quite easily destroy the incentive to create and produce new inventions. Finally, the two deepest mysteries of cooperation are the men who once lived and the men who will live, the voiceless majority. It is probably ridiculous to ignore what our ancestors would wish us to do if they were alive, and probably fatal to ignore what our progeniture will wish we had done.

The practitioner may feel that the academic has strayed far away in this discussion of the ethics of the profession, and to some extent this is true, since

---

[22] E. A. Singer, Jr., *On the Contented Life*, Henry Holt and Co., New York (1936), p. 145.

the academic is trying to get a broad perspective, to see what the whole forest looks like. There is no *a priori* reason why every academic concern should be tomorrow's practitioner's problem. But in the present case the practitioner does face much the same issue as the academician in a specific context. Many managers tend to pay attention to one productive measure of their organization—gross sales or items produced, number of graduates, number of people removed from the poverty class, and so on. They are proud of a record which moves these measures upward. The unwary operations researcher is apt to find himself formulating problems in the manager's terms, and to find his downfall when management changes from expansion to contraction.

Returning to the broader perspective, we need to ask to what extent any one of us ought morally to be concerned about lives beyond our own life spans. Today's concern with the ecology of the environment seems to say that we should. But why? What makes me wish for the power of those of the past who are forever powerless or those of the future who only will come to power in an age when I too am powerless? There must be something deeper than a mere enabling philosophy.

This "something beyond personal power" has often been called morality. Morality is that force which takes us beyond the boundaries of the system which is directly relevant to our lives. If one looks at the Ten Commandments, it is clear that each one of them is a prescription not to do something which normally would be rather natural and beneficial. Immanuel Kant caught this spirit of morality in a very elegant manner. He believed that morality as a force ("principles") is applicable to all Wills; i.e. to the totality of humanity. His formulation of the moral principle is: "Make only those decisions which treat humanity (in you or in another) as an end, never as a means only."[23]

Kant's moral law, although it universalizes the motivation for consideration of all men, dead, living and to live, nevertheless poses a paradox for the profession of OR. It is difficult to conceive of an OR recommendation which does not treat some people as means only. For example, a great deal of OR consists in reducing costs, where, at least in principle, the savings mean firing or re-allocating personnel. Since the operations researcher rarely takes these people into account, it seems reasonable to say that he "treats them as means

---

[23] *Fundamental Principles of the Metaphysic of Morals* (1785). Kant is more famous for another version of this principle, the categorical imperative: make decisions as though the basic policy of the decision were a universal policy applicable to all men ("Universal Law of Nature"). Kant regarded this version as more fundamental, because, he says, all the usual moral laws follow from it. But it is interesting to note how a contemporary development, game theory, dramatically shows up the fallacy of Kant's reasoning. Deception, Kant says, cannot be made into a universal policy, because then no-one could be deceived if he knew that all men were deceiving; thus "thou shalt not lie" was supposed to follow from his categorical imperative. But game theory tells us that if we are engaged in the universal policy of deception, we should use a mixed strategy, and no contradiction results; indeed, it may be that Nature and man together do play such a game.

only, not as ends." Even in the public sector, the operations researcher will find that, with all the best intent in the world, his plans nonetheless are immoral according to Kant's law.

Another example of the possible immorality of OR is the frequent collaboration between OR and management in instituting changes in organizations without any participation whatsoever on the part of the rest of the people concerned. One can make a plausible argument which would have wide acceptance today, that a part of what Kant calls "humanity in a person" consists in that person having a strong share in the decisions that affect his life. To the extent that managers and their collaborators prevent such participation, they are treating humanity in another as a "means only."

It needs emphasizing again that the issue of morality and OR is an academic matter, an issue dealing with the preparation for the profession. There is, of course, the question whether a moral code should be imposed on the practitioners of the profession, as it is in medicine, psychology and the law. But experience shows that such moral codes create no dilemma or mystery for the profession. They tend, in fact, to amplify the second of Blauch's conditions, namely, service to the needs of the people rather than to personal gain. On the whole, I do not regard the writing of such moral codes to be a problem of academic concern.

Now the deeper problem of morality, the hidden evil of doing good, is certainly amenable to study. Kant himself, with great foresight, believed he saw a solution.[24] His notion was that the principle of seeking happiness, which in OR we would call maximization of the measure of performance, is always partially at odds with the moral law. But, he thought, the two may be made to converge "in the limit," so that he was in effect suggesting a superior measure of performance. At the lower level, we use cost–benefit, or net profit, or social indicators; at the higher level we estimate the dispersion between the plans such measures generate and the plans which morality generates. The closer the two plans, the "better" is the planning function.

Whether we should be satisfied with Kant's notion of progress does require more study, as does the whole topic of morality and planning. For one thing, the moral side of planning appears to preclude any trade-off principle, since one does not pay for evil by doing good. The manner in which the "superior scoring system" would be designed is at this time very obscure.

But there is one very important aspect of Kant's suggestion which becomes another mystery of OR as a profession. Most practitioners pray that their mistakes will not come back to haunt them, and the astute practitioner tries to create an environment in which no error will ever prove fatal. One might label

---

[24] In the *Critique of Practical Reason* (1788); see, in particular, the section on "The Immortality of the Soul as a Postulate of Pure Practical Reason." Modern man is more inclined to accept the principle of the immortality of mankind than the immortality of each rational being.

such efforts as attempts to create planning stability, e.g. by the right kind of friendships or trusts, or by avoidance of very risky alliances.

The profession of OR faces much the same problems in the large. Not only will mistakes be made by operations researchers, but much more to the point, there may be forces at work which will negate all the most strenuous and excellent efforts of applied science to improve society. Hence the mystery is: what are the characteristics of the whole system which guarantee that no such calamity will occur, and that "improvement" can be real rather than illusory? It is certainly in keeping with one philosophical tradition[25] to call these characteristics God. Theology is another aspect of the academician's concern for the profession of OR.

SECURING

We come finally to the last of the terms of OR's definition, "securing." It needs to come last, because OR as a profession is not primarily interested in persuading decision makers to adopt its recommendations; it seeks implementation only when the practitioner has sound scientific grounds for believing that his recommendation is a real improvement in the social system.

Much has been written on implementation,[26] and there is no need here to review the results. I am more concerned with an aspect which has not been discussed, and which does constitute another basic mystery.

It must be admitted that OR as a profession is based on a philosophy which is not held valid by many conscientious people, both old and young; indeed, many people regard OR's philosophy to be dangerous if not subversive. We have already alluded to the morality issue, but there is another aspect which is equally important. This might be called constituency decision making. In its ideal form, the idea is that each public or private decision maker is responsible to the wishes of his constituency, which decides whether or not he is to continue his role of decision making. Obviously, the decision maker's main measure of performance will be the probability that he will remain in his role (i.e. be re-elected or promoted or maintained). The constituency, in the eyes of the operations researcher, need not be the client; nor does the constituency have the ability to perform the required analysis. Constituencies tend to be impressed by sheer numbers: number of students graduated, number of acts of violence, number of dollars of sales, and so on. The operations researcher well knows the pitfalls of using such numbers as a basis of decision making. The name of the constituency game is politics, and the chief commodity is

---

[25] See, for example, Descartes, *ibid*.
[26] C. West Churchman and A. H. Schainblatt, "The Researcher and the Manager: A Dialectic of Implementation", *Management Science*, **11**(4), February 1965.

political power. Maximizing political power is not a basic goal of OR's philosophy.

Here again the profession has to find a way to live with its opposition, with the expectation of a convergence over the long run. The method also is obscure, and has to be learned, if at all, through experience. Once the practitioner has learned how to adapt his behaviour to his opposition (i.e. to political power structures) while still maintaining his overall goal of system improvement, then he has taken the essential step in "securing."

CONCLUSION

Such an account of the mysteries of the profession might run the danger of creating a malaise among both the practitioners and the academics. But this would be a badly mistaken attitude. All professions face similar deep mysteries. The "body of erudite knowledge" must include an inventory of items which we know we do not know.

What should OR do about its mysteries, its "irrational side," other than appreciate it? To make a series of recommendations with assurance is obviously contrary to the spirit of the paper itself. The following suggestions are intended mainly to illustrate the points made earlier.

1. There is above all the very personal side of OR, where each practitioner should develop his own feelings and ideas about the profession. I should say it's probably a healthy sign, on the whole, whenever the practitioner begins to realize that he doesn't really know what OR is all about and appreciates and enjoys this realization.

2. The societies are hampered from doing anything very different because their organizational structure and form of meeting has become so stylized. Many of us in the early days of ORSA and TIMS dreamt of experimentation, with journals, with meetings, with organization. Try a year without *Management Science*, replacing it by a communication system of letters and working papers (including letters of recommendation for young professors). Hold a meeting without any announced program. Abolish the TIMS council and hold instead a series of self-evaluation meetings which begin with the invocation: "We have failed as a society; therefore . . ." More practically, hire an organization to determine why TIMS and ORSA cannot apply OR to themselves.

3. Publish papers on "failures which learn," in order to develop the value of uncertainty as the pathway to understanding.

4. Hold "morality meetings" where there are no experts.

5. Assess the relevance of OR and MS to (a) non-military local, national and international problems, (b) the youth, (c) the conservative lower middle class, (d) top management of firms.

6. Experiment with the schools. For example, form a consortium of organizations (firms, government agencies, unions, churches, etc.), and call them a "school of management." Each organization separately pursues its own goal; all organizations collectively pursue the goal of preparing people to manage or "do OR." How would they organize themselves to accomplish this task of preparation?

7. Make some models of the tactics and strategies of OR teams. Include in these the essence of "faith, hope and charity."

And, last, remember that the joy of OR is that it is in the center of the deepest mysteries of the human race, because, academically speaking, it has taken on the whole system. It could only have come into existence in the twentieth century: as everyone knows, the greatest discovery of our century is the place called the Whole World.

Chapter 2

The Future of Operational Research is Past

RUSSELL L. ACKOFF

INTRODUCTION

A few years ago I was asked to speak at the Joint Annual Meeting of the Operations Research Society of America and the Institute of Management Sciences. I characterized that occasion as a wake for the profession, whichever name it chose to use. In my opinion, American Operations Research is dead even though it has yet to be buried. I also think there is little chance for its resurrection because there is so little understanding of the reasons for its demise.

This lack of understanding is well reflected in a recent article by John R. Hall Jr and Sydney W. Hess entitled "OR/MS Dead or Dying? RX for Survival" that appeared in *Interfaces* (1978). The authors prescribed five treatments:

1. . . . practitioners could be more effective if more of the academics' new discoveries in OR/MS theory were made truly accessible to them. The use of short (two-page) readable summaries—refereed to protect the academics' interest—could help to move theory into practice.

2. It would also help if some academics would show less disdain for problems they have "solved before" and recognize the importance to practice of steps outside the problem-solving process (such as preparation of examples and demonstrations of techniques on real problems).

Reprinted by permission from *Journal of the Operational Research Society*, Volume 30, 1979

3. Assistant professors could be brought in to help write up the case studies that older practitioners are too busy (or too lazy) to write up.

4. Academics can be given part-time or on-site jobs with companies in their areas.

5. Internship programmes can also foster closer relationships between academics and non-academic professionals.

These recommendations make it clearer that the only thing that Hall and Hess find wrong with OR/MS is the relationship between academics and non-academic practitioners. This position is in sharp contrast with that taken by K. D. Tocher. In a recent article (1977) he questions deeply the adequacy of what Thomas Kuhn would call "the paradigm of OR," and doing so Tocher sows the seeds of revolution, not merely superficial changes. Less generally, but no less tellingly, Jonathan Rosenhead (1978) recently called into question the suitability of the OR paradigm in the area of health-service planning. For a number of years now Neil Jessop, John Stringer, John Friend and their colleagues at IOR (1967, 1969, 1974) have done likewise in areas involving the interactions of autonomous organizations. In a very recent issue of this society's journal, K D Radford (1978) offered a sketch of a new paradigm for OR.

Because there is more questioning of the paradigm in the UK than in the United States, I have the impression that Operational Research, unlike Operations, may not yet be dead. Perhaps in the land of its birth OR may have a renaissance, but, in my opinion, not without a radical transformation. In this, the first of my presentations, I deal with the death of OR. In the second (1979), I consider how it might be resurrected.

THE DENOUEMENT

The life of OR has been a short one. It was born in the UK late in the 1930s. By the mid-1960s it had gained widespread acceptance in academic, scientific, and managerial circles. In my opinion this gain was accompanied by a loss of its pioneering spirit, its sense of mission and its innovativeness. Survival, stability and respectability took precedence over development, and its decline began.

I hold academic OR and the relevant professional societies primarily responsible for this decline and since I had a hand in initiating both, I share this responsibility. By the mid-1960s most OR courses in American universities were given by academics who had never practised it. They and their students were textbook products engaging in impure research couched in the language, but not the reality, of the real world. The meetings and journals of the relevant professional societies, like classrooms, were filled with abstractions from an imagined reality. As a result OR came to be identified with the use of mathematical models and algorithms rather than the ability to formulate management problems, solve them, and implement and maintain their solutions in turbulent environments. This obsession with techniques, combined with unawareness of or indifference to the changing demands being made of managers, had three major effects on the practice of OR.

First, practitioners decreasingly took problematic situations as they came, but increasingly sought, selected, and distorted them so that favoured techniques could be applied to them. This reduced the usefulness of OR, a reduction that was well recognized by executives who pushed it further and further down in their organizations, to where such relatively simple problems arose as permitted the application of OR's mathematically sophisticated but contextually naive techniques. According to Hall and Hess (1978):

> . . . this decline in visibility has not stemmed from a wave of firings or other reductions in OR/MS ranks. Instead OR/MS talent is increasingly being dispersed to the various corporate functions. The original reason for centralization was that OR/MS was felt to need protection to establish itself. Today, the only companies still maintaining central OR groups are those that are large enough to be able to use "internal consultants" who are available to back up the analysts down the line.

The dispersion that Hall and Hess note is a fact, but their reasons for it are a fiction. I submit that OR was once a corporate staff function, because corporate executives believed it could be useful to them. It was pushed down because they no longer believed this to be the case, and they correctly perceived that if it had any use, it was in the bowels of the organization, not the head. My observation of a large number of American corporations reveals that when it could no longer be pushed down, it was pushed out.

A second effect of the technical perversion of OR derived from the fact that its mathematical techniques can easily be taught by those who do not know where, when and how to use them. This, together with the fact that in the late 1960s use of quantitative methods became an "idea in good currency," resulted in these techniques being taught widely in schools of business, engineering and public administration, among others. This has deprived OR of its unique incompetence; an increasing portion of it is done by those who do not identify with the profession.

These non-professionals are not as obsessed with the techniques nor as immune to reality as the professionals. When required to make a choice, they are more likely to embrace reality than techniques; therefore, they tend to move up in their organizations, not down.

According to Hall and Hess, the decline of visibility of professional OR in organizations "is more a sign of institutional acceptance than a sign of real decline." If one were to take this criterion seriously, one would be forced to conclude that such professions as economics and engineering, which have not declined in visibility, enjoy less institutional acceptance than OR. No. What this dispersion signifies is that OR has been equated by managers to mathematical masturbation and to the absence of any substantive knowledge or understanding of organizations or their management.

The third effect of OR's immersion in techniques is that those who either practise or preach it have come to be more and more like each other. The original interdisciplinarity of OR has completely disappeared. In his recent presidential address to the Operational Research Society, Professor Michael Simpson (1978) correctly referred to OR as a discipline. OR's isolation from other disciplines was (and is) encouraged by professional societies. In several countries, including the UK, serious consideration has been given to registering only qualified practitioners and to accrediting academic programmes. Nothing could be more effective in removing whatever vestiges of interdisciplinarity there are in the practice of OR.

In the first two decades of OR, its nature was dictated by the nature of the problematic situations it faced. Now the nature of the situation it faces is dictated by the techniques it has at its command. The nature of the problems facing managers has changed significantly over the last three decades, but OR has not. It has not been responsive to the changing needs of management brought about, to a large extent, by radical changes taking place in the environment in which it is practised. While managers were turning outward, OR was turning inward—inbreeding and introverting. It now appears to have attained the limit of introversion: a catatonic state.

Many practitioners do not accept my characterization of the state of OR or the environment in which it is practised. Supporting evidence and argument are required. I tried to provide them in my book *Redesigning the Future* (1974a), but here I summarize very briefly some of the essential points made there.

THE CHANGING ENVIRONMENT OF OR

I believe that the Second World War marked the beginning of the end of what might be called the *Machine Age*, an age that began with the Renaissance. In the Renaissance, man's attention shifted from death to life and the world in which it took place. Like a child, man sought understanding by means of a three-step process; first, taking apart the things he wanted to understand, then trying to understand how these parts worked, and finally assembling his understanding of the parts into an understanding of the whole. This process is called analysis. It was the dominant mode of thought in the Machine Age.

The use of analysis raised several fundamental questions around the answers to which the world-view and science of the Machine Age were organized. First, if in order to understand how something works we must take it apart and seek understanding of its parts, how do we acquire understanding of its parts? To analysts the answer to this question was obvious: by taking the parts apart. But if we can only understand something by understanding its parts, and if we can only understand its parts by taking them apart, how can we gain ultimate or complete understanding of anything? Machine Age man, who believed in the possibility of complete understanding, also believed it could be derived from understanding ultimate indivisible parts, *elements*. The doctrine based on these beliefs is called *reductionism*. Its many manifestations are familiar; for example, atoms, chemical elements, cells, directly observables, basic needs, instincts, phonemes, and so on. Elements were the holy grail of the analytical crusade.

Once an understanding of parts is acquired, an understanding of the whole can be achieved only if the relationships between the parts are understood. It is not surprising that Machine Age man believed that one elementary relationship was sufficient for this purpose: *cause and effect*. His exclusive commitment to this relationship yielded a *deterministic* concept of the universe, one in which everything that occurs is taken as the effect of a preceding cause. The possibility of complete understanding of the universe required postulation of a first cause, God. The universe and everything in it, including man and society, were thus conceptualized as machines or machine parts created by God to do His work.

It was natural for men who so viewed the universe, and who believed that they had been created in the image of God, to try to imitate Him, however unconsciously, by creating machines to do their work. The product of this effort was the Industrial Revolution.

Formulation of a new world-view was brought about in part by the growing preoccupation, in the second quarter of this century, with *systems*, their growing complexity and the increasing difficulty of managing them effectively. This preoccupation led to the realization that systems are wholes which lose their essential properties when taken apart. Therefore, they are wholes that cannot be understood by analysis. This realization, in turn, gave rise to *synthetic* or *systems thinking*. Three steps are involved in this process. First, a thing to be understood is conceptualized as a part of one or more larger wholes, not as a whole to be taken apart. Then understanding of the larger containing system is sought. Finally, the system to be understood is explained in terms of its *role* or *function* in the containing system. Analysis of a system reveals its structure and how it works; it yields know-how, knowledge, not understanding. It does not explain why a system works the way it does. Systems thinking is required for this.

Such thinking has produced the doctrine of *expansionism* which, in contrast to reductionism, asserts, first, that ultimate understanding of anything is an ideal that can never be attained but can be continuously approached; and, second, that understanding, in contrast to knowledge, flows from larger to smaller systems; not, as analysis assumes, from smaller to larger.

At the turn of this century the American philosopher of science, E. A. Singer Jr (1959), formulated an alternative to the deterministic cause–effect relationship and called it *producer–product*. Others have called it *non-deterministic* or *probabilistic causality*, or *directive correlation* (Sommerhoff, 1950). Whereas a classical cause was both necessary and sufficient for its effect, the Singerian producer was only necessary, not sufficient, for its product. Singer showed that slicing the universe with producer–product yielded a view of it as different from that obtained by slicing it with cause-and-effect, as the view of the interior of an orange obtained by slicing it horizontally is from the view of it obtained by slicing it vertically. The universe that appears to be mechanistic when sliced by cause-and-effect appears to be *teleological* when sliced by producer–product. Moreover, the teleology revealed is *objective*: such properties and phenomena as free will, choice, function, role and purpose can be operationally defined, observed and measured.

Systems thinking, expansionism and objective teleology provide the intellectual foundation for what may at least tentatively be called the *Systems Age*. The world-view they yield does not discard that of the Machine Age but incorporates it as a special case. Machines are understood as instruments of purposeful systems: purposeful systems are no longer conceptualized as machines. The Post Industrial Revolution is as logical a consequence of systems thinking as the Industrial Revolution was of mechanistic thinking. In this second revolution man seeks to develop and use instruments that do *mental* rather than physical work: artifacts that *observe* (generate symbols), communicate (transmit symbols) and *think* (process symbols logically). Together these technologies make possible the mechanization of *control, automation*.

Systems thinking brings special attention to organizations: purposeful systems that contain purposeful parts with different roles or functions, and that are themselves parts of larger purposeful systems. This focus reveals three fundamental interrelated organizational problems: how to design and manage systems so that they can effectively serve their own purposes, the purposes of their parts, and those of the larger systems of which they are part. These are the *self-control*, the *humanization* and the *environmentalization* problems, respectively.

Now OR has been and is almost exclusively concerned with organizational self-control. It has virtually ignored the other two types of problem and the relationship between them and self-control. Furthermore, it employs a Machine Age approach to the self-control problem. Its method is analytical and its models are predominantly of closed mechanical systems, not of open purposeful systems. This is clearly revealed when one considers OR's use of two concepts: *optimization* and *objectivity*.

OPTIMIZATION IN OR

I begin this discussion of optimization by retelling one of what my students call "Ackoff's Fables" (1977). Two years ago, an OR group that was highly placed in an important public agency asked me to review one of its major projects. Most of the members of the group had received degrees in OR from three of the major centres of OR education in the United States.

The project involved a very large intrasystem distribution problem. Those who worked on it were very proud of the number of variables and constaints included in the linear programming transportation model they had developed. As usual, the researchers complained of the fact that they had not been able to obtain either the quantity or quality of data that they would have liked. As a result it had been necessary for them to engage in a bit of data enrichment.

After the team members had presented the problem, the model and their way of solving it, they showed me what they referred to as their "evaluation of the results." Over a reasonably long period of time they had recorded the decisions actually made and implemented by the responsible managers and had fed these decisions into their model and had calculated the total related operating costs. They had then compared these costs with those associated with the optimal solution derived from the same model.

Lo and behold! The optimal solutions were consistently better than those of the managers. Using these differences they had estimated an annual saving which they had used successfully in convincing management to adopt their model and optimizing procedure.

Of minor significance was the fact they had not taken into account the not insignificant costs of their research and its implementation. Also of minor significance was the fact that they also had not taken into account the unreliability and inaccuracy of the data about which they had complained. Of *major* significance, however, was the fact that even if these costs had been taken into account, their evaluation would have been a *farce*.

The optimal solution of a model is *not* an optimal solution of a problem unless the model is a perfect representation of the problem, which it never is. Therefore, in testing a model and evaluating solutions derived from it, the model itself should never be used to determine the relevant comparative performance measures. The only thing demonstrated by so doing is that the minimum or maximum of a function is lower or higher than a non-minimum or non-maximum.

All models are simplifications of reality. If this were not the case, their usefulness would be significantly reduced. Therefore, it is critical to determine how well models represent reality. In this project the team had not done so.

I put the following question to its members: Suppose you could not conduct an adequate test of your model, what would you do? After considerable squirming the group's leader said he would ask managers to accept it *on faith.* *Voila* and Q.E.D.!

This was not the end of the matter. The researchers went on to tell me how the managers had invariably modified the optimal solution to take into account factors that were not taken into account in the model. Furthermore, the team confessed that it had not carried out any analysis of the nature of the adjustments made by managers or their effects. When I pressed for an explanation of this oversight, I was told that the nature of the factors considered by the managers precluded their inclusion in a mathematical model. *Voila* again!

Then came the climactic revelation. After about six months the managers had discontinued use of the model because of a significant change in the environment of the system. This change was political in character. When I asked why they had not tried to incorporate the relevant politics into their model, I was told that such changes are neither quantifiable nor predictable.

It should be apparent by now that if the researchers had, in fact, solved a problem, it was not the problem that the managers had.

The Need for Learning and Adaptation

The structure and the parameters of problematic situations continuously change, particularly in turbulent environments. Because optimal solutions are very seldom made adaptive to such changes, their optimality is generally of short duration. They frequently become less effective than were the often more robust solutions that they replace. Let us call this crossover point the moment of death of the solution. Donald A. Schon (1971) has convincingly argued that the life of solutions to many critical social and organizational problems is shorter than the time required to find them. Therefore, more and more so-called optimal solutions are still-born. With the accelerating rate of technological and social change dramatized by Alvin Toffler (1971) and others, the expected life of optimal solutions and the problems to which they apply can be expected to become increasingly negative.

For these reasons there is a greater need for decision-making systems that can learn and adapt quickly and effectively in rapidly changing situations than there is for systems that produce optimal solutions that deteriorate with change. Most operational researchers have failed to respond to this need. As a consequence, the application of OR is increasingly restricted to those problems that are relatively insensitive to their environments. These usually involve the behaviour of mechanical rather than purposeful systems and arise at the lower levels of the organization; hence the movement of OR down to them.

The Omission of Aesthetics

There is a second very subtle deficiency in OR's concept of optimality that derives from the concept of *rationality* on which it is based. The conventional concept of an optimal solution to a problem is one that maximizes expected value. Expected value is expressed as a function of three types of variable: first, the *probabilities of choice* associated with each of the available courses of action; second, the *efficiencies* of each of these courses of action for each possible outcome; and third, the values of each of these outcomes. The probabilities of choice that maximize the expected value are said to be both a rational and optimal choice. Rationality and optimality so conceived are seriously deficient because they do not take into account two other types of variable. Let me explain.

A positively valued outcome is called an *end* or *objective*. Any course of action that has some probability of producing an end is called a *means*. In OR's concept of optimality the value of a means is taken to lie exclusively in its efficiency for ends, that is, the value of a means is taken to be purely *instrumental, extrinsic*. On the other hand, the value of an end is taken to lie in the satisfaction its attainment brings, to be purely *non-instrumental, intrinsic*. OR does not acknowledge, let alone take into account, the intrinsic value of means and the extrinsic value of ends.

Means and ends are relative, not absolute, concepts. Every means is also an end and every end is also a means. For example, going to school is a means of obtaining an education, an end. But obtaining an eduction is also a means of increasing one's income, an end. Increasing income, in turn, is a means of supporting a family, and so on.

Every means has intrinsic value because it is also an end, a potential source of satisfaction. And every end has extrinsic value because it is also a means; it has consequences.

That means have intrinsic value is commonplace knowledge. For example, we have preferences among shoes that are identical in all respects except for colour. We like certain colours more than others. Such preferences among means have nothing to do with their efficiencies but with the satisfaction their use brings. We often prefer a less efficient means because of the satisfaction its use brings. Persistent efficiency-independent preferences among means are called *traits*. Traits, in turn, are elements of that general characteristic of personality called *style*. Style has to do with the satisfactions we derive from what we do rather than what we do it for. It is apparent to all but (apparently) an optimizer that the pursuit of an objective is often more satisfying than its attainment. Herein, of course, lies the attractiveness of games.

To the extent that OR's concept of optimality fails to take the intrinsic value of means, traits and style into account, it is seriously deficient. How they can be taken into account is much too big a subject to deal with here (Ackoff and Emery, 1972; Ackoff, 1975). But let me say a little about it.

In 1936 the eminent psychologists G. W. Allport and H. S. Odbert identified 17 953 traits. It is apparent, therefore, that it is not feasible to measure, let alone include in a model, every relevant aspect of the styles of the decision makers and all others who hold a stake in a decision. This presents a problem that is taken up elsewhere (Ackoff, 1979).

Now consider ends. Every end that is less than an ideal has consequences with respect to which it can be considered a means. Every consequence of an outcome is itself a means to further consequences, and so on to an ultimate consequence. A maximally desired ultimate consequence, of course, is an ideal which is the only kind of an end that can have purely intrinsic value. Therefore, the instrumental value of any end that is less than an ideal lies in the amount of progress towards one or more ideals that its attainment represents. For example, if an ideal of science is omniscience, then at least part of the extrinsic value of the outcome of any scientific research lies in how much it advances us toward this ideal.

Again, to the extent that OR's concept of optimality fails to take extrinsic value of ends, progress towards ideals, into account, it is seriously deficient.

In a recent article (1975) I tried to show that non-instrumental values of means and instrumental values of ends are aesthetic in character, and that aesthetic, as well as ethical, values should be incorporated into our theories of decision making. My reasons for doing so were not philosophical; they were pragmatic.

I believe the current world-wide concern with deteriorating *quality of life*, and of such aspects of life as work and education, derives from decreasing stylistic satisfaction and loss of a sense of progress. More and more people are coming to realize that optimization of all the quantities of life does not optimize the quality of life and that growth is a limiting objective.

In addition, there is a widespread belief that much of the accelerating rate of change is getting us nowhere. There is a diminishing sense of progress towards such ideals as peace of mind, peace on earth, equality of opportunity, individual freedom and privacy and the elimination of poverty. A sense of progress towards ideals gives meaning to life, makes choice significant. But today more and more people believe either with Jacques Ellul (1967) that they are no longer in control of their futures, or, as the Nobel laureate George Wald (1969) wrote, with part of the younger generation, that there may be no future. For them choice is meaningless. Quality of life is degraded by resignation to a future that is believed to preclude progress towards ideals.

Those of us who are engaged in helping others make decisions have the opportunity and the obligation to bring consideration of quality of life—style and progress—into their deliberations. OR has virtually ignored both the opportunity and the obligation.

Beyond Problem Solving

My third point about problem solving is as obvious as my second point about style and progress was obscure. Managers are not confronted with problems that are independent of each other, but with dynamic situations that consist of complex systems of changing problems extracted from messes by analysis; they are to messes as atoms are to tables and chairs. We experience messes, tables, and chairs; not problems and atoms.

Because messes are systems of problems, the sum of the optimal solutions to each component problem taken separately is *not* an optimal solution to the mess. The behaviour of a mess depends more on how the solutions to its parts interact than on how they act independently of each other. But the unit in OR is a problem, not a mess. Managers do not solve problems; they manage messes.

Effective management of messes requires a particular type of *planning*, not problem solving. The inappropriateness of OR modelling to the type of planning required has been presented effectively by K. D. Tocher (1977) and Jonathan Rosenhead (1978) in the articles already referred to. Furthermore, the *design* (or redesign) of organized systems so as to reduce or eliminate messes is not a preoccupation of OR. Planning and design are predominantly synthesizing, rather than analytic, activities; they involve putting things together rather than taking them apart. Moreover, there is no such thing as an optimal plan for, or design of, a purposeful system in a dynamic environment. The objective of such efforts should be to produce systems that can pursue ideals effectively and do so in a way that provides continuing satisfaction to the participants.

The Paradigmatic Dilemma of OR

Now for my fourth point; the type of model employed in OR implies a particular paradigm of problem solving. It consists of two parts: *predicting the future* and *preparing for it*. Clearly, the effectiveness of this approach depends critically on the accuracy with which the future can be predicted. It helps us little, and may harm us much, to prepare perfectly for an imperfectly predicted future. It is important, therefore, to understand the conditions under which perfect prediction is possible in principle, if not in practice.

Perfect prediction is possible under two sets of conditions; first, when nothing changes. Of course, if nothing could change, choice, hence problems, would not exist. At best we would be restricted to changing our own behaviour and only that behaviour which had no effect on anything external to us. Moreover others in our environment would not be able to change any of their behaviour that affects anything other than themselves, because this would constitute a change in our environment. Clearly the world is not like this. If nothing else, what we do affects others, what they do affects us.

The second set of conditions under which perfect prediction would be possible is that the behaviour of that which we predict occurs in accordance with deterministic causal laws, and that we know perfectly these laws and the structure of whatever it is that we are predicting; that is, if the world were like what the Machine Age thought it was like, and we had such complete knowledge of it as that Age believed was within our grasp. But if what we can predict perfectly is necessarily determined, then we can do nothing about it; that is, we cannot change what can be predicted perfectly. But can we not prepare ourselves for it?

Some will point out that we can prepare for the weather although we cannot affect it; and it is conceivable that the weather behaves mechanistically even though we do not yet understand it well enough to predict it accurately. This argument holds only because apparently we are not a part of the weather system. The organizations and institutions for which we work, however, are part of the socio-economic system that we try to predict, hence their preparations and those of others affect that system. This is why the behaviour of containing systems cannot be predicted accurately.

To avoid the dilemma deriving from the predict-and-prepare paradigm, the operational researcher implicitly assumes that the environment of the system he deals with, the containing system, is deterministic in nature—hence is predictable in principle if not in practice—but that the system he is dealing with has choice, is purposeful. This amounts to assuming that the containing system behaves mechanistically, but that the contained system being manipulated is teleological. Now one of the things we have never been able to conceptualize is a machine that has purposeful parts, and for good reason; it involves a contradiction. Thus there is a critical type of indeterminacy inherent in the paradigm employed by OR: to the extent we can predict accurately the behaviour of a system of which we are a part, we cannot prepare effectively for it; and to the extent that we can prepare effectively, we cannot predict accurately what we are preparing for.

OR lives with this paradigmatic dilemma by keeping it unconscious and continues to try simultaneously to improve its predictions and its preparations.

There is a way out of this dilemma, but it requires a change of paradigm. If we can prepare for the future, we can affect it. Therefore, the paradigm of OR should be one that involves "designing a desirable future and inventing ways of bringing it about." The future depends at least as much on what we and others do between now and then as it does on what has already happened. Therefore, we can affect it, and by collaboration with others—expanding the system to be controlled—we can increase our chances of "making it happen." The wider the collaboration, the more closely we can approximate the future we have jointly designed. It is this perception by Fred Emery and Eric Trist (1973) that gave rise to their work in social ecology.

Prediction and preparation were the principal modalities of the Machine Age; design and invention are emerging as the principal modalities of the Systems Age. Prediction and preparation involve passive adaptation to an environment that is believed to be out of our control. Design and invention involve active control of a system's environment as well as the system itself.

The models currently employed by OR are evaluative in nature; they enable us to compare alternative decisions or decision rules that are "given." In design and invention, however, the alternatives are "taken," created. Creative solutions to problems are not ones obtained by selecting the best from among a well- or widely-recognized set of alternatives, but rather by finding or producing a new alternative. Such an alternative is frequently so superior to any of those previously perceived that formal evaluation is not required. If it is, however, then the evaluative models of OR may have a use. The challenge, therefore, is not so much to improve our methods of evaluation, but to improve our methods of design and invention.

The point of the view I have expressed up to this point is not that OR's concept of problem solving is useless, but that it should have been taken as a starting-point of OR's development, not as its end-point. To have taken it as the end-point was to have aborted OR's development and to have initiated its retreat from reality.

The Disciplinarity of OR

My fifth point relates to an allegation I made earlier: that although OR began as an interdisciplinary activity, it has become uncompromisingly unidisciplinary. This, I believe, has contributed significantly to its decline.

Colin Cherry (1957) observed that up until the time of Leibniz one person could know the entire body of scientific knowledge. As science expanded it became necessary to subdivide both its pursuit of knowledge and the knowledge it produced. Disciplines began to emerge, slowly at first, but with increasing speed. A few years ago the US National Research Council had identified about one hundred and fifty of them.

Subjects, disciplines, and professions are categories that are useful in filing scientific knowledge and in dividing the labour involved in its pursuit, but they are nothing more than this. Nature and the world are not organized as science and universities are. There are no physical, chemical, biological, psychological, sociological or even operational research problems. These are names of different points-of-view, different aspects of the same reality, not different kinds of reality. Any problematic situation can be looked at from the point-of-view of any discipline, but not necessarily with equal fruitfulness. The higher in the evolutionary scale is the object of study, the larger is the number of disciplines that are likely to make a constructive contribution to that study. For example, a doctor may see the incapacity of an elderly woman as a result of her weak heart; an architect, as deriving from the fact that she must walk up three flights of steep stairs to the meagre room she rents; an economist, as due to her lack of income; a social worker, as a consequence of her children's failure to "take her in"; and so on. Planning such an old lady's future ought to involve all these points-of-view and many others. Progress in handling messes, as well as problems, derives at least as much from creative reorganization of the way we pursue knowledge and the knowledge we already have as it does from new discoveries. Science's filing system can be reorganized without changing its content, but doing so can increase our access to and understanding of that content.

The world is in such a mess largely because we decompose messes into unidisciplinary problems that are treated independently of each other. Effective treatment of messes requires the application of not only Science with a capital "S," but also all the arts and humanities we can command. OR provides no such treatment. Its interdisciplinarity is a pretension, not a reality.

OBJECTIVITY IN OR

OR does not incorporate the arts and humanities largely because of its distorted belief that doing so would reduce its *objectivity*, a misconception it shares with much of science. The meaning of *objectivity* is less clear than that of *optimality*. Nevertheless, most scientists believe it is a good thing. They also believe that objectivity in research requires the exclusion of any ethical–moral values held by the researchers. We need not argue the desirability of objectivity so conceived; *it is not possible*. Since my argument to this effect has already appeared (1974b), I repeat only its main points here.

Most, if not all, scientific inquiries involve either testing hypotheses or estimating the values of variables. Both of these procedures necessarily involve balancing two types of error. Hypotheses-testing procedures require use of a significant level, the significance of which appears to escape most scientists. Their choice of such a level is usually made unconsciously, dictated by convention. This level, as many of you know, is the probability of rejecting a hypothesis when it is true. Naturally, we would like to make this probability as small as possible. Unfortunately, however, the lower we set this probability, the higher is the probability of accepting a hypothesis when it is false. Therefore, choice of a significance level involves a value judgment by the scientist about the relative seriousness of these two types of error. The fact that he usually makes this value judgement unconsciously does not attest to his objectivity, but to his ignorance.

There is a significance level at which any hypothesis is acceptable, and a level at which it is not. Therefore, statistical significance is *not* a property of data or a hypothesis but is a consequence of an implicit or explicit value judgment applied to them.

The choice of an estimating procedure can also be shown to require the evaluation of the relative importance of negative and positive errors of estimation. The most commonly used procedures are "unbiased"; therefore, they provide best estimates only when errors of equal magnitude but of opposite signs are equally serious—a condition I have never found in the real world.

Those who conduct research in which the consequences of error are very difficult to identify often excuse themselves from giving these errors conscious consideration by calling their research "pure," "fundamental," or "basic." These labels do not change the fact that in drawing any conclusion from any type of research, a judgment about the relative seriousness of different types of error is necessarily involved.

The prevailing concept of objectivity is basd on a distinction between ethical–moral man, who is believed to be emotional, involved and biased, and scientific man, who is believed to be unemotional, uninvolved and unbiased. The scientist is expected to deposit his ethics and morality, his "heart," at the door to his workplace, but to take his "head" with him. This expectation obviously assumes the separability of head and heart, of science and values. I find this assumption incredible in light of what science and philosophy have revealed about the nature of man. To make this assumption is equivalent to assuming that because we can look at and discuss the head and tail of a coin separately, we can separate them.

Immanuel Kant (1929) showed that thought and observation could not be separated. C. G. Jung (1926) argued that neither thought nor observation could be separated from feeling, the source of value judgments. C. West Churchman (1961), I believe, showed the validity of this argument. To think of objectivity in terms of thoughtless and feelingless observations, as some classical empiricists did, is to think of the scientist as a camera or tape-recorder. To think of objectivity is observationless and feelingless thought, as some classical rationalists did, is to think of the scientist as an unprogrammed computer. The scientist can no more act like a machine than a machine can act like a scientist.

Objectivity is *not* the absence of value judgments in purposeful behaviour. It is the social product of an open interaction of a wide variety of subjective value judgments. *Objectivity* is a *systemic property of science taken as a whole, not a property of individual researchers or research*. It is obtained only when all possible values have been taken into account; hence, like certainty, it is an ideal that science can continually approach but never attain. That which is true works, and it works whatever the values of those who put it to work. It is *value-full*, not value-free.

This concept of objectivity has an important implication for OR. The clients of OR are usually organizations. These organizations have purposes of their own, and so do their parts and the larger systems of which they are part. Therefore, organizations clearly have responsibilities to themselves, their parts and their containing systems. These purposes are often in conflict. Such conflicts are frequently conceptualized by managers and the researchers who serve them as games to be won. In my opinion, such a formulation is irresponsible, unprofessional and unethical.

It seems to me that it is the responsibility of managers and their researchers to try to dissolve or resolve such conflicts and serve all of an organization's stakeholders in a way that reflects the relative importance of the organization to them, not their relative importance to the organization. This cannot be done without involving them or their representatives in the organization's decision making. To fail to take all stakeholders into account, as OR usually does, is to devalue those who are not considered or involved in the decision process but who are affected by it. Their exclusion is a value judgment, one that appears to me to be immoral. Science has a moral responsibility to all those who can be affected by its output, not merely to those who sponsor it.

SUMMARY

Now let me attempt a constructive summary. I have tried to make the following points.

First, there is a greater need for decision-making systems that can learn and adapt effectively than there is for optimizing systems that cannot.

Second, in decision making, account should be taken of aesthetic values—stylistic preferences and progress towards ideals—because they are relevant to quality of life.

Third, problems are abstracted from systems of problems, messes. Messes require holistic treatment. They cannot be treated effectively by decomposing them analytically into separate problems to which optimal solutions are sought.

Fourth, OR's analytic problem-solving paradigm, "predict and prepare," involves internal contradictions and should be replaced by a synthesizing planning paradigm such as "design a desirable future and invent ways of bringing it about."

Fifth, effective treatment of messes requires interaction of a wide variety of disciplines, a requirement that OR no longer meets.

Sixth and last, all those who can be affected by the output of decision making should either be involved in it so they can bring their interests to bear on it, or their interests should be well represented by researchers who serve as their advocates.

In another article (1979) I consider what can be done to take these points into account.

POSTSCRIPT

Let me close with a very personal postscript. I doubt the persuasiveness of the arguments I have presented here. In the early 1970s I persistently argued similarly with the faculty in OR that I had assembled at the University of Pennsylvania. Despite three years' effort I was unable to convince them of the need for radical change. A minority of the faculty and I felt this need for change so deeply that we separated from the OR faculty and initiated a new graduate programme in what we called "Social Systems Sciences." This name was selected for three reasons. First, it was the only one we proposed that no other department of the university objected to, for obvious reasons. Second, we could not conceive of a profession, a discipline or a society using such an awkward name, and we wanted to preclude such use. Finally, it suggests, however vaguely, what we are about. Nevertheless, we would not have changed the name if we could have changed OR.

If I could not persuade a faculty that I had assembled to change its concept of OR, you can understand why I am not very hopeful here. But I would point out one thing. The OR Programme at Pennsylvania is only a fraction of the size it was when the separation occurred and it no longer has a research centre associated with it. The new programme in Social Systems Sciences is now much larger than the programme in OR is or ever was. Of course this does not prove that I was right; but it does suggest that if I was wrong, it was not a costly error.

REFERENCES

Ackoff, R.L. (1974a). *Redesigning the Future*, John Wiley, New York.
Ackoff, R.L. (1974b). The social responsibility of operational research, *Opl Res. Q.*, **25**, 361–371.
Ackoff, R.L. (1975). Does quality of life have to be quantified, *Gen. Syst.*, **IX**, 213–219.
Ackoff, R.L. (1977). Optimization + objectivity = opt out, *Eur. J. Opl Res.*, **1**, 1–7.
Ackoff, R.L. (1979). Resurrecting the future of operational research. *J. Opl Res. Soc.*, **30**, 189–200.
Ackoff, R.L., and Emery, F.E. (1972). *On Purposeful Systems*, Aldine-Atherton, Chicago.
Allport, G.W., and Odbert, H.S. (1936). Trait-names; a psycholexical study, *Psych.Mon.*, **211**.
Cherry, C. (1957). *On Human Communication*, John Wiley, New York.
Churchman, C.W. (1961). *Prediction and Optimal Decision*, Prentice-Hall, Englewood Cliffs, NJ.
Emery, F.E., and Trist, E.L. (1973). *Towards a Social Ecology*, Plenum Press, London.
Ellul, J. (1967). *The Technological Society*, Vintage Books, New York.
Friend, J.K., and Jessop, W.N. (1969). *Local Government and Strategic Choice*, Tavistock, London.

Friend, J.K., Power, J.M., and Yewlett, C.J.L. (1974). *The Inter-Corporate Dimension*, Tavistock, London.

Hall, J.R. Jr., and Hess, S.W. (1978). OR/MS dead or dying? RX for survival, *Interfaces*, 8, 42–44.

Jung, C.J. (1926). *Psychological Types*, Harcourt and Brace, New York.

Kant, I. (1929). *Critique of Pure Reason*, Macmillan, London.

Radford, K.J. (1978). Decision-making in a turbulent environment, *J. Opl Res.Soc.*, **29**, 677–682.

Rosenhead, J. (1978). Operational research in health services planning, *Eur. J. Opl Res.*, **2**, 75–85.

Schon, D.A. (1971). *Beyond the Stable State*, Random House, New York.

Simpson, M.G. (1978). Those who can't?, *J. Opl Res. Soc.*, **29**, 517–522.

Singer, E.A. Jr. (1959). *Experience and Reflection*, University of Pennsylvania Press, Philadelphia.

Sommerhoff, G. (1950). *Analytical Biology*, Oxford University Press, London.

Stringer, J. (1967). Operational research for multiorganizations, *Opl Res. Q.*, **18**, 105–120.

Tocher, K.D. (1977). Systems Planning, *Phil. Trans. R. Soc. Lond.*, **A287**, 425–441.

Toffler, A. (1971). *Future Shock*, Bantam Books, New York.

Wald, G. (March 8, 1969). A generation in search of a future, *The Boston Globe*, Boston.

Chapter 3

From Optimizing to Learning: A Development of Systems Thinking for the 1990s

PETER B. CHECKLAND

INTRODUCTION

Operational research (OR) is one of those bodies of theory and practice whose concern might be described as "rational intervention in human affairs." This concern it shares with several other disciplines, including systems engineering (Hall, 1962), RAND systems analysis (Optner, 1973), soft systems methodology (Checkland, 1981) and the so-called policy sciences (Lasswell and Lerner, 1951). All face a more complex situation than that facing the natural scientist, who plays his game against nature's unchanging phenomena; yet all hope to make use of the organized rational thinking which is characteristic of the whole intellectual enterprise which is natural science. Any approach to rational intervention in human affairs has to accept that in studying purposeful human action and in trying to bring about change in human situations, it is not simply a matter of setting to work to discover "laws" governing the phenomena in question. Autonomous human beings could, in principle, deliberately act in a way which could either confirm or refute any supposed "laws" of human affairs.

This means that the would-be rational intervener in human affairs cannot separate theory and practice in the way that the natural scientist can. Such intervention requires a steady interaction between theory and practice in a

Reprinted by permission from *Journal of the Operational Research Society*, Volume 36, 1985

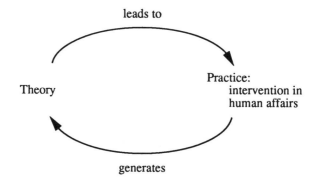

leads to

Theory

Practice:
intervention in
human affairs

generates

Figure 3.1 Groundlessness in management science—neither theory nor practice is prime

process of inquiry. The state of the subject, or discipline, is then best thought of as an account of the history and present state of that process. The Operational Research Society conference on "Systems Thinking in Action" (1985) of which this presentation was a part was an opportunity to examine some of that history and to delineate the current state of the process. In criticizing the selection of speakers for the conference in question, Rivett (1985) makes a false assumption that "theory" and "practice" are the concern of two different groups of people, namely "academics" and "practitioners." Both groups need to act in a way which makes *sure* the assumption is false! "Practitioners" need also to be reflective about their actions (many are); "academics" need also to engage in practice (many do).

The process by which OR, systems engineering, systems analysis etc. are generated as bodies of knowledge is shown in Figure 3.1. It is not as trivial a picture as it might appear. It emphasizes the *groundlessness* underlying these disciplines. Theory leads to practice; but the practice is itself the source of the theory; neither is prime; the process generates itself. (The only way, in fact, to avoid involvement in this complex, rewarding, but trying process is to focus on that theory which is applicable not to human affairs in all their richness but merely to the logic of situations. This leads to the OR techniques and algorithms. It is a route which has been followed to excess, especially in the textbooks of the subject.)

This paper, concerned with the recent history of attempts rationally to intervene in human affairs, and with the present state of the art-cum-science, will propose a framework which makes sense of the history and can also be used to examine accounts of any attempts to do OR, systems engineering, systems analysis etc.

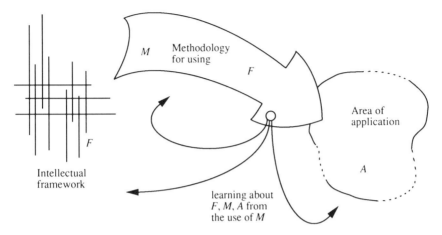

Figure 3.2   The organised use of rational thought

UNDERSTANDING RATIONAL INTERVENTION IN HUMAN AFFAIRS

Keynes suggested that people who described themselves as practical men, proud to be uncontaminated by any kind of theory, always turned out to be the intellectual prisoners of the theoreticians of yesteryear (Keynes, 1936). Whether we agree or not with Keynes' assertion, it is useful in that it reminds us that all practical action is theory-laden, in the sense that if we observe any apparently purposeful human action, we can always ask of it: "What intellectual framework would in logic make this particular action meaningful?" (This question is independent of whether the doer is conscious of the deduced framework.) This linking of ideas and their use in action suggests that it would be useful to make a distinction between, on the one hand, a basic set of ideas, and on the other, a process (or methodology) for applying those ideas in an organized way to some particular area of application. This gives us Figure 3.2 as an expansion of Figure 3.1. We now have some linked ideas in a framework F, a way of applying these ideas in the methodology M, and an application area A. A is indicated without sharp boundaries to remind us that when A is human affairs, the application of F, through M, may lead us into byways not initially expected (Checkland, 1984). Having used M, then, we may hope for and may reflect upon what learning has been acquired, learning about all three elements: F, M and A. This is a very general model of the organized use of rational thought, and applies not only to OR but to applied natural science as well. For example, in the pharmaceutical industry in the 1980s, one definition of A is the search for economy of experimentation in seeking useful drugs; quantum theory provides an F well-tested in other fields of science; and modern sophisticated computer graphics provides a new M in which models of molecular orbitals may be created and manipulated on the computer screen. In the chosen area of this paper, A is rational intervention in human affairs; F can be provided by systems ideas; and M is the methodology of OR, systems engineering etc.

The argument of this paper is that M *has begun to change in the last decade,* having been initially established in a particular form in the 1950s and 1960s.

"OPTIMIZING": "HARD" SYSTEMS THINKING—THE 1950s AND 1960s

In the years after the Second World War, when lessons from military operations were applied to industrial companies and government agencies, an interest in systems ideas developed in many fields. (That interest was signalled by the founding in 1954 of the Society for General Systems Research, a group of people interested in the application of systems thinking across the boundaries of traditional disciplines.) Ideas about system control were generalized across disciplines in cybernetics, the study of the underlying logic of the control of systems of any kind (Wiener, 1948). In the language of this paper, F (Figure 3.2) now contained the notion of optimizing the structure and behaviour of systems and maintaining them in that state. But if this notion is to be applied to "human systems," then some concept of the nature of the latter is needed: a view has to be taken on what it is in "human systems" that can be "engineered." The answer adopted in the 1950s and 1960s was: *goal seeking.* It was assumed that any human activity could be regarded as a goal-seeking system, and the thinking which constitued F and M could be condensed into:

1. Define the system of concern.
2. Define the system's objectives.
3. Engineer the system to meet those objectives.

This has been a coherent and powerful strand of thinking in the last 30 years: it is the "hard" paradigm of systems thinking (Checkland, 1981, 1983). This paradigm is succinctly expressed in Ackoff's assertion written in 1957:

> All problems ultimately reduce to the evaluation of the efficiency of alternative means for a designated set of objectives.

That is the belief which drives work within the "hard" tradition. It is the basic idea which underlies one of the largest and most influential bodies of work in management science, that of Herbert Simon. This example is used here because it has been the subject of recent public discussion at the IFORS conference, OR '84 (Brans, 1984; Checkland, 1985).

That conference included a "round-table," whose billing derived from the title of Simon's (1960) well-known book. The discussion considered the question: "Is the new science of management decision still new?" Zannetos (1984) started the round-table by presenting a paper which reviewed Simon's work. He neatly summarized Simon's legacy as:

> A theory of problem solving, programs and processes for developing intelligent machines and approaches to the design of organization structures for managing complex systems.

In seeking a true science of administrative behaviour and executive decision making, Simon shrewdly abandoned the notion of optimizing. He pointed out that the abstraction from reality necessary to facilitate mathematical manipulation of OR models runs the danger of convincing the analyst that the simplified problem was the problem he wanted to solve all along (Simon, 1960, p. 18); and in any case such abstraction isolates problems which in fact occur in rich contexts which are themselves part of the problem (Zannetos, 1984). March and Simon (1958), in developing a behavioural theory of the firm, used the notion of managers searching not for optimum solutions but for ones which were good enough in the perceived situation, the search itself being "motivated by the existence of problems as indicated by gaps between performance and goals" (Zannetos, 1984, p. 73).

Thus, although the concept of optimizing is wisely dropped in relation to human affairs, the core idea underlying the search for heuristics for real-world problem solving is that of goal seeking as a model of human behaviour. This is clear also in another of Simon's major contributions, the work written jointly with Newall on GPS (general problem solver), a heuristic computer program which seeks to simulate human thought in problem solving (Simon and Newall, 1972). The whole of this 700-page volume is built upon the concept that problem solving is a search for an end we already know to be desirable. That idea is the crucial concept underlying the whole of Simon's great contribution to management science. In his words:

> Problem solving proceeds by erecting goals, detecting differences between present situation and goal, finding in memory or by search tools or processes that are relevant to reducing differences of these particular kinds, and applying these tools or processes. Each problem generates subproblems until we find a subproblem we can solve—for which we already have a program stored in memory. We proceed until, by successive solution of such subproblems, we eventually achieve our overall goal—or give up. (Simon, 1960, p. 27)

My purpose here is to illustrate the centrality of the concept of goal seeking in the management science thinking of the 1950s and 1960s. Simon provides a good example simply because his work has been so important. At the IFORS round-table I suggested in the discussion that a good way to pay tribute to Simon's work would be to try to build beyond it by rejecting the use of the idea upon which it was based, namely goal seeking. This did not appeal to the speakers. Both Zannetos and, in discussion afterwards, Simon himself argued that although it is the case that in real life the goals *change all the time*, the concept of goal seeking is still useful for analytical purposes.

My suggestion had been that Vickers' concept of *relationship maintaining* was more fruitful than that of goal seeking, being not only closer to reality but also overcoming the problem of treating as fixed an element you know is really continually changing. Vickers' ideas can in fact be used to examine the newer versions of systems thinking which have emerged in the last decade or so. They modify both the framework (*F*) and the methodology (*M*) of Figure 3.2.

"LEARNING": "SOFT" SYSTEMS THINKING—THE 1970s TO THE 1990s?

Appreciative Systems

It is noticeable that heuristic programming, as in Simon's GPS project, like much work in artificial intelligence, has so far concentrated on the solution of trivial problems for which goal statements are unambiguous. The much-studied game of chess, for example, provides such a problem: the goal is to win the game, and you either achieve that goal within the rules of the game or fail to achieve it. The work can then concentrate on the logic of the game and its rules. However, situational logic is much simpler than real-life problem situations, in which different logics (associated with different actors and outlooks) interact intermittently. In understanding the "hard" tradition of systems thinking and trying to go beyond it, it is useful to start from real-world experience and see what patterns can be discerned in it. The work of Geoffrey Vickers does this, and provides an introduction to the "soft" tradition of systems thinking which complements the "hard" one.

Vickers was neither a "practitioner" in any management science sense nor an "academic" in a professional sense. But he was a splendid example of a reflective adviser and manager who had both a wide experience of the world of affairs and an insatiable curiosity which led him to think hard and long about his experiences in order to "make sense," as he put it, of his professional life. Born in 1894, he was, after the First World War, a partner in a firm of solicitors in the City of London. During the Second World War, he was Director of Economic Intelligence at the Ministry of Economic Warfare. After the war, he became legal adviser to the National Coal Board, then Board Member responsible for manpower, training, education, health and welfare. Other public posts followed; then in retirement Vickers started a new career, that of making sense of 40 years experience of what he termed "governance": the exercise of judgment, the weighing of moral issues, the creation of form. This mental activity he regarded as common to statesmen, judges, artists, doctors and business executives (Vickers, 1961). Vickers made sense of his experience through the development of the idea of "appreciation" and its exercise in "appreciative systems." His richly written books, published between 1959 and 1983, record the story of his thinking (the most important being *The Art of Judgment* in 1965, *Freedom in a Rocking Boat* in 1970 and *Human Systems are Different* in 1983); Blunden (1985) provides an insightful short introduction to his ideas.

The title of Vickers' last book (*Human Systems are Different*) is significant. He argued steadily that the human and social sciences are intrinsically different from the natural sciences. In a discussion at the Silver Anniversary Meeting of the Society for General Systems Research in London in 1979, he gave the following illustration of his grounds for taking that view. Ptolomy and Copernicus offer completely different theories concerning the structure of the solar system. The actual structure is entirely unaffected by belief in either theory, but when Marx produces a theory of a cultural artefact, namely "history," then history is changed as a result of allegiance to the theory. Vickers was thus wholly opposed to Simon's notion of creating quasi-natural sciences of cultural artefacts (what Simon, 1969, calls *The Sciences of the Artificial*). And Vickers' development of the concept of "appreciative systems" starts from a rejection of goal seeking as an adequate model of human behaviour. Hence we can use the work of Simon and Vickers to represent the polarity in systems thinking.

In the 1950s, Vickers was influenced by systems thinking and cybernetics, and found them very useful in understanding the social process of "governance." His interest in systems ideas was humanistic rather than technological:

> While I was pursuing these thoughts, everyone else who was responding at all was busy with man-made systems for guided missiles and getting to the moon or forcing the most analogical mental activities into forms which would go on digital computers. "Systems" had become embedded in faculties of technology and the very word had become dehumanized. (Vickers, 1979)

Vickers re-humanized the word "systems" in the concept of appreciation, a concept which begins with his rejection of both the goal-seeking model and that version of the cybernetic model in which standards are set from outside the system. His books give discursive accounts of the nature of an appreciative system. The most succinct account is in a letter he wrote to me in 1974 when he and I were discussing soft systems methodology as a practical orchestration of the process of appreciation. He wrote:

It seems to me in retrospect that for the last twenty years I have been contributing to the general debate the following neglected ideas:

(i) In describing human activity, institutional or personal, the goal-seeking paradigm is inadequate. Regulatory activity, in government, management or private life consists in attaining or maintaining desired relationships through time or in changing and eluding undesired ones.

(ii) But the cybernetic paradigm is equally inadequate, because the helmsman has a single course given from outside the system, whilst the human regulator, personal or collective, controls a system which generates multiple and mutually inconsistent courses.

(iii) From (i) and (ii) flows a body of analysis which examines the "course generating" function, distinguishes between "metabolic" and functional relations, the first being those which serve the stability of the system (e.g. budgeting to preserve solvency and liquidity), the second being those which serve to bring the achievements of the system into line with its multiple and changing standards of success. This leads me to explore the nature and origin of these standards of success and thus to distinguish between norms or standards, usually tacit and known by the mismatch signals which they generate in specific situations, and values, those explicit general concepts of what is humanly good and bad which we invoke in the debate about standards, a debate which changes both.

(iv) This leads to the concept of "appreciation," a mental, evaluative act in which conflicting norms and values determine what "facts" perceived or envisaged demand attention because they are seen to be relevant to particular norms and values.

(v) This identification of a familiar mental activity leads to its further analysis and to a suggestion for conceptualizing it in a way which will include both its fact finding and its evaluative function and will thus escape the sterilising isolation of the cognitive function which has marked most of the study of thinking. This in turn shows that its contents are systematically related and form a system which enables, limits and characterises how the agent will discriminate his situation, what he will make of it and what "match" or "mismatch" signals it will set resonating in him.

(vi) By this stage I am trying explicitly to formulate an epistemology which will account for what we manifestly do when we sit round board tables or in committee rooms (and equally though less explicitly when we try, personally for example, to decide whether to accept the offer of a new job). At this point I find myself in conflict with some, I think outdated, concepts derived from the earlier history of the natural sciences and their methods, and more generally, from the attempt to apply these to what Simon calls the sciences of the artificial.

Up to the middle of paragraph (iii) above, I am offering a critique of current theories of decision-making and policy making which does not explicitly need the concept of appreciation. From there on I am developing an epistemological theory which uses decision-making and policy making as its examples but is basically concerned with the nature of human understanding and human value judgement. My personal interest lies chiefly in this second area, but the people who read my books live chiefly in the first.

Thus, in summary, an appreciative system is a cultural mechanism which maintains desired relationships and eludes undesired ones. The process is cyclic and operates like this: our previous experiences have created for us certain standards or norms, usually tacit (and also, at a more general level, values, more general concepts of what is humanly good or bad); the standards, norms and values lead to readinesses to notice only certain features of our situations; they determine what "facts" are relevant; the facts noticed are evaluated against the norms or standards, so that future experiences will be evaluated differently. Thus Vickers (1970) argues that our human experience develops within us:

> . . . readinesses to notice particular aspects of our situation, to discriminate them in particular ways and to measure them against particular standards of comparison, *which have been built up in similar ways.* (italics added)

These readinesses are organized circularly into an appreciative system which creates for all of us, individually and socially, our appreciated world. We fail to see this clearly, in Vickers' view, because of the concentration in our science-based culture on linear causal chains and on the notion of goal seeking.

Vickers wrote consistently against the adoption of what he regarded as a poverty-stricken model of human behaviour, namely goal seeking. He argued for the concept of *relationship maintaining* as the basis of a richer and more realistic model. His work thus provides an intellectual base for new versions of *F* and *M* in Figure 3.2.

Let me end this brief introduction to Vickers' ideas with a lethally elegant paragraph from *Freedom in a Rocking Boat* (1970, p. 128):

> The meaning of stability is likely to remain obscured in Western cultures until they rediscover the fact that life consists in experiencing relations, rather than in seeking goals or "ends." The intrinsic confusion about means and ends arises from the fact that no end can ever be more than a means, if an end is equated with a goal. To get the job or marry the girl is indifferently an end, a means and a goal; it is an opportunity for a new relationship. But the object of the exercise is to do the job and live with the girl; to sustain through time a relationship which needs no further justification but is, or is expected to be, satisfying in itself.

Soft Systems Methodology

Vickers made no claims for the idea of appreciative systems beyond its value in *understanding* the social process which characterizes human affairs. His aim was understanding rather than intervention: in the terms of Figure 3.2, he provides a new *F* rather than an *M*. Nevertheless, during the years in which Vickers was developing his ideas and writing his books a methodology for rational intervention in human affairs was being developed which maps onto the idea of appreciative systems (Checkland, 1981, pp. 261–264). I refer to soft systems methodology (SSM), which can be seen as the orchestration of the operation of an appreciative system in a human situation perceived as problematic. SSM has been fully described elsewhere (Checkland, 1981; Wilson, 1984). Here, only enough of its content will be described to make clear the link with Vickers' ideas and to make possible the final discussion in this paper of the relation between the two versions of M related to rational intervention in human affairs: the "hard" and "soft" traditions of systems thinking.

SSM was developed because the methodology of systems engineering, based on defining goals or objectives, simply did not work when applied to messy, ill-structured, real-world problems. The inability to define objectives, or to decide whose were most important, was usually part of the problem. The methodology which emerged has the general shape indicated in Figure 3.3. Its most important characteristics are as follows:

1. It moves from finding out about a problem situation to taking action in the situation: it does so by carrying out some organized explicit systems thinking about the real-world situation.

2. Some human activity systems *relevant* to exploring (not *of*) the situation are carefully named in "root definitions" (RDs) (Checkland, 1981, pp. 115–119, 166–177, 215–221). The RDs explicitly name a number of features of the relevant systems, the CATWOE elements as defined in Figure 3.3.

3. Each RD makes plain its *Weltanschauung*, the point of view from which the (human activity) system is described—since one man's "terrorism" is another's "freedom fighting."

4. Conceptual models of the systems named in the RDs are built (Checkland, 1981, pp. 169–177 and Appendix 1). They are models of purposeful activity considered *relevant to* debate and argument about the problem situation. They are not at this stage thought of as designs.

5. The debate about the situation is structured by *comparing* models with perceptions of the real world. The aim of the debate is to find some possible changes which meet two criteria: systemically desirable *and* culturally feasible in the particular situation in question.

6. Definition of desirable and feasible changes gives a new problem situation (how to implement), and the cyclic process can begin again.

7. SSM thus seeks *accommodation* among conflicting interests.

8. SSM is doubly systemic. It is itself a cyclic learning process; and it uses *systems* models within that process.

SSM can be mapped onto the appreciative system concept both at a general level and more specifically. At a general level, both accept that in social life there are multiple realities. Our perceptions of cultural artefacts are acquired

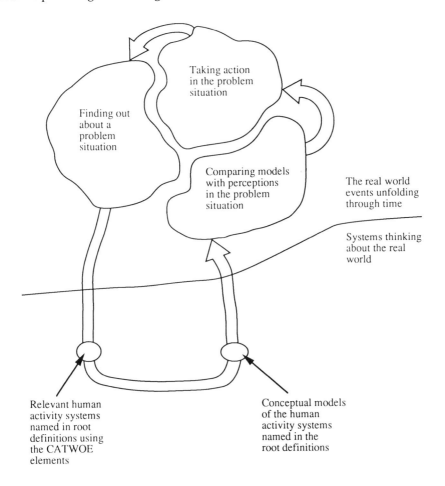

CATWOE

C ("customers")	Who would be victims or beneficiaries of this system were it to exist?
A ("actors")	Who would carry out the activities of this system?
T ("transformation process")	What input is transformed into what output by this system?
W ("Weltanschauung")	What image of the world makes this meaningful?
O ("owner")	Who could abolish this system?
E ("environmental constraints")	What external constraints does this system take as given?

Figure 3.3 The nature of soft systems methodology (SSM)

within taken-as-given assumptions about the world which are themselves built up by our experiences in the world. (It is that which results in one man's "terrorism" being another's "freedom fighting.") Because of it, models of human activity systems in SSM do not pretend to be models *of* the world, only models which embody a particular stated way of viewing the world. Given a set of such models, comparing them against the different perceptions of the problem situation which different concerned people may "own" articulates in a formal way the process Vickers calls "appreciation." The debate which SSM engineers through the comparison phase reveals the norms, the standards, the values extant in the problem situation *and contributes to their changing*. It is virtually impossible to perform the comparison phase of SSM without modifying the readinesses of the participants to perceive the world in a particular way. "Appreciative settings" will be revealed, as will the degree to which they *are* changing, *could* be changed or—in the framework of stated *Weltanschauungen*—*should* be changed.

This learning which occurs through the use of SSM ensures that the process is a cyclic one, in principle a never-ending one. In articulating in a formal way the process of "appreciation," SSM shares with Vickers an epistemology which extends—or subverts—that of the "hard" paradigm of goal seeking, with its time-bound language of "goals" which are "achieved" and "problems" which are "solved" out of existence.

The idea of "appreciative systems," together with the practice of SSM, which can be seen as a formal practical expression of it, thus helps to define a strand of systems thinking usefully different from that developed in the 1950s and 1960s. It includes not only the work of Vickers and the development of SSM; other work can broadly be related to it, even though the history of ideas is never clear-cut: for example, the work of Churchman (1971), Ackoff (1957, 1974), Mason and Mitroff (1981), Thompson (1979) and Eden *et al.* (1979) can be seen as contributing to and helping to create the "soft" tradition.

It remains finally to relate these two paradigms of systems thinking, "hard" and "soft," to each other.

THE RELATION BETWEEN THE TWO TRADITIONS

It has been argued here that it is useful to examine the state of thinking and practice concerned with rational intervention in human affairs in the language of Figure 3.2. What is the intellectual framework, F? What is the methodology, M, which applies it? If we address those questions, then we can make sense of the last 30 years in "management science," broadly defined, as representing a shift from one version of F and M to another. But it would be wrong to regard the newer thinking as in some way replacing the earlier, and equally wrong to imagine that the "hard"/"soft" distinction defines two groups of people: it defines two sets of ideas, which anyone can use. The thinking of the 1950s and 1960s, and its victories, remain with us. That thinking and its methods are there to be used when appropriate; it is simply that there are now some additional ideas and methodology complementary to that developed in the years after the Second World War.

This implies that there will be judgments to be made concerning the systems thinking appropriate in particular situations in human affairs. And that directs attention to a comparison between "hard" and "soft" systems thinking in order that those judgments may be well informed. The final aim of this paper is to examine "hard" and "soft" systems thinking together and to establish their relationship.

The nature of the "hard" tradition can be summarized as follows: it seeks to make possible the efficient achievement of goals or objectives, taking goal-seeking to be an adequate model of human behaviour; it assumes that the world contains systems which can be "engineered," hence that models of those systems can be made; it talks the language of "problems" and "solutions" which eliminate problems.

The "soft" tradition does not regard goal seeking as an adequate model for much of what goes on in human affairs; it does not assume that the rich complexity of the world can be captured in systemic models, and hence regards system models produced within the "hard" tradition not as "models of X" but only as "models of the logic of X." Hence the "soft" tradition regards system models as models relevant to arguing about the world, not models of the world; this leads to "learning" replacing "optimizing" or "satisficing"; this tradition talks the language of "issues" and "accommodations" rather than "solutions."

These differences are summarized in Table 3.1, which also lists the obvious advantages and disadvantages of each tradition. Table 3.1 shows the complementarity of the two bodies of thought; but what is their mutual relationship?

There are undoubtedly situations in which the language of "problems" requiring "solutions" is appropriate. If you are a mail-order company whose catalogue generates orders which then take months to fulfil because of inadequate stocks, or a library with a significant proportion of the stock not catalogued, then you have a problem which calls for a system to be engineered to solve it. Nobody would argue with this because at this basic operational level there is very often a complete consensus on what needs to be done and what constitutes efficiency in doing it. However, at levels above the operational, consensus quickly breaks down. Discussing the potential product range of the mail-order company, or how the library's budget should be spent, will quickly reveal different perceptions of the relevant worlds: what at the operational level may be agreed problems quickly become, at higher levels, issues created by clashing norms, values and *Weltanschauungen*. This suggests that the relation between "hard" and "soft" systems thinking is not like that between apples and pears: it is like that between apples and fruit. The well-defined problem needing solution is the special case within the general case of issues calling for accommodations. The history of the development of SSM

Table 3.1 The "hard" and "soft" traditions of systems thinking compared

The "hard" systems thinking of the 1950s and 1960s	The "soft" systems thinking for the 1980s and 1990s?
Oriented to goal seeking	Oriented to learning
Assumes the world contains systems which can be "engineered"	Assumes that the world is problematical but can be explored by using system models
Assumes system models to be models of the world (ontologies)	Assumes system models to be intellectual constructs (epistemologies)
Talks the language of "problems" and "solutions"	Talks the language of "issues" and "accommodations"
ADVANTAGES Allows the use of powerful techniques	*ADVANTAGES* Is available to both problem owners and professional practitioners; keeps in touch with the human content of problem situations
DISADVANTAGES May need professional practitioners	*DISADVANTAGES* Does not produce final answers
May lose touch with aspects beyond the logic of the problem situation	Accepts that inquiry is never-ending

reflects this. Occasionally what "the system" consisted of was obvious, in the sense that there was no disagreement about it. More often there were multiple possible definitions of both "the system" and how to conceptualize it. The concept of root definition had to replace that of the simple objectives of the system. And it was found necessary to define a root definition richly, naming several elements: the transformation process it embodies: the *Weltanschauung* which makes this perception meaningful; the system's victims or beneficiaries; its actors; its owners; and the environmental constraints which it takes as given (i.e. the CATWOE elements). Occasionally, in the special case, these elements condensed into unproblematic "objectives."

Thus, using the example of SSM, we see that "soft" systems thinking is the general case of which "hard" systems thinking is the occasional special case, a relationship shown in Figure 3.4.

CONCLUSION

If we ask what is the single most marked change in moving from the special ("hard") case of an unproblematic system which can be engineered to the

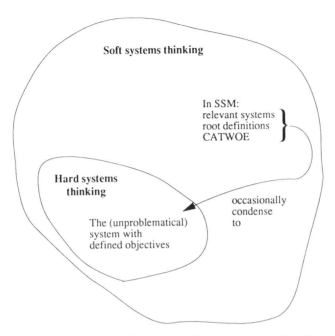

Figure 3.4   The relation between the two traditions of systems thinking

general ("soft") case of an issue-based situation in which accommodations must be sought, it is probably best thought of as the shift from thinking in terms of models of (parts of) the world to models relevant to arguing about the world. Applied social science (which intervention in human affairs is bound to be) normally has to deal in the latter. It is interesting to note how clearly Keynes saw this in the case of economics. He put it to R. F. Harrod in 1938 during the discussion of the latter's presidential address to the Royal Economic Society:

> It seems to me that economics is a branch of logic, a way of thinking; and that you do not repel sufficiently firmly attempts . . . to turn it into a pseudo-natural science . . . Economics is a science of thinking in terms of models joined to the art of choosing models which are *relevant to* the contemporary world. It is compelled to be this, because, unlike the typical natural science, the material to which it is applied is, in too many respects, not homogeneous through time. (Keynes, 1938, *italics added*)

Everything said here about economics applies with equal force to management science. Valiant efforts have been made to "turn it into a pseudo-natural science." The result has been useful models of *one aspect* of situations arising in human affairs, namely their logic. Because the material to which management science is applied "is, in too many respects, not homogeneous through time," we need the extension of "hard" systems thinking which the "soft" tradition is beginning to supply. It will help us to be better armed, intellectually, to face the problems of the 1990s.

REFERENCES

Ackoff, R.L. (1957). Towards a behavioural theory of communication, in *Modern Systems Research for the Behavioural Scientist* (Ed. W. Buckley), pp. 209–218, Aldine, Chicago.
Ackoff, R.L. (1974). *Redesigning the Future*, John Wiley, New York.
Blunden, M. (1985). Vickers' contribution to management thinking, *J. Appl. Syst. Anal.*, **12**, 107–112.
Brans, J.P. (Ed.) (1984). *Operational Research '84: Proceedings of the Tenth International Conference on Operational Research*, North-Holland, Amsterdam.
Checkland, P.B. (1981). *Systems Thinking, Systems Practice*, John Wiley, Chichester.
Checkland, P.B. (1983). OR and the systems movement; mappings and conflicts. *J. Opl Res. Soc.*, **34**, 661–675.
Checkland, P.B. (1984). Systems thinking in management: the development of soft systems methodology and its implications for social science, in *Self-organization and Management of Social Systems* (Eds. H. Ulrich and G. J. B. Probst), Springer, Berlin.
Checkland, P.B. (1985). Conferences, as process and product: thoughts from IFORS '84, *J. Appl. Syst. Anal.*, **12**, 113–116.
Churchman, C.W. (1971). *The Design of Inquiring Systems*, Basic Books, New York.
Eden, C., Jones, S., and Sims, D. (1979). *Thinking in Organizations*, Macmillan, London.
Hall, A.D. (1962). *A Methodology for Systems Engineering*, Van Nostrand, Princeton, NJ.
Keynes, J.M. (1936). *The General Theory of Employment, Interest and Money*, Macmillan, London.
Keynes, J.M. (1938). Quoted in D. E. Moggridge (1976), *Keynes*, p. 26, Fontana, London.
Lasswell, H.D., and Lerner D. (Eds) (1951). *The Policy Sciences: Recent Developments in Scope and Method*, Stanford University Press, California.
March, J.G., and Simon, H.A. (1958). *Organisations*, John Wiley, New York.
Mason, R.D., and Mitroff, I.I. (1981). *Challenging Strategic Planning Assumptions*, John Wiley, New York.
Optner, S.L. (Ed.) (1973). *Systems Analysis*, Penguin, Harmondsworth.
Rivett, P. (1985). Letter to O.R. Newsletter, **14**, 13.
Simon, H.A. (1960). *The New Science of Management Decision*, Harper & Row, New York.
Simon, H.A. (1969). *The Sciences of the Artificial*, MIT Press, Cambridge, Mass. (2nd edition 1981).
Simon, H.A., and Newell, A. (1972). *Human Problem Solving*, Prentice-Hall, Englewood Cliffs, NJ.
Systems Thinking in Action, O.R. Society National Event, Henley, April 1985.
Thompson, M. (1979). *Rubbish Theory: Creation and Destruction of Value*, Oxford University Press, London.
Vickers, G. (1961). Judgment, in *The Vickers Papers* (1984), Harper & Row, London.
Vickers, G. (1965). *The Art of Judgment*, Chapman & Hall, London.
Vickers, G. (1970). *Freedom in a Rocking Boat*, Allen Lane, London.
Vickers, G. (1979). Letter to Guy Adams, quoted in M. Blunden (1984), Geoffrey Vickers—an intellectual journey, in *The Vickers Papers*, Harper & Row, London.
Vickers, G. (1983). *Human Systems are Different*, Harper & Row, London.

Wiener, N. (1948). *Cybernetics*, MIT Press, Cambridge, Mass.
Wilson, B. (1984). *Systems: Concepts, Methodologies and Applications*, John Wiley, Chichester.
Zannetos, Z.S. (1984). Decision sciences and management expectations: fulfilled, frustrated and yet-to-come, in *Operational Research '84: Proceedings of the Tenth International Conference on Operational Research* (Ed. J.P. Brans), North-Holland, Amsterdam.

NOTE

Since this paper was written an account of the last decade's development of SSM has been given in Checkland, P. and Scholes, J. (1990). *Soft Systems Methodology in Action*, Wiley, Chichester, 329 pp.

Part Two

The Break with Soft Systems Thinking

Commentary

In the 1970s and 1980s, soft systems thinking gained the respect of a wide variety of people from both the academic and business communities. The main ideas offered a powerful and accessible alternative, especially because they were well thought out and clearly presented. A result of this careful documentation was an increase in the transparency of the new ideas, and their exposure to possible new criticism. It turned out that genuine concern did emerge in the 1980s. The worries were fundamental and wide ranging, aimed at the core of the methodological and epistemological tenets of the soft approach. A set of papers expressing this concern has been brought together in this section. They represent "The Break With Soft Systems Thinking" and the emergence of critical systems thinking, as we shall now find out.

There were two main concerns. First, that the interpretive theory underpinning soft systems thinking is inadequate for understanding and acting in social situations where there are inequalities in power and economic relations. Second, that the idea of complementarity in the form of hard being a special case of soft would lead to denaturing of hard by soft tenets. We will trace these lines of argument through six key articles.

The first two papers in this section are solely concerned with the idea of emancipatory systems practice. The remaining papers unravel a critically reflective approach to complementarity as well as covering emancipatory issues.

The first contribution is Thomas and Lockett's "Marxism and Systems Research: Values in Practical Action" (1979). This leader is particularly fitting because critical systems thinking is founded on a tradition that begins with Karl Marx's critique of political economy. Our contributing authors analyse the main differences between soft systems thinking and the Marxist pole. The essential disparity is one of commitment. With Marx there are explicit value commitments which challenge power, wealth and authority. Soft systems, on the other hand, claims a political and ideological neutrality. The ideas, it is argued, are available in principle to any interest in society. Methodologies do not serve any particular group or class. Conflict is played down in favour of

---

Critical Systems Thinking: Directed Readings. Edited by R. L. Flood and M. C. Jackson
© 1991 John Wiley & Sons Ltd

consensus. On analysis, however, we find that existing structures of power and authority are favoured. It is inevitable that methodologies without an emancipatory commitment to penetrate power structures will lead to output which reflects the interests of managerial or dominant groups in society. Thomas and Lockett argue, therefore, that soft systems is limited to the special case where conflict between people is not subject to the domination of any one interest. Whilst this criticism is valuable, it was not until Ulrich contributed critical systems heuristics that emancipatory methodological principles were born.

Ulrich's article "Critical Heuristics of Social Systems Design" (1987) outlines the basis of an approach which deals with the normative implications of problem definition and systems design. The aim is to help us to gain essential insights into the conditions that would allow us to justify disputed validity claims. Ulrich introduced the idea of argument "break-offs," where every chain of argumentation starts and ends with some judgement, the rational justification of which must remain an open question. Critical systems heuristics deals critically with justification break-offs. It practises practical reason.

In his paper, Ulrich introduces critical systems heuristics. He stresses that boundary judgements are the key concern. Any plan can be critically considered in terms of boundary judgements, in an "is" mode (what is the rationality of the plan?) and an "ought" mode (what ought to be the rationality of the plan?). "Is" and "ought" can be used in a critical evaluation of any plan, focusing particularly on clients, decision makers, planners and witnesses. "Is" questions aim at determining a design's effective normative implications in the light of "ought" answers, that is to say, without any illusions of objectivity. This helps us to evaluate the normative content of planning, while at the same time laying open the normative basis of the evaluation itself.

Jackson in "Social Systems Theory and Practice: The Need for a Critical Approach" (1985) pursues a similar line to Thomas and Lockett's critique of soft systems thinking. His thesis highlights a need for an appropriate radical, or emancipatory, approach in special cases where inequalities are found to be characterised by power relations. For example, he agrees with interpretivists (soft systems thinking) that the social world is a socially constructed phenomenon, created by people, but adds that people are not necessarily aware of what they are doing or able to create exactly the world they want to construct. Further, people have conflicting aims and can bring different resources to bear. These may be linked to economic and social forces which need to be changed before we can pursue the soft systems aim of changing ideas; i.e. in certain contexts ideas may be coerced and will not readily develop and change. Jackson points to Marx's critique of political economy as the exemplar for critical social science. Nowadays, however, the institutional framework has become increasingly important. Marx's ideas thus need to be complemented with a critique of alienation in the institutional realm of society. Habermas has contributed in this respect with a theory of communication free from distortion, the ideal speech situation and communicative competence. Psychoanalysis is also introduced as a way of dealing with false consciousness, of getting beneath explanations offered by subjects.

In this discussion, Jackson is preparing the ground for an approach such as critical systems heuristics, but he does not stop there. Jackson begins to cultivate another significant contribution of Habermas, his knowledge-constitutive interests. For "problem solving," this suggests that methods of inquiry must be suitable for the "system" of concern. Natural science methods cannot simply be taken over to the domain of the social sciences. They are suitable for a "class" of social systems where agreement on what is to be done encounters little resistance. Similarly, soft approaches are only suitable for a "class" of social systems which are characterised by disagreement but not by dominant power relations. Coercive contexts demand a radical or emancipatory attitude and commitment. In essence, Jackson is saying that we must evaluate the suitability of various methods of inquiry for use in social systems science. This is the critical call for complementarity through critical reflection.

At about the same time, Jackson and Keys published "Towards a System of Systems Methodologies" (1984). This was the first genuine attempt to work out a critically reflective approach to complementarity. Jackson and Keys' notion of complementarity is about the competence of methods in particular problem contexts. Each one, it is argued, has a definable area of competence which is different from others. The framework which is developed encourages mutual respect between approaches, an understanding of their limitations and asks the questions "which methodology, when and why?" The paper tackles these questions in two sections. First, a systematic analysis of problem contexts is presented. Second, an analysis of methodologies most suitable for "classes" of problem context is set out. A system of systems methodologies, which relates methodology to context, is then drawn up using the findings of the two sections. The system of systems methodologies is the first methodological realisation of critical systems thinking. Surprisingly, however, the authors present the ideas at a methodological level only, making no reference to Habermasian critical theory which evidently is the underpinning rationality.

Jackson and Keys were aware that their effort was a first call for a coordinated research programme to deepen understanding of different problem contexts. This was responded to by authors such as Oliga, Flood and Ulrich, as we shall see below.

"Methodological Foundations of Systems Methodologies" (1988) is Oliga's comprehensive epistemological inquiry that complements Jackson and Keys' methodological one. Oliga recognises significant developments in types of problem solving methodology. The hard/soft argument gave the impetus for one line of inquiry and debate about the nature of methodologies, whilst the critical interjection stimulated another. Oliga pointed out the common features of these lines of development. First is further advancement of design and application of systems-based methodologies. Second is their raising of a number of controversial issues. Resolving these current controversies, he continues, depends on a serious attempt to reconsider underlying metatheoretical assumptions and concerns. He launches into a thorough analysis of three methodological foundations—empiricism, hermeneutics and critique—concluding that critique does not deny the legitimacy of human interests (Habermas) underlying empiricist and hermeneutic methodological foundations. Rather, in the context of contemporary social formations, Oliga argues that critique attempts to transcend their alterable, historical and essentially ideological limitations. After identifying hard approaches with empiricism, soft approaches with hermeneutics, he then assesses critically the nature and limits of systems approaches to problem solving, focusing on their epistemological *and* ethical claims.

Although Oliga does not come down on the side of either the soft or critical position in the complementarist debate, he does sound a number of very useful warnings about contingency. He says that any "contingency" framework can all too easily pose as unproblematic, without questions being raised about how and why it arose—becoming pigeon-holing rather than critical. Frameworks such as the system of systems methodologies therefore must be conceived as ideal types. With his article, Oliga had paved the way for further and more pointed epistemological investigations.

Flood and Ulrich set out in their "Testament to Conversations on Critical Systems Thinking Between Two Systems Practitioners" (1990) a comprehensive epistemological analysis for both the emancipatory and complementarist lines of development. They identify changes in systems thinking as epistemological breaks. The shift from hard to soft reflects a break from positivism to interpretivism, whilst critical systems thinking is a break from interpretivism to critical theory. The paper offers a thorough exploration of the main characteristics of positivism, interpretivism and critique. The authors are particularly careful to document the legitimacies and limitations of non-reflective positivism (argued to be untenable) and non-reflective interpretivism (argued to be impoverished). An important contribution of the conversation, which adds clout to the critical systems endeavour, is the recognition that systems thinking implies emancipation and critique when interpreted according to its original critical intent (as developed by Kant). The systems idea and critique therefore form a singularity (a set of logical comprehensive ideas and concepts), and it is only from this singularity that systems thinking and systems intervention can be assumed adequate (yet open to critique itself).

In summary (also see Table 1), the soft systems school developed a tradition opposing hard systems thinking. Two paradigms were distinguished. The soft paradigm argued that hard is a subset of soft, but is useful only in special restricted cases. This is an isolationist interpretation of complementarism.

Table 1

School of thought	Critique	Ideology	Complementarist
Hard	Falsification of theories	Conservative in all cases	No, uses "the optimal" method
Soft	Exposition of ideas	Conservative in the face of domination by political and economic élites and inequalities	Superficially, by subsumption of hard methods
Critical	Emancipatory and complementarist	Emancipatory in all cases	Yes, critically reflective

The emerging critical school rejected this idea, arguing that complementarity means reflective use of methodology by analysis of underlying theoretical assumptions and assessing their relevance to the social context at hand. Furthermore, the critical school argued, carrying out such an analysis on soft systems approaches showed its underlying principles to be relevant in special cases where there are conflicting views which are not resolved through coercive means. An open and conciliatory approach was called for which respects the strengths and weaknesses of methodologies and their epistemological underpinnings. A reflective approach would then challenge the foundationless soft-critical notion that viewpoints are equally relevant and thus we only need to create discursive conditions for expression of the ideas. The soft school did not take heed of Marx's appreciation that social material conditions can lead to social structures where ideas cannot be freely debated. It also neglected one of the main lessons laid out by Churchman, that ethical and moral judgements have to be made. Relativism assumed in soft systems thinking will give way to "the most relevant," and what is "most relevant" in coercive contexts, we know, will be decided by the most powerful, no matter what ethical or moral position they represent. Soft systems is therefore conservative in the face of domination and political and economic inequalities.

The arguments for a break with soft systems thinking had been forged. The criticisms were comprehensive, and so the next challenge was to take critical systems thinking into an era of development with new research programmes to confront wider debates such as post-modernism in social theory. This was accompanied by the development of a pragmatic version of critical systems thinking called "Total Systems Intervention," or "creative problem soliving." The remaining part of this book provides an insight into the new era which is still unfolding. A number of recent and new articles are presented that take systems thinking into an exciting new wave of development.

Marxism and Systems Research: Values in Practical Action

ALAN R. THOMAS AND MARTIN LOCKETT

SCIENTIFIC METHOD AND MARXIST METHOD

The dominant paradigm for the application of knowledge to practical human problems is that based on classical scientific method derived from the physical sciences. It can be summed up in the belief that similar "scientific" thought-processes can be applied equally to getting a person to the moon and to solving problems of the inner city or drought-stricken areas in Africa. This dominant paradigm includes:

1. a positivist view of knowledge;
2. validation through the activity of a scientific community;
3. separation of "facts" from values; and hence
4. separation of the process of generating knowledge from the practical application of that knowledge.

The fourth aspect has been prominent in Western thought since the time of Greek philosophers such as Socrates. More recently, theorists associated with the rise of science saw such a division between theory and action as essential: thus Descartes (1912) argued that ". . . the knowledge of the understanding ought always to precede the determination of the will." Today we can see this

Reprinted by permission from *Proceedings of the 23rd Annual Conference of the International Society for General Systems Research.* © ISGSR 1979 separation reflected in the institutional division between science and engineering, and between academic research and its application.

Although many criticisms of classical scientific method are of recent origin in the natural sciences (e.g. Kuhn, Feyerabend), Marxism has been a major alternative in the social sciences for some time. Although some of its proponents see Marxism in a more traditional scientific framework, this interpretation is largely inconsistent with the works of Marx and many subsequent Marxists, concentrating on certain theoretical conclusions and neglecting the methodological contribution of Marxism. In particular Marxism sees knowledge as both generated by social activity and validated by practical social action. For, argued Marx, in his *Theses on Feuerbach* (in Feuer, 1969), "The question whether objective truth can be attributed to human thinking is not a question of theory, but is a *practical* question." So, practice and theory have to be linked and for Marx this was a question of social change for "The philosophers have only *interpreted* the world in various ways; the point, however, is to change it." This "unity of theory and practice" Marx called *praxis*, and, according to Lefebvre (1968), "Its theoretical aim and its practical aim—knowledge and creative action—cannot be separated."

Although Marxists may talk of the "discovery of laws of social development," these are not to be seen as of general validity and in particular are related to a specific mode of production (e.g. the capitalist or feudal). In *Anti-Duhring* Engels (1975) argued that in the historical (or social) as opposed to the natural and biological sciences,

> . . . knowledge is here essentially relative, inasmuch as it is limited to the investigation of interconnections and consequences of certain social and state forms which exist only in a certain epoch and among certain peoples and are by their very nature transitory.

If such knowledge leads to "predictions," it must be realised—as A. Rapoport (1974) points out—that whereas predictions in a natural science are "independent of human will and volition . . . the predictions of Marxist theory are of a different sort. Their realisation could be assured only by the interference of purposeful human action."

Though such a view of knowledge would be rejected as contradictory by the standards of classical scientific method, it can be argued that it is consistent by the standards of a different type of method. So, argues Lefebvre (1968):

> Is not dialectical materialism therefore both a science and a philosophy, a causal analysis and a world-view, a form of knowledge and an attitude to life, a becoming aware of the given world and a will to transform this world, without any one of these characteristics excluding the other?

So, Marxism is clearly a rather different approach from that of classical scientific method both to practical human problems and to the generation and validation of knowledge. Many writers and commentators regard positivist scientific method and Marxist method as effectively the only two possible frameworks. One such is the anthropologist Bastide (1973), who sums up how Marxist method is distinguished from the prevailing "Cartesian" model as follows:

> The truth is that which our revolutionary action verifies . . . theoretical knowledge develops at the same time as practical knowledge. . . . Human intervention in social reality is both action and science at once, since it permits us at the same time to change the world, and, in changing, to discover it.

SYSTEMS ACTION RESEARCH

In terms of the process of generation and validation of knowledge, such a rigid contrast between Marxism and conventional scientific method ignores the contribution of other methodologies which stress the integration of "theory" and "practice." In particular, it ignores the development of action-research, defined by R. N. Rapoport (1970) as aiming to ". . . contribute both to the practical concerns of people in an immediate problematic situation and to the goals of social science by joint collaboration within a mutually acceptable ethical framework." The methodological basis of such action-research need not be Marxist: in a recent analysis of its "scientific merits," Susman and Evered (1978) argue that there are five non-positivist frameworks within which action-research can be justified and do not include Marxism within this list. Oquist (1978) in contrast sees some interpretations of Marxist method to be generally consistent with ideas of action-research; the exception he analyses is Althusserian structuralist Marxism.

One particular development of action-research has been by those explicitly advocating, or strongly influenced by, systems theory. Such systems methodologies are similar to Marxism in that they use action to validate analysis. Again, like Marxism, they see themselves as scientific yet as an alternative paradigm to that based on classical scientific method. For they are certainly regarded by their promoters as more than mere techniques or just new areas of application of knowledge generated and validated within a more conventional scientific method. In this respect all action-research has similarities with Marxism, although the level of both analysis and action to validate the theory is typically different: that of the organization—or perhaps, the community—for most action-research, and of the mode of production or society for Marxists.

SIMILARITIES BETWEEN SYSTEMS AND MARXISM

One can also see other similarities which are more than superficial between systems methodologies and Marxist method. These are in several areas: holism, meta-disciplinary perspective, multi-causality, and emphasis on change.

Holism

Both Marxists and systems methodologists stress holistic rather than reductionist principles. Systems theory attempts a holistic analysis almost by definition. For example, Mayon-White (1978) suggests that the "systems paradigm" consists of only two concepts: *system* and *holism*. In the case of Marxism, the frequent allegation of economic determinism clouds the picture. However, a closer look shows that Marxism also offers a holistic perspective. In part, this arises from the generally higher level of analysis typically used in Marxism. But this is not all: for example Engels (1975) states in general terms "The world clearly constitutes a single system, i.e. a coherent whole," whilst Marx argued that

> . . . production, distribution, exchange and consumption . . . are all elements of a totality, distinctions within a unity. Production predominates . . . but there is interaction between the various elements. This is the case in every organic whole . . . (quoted in Bottomore and Rubel, 1963)

Also, like many systems theorists, Marx made use of organic analogies to stress the importance of holism, for example his argument in *Capital* that ". . . the present society is no solid crystal, but an organization capable of change, and constantly changing" (in Feuer, 1969).

Meta-disciplinary perspective

Both Marxism and systems theory are not confined to a particular discipline. Checkland's (1979a) description of "systems" as a "meta-discipline, one which can talk about the subject matter of any other discipline" is echoed in Marxist analyses of other disciplines. In particular both systems and Marxism can be used (i) as a distinctive perspective within existing disciplines, and (ii) as an overall framework for investigation. So, for example, Gaines (1977, quoted in Lafreniere, le Guyader and Moulin, 1979) at a major international conference on "applied general systems research" argued that: "General Systems Theory is essentially a dialectical method rather than a discipline and it is characterised by the freedom it enjoys to assimilate change at any level."

Multi-causality

The cause-and-effect model of classical scientific method is recognised as inappropriate in many cases by both Marxism and systems. Engels (1975) argued that:

> . . . cause and effect are conceptions which hold good only in their application to individual cases. In their general connection with the universe as a whole they run into each other, and they become confounded when we contemplate that universal action and reaction in which causes and effects are eternally changing places, so that what is effect here and now will be cause there and then, and *vice versa*.

For systems methodologists, ideas of multi-causality are also important and multi-causality may even rank with holism as one of the defining concepts of systems thinking.

Emphasis on change

Linked with their rejection of positivist scientific method, both systems methodologists and Marxists emphasise change—as a relatively universal phenomenon and as the object of analysis and action. For Marxists, the study of society leads one to see the possibilities of change which action, particularly by social classes, can bring about. Within capitalist societies and in a transition to socialism, they specifically emphasise the role of the working class in transforming society and social relations.

Similarly, systems methodologies are concerned with change—though, as we have noted above, often at the organisational level. Thus, Naughton (1979) talks of

> . . . a common misconception about the nature of "soft" systems research— namely the notion that such research has the general characteristics of a (would-be) "science", in other words, a discipline the main goal of which is *explanation*.

In fact, he continues, "soft-systems research is more accurately viewed as a kind of social technology." Rather than seeking to discover general laws or underlying truths, systems research seeks improvement to specific situations or the development of methods aimed at utility, as in Checkland's (1972) "feasible, desirable change" or Ackoff's (1979) "continuous and improving control." In this, as Checkland (1972) recognizes and as remarked above, it is in line with the action-research tradition in social science. Susman and Evered (1978) sum this up as follows:

. . . the ultimate sanction is in the perceived functionality of chosen actions to produce desirable consequences for an organization. Action research constitutes a kind of science with a different epistemology that produces a different kind of knowledge, a knowledge which is contingent on the particular situation. . . .

So Marxism and "soft" systems methodologies have much in common in their relationship to positivist scientific method. The latter is concerned with the formulation of general laws and the discovery of objective "truth," seeks validation by reference to a "scientific community," and separates the method of scientific investigation from the application of scientific knowledge to practical action. In contrast, both the Marxist and the soft systems methods seek to analyse specific situations and rely on practical action and its results simultaneously for the generation of knowledge and its validation.

THE "PROBLEM OF ENDS"

Much of the similarity stems from the fact that both Marxism and "soft" systems methodologies reject the separation of fact and value in analysis, expressed for example by Weber's view that, although the area of investigation will be affected by one's values, the analysis itself should seek to exclude these. Holding to this separation causes great difficulties for those attempting to apply classical scientific method to practical human problems. In particular, it makes it extremely difficult to deal with human "ends" in a rigorous "scientific" manner.

On the one hand, it is possible to use classical scientific method to try to establish general laws of society which transcend those questions of value which govern the free behaviour of individuals and groups. However, any such attempt to formulate "facts" about "social forces" appears to deny the undoubted capability of people to change those forces by deliberate action to suit their chosen ends. In Bastide's (1973) words, ". . . man is free and can counter determinism, while nature submits to it."

On the other hand, it is possible in a given situation to perform a scientific analysis of cause-and-effect, and to calculate the most appropriate means of obtaining a particular, desired, effect. This would be the type of work undertaken by the engineer, applied social scientist, "hard" systems methodologist or operational researcher. The determination of "ends"—that is, which effect is desired—is a question of values, perhaps a moral and political question, but in any case is not a scientific question and has to be regarded as taking place separately from, and externally to, that analysis.

In some cases, there is an attempt to determine ends themselves "scientifically", thereby giving objective status to value judgements. For example, attempts have been made in a cost–benefit framework to reduce all aspects of a public project appraisal to a single dimension, and to base this reduction on a scale of "social utility" derived from observation of individuals' behaviour. Thus, the value to be attached to noise nuisance or to loss of life in accidents is derived from surveys of property values or insurance companies' returns, respectively. De Neufville and Stafford (1971) provide a good example of this approach, stating for example that ". . . the determination of the appropriate discount rate is . . . more complex to estimate than . . . the stability of an earth embankment. But it is not therefore more vague."

The point is not simply to criticize this approach, but to realize that the difficulties begin to arise when dealing with what Ackoff (1971) terms "purposeful" systems, which can choose their own goals, and in which the ends, or goals, of actors are both a subject of study and a determinant of action. Classical scientific method aims ideally at objective observation, which effectively means treating all systems *as if* they were "purposive," thus denying the possibility of studying deliberate efforts at organization or at bringing about change in society. However, a rigid separation of ends and means, and of facts and values, is not possible in purposeful systems. In fact, since such systems both initiate new behaviour and react to external pressures, an observer may be unable to distinguish goal-seeking behaviour from relationship-maintaining behaviour from externally determined behaviour.

MARXISM IS COMMITTED: WHAT OF SYSTEMS?

Both "soft" systems methodologies and Marxism, with their combination of analysis and action, deal with purposeful systems by direct involvement in them. This would seem to entail giving up the ideal of objective, detached observation. Certainly Marxists are relatively clear about their political and ideological stance—identification with what they see as the real interests of the working class; i.e. a transition to a socialist society whose creation in practice is in turn a validation of Marxist theory. In contrast, soft systems methodologies have no explicit value commitments to resolve the difficulties over ends and means, although it may have been these very difficulties that prompted their development from "hard" methodologies. Instead, they often stress their political and ideological neutrality. While a particular piece of systems analysis may not be objective, the methods are specifically seen as available in principle to any interest in society, and soft systems methodologists do not see their methodologies as serving any particular social group or class.

Thus Checkland (1972) claims that his work ". . . is relevant to any human activity which is purposeful", adding "It need hardly be stated, one hopes, that it is not restricted to 'management' interpreted in a class sense."

Similarly, Ackoff (1979) argues that ". . . there are no experts when it comes to answering the question: what ought a system to be like? Here *every stakeholder's opinion is as good as any other's*" (emphasis added). He adds that his methodology "tends to generate a consensus among the participants."

This idea of a neutral method which may be used (or presumably abused) by a whole variety of groups, organizations or even individuals, is similar to the use/abuse model of the natural sciences which has come under criticism (e.g. in *Radical Science Journal*) for neglecting the *practice* of the activity of research. One notable example of a soft systems methodology is that of Peter Checkland and the Lancaster University Systems Department based on over 100 projects in the "real world" (Checkland, 1972). This methodology is analysed below in some detail from the point of view of determining its neutrality, or otherwise, in *practice*.

THE CHECKLAND METHODOLOGY

Checkland's methodology is developed from "hard" systems methodologies, particularly that of Jenkins (1969), which explicitly accepts existing structures of authority and power in its unitary view of management. In Jenkins' approach according to Checkland (1972), ". . . the whole activity is aimed at helping a manager, so it is at least implicit that he will himself profoundly influence the choice of system engineered to solve his problem . . ." Though Checkland rejects systems *engineering* in favour of a more conceptual approach, he nowhere indicates any profound difference from this idea of helping a manager—or more precisely, the *client* of the action-research—stressing that

> The work is thus concerned with problems of "management," in the broad sense that much human activity involves planning, doing and monitoring, and that some aspects of what is seen as "a problem" are likely to be a mismatch between intention or expectation, and outcome . . .

However, Checkland certainly goes beyond the simple unitary view of management implied by "hard" systems thinking of the type which he characterizes as ". . . based upon the assumption that the problem task . . . is to select an efficient means of achieving a known and desired end" (Checkland, 1978). His own methodology was designed to overcome the inadequacies of "hard" systems methodologies in areas where ". . . there is no agreement on needs, objectives, measures of performance, etc." (Checkland, 1972). In such cases, definition of the problem is the major step towards resolving it, and cannot be assumed as a given first step (Checkland, 1977). However, this view that "a problem defined is a problem solved" plays down conflicts of real interest—a Marxist might, for example, define a major problem of capitalism, without thereby moving very far towards the perceived solutions. This playing-down of conflicts of real interests is reflected in Checkland's (1972) analysis of *why* "needs, objectives, measures of performance etc." differ as resulting from incompatible *world-views*, or from not emphasising the relational aspects of goals ("on-going relationships through time") when these are more appropriate than a means/end model of goal-seeking. One cannot avoid the conclusion that Checkland assumes an overall basis of consensus and no fundamental conflicts—even if specific interests and perceptions differ—in short what might be called a liberal pluralist view. (For a full discussion of unitary, pluralist and conflict frames of reference, see Fox, 1973). In practice, such a view also accepts existing structures of authority and power, although the role of management may be seen in terms of balancing interests against each other, and forging compromises, rather than in terms of leading a "team" effort.

Certainly, any systems methodologists concerned with management, and hence decision-making, must have as their clients those who already have some power in the problem situation. For one thing, if they do not, then there is no possibility of the methodology being effective, and, for that matter, no possibility of any action-research results being validated. Further, as theorists of power such as Silverman (1970) and Lukes (1974) have noted, one of the most far-reaching exercises of power is in the structuring of the world-views of others, which in turn will be reflected in the definition of a problem. Whilst the analyst in a systems study may, and often will, disagree with a definition of the problem by the client, his or her alternative definition must be acceptable to the client—at least if the action-research is to continue.

Thus in practice, if one is to engage in action-research in a "mutually acceptable ethical framework", one's clients and hence one's analyses will reflect the interests of dominant groups in society. One might add that, however much one's methodology is not in principle restricted to "'management'. . . in a class sense," in practice in a class society it will reflect management in a class sense. Political and ideological neutrality cannot be preserved in practice, despite implicit claims to neutrality.

If one looks closer at the situations in which the methodology has been developed and applied, this is clear. Although we do not have details of the 100 projects mentioned by Checkland, it is interesting that his three major examples in his 1972 paper are all from management consultancy, two initiated at director level and the other by a corporate planning group reporting to the managing director. This is also true of the main examples in Checkland's later papers (e.g. Smyth and Checkland, 1976; Checkland, 1979b)—although hypothetical and illustrative examples are given of how the methodology might be applied in other contexts. There is also a concentration on the organizational level, which one could argue is the level which is of most concern to management. This contrasts with the non-organizational level of analysis implied, by, say, studying the provision of adequate, cheap housing for people

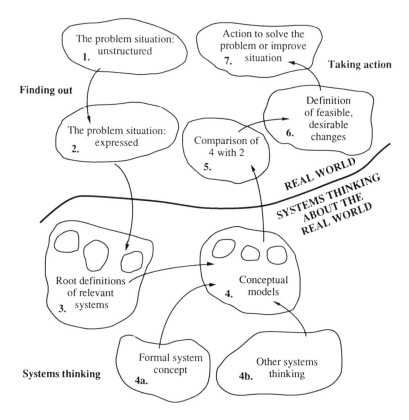

Figure 4.1 The systems methodology for ill-structured problems (adapted from Checkland, 1979b)

in a particular area—although there have been attempts to apply the methodology to such areas. Checkland (1972) admits that areas where inter-organizational relations are basic will involve more fundamental conflicts of interest, and we examine below the extension of the application of this methodology to such areas.

If we look in more detail at the methodology, we can see some of these factors analysed above—particularly in the area of validation.

Figure 4.1 shows the methodology as a sequence of stages. Checkland (1979b) comments, however, that ". . . the use of the methodology will frequently entail a less straightforward sequence, as well as much recycling between activities as perceptions are enriched."

In practice the methodology stresses removing one's view from existing reality to some extent, but not too far. To start with one builds up an "expression" of the problem situation *not* in systemic terms, for such an

approach "almost always leads to the identification of organizational groupings—departments or functions—as systems, which may or may not be
appropriate" (Checkland, 1972).

There is very little discussion in any of the papers on the methodology about
the validation of this "expression" stage. Checkland (1972) indicates certain
questions which the analyst should be able to answer "convincingly and in
some depth" before finishing this phase ("if only temporarily"). These include
questions which are effectively about internal power relations within the client
organization such as "*By whom* are resources deployed?" and "How is this
resource deployment *monitored and controlled?*" (Checkland's emphasis). The
briefest reflection shows that the information available to the analyst to
perform the "expression" of the problem situation must be controlled through
the same power relations that he is trying to "express." Certainly the control
of information is an even more straightforward use of power than the
moulding of world views discussed above. And who will the analyst be trying
to "convince"?

In an attempt to extend the methodology to a "supra-institutional" problem,
that of the art world, Cornock (1977) recognized that

> a would-be descriptive expression . . . produced with the intention of providing
> (a) neutral picture . . . was neither descriptive of the facts nor neutral! Instead,
> . . . the writer had produced . . . a model . . . based on a point of view . . .
> reflecting the writer's engagement in the activities . . .

Even within an organization, an analyst surely has to recognize that his
"expression" is bound to be coloured both by the information made available
to him by the very "client" he has to convince, and by his own preconceptions.

Checkland (1972) does not discuss problems of what constitutes a valid
"expression," contenting himself with a statement that this phase "may be
taken to be complete when it is possible to postulate a root definition of the
basic nature of the system or systems thought to be relevant to the problem
situation." Validation is thus shifted into the next, key, phase, that of
formulating a *root definition* (RD). Such RDs are not right or wrong, rather they
may be more or less insightful.

It is important to realize why Prevost (1976) is quite wrong in arguing that
Checkland's "Root Definition" is virtually identical with the concept of
function in functionalist social science theory. Prevost argues from this point
that the Checkland methodology has an inherent "static and conservative
bias." The RD, however, is neither a statement of what the purpose of the
organization (or part of it) *is*, nor of what its purpose *should* be. As Naughton
(1979) points out, "the idea behind the postulation of a relevant system in the
first place is *not to contribute to the maintenance of a given state*". Rather it is "to
explore the *consequences* of postulating a particular systemic entity within the

problem situation." Thus, although an RD in itself is clearly designed as a statement which must embody a unitary point of view, it is a hypothetical "If . . ." statement not designed to carry overtones of approval or disapproval. It does not, therefore, imply a unitary frame of reference for the problem as a whole.

However, the RD must relate, at least at a distance, to the perceptions of the "client." Checkland (1976) acknowledges this in his discussion of problems in formulating RDs. He describes the formulation of an RD in a large corporation with a power struggle between the centre and semi-autonomous divisions. An RD (which might be seen as essentially a potentially adroit political compromise)

> described a manufacturing business system characterized by being neither cen-
> tralised nor decentralised as such, but managed with the intentions that the
> divisions should be autonomous but with the centre intervening to ensure that
> the interactions between divisional decisions were not inimical to the corporation
> as a whole.

Whilst clearly reflecting existing patterns of power relationships, the RD could not resolve the "power struggle between the centre and divisions" for it "failed to carry managers within the centre, where internal power struggles were being played out." Thus the principle of validation by reference to the perceptions of actors in the situation, and overall those of management, is clear even at this stage.

In the case of "supra-institutional" problems, it is interesting that Checkland (1972) suggests that one should ". . . tease out and formulate root definitions *as if* they could be made manifest in an organization." He gives as an example a project which in fact led to a root definition as follows:

> . . . a system for the management of the uses of the Uplands of Northern England
> and Southern Scotland on behalf of a client who will not otherwise be repre-
> sented, namely the community as a whole, this including future generations as
> well as the present community. (Collins, 1977)

This type of RD is clearly even more hypothetical than the earlier types. However, it may be indicative that Checkland apparently implies that an RD involving defining the common interest of a community could more readily be "made manifest" within an organization than in the domain of a publicly owned problem.

From the RD, one must "logically derive" a *conceptual model* (CM) as a picture, as objective as possible, of what is implied by the root definition (Checkland, 1972) to help structure one's thinking. The emphasis on the "logical derivation" of the CM solely from the RD can be criticised on logical grounds, for one requires a range of knowledge of practices and "theories-in-use" (Argyris and Schon, 1978), the implicit theories held by those involved (see Prevost, 1976, Naughton, 1979). However, more important is the continuation of the unitary nature of the RD—although, once again, a CM is not meant as a prescription, and indeed, Checkland (1972) states that a CM is likely to be "antiseptic" and "inhuman." Checkland's other criterion for a CM, apart from its logical derivation from the RD, is that it must satisfy eight "formal system" properties. Numbers 1, 2 and 7 are particularly significant. In any "formal system" S:

1. "S has an objective, a mission, a definition of a final desirable state, or an on-going purpose.
2. "S has a measure of performance. . . ."
7. "S contains a decision-taking process."

This also stresses the role of management in an organizational framework: for example, one project in an industrial firm "illustrated the value of the notion in the 'formal system' model . . . that a system boundary is defined by the area within which a decision-taking body can exercise authority." Again at this stage, Checkland argues that one should not try to put forward ideal models of the system, as "The art of conceptualisation lies in cleaving to the implications of the RD while at the same time being not unaware of the reality: the art lies in finally achieving a bridgeable gap between the conceptual model and the problem situation."

Interestingly, Wilson (1979), in what he explicitly states is an application of the Checkland methodology to management control systems, suggests that a conceptual model derived from a root definition could be used directly for the design of such systems in "green-field" situations. In the more usual case of trying to improve an existing system, Wilson's RD "expresses the 'manifest purposes' of the organization studied," and his CM is to be revised until eventually it is a ". . .'required activity' description of the area under review." Thus Wilson adapts the Checkland methodology quite readily so that the RD and CM do in fact become statements of management purposes and ideals in a clearly unitary framework. Checkland himself recognises that his methodology readily assumes a unitary view. In fact he sees (1979b) a major error in the application of his methodology being ". . . a tendency to formulate Root Definitions which contain several transformations and express several *Weltanshauungen*," and adds: "It is virtually impossible to build a model from such definitions. . . ." Thus he suggests that a number of models could be developed: "What we can do is to select a number of perceptions relevant to the problem situation and model these in the form of models of human activity systems each expressing a particular *Weltanschauung*."

Cornock (1977) takes this further, recognising that at least within multiorganizational systems there will be potentially contradictory world-views. Interestingly, Cornock ascribes his difficulties to the "public ownership" of the (perceived) problem he is tackling. He contrasts this with problems with single owners and those with multiple owners, such as, for example, "the mechanization of a technology which threatens part of a labour force with unemployment," where a manager would be "drawn into conflict with those who are affected by his 'solutions'." Cornock goes on:

> Problem-solving of this kind, though more complex than cases in which the problem can from the start be reduced to a decision on the choice of means to achieve a defined objective (i.e. with a single owner), is itself relatively straightforward compared with the task of tackling problems whose ownership lies with the public as a whole.

The implication remains that within an organization conflicting interests can always be resolved, though there may be several differing legitimate ways of looking at problems. The idea that conflicts of real interest might "spill over" from the wider society into an organization seems too radical to contemplate. Naughton (1979) argues that although "the Checkland system does indeed often lead to rather conventional and 'bureaucratic' agendas for change," this is not necessarily an inherent characteristic of the methodology, and that "there is nothing in the methodology *per se* which forbids" radical or, at least, imaginative, conceptual models. However, after developing the CM it must be compared with the (perceived) reality of the problem situation. This involves validation by reference to "the perceptions of managers and other actors in the situation" (Naughton, 1979). Wilson (1979) reports on a specific successful application of the methodology as follows:

> The decisions concerning . . . responsibilities were made by senior line managers concerned. Thus what emerged from the analysis was an organization structure that *they* had developed (and hence felt they owned) rather than one imposed either from outside or from above . . .

However, Checkland (1972) states "it is worth special efforts to ensure that the conceptualisation and comparison stages are accepted by the client only as a way of viewing the problem situation in a structured way." Out of this comparison of the CM and reality come proposals for change which are referred to the client, for "a debate in which only those who live in the problem situation can select a change to be implemented." Such changes, Checkland (1976) argues, must be both desirable and feasible for those involved—but this in practice implies leaving the choice to existing decision-making processes. In line with pushing a conceptual rather than system design approach, "the whole bias of the methodology is . . . in favour of the *on-going purposeful maintenance of relationships*." In practice, this is likely to mean sufficient change to maintain and reinforce the control of the client group.

Thus rather than seeing the Checkland methodology as necessarily "static and conservative," it can be better seen as an attempt to stimulate the creation of mechanisms which can cope dynamically with a changing organisational environment and internal problems—in other words, the promotion of adaptive methods for preserving those existing relationships which are seen as important.

In practice such a methodology is therefore "managerialist" (in its orientation), "technocratic" and "reformist" (rather than conservative or revolutionary) in its practice if not in its explicit theoretical orientation. Broadly speaking, such an analysis is applicable to other "soft" systems methodologies—for such characteristics may well be a major factor in providing finance and access to systems action-researchers, and in making the conclusions of their studies both relatively acceptable to, and effective for, their clients. Certainly it would seem that such methodologies, to be effective, must lead to action, so that research on behalf of relatively powerless groups can never be validated fully.

For example, Ackoff (1974, 1979), argues that in a problem situation one should "Enlarge it by focusing on and formulating the largest relevant mess (system of problems) over which the management served has some control or influence . . ." enabling it to be brought "under continuous and improving control." He maintains that one should try to create an "idealised design" of a system which is both technologically and operationally reasonable if installed and that at such a stage "no attention should be given to whether or not it can be brought into existence." By such a methodology he hopes to overcome some of the problems of conflicts of interests and views. For his methodology "facilitates participation, . . . tends to generate a consensus among the participants, mobilises them and releases suppressed creativity and focuses it on organizational development." On the surface, such a methodology seeks to change relationships between those involved. In practice, however, Ackoff seems more concerned that management should not leave planning to specialised departments and appears to see participation as a means of easing acceptance of plans in the implementation stage. Such participation, as Mulder (1971) and others (e.g. Hovels and Nas, 1977) have argued, may in fact increase the power of managers and experts rather than equalising power relationships.

CONCLUSIONS

We have shown that, in practice, it is untenable to claim ideological or political "neutrality" for "soft" systems methodologies such as the Checkland methodology. The practical application of such methodologies cannot be value-free.

This applies even to those cases where deliberate efforts have been made to incorporate conflicts of interest to some extent into the analysis, for example, Ackoff's work, and Cornock's modification of the Checkland methodology. However, Ackoff (1979) still feels that "ultimate values" are likely to create consensus where "short run objectives" may fail, whilst Cornock (1977) sees a more informed debate between those involved being the desirable outcome. In this he follows Churchman (1971), who wrote:

> . . . it seems at least plausible to argue that the "verification" of a research project of a dialectical inquirer is not the establishment of a solution, but the creation of a more knowledgeable political process in which the opposing parties are more fully aware of each others' *Weltanschauungen* and the role of data in the battle for power.

However, the whole question of the role of information as a power resource and the multi-faceted nature of power is played down even in these more politically pluralist methodologies. The apparent radicalism of Ackoff's participatory approach does not in practice challenge existing relationships of power and authority any more than does the Checkland methodology.

Overall, then, such methodologies can be characterised as *managerialist, technocratic,* and *reformist.*

In contrast, Marxism has explicit value commitments which have clearly structured the concepts used in analysis and which challenge existing patterns of power, wealth and authority, at least in capitalist societies. Such a position is thus more consistent than that of the systems methodologies. To achieve a similar degree of consistency, systems theorists and practitioners must make a choice between two alternatives.

The first is to be explicit about the values adopted in their action-research and to adopt a clear ideological and political commitment—which could even be Marxist.

The second alternative is to continue to use existing methodologies whilst accepting that their historical development and practical application implies an acceptance of existing relationships and a commitment to piecemeal change controlled by clients. Such an acceptance means that claims to ideological neutrality should be dropped.

So, we argue that the application of systems ideas to social problems through action-research cannot be ideologically or politically neutral. Many of the uses of systems methodologies will be intended to promote changes to "improve the human condition," and these can be based on a range of value commitments. But in such action research it is inconsistent to disguise these commitments and values as "science" (even in a non-positivist sense)— although this may for some provide a convenient justification for presenting consultancy as research.

REFERENCES

Ackoff, R.L. (1971). Towards a system of systems concepts, *Mgmt. Sci.*, **17**, 11–19.
Ackoff, R.L. (1974). The systems revolution, *Long Range Planning*, **7**, 2–26.
Ackoff, R.L. (1979). Resurrecting the future of operational research, *J. Opl Res. Soc.*, **30**, 189–200.
Argyris, C., and Schon, D.A. (1978). *Organizational Learning*, Addison Wesley, Reading, Mass.
Bastide, R. (1973). *Applied Anthropology*, Croom-Helm, London.
Bottomore, T.B., and Rubel, M. (Eds). (1963). *Karl Marx: Selected Writings in Sociology and Social Philosophy*, Penguin, Harmondsworth.
Checkland, P.B. (1972). Towards a systems-based methodology for real-world problem-solving, *J. Syst. Eng.*, **3**, 87–116.
Checkland, P.B. (1976). Systems methodology in problem solving: some notes from experience, *Third European Meeting on Cybernetics and Systems Research*, Vienna.
Checkland, P.B. (1977). The problem of problem-formulation in the application of a systems approach, *International Conference on Applied General Systems Research*, Binghampton, NY.
Checkland, P.B. (1978). The origins and nature of "hard" systems thinking, *J. Appl. Syst. Anal.*, **5**, 99–110.
Checkland, P.B. (1979a). The shape of the systems movement, *J. Appl. Syst. Anal.*, **6**, 129–135.
Checkland, P.B. (1979b). Techniques in "soft" systems practice. Pt 2: Building conceptual models, *J. Appl. Syst. Anal.*, **6**, 41–49
Collins, J.H. (1977). Use of systems concepts in the description of the management problems in the Uplands of Northern England and Southern Scotland, *Agricultural Syst.*, **2**, 139–152.
Cornock, S. (1977). Understanding supra-institutional problems: systems lessons drawn from an application of the Checkland methodology, Discussion paper, Leicester Polytechnic (Department of Fine Art).
Churchman, C.W. (1971). *The Design of Inquiring Systems*, Basic Books, New York.
De Neufville, R., and Stafford, J.H. (1971). *Systems Analysis for Engineers and Managers*, McGraw-Hill, London.
Descartes, R. (1912). Meditations on the first philosophy, in *A Discourse on Method*, Dent, London.
Engels, F. (1975). *Anti-Duhring*, Lawrence and Wishart, London.
Fox, A. (1973). Industrial relations: a social critique of pluralistic ideology, in *Man and Organisations* (Ed. J. Childs), Allen and Unwin, London.
Feuer, L.S. (Ed.) (1969). *Marx and Engels: Basic Writings on Politics and Philosophy*, Fontana, London.
Hovels, B.W.M., and Nas, P. (1977). *Works Councils in Practice*, Institut voor Toegepaste Sociologie, Nymegen, Netherlands.
Jenkins, G.M. (1969). The systems approach, *J. Syst. Eng.*, **1**, 3–49.
Lafreniere, L., le Guyader, H., and Moulin, T. (1979). An account of the International Conference on Applied General Systems Research: Recent Developments and Trends, Binghampton, NY, *J. Appl. Syst. Anal.*, **6**, 107–112.
Lefebvre, H. (1968). *Dialectical Materialism*, Vintage, New York.
Lukes, S. (1974). *Power: a Radical View*, Macmillan, Basingstoke.
Mayon-White, W.M. (1980). The systems community and its paradigm, in *Progress in*

Cybernetic and Systems Research (eds. E.R. Pichler and P.F. de Hanika), pp. 333–35, Hemisphere, Washington.

Mulder, M. (1971). Power equalization through participation?, *Admin. Sci. Q.*, **16**, 31–38.

Naughton, J. (1979). Functionalism and systems research: a comment, *J. Appl. Syst. Anal.*, **6**, 69–74.

Oquist, P. (1978). The epistemology of action research, *Acta Sociologica*, **21**.

Prevost, P. (1976). Soft systems methodology, functionalism and the social sciences, *J. Appl. Syst. Anal.*, **5**, 65–73.

Rapoport, A. (1974). *Conflict in Man-Made Environments*, Penguin, Harmondsworth.

Rapoport, R.N. (1970). Three dilemmas of action-research, *Hum. Relat.*, **23**, 499–513.

Silverman, D. (1970). *The Theory of Organisations*, Heinemann, London.

Smyth, D.S., and Checkland, P.B. (1976). Using a systems approach: the structure of root definitions, *J. Appl. Syst. Anal.*, **5**, 75–83.

Susman, G.I., and Evered, R.D. (1978). An assessment of the scientific merits of action research, *Admin. Sci. Q.*, **23**, 582–603.

Wilson, B. (1979). The design and improvement of management control systems, *J. Appl. Syst. Anal.*, **6**, 51–67.

Critical Heuristics of Social Systems Design

WERNER ULRICH

APPLIED SCIENCE AND THE PROBLEM OF JUSTIFICATION BREAK-OFFS

OR as an Applied Science

The stuff of applied disciplines such as OR/MS is what epistemologists call the "context of application," in distinction to the so-called "context of justification." Epistemologists such as Karl R. Popper (1961, 1968, 1972) have claimed that the context in which science is applied is relatively irrelevant for the justification of its propositions. In distinction to this position, I propose to understand—and indeed define—applied science as *the study of contexts of application*. Of course this definition renders the distinction between the two contexts obsolete. From an applied-science point of view, the distinction is really quite inadequate: To justify the propositions of applied science can only mean to justify its effects upon the context of application under study. The key problem that makes applied science, as compared with basic science, so difficult to justify lies in the *normative content* that its propositions gain in the context of application.

By "normative content" I mean not only the value judgments—the normative premises—that inevitably flow into practical propositions such as recommendations for action, design models, planning standards or evaluative judgments, but also their normative implications in the context of application;

Reprinted by permission from *European Journal of Operational Research*, Volume 31, 1987 i.e. the life-practical consequences and side-effects of the "scientific" propositions in question for those who may be affected by their implementation.

Speaking of the "context of application" is a scientifically neutral way to say that applied science, whenever it really gets applied, tends to affect citizens that have not been involved in the scientific justification of its propositions. What does it mean to be scientific, or to "justify" the propositions of applied science, in view of the uninvolved being affected?

The Problem of Practical Reason

Basically, the answer is to understand "justification" no longer as the business of the involved only, but as the common task of both the involved and the affected. Hence a *dialogical concept of rationality* must replace the conventional "monological" understanding of rational justification. Whereas the latter relies on deductive logic and empirical corroborations or falsification attempts on the part of the involved, the former must be grounded in a model of rational discourse that would explain the conditions for reaching "rational" (as opposed to merely factual) consensus among all the involved and the affected in regard to the "rightness" (acceptability) of a design's normative content.

The problem of how rational discourse can redeem the validity claims of practical propositions—their claim to secure improvement *and* to be rationally justifiable—is known as the *problem of practical reason*. The branch of philosophy dealing with this problem, practical philosophy, has recently experienced a considerable renaissance. Contemporary practical philosophers such as Paul Lorenzen (1969), Lorenzen and Schwemmer (1975) and Jürgen Habermas (1971, 1973, 1975, 1979; see also McCarthy, 1978) have developed "ideal" models of practical discourse. They give us essential insights into the conditions that would allow us to justify disputed validity claims. The problem is only that these models, *because* they are ideal designs for rational discourse, are impractical (not realizable). They assume ideal conditions of rationality that will always remain counter-factual. In fact they presuppose what they are supposed to produce, namely, rational argumentation—the ability and will of all participants to argue cogently and to rely on nothing but the force of the better argument. Most importantly they do not take into account the *inevitability of argumentation break-offs*. In practical discourse, just as in conventional "monological" justification strategies, every justification attempt must start with some material premises and end with some conclusions that it cannot question and justify any further. In other words, every chain of argumentation starts and ends with some judgments the rational justification of which must remain an open question.

CRITICAL HEURISTICS, OR HOW TO DEAL
CRITICALLY WITH JUSTIFICATION BREAK-OFFS

From what has been said it follows that the crucial problem for any applied scientist seeking to justify his propositions is the question of how to deal critically with the justification break-offs that inevitably flow into these propositions. As long as he does not learn to make transparent to himself and to others the justification break-offs flowing into his designs, the applied scientist cannot claim to deal critically with the normative content of these designs.

Critical Heuristics (or by its full name: Critical Heuristics of Social Systems Design) is a new approach to both systems thinking and practical philosophy, an approach that aims to help the applied scientist in respect to this task. It does not seek to prove theoretically why and how practical reason is possible (as do all presently known "schools" of practical philosophy) but rather concentrates on providing planners as well as affected citizens with the heuristic support they need to *practice* practical reason; i.e. to lay open, and reflect on, the normative implications of systems designs, problem definitions, or evaluations of social programs.

In order to achieve this purpose, critical heuristics takes three requirements to be essential:

1. to provide applied scientists in general, and systems designers in particular, with a clear understanding of the meaning, the unavoidability and the critical significance of justification break-offs;

2. to give them a conceptual framework that would enable them systematically to identify effective break-offs of argumentation in concrete designs and to trace their normative content; and

3. to offer a practicable model of rational discourse on disputed validity claims of such justification break-offs, that is to say, a tool of cogent argumentation that would be available both to "ordinary" citizens and to "average" planners, scientists, or decision takers.

For each of these three basic requirements, critical heuristics offers a key concept. I can only give a brief introduction here; for a more complete explanation, the reader is referred to the main sources (Ulrich, 1983, 1984); for a helpful review see Jackson (1985). The application of these concepts has been illustrated in two earlier case studies (Ulrich, 1981b; 1983, Chapters 7 and 8).

KEY CONCEPT NO. 1: JUSTIFICATION BREAK-OFFS
AS BOUNDARY JUDGMENTS
(WHOLE SYSTEMS JUDGMENTS)

Systems science offers a concept that is helpful to understanding the meaning of justification break-offs, though unfortunately its critical significance is not always adequately understood. I mean the well-known concept of *boundary judgments*.

Whenever we apply the systems concept to some section of the real world, we must make very strong *a priori* assumptions about what is to belong to the system in question and what is to belong to its environment. The boundary judgments representing these assumptions can therefore be understood in a twofold, and complementary, way:

1. as *whole systems judgments*[1], i.e. the designer's assumptions about what belongs to the section of the real world to be studied and improved and what falls outside the reach of this effort;

2. as *justification break-offs* with regard to the demarcation of the context of application that is to be relevant when it comes to justifying the normative implications of a design for those affected by its effects.

In contemporary systems science, the problem of boundary judgments is either entirely ignored (typically in textbook exercises and case studies) or else it is discussed in terms of formal criteria of modelling, rather than in terms of the normative content of whole systems judgments and corresponding justification break-offs. Frequently, models of "systems" are presented as if the boundaries were objectively given, and the model itself does not tell us whether the boundaries in question have been adequately chosen. If the problem is discussed at all, it is seen merely from a modelling point of view: so as to facilitate the modelling tasks, boundaries are determined according to the availability of data and modelling techniques. But even from a merely technical modelling point of view, this way of dealing with the problem of boundary judgments is inadequate. First, the implicit criterion is that everything that cannot be controlled or is not known falls outside the boundaries of the model, so that the model itself looks neat and scientific. In point of fact, the reverse criterion should be applied: we cannot understand the meaning of the model (and hence, the system in question) if we do not understand the model-environment. Hence aspects that are not well understood ought to be

---

[1] A concept I owe to C. West Churchman, see especially Churchman (1970). Cf. in this context his "ethics of whole systems" in *Challenge to Reason* (1968). Cf. also Ulrich (1983, pp. 226–230) and *passim* (see index to the book).

considered as belonging to the system in question rather than to its environment, at least until their significance has been studied. Second, such studying of boundary questions must not be restricted to the "is" (or "will be") but must always include the "ought." Whether or not a certain boundary judgment is rational depends less on what boundaries are presently established than on what the boundaries should be, given the purpose of the model (the systems map or design). The normative content of the answer to the question of what the boundaries should be cannot be justified by referring to data availability, to presently accepted boundaries, or to the success of purposive–rational action. The normative content can be justified only through the voluntary consent of all those who might be affected by the consequences. Hence all the citizens affected, be they involved in the process or not, ought to be regarded as being part of the context of application.

Such an openly and critically normative understanding of boundary judgments has far-reaching implications for systems science and systems design. To mention but two of them:

1. Systems science will have to employ a new, "critically-normative"[2] concept of what represents an adequate definition (map, design) of a system: *a system is "adequate" if it makes explicit its own normative content.*[3]

2. The designer (applied scientist) will have to aim not at an objective but at a *critical solution to the problem of boundary judgments.* That is to say, it is his responsibility to secure the transparency of the boundary judgments on which he relies and to trace their possible normative consequences; but he cannot delegate to himself the political act of positively sanctioning these consequences—only the affected can. No standpoint, not even the most comprehensive systems point of view, is ever sufficient to validate its own implications. The rationality of a systems design is to be measured not by the degree to which it fulfils the impossible role of providing an elitary justification of its own normative implications, but rather by the degree to which it renders explicit the underlying justification break-offs and thus enables both those involved in and those affected by the design to reflect and discourse on the validity and legitimacy of these break-offs.

---

[2] I call a discipline "critically normative" if it offers methodical help not only in formulating and justifying scientific propositions but also in laying open the normative implications of the standpoint from which it derives and justifies its propositions, rather than misunderstanding or representing this standpoint as objective. Cf. Ulrich (1984, p. 327).

[3] Cf. Ulrich (1983, p. 229). I have argued against the failure of contemporary systems science to employ the systems idea in a critically-normative manner—i.e. as a tool of practical rather than merely instrumental (or functional) reason—on various occasions and from different points of view; see e.g. Ulrich (1977, p. 1100 ff, 1980, 1981a, 1983, p. 21ff, p. 222ff, p. 326ff and *passim*, 1987a, b)

Table 5.1 Checklist of boundary questions, the answers to which inevitably flow as normative premises into any concrete systems designs

1. Who ought to be the *client* (beneficiary) of the system S to be designed or improved?
2. What ought to be the *purpose* of S; i.e. what goal states ought S be able to achieve so as to serve the client?
3. What ought to be S's *measure of success* (or improvement)?
4. Who ought to be the *decision taker*, that is, have the power to change S's measure of improvement?
5. What *components* (resources and constraints) of S ought to be controlled by the decision taker?
6. What resources and conditions ought to be part of S's *environment*, i.e. should not be controlled by S's decision taker?
7. Who ought to be involved as *designer* of S?
8. What kind of *expertise* ought to flow into the design of S; i.e. who ought to be considered an expert and what should be his role?
9. Who ought to be the *guarantor* of S; i.e. where ought the designer seek the guarantee that his design will be implemented and will prove successful, judged by S's measure of success (or improvement)?
10. Who ought to belong to the *witnesses* representing the concerns of the citizens that will or might be affected by the design of S? That is to say, who among the affected ought to get involved?
11. To what degree and in what way ought the affected be given the chance of *emancipation* from the premises and promises of the involved?
12. Upon what *world-views* of either the involved or the affected ought S's design be based?

KEY CONCEPT NO. 2: *A PRIORI* CONCEPTS OF PRACTICAL REASON

In order to facilitate the systematic identification and examination of justification break-offs, critical heuristics has developed a checklist of twelve *boundary questions*. They aim at boundary judgments that inevitably flow into any systems design. By means of these questions, both the involved and the affected can question a design's normative content and challenge the "objective necessities" by which the other side may seek to justify or to dispute the underlying boundary judgments.

The twelve boundary questions[4] are given in Table 5.1. They are organized into four groups of boundary judgments, each group comprising three kinds of categories.

The first group asks for the *sources of motivation* flowing into the design in

---

[4] The list is partly inspired by similar efforts on the part of C. West Churchman and Peter B. Checkland, though its justification in critical heuristics is independent of the two authors. Cf. Churchman (1971, p. 43; 1979, p. 79 ff) and Checkland (1981, p. 223 ff).

question: Who contributes (ought to contribute) the necessary sense of direction and "values"? What purposes are to be served? Given a tentative planning purpose, whose purpose is it?

The second group is to examine the *sources of control* built into a design: Who contributes (ought to contribute) the necessary means, resources, and decision authority (i.e. "power")? Who has (ought to have) the power to decide?

The third group of questions is to trace the *sources of expertise* assumed to be adequate: Who contributes (ought to contribute) the necessary design skills and the necessary knowledge of "facts"? Who has (ought to have) the know-how to do it?

The fourth group, finally, helps reflect on the *sources of legitimation* to be considered: Who represents (ought to represent) the concerns of the affected? Who contributes the necessary sense of self-reflection and "responsibility" among the involved? How do the involved deal with the different world-views of the affected?

In short, the first group of boundary questions asks for the *value basis* of the design; the second for its *basis of power*; the third for its basis of *know-how*; and the fourth for its *basis of legitimation*.

The three questions of each group refer to the following three kinds of *categories*: the first question refers to *social roles* of the involved or the affected, the second to *role-specific concerns*, and the third to *key problems* or crucial issues in determining the necessary boundary judgments relative to the two previous categories.[5]

The critical relevance of these categories and corresponding boundary questions may best be seen by contrasting each "ought" with the pertaining "is" judgment:

1. Who *is* the actual client of S's design; i.e. who belongs to the group of those whose purposes (interests, values) are served, in distinction to those who do not benefit but may have to bear the costs or other disadvantages?

2. What is the actual purpose of S's design, as being measured not in terms of the declared intentions of the involved but in terms of the actual consequences?

3. What is, judged by the design's consequences, its built-in measure of success?

4. Who is actually the decision taker; i.e. who can actually change the measure of success?

5. What conditions of successful planning and implementation of S are really controlled by the decision taker?

---

[5] For a more detailed introduction of the twelve critically-heuristic categories, as well as the complementary quasi-transcendental ideas of critical heuristics not introduced here, see Ulrich (1983, p. 253 ff). Regarding the epistemological status of the ideas and categories, cf. Ulrich (1983, p. 231 ff).

6. What conditions are *not* controlled by the decision taker; i.e. what represents "environment" to him?

7. Who is actually involved as planner?

8. Who is involved as "expert," of what kind is his expertise, what role does he actually play?

9. Where do the involved seek the guarantee that their planning will be successful? (In the theoretical competence of experts? In consensus among experts? In the validity of empirical data? In the relevance of mathematical models or computer simulations? In political support on the part of interest-groups? In the experience and intuition of the involved? etc.) Can these assumed guarantors secure the design's success, or are they false guarantors?

10. Who among the involved witnesses represents the concerns of the affected? Who is or may be affected without being involved?

11. Are the affected given an opportunity to emancipate themselves from the experts and to take their fate into their own hands, or do the experts determine what is right for them, etc.? That is to say, are the affected used merely as means for the purposes of others, or are they also treated as "ends-in-themselves" (Kant), as belonging to the client?

12. What world-view is actually underlying the design of S? Is it the view of (some of) the involved or of (some of) the affected?

Contrasting "is" and "ought" boundary judgments provides a systematic way to evaluate the normative content of planning while at the same time laying open the normative basis of the evaluation itself: The "is" questions aim at determining a design's effective normative implications in the light of the "ought" answers, that is to say, without any illusion of objectivity.[6]

It remains to be explained why the title to this section speaks of *a priori concepts of practical reason*. First, the suggested boundary questions represent mere "forms of judgments," that is, they are in need of being substantiated with respect to both their empirical and normative content. Second, they can help to fill critically-heuristic categories such as "client", "purpose," etc. with empirical and normative content, but not to *justify* this content. The boundary judgments identified or postulated remain dependent for their justification on a discursive process of consensus formulation—a rational discourse—among the involved and the affected.

As previously suggested, contemporary models of ideal discourse do not provide a practicable way to redeem disputed validity claims of justification break-offs; it remains to be shown how practical discourse can secure at least a critical solution to this problem.[7]

---

[6] I have sought to illustrate this double employment of the suggested categories in two case studies; see Ulrich (1981b, or 1983, p. 343 ff ("Project Cybersyn" in Allende's Chile, 1971–73)) and (1983, p. 372 ff (health systems planning)).

[7] For a thorough introduction see Ulrich (1983, Chapter 5, especially p. 301 ff).

KEY CONCEPT NO. 3: THE POLEMICAL EMPLOYMENT OF BOUNDARY JUDGMENTS

The concepts that have been introduced thus far are to provide a tool of reflection for tracing the normative implications of systems designs. But they cannot guarantee such reflection. How then can affected citizens cause the involved decision takers, planners, and experts to reflect on a design's normative content if the involved are not willing to do so on their own? On the other side, how can the conflicting demands on democratic participation (of the affected) and of cogent argumentation (on the part of everybody involved, including the witnesses of the affected) be reconciled so that ordinary citizens can bring in their personal concerns without being convicted of lacking rationality or cogency?

Critical heuristic's basic conjecture in this regard may by now seem familiar: Any use of expertise presupposes boundary judgments with respect to the context of application to be considered. No amount of expertise or theoretical knowledge is ever sufficient for the expert to justify all the judgments on which his recommendations depend. When the discussion turns to the basic boundary judgments on which his exercise of expertise depends, the expert is no less a layman than are the affected citizens.[8]

It follows that every expert who justifies his recommendations, or the "objective necessities" he may disclose in the name of reason, by referring to his expertise *without* at the same time laying open his lay status relative to the underlying boundary judgments can be convicted of a dogmatic or cynical employment of boundary judgments. *Dogmatically* he employs them if he fails to recognize this lay status in respect to boundary judgments and hence asserts their objective necessity; *cynically*, if he very well sees through their character as justification break-offs but against his better judgment conceals them behind a facade of objectivity or pretends other than the true ones to be his boundary judgments.

Now anybody who is able to comprehend the unavoidability and the meaning of boundary judgments in general can also learn to see through—

---

[8] I find an interesting addition to this conclusion in Paul Feyerabend's new introduction to the revised German version of *Science in a Free Society* (1978). He observes that experts are often quite unable to justify routine procedures and routine arguments on which their claim for rationality depends; in discussing the assumptions underlying these procedures, they are indeed laymen. Our concept of boundary judgments suggests one possible explanation: the expert's routine procedures and arguments embody the basic boundary judgments by means of which problems are bounded in such a way that they fit his domain of competence. What falls outside this domain is relegated to an "irrelevant" or "irrational" ("merely subjective") status. The subjective, indeed dogmatic, character of such boundary judgments is then concealed behind a facade of routine procedures and professional authority ("all experts agree that this is the way to do it," or "we don't know any other way to do it").

and to make transparent to others—the dogmatic or cynical character of the "objective necessities" disclosed by experts in specific contexts of application. To this end, concerned citizens and professionals will have to master two tasks of argumentation:

1. They must be in a position to demonstrate that the boundary judgments of the involved cannot be justified rationally, i.e. cogently.

2. They should be able to translate their own subjective way of being affected by the boundary judgments in question into rational, cogent argumentation.

How can ordinary citizens without any special expertise or "communicative competence" (as required by the ideal models of rational discourse) accomplish this apparent squaring of the circle? My answer is: by means of *the polemical employment of boundary judgments.*

Immanuel Kant, in his discussion of the "polemical employment of reason" (1787, B767), calls *"polemical"* an argument that is directed against a dogmatically asserted validity claim and which does *not* depend for its cogency on its own positive justification. A polemical argument has only critical validity; but in regard to this merely critical intent, it must be rational, i.e. cogent. Thus the polemical employment of reason, as understood by Kant, has nothing in common with "polemics" in the contemporary, vulgar meaning of the term; it aims at the cause rather than at the person, and it must be logically compelling.

The use of boundary judgments for merely critical purposes almost ideally fulfils this condition: boundary judgments that are introduced overtly as personal value judgments entail no theoretical validity claim and hence do not require a theoretical justification. Hence no theoretical knowledge or any other kind of special expertise or "competence" is required. Indeed, it is not even necessary to pretend that a boundary judgment used polemically may not be false or merely subjective. What matters is only that no one can demonstrate the objective impossibility (and hence, irrelevance) of a polemical statement any more than its proponent can demonstrate its objective necessity.

Now the crucial point is this. So long as affected citizens employ their boundary judgments for critical purposes only—i.e. without asserting any positive validity claims—they can secure for themselves an advantage of argumentation by imposing the burden of proof upon the involved experts: as against the expert's boundary judgments, they can with equal right and with overt subjectivity advance their own boundary judgments, thereby embarrassing the expert for being unable to prove the superiority of *his* boundary judgments by virtue of his expertise. In this way, they can demonstrate three essential points:

1. that boundary judgments do play a role in the expert's propositions;
2. that his theoretical competence is insufficient to justify his own boundary judgments or to falsify those of his critic;
3. that an expert who seeks to justify his recommendations by referring to his competence or by asserting "objective necessities" argues either dogmatically or cynically and thereby disqualifies himself.

Thus the polemical employment of boundary judgments enables ordinary people to expose the dogmatic character of the expert's "objective necessities" *through their own subjective arguments*, without even having to pretend to be objective or to be able to establish a true counterposition against the expert. Therein, I believe, lies the enormous significance of Kant's concept of the polemical employment of reason for a critically-heuristic approach to planning, an approach that would actually mediate between the conflicting demands of democratic participation (of all affected citizens) and those of rational, cogent argumentation (on the part of the involved planners and experts).

To be sure, as soon as the affected claim positive validity for their boundary judgments, they lose their advantage of argumentation and disqualify themselves no less than the experts do. But it would be to mistake the situation if the polemical employment of boundary judgments were considered to produce a mere "symmetry of helplessness."[9] The polemical employment of reason secures to both sides an equal position for reasonable dialogue: each side, if only it renounces the dogmatic or cynical employment of boundary judgments, can now argue its case and work toward mutual understanding about the premises and consequences of planning, by advancing its own good grounds, i.e. "facts" and "values" capable of consensus such as existential needs of all individuals, ecological knowledge, ethical principles, principles of constitutional democracy, and so on. The fact that ultimate justifications remain impossible provides no sound reason for renouncing any effort to bring in one's own good grounds. Nor does it provide the other side with a good ground to refuse entering upon such an effort: scepticism, turned into an argument against any argumentative effort, is no less dogmatic than the expert's reference to "objective necessities." Hence a "symmetry of helplessness" arises only with respect to dogmatic or cynical argumentation attempts; for the rest, an essential condition of rational discussion is secured, namely, the possibility of "competent" participation of affected citizens in the process of unfolding the normative implications of planning.

Opening up the applied disciplines for such a process of unfolding is certainly no royal way to solve the problem of practical reason; but it might be an important step towards dealing critically with the justification break-offs that inevitably flow into the definition of specific contexts of application to be

---

[9] A concept coined by Horst Rittel in a different context; cf. (1963, p. 14).

considered. It is only thus that applied science can hope to fulfil its mission—
to secure improvement of the human condition, by studying contexts of
application of human knowledge and design.

REFERENCES

Checkland, P.B. (1981). *Systems Thinking, Systems Practice*, John Wiley, Chichester.
Churchman, C.W. (1968). *Challenge to Reason*, McGraw-Hill, New York.
Churchman, C.W. (1970). Kant—a decision theorist? *Theory and Decision*, 1, 107–116.
Churchman, C.W. (1971). *The Design of Inquiring Systems*, Basic Books, New York.
Churchman, C.W. (1979). *The Systems Approach and its Enemies*, Basic Books, New York.
Feyerabend, P. (1978). *Science in a Free Society*, New Left Books, London. (Revised
German version: *Erkenntnis für freie Menschen*, veränderte Ausgabe, Suhrkamp,
Frankfurt am Main, 1980.)
Habermas, J. (1971). Vorbereitende Bemerkungen zu einer Theorie der kommunikativen
Kompetenz, in *Theorie der Gesellshaft oder Sozialtechnologie—Was leistet die Systemfor-
schung?* (Eds J. Habermas and N. Luhmann), Suhrkamp, Frankfurt am Main.
Habermas, J. (1973). Wahrheitstheorien, in *Wirklichkeit und Reflexion* (Ed. H. Fahren-
bach), Neske, Pfullingen, Germany.
Habermas, J. (1975). A postscript to knowledge and human interests, *Phil. Social Sci.*, 3,
175–189.
Habermas, J. (1979). What is universal pragmatics?, in *Communication and the Evolution
of Society* (Ed. J. Habermas), Beacon Press, Boston, Mass.
Jackson, M.C. (1985). The itinerary of a critical approach: review of *Critical Heuristics of
Social Planning* by W. Ulrich, *J. Opl Res. Soc.*, 36, 878–881.
Kant, I. (1787). *Critique of Pure Reason*, 2nd edition, translated by N. Kemp Smith, St
Martin's Press, New York, 1965.
Lorenzen, P. (1969). *Normative Logica and Ethics*, Bibliographisches Institut, Mannheim,
Germany.
Lorenzen, P., and Schwemmer, O. (1975). *Konstruktive Logik, Ethik und Wissenshaftstheo-
rie*, Bibliographisches Institut, Mannheim, Germany.
McCarthy, T. (1978). *The Critical Theory of Jürgen Habermas*, MIT-Press, Cambridge,
Mass.
Popper, K.R. (1961). *The Logic of Scientific Discovery*, Basic Books, New York (original
edition, *Logik der Forschung*, Springer, Wien, 1935).
Popper, K.R. (1968). *Conjectures and Refutations: The Growth of Scientific Knowledge*, Basic
Books, New York (original edition, Routledge & Kegan Paul, London, 1963).
Popper, K.R. (1972). *Objective Knowledge*, Clarendon Press, Oxford.
Rittel, H. (1963). Überlegungen zur wissenschaftlichen und politischen Bedeutung der
Entscheidungstheorie, mimeographed paper, revised version in H. Krauch *et al.*
(Eds), *Forschungsplanung*, Oldenburg, Munich and Vienna.
Ulrich, W. (1977). The design of problem-solving systems, *Mgmt. Sci.*, 23, 1099–1108.
Ulrich, W. (1980). The metaphysics of design: a Simon-Churchman debate, *TIMS/ORSA
Interfaces*, 10, 35–40.
Ulrich, W. (1981a). Systemrationalität und praktische Vernunft, Gedanken zum Stand
des Systemansatzes, translator's introduction to the German version of Churchman
(1979), *Der Systemansatz und seine "Feinde"*, Paul Haupt, Bern, 1981.
Ulrich, W. (1981b). A critique of pure cybernetic reason: the Chilean experience with
cybernetics, *J. Appl. Syst. Anal.*, 8, 33–59.

Ulrich, W. (1983). *Critical Heuristics of Social Planning: A New Approach to Practical Philosophy*, Paul Haupt, Bern/Stuttgart.

Ulrich, W. (1984). Management oder die Kunst, Entscheidungen zu treffen, die andere betreffen, *Die Unternehmung, Schweizerische Zeitschrift für betriebswirtschaftliche Forschung und Praxis*, **38**, 326–346.

Ulrich, W. (1987a). The metaphysics of social systems design, in *Decision Making about Decision Making: Metamodels and Metasystems* (Ed. J. P. van Gigch), pp. 219–226, Abacus Press, Tunbridge Wells, England, and Cambridge, Mass.

Ulrich, W. (1987b). Systemtheorie der Planung, in *Handwörterbuch der Planung* (Ed. N. Szyperski), Poeschel, Stuttgart.

Chapter 6

Social Systems Theory and Practice: The Need for a Critical Approach

MICHAEL C. JACKSON

INTRODUCTION

Much of the success of science in explaining, predicting and controlling natural systems can be attributed to the well understood methods that exist for producing and testing theory in the natural sciences. The successful development of social systems science is similarly likely to depend on the elucidation of methods of inquiry suitable to the systems of its concern. Unfortunately the successful methods employed by natural scientists cannot be simply taken over and used in social systems science. Systems scientists who attempt to do this risk operating with wholly inappropriate tools when dealing with social systems. Alternative methods of inquiry have been developed in the "soft" systems tradition which are more appropriate for use in relation to one large class of social systems. However, there are many social systems for which even these soft systems approaches are inappropriate. For such social systems there is a need for a more radical and critical approach to producing and verifying social systems science. This paper seeks to demonstrate the need for a critical approach in relation to one class of social systems and shows how only this kind of approach can take account of the special characteristics of this category of social system.

The purpose of the paper is to evaluate the suitability of various methods of

Reprinted by permission from *International Journal of General Systems*, Volume 10, 1985 inquiry for use in social systems science. In particular the need for a critical method of inquiry in relation to an important category of social systems will be demonstrated. The starting point is an account of the scientific method given by N. Rescher (1979). The aim of summarising Rescher's account is to establish the importance of method in the development of science and to show that there would be difficulties in applying even this sophisticated version of scientific method in social systems science.

In the next section, consideration is given to how "hard" systems theorists try to gain knowledge about systems and to use it to intervene in social systems. The procedures they adopt are very similar to the natural scientific method and the argument will be that these procedures will only rarely be applicable for social systems. In a further section the soft systems tradition of thought will be considered. The methodologies explicated are seen as an important advance on hard systems approaches because they recognise that systems in which human beings play an important part must be treated differently from "hard" systems. Nevertheless, soft systems methodologies themselves have a restricted domain in which they can be used successfully. In the final part it is argued that an approach to social systems science based on the critical theory of J. Habermas is necessary if the apparently contradictory nature of certain types of social system is to be understood and if successful practice is to result from this understanding.

SCIENTIFIC METHOD AND ITS POSSIBLE APPLICATION TO SOCIAL SYSTEMS

It is useful to consider first the methods used for producing and testing theory in the natural sciences. These methods are "well understood" in the sense that the elements comprising the scientific method—observation, analysis, experiment, formulation of hypotheses, testing, development of theory—have been recognised for many centuries. All these elements are recognised as essential, although disputes do continue about the relative importance of the various elements in the method. In the traditional view, science proceeds by experiment and analysis to formulate hypotheses concerning the real-world. Further testing leads to the adoption of some of these hypotheses as scientific laws. These laws are then integrated in a scientific theory. Another version of the scientific method, that of K. R. Popper (1972), affords primacy to theory, since some theory is presupposed by any observation. An account of the scientific method given by Rescher (1979) is the one that will be followed here. This account, in which the concept of "cognitive system" assumes paramount importance, is particularly relevant in relation to questions about systems theory (see Jackson, 1981).

Rescher notes the tendency of human beings to organise their knowledge in cognitive systems. These are structured frameworks linking various elements of knowledge into cohesive wholes. They express certain intellectual norms—simplicity, regularity, uniformity, comprehensiveness, unity, harmony, economy; norms which men have found useful in thinking about the world and making their way in the world. According to the traditional view of science, cognitive systems play little part in the production of knowledge. In Rescher's epistemology, however, cognitive systems are elevated to a most important function. They undergo what he calls the "Hegelian Inversion" and are transformed from being merely the organised expression of what is accepted on other criteria to be true, to being actual arbiters of what is acceptable as true. Thus a hypothesis does not become a scientific law because of repeated observation and experiment but only when it can be integrated into a systematic body of scientific knowledge—a cognitive system. Only if a thesis coheres systematically with the rest of what is known is it accepted as part of real knowledge. The truth is that which can by systematized. This principle, combined with a "network" model of how cognitive systems are constructed, is what Rescher calls "coherentism."

At the centre of the scientific method, then, are cognitive systems. These systems judge the worthiness of new truth candidates and continually develop in the search for greater systematicity. Rescher now has to justify science proceeding along these lines. The scientific theses which emerge from this method are acceptable, he argues, *just because* they are produced by an appropriate method—the systems/scientific method. This of course throws the whole burden of justification onto the method itself. Rescher argues that coherentism can be regarded as a legitimate method because it is subject to two types of control—theoretical control and applicative control. The theoretical control stems from the "self-monitoring" of coherentism as a theory. Thus, with coherentism, systematicity is the starting point of inquiry but it is not necessarily the end of inquiry. If the results produced by using the criteria of systematicity reveal the world to be unsystematic, then the guiding principles of the inquiry (those original criteria) can still be abandoned. The applicative control of a method concerns its success or failure in producing results which facilitate the prediction and control of the object of study. A method is justified if its results can underwrite successful practice. As was shown, coherentism underpins the scientific method and science has had dramatic success in the prediction and control of natural phenomena. This justifies coherentism as a method. It also suggests to Rescher that nature itself must be orderly. It follows that with the development of our systematising endeavours (using the feedback provided by the theoretical and applicative controls) there should develop a growing conformity between these endeavours and the real world.

Let us accept that coherentism is a good account of the process of knowledge production in the natural sciences and that Rescher shows how this method can be justified. It must now be asked whether the coherentist method can similarly be adopted to produce and test knowledge about social systems and whether its use can be justified in the same way.

A first step might be to consider whether it is equally justifiable in the social as well as the natural sciences to employ cognitive systems as the arbiters of what is acceptable as true. It might be objected that coherentism simply is not an appropriate method of inquiry in the social sciences. Social systems are the consequence, intended or otherwise, of the action and interaction of human beings. They are made up of groups with diverse and often conflicting aims and intentions. Can this reality be represented in a discipline based upon the canons of systematicity—simplicity, regularity, uniformity, comprehensiveness, unity, harmony and economy? Coherentism would seem to require conceptualisations in which conflict and contradiction are absent. Cognitive systems constructed according to coherentist principles would surely misrepresent the reality they were trying to depict. If as T. Adorno (the Frankfurt School sociologist) believed, society is full of contradictions,

> The sociological mode of procedure must bow to this. Otherwise, out of a puristic zeal to avoid contradiction, it will fall into the most fatal contradiction of all, namely that existing between its own structure and that of its object. (Adorno, 1976)

The coherentist method can be seen as encouraging the social sciences to fall into this most fatal contradiction.

A second step in evaluating the applicability of Rescher's version of the scientific method to the social sciences might be to consider whether the two controls on the method are equally valid when it is applied to social systems.

The theoretical control seems suspect enough even when applied to natural systems. The requirement is that the canons of systematicity be used in theory construction, but that ultimate belief in their efficacy be withheld until the world is actually revealed to be systemic. But surely, if one goes into the world seeking order and system, one is likely to find it. This weakness is considerably exaggerated when dealing with social phenomena, since it is usually much more difficult to establish incontrovertibly that a social scientific theory has been falsified. It is to be expected, then, that theorists who employ systems ideas in the social sciences will discover and continue to believe in a world which is systemic. A book by R. Lilienfeld (1978) suggests that this is the case. Lilienfeld has demonstrated that almost all of what passes as systems theory in the social sciences is "functionalist" in orientation. The social world is taken to exist as an objective reality and studied as if it were a "second nature" (Bauman, 1977). The primary focus of interest is on regulation; the study of social order and those aspects of the social world which help maintain social order. The work of Henderson, Bertalanffy, Parsons, Merton, Deutsch and Easton (among others) is examined in some detail and is found to fall squarely into the functionalist paradigm. Issues which other theorists stress—such as the existence of conflict, power, coercion and change in social systems—seem to get ignored.

The second control over coherentism as a method is the applicative control. The method is justified if it produces results which aid the prediction and control of the object of study. On the basis of this control it is arguable that coherentism has failed as a method for the social sciences. The complexity of social phenomena and the unpredictability of human beings have, perhaps fortunately, frustrated attempts to predict and control social systems.

There is, however, an even more important point. The applicative control is particularly ill-suited to the social sciences and simply cannot be used as a criterion of the success of a method in the social sciences. This is because of the close link between theory and practice in these disciplines. Thus, a particular élite in society, believing in some coherentist social theory and searching for order in social life, might be tempted to use compulsion to bring social practice into line with their theory. If the compulsion worked they would certainly be better able to predict and control social reality. Ironically this would, on the basis of the applicative control, confirm the scientific stature of the theory. As R. Bahro (1978, p. 245) says of the Soviet ideology: "It *appears* as 'true' and 'scientific' precisely to the extent that the compulsion functions effectively."

This summary of Rescher's account of the scientific method will, I hope, have established the importance of method in scientific development. However, the discussion of the relevance of coherentism to social systems reveals that even this very sophisticated version of the scientific method cannot simply be taken over and used in the social sciences. The methods systems theorists employ to gain knowledge about social systems and to intervene in social systems looks as if it should be an interesting area of study.

HARD SYSTEMS METHODOLOGIES APPLIED TO SOCIAL SYSTEMS

In this section attention will be given to the methods used by "hard" systems researchers to seek knowledge about systems and to use that knowledge to improve or design systems. The question will be asked whether these methods are appropriate when social systems are the object of concern. Brief consideration will also be given to general system theory, cybernetic and socio-technical approaches.

Hard systems thinking can, following P.B. Checkland (1978), be seen as made up of three strands. These three strands are the methodologies of "systems engineering" (A.D. Hall, H. Chestnut, G.M. Jenkins etc.), "systems analysis" (the RAND Corporation etc.) and traditional "operational research" with what R.L. Ackoff (1979a) calls its "predict and prepare" paradigm. What makes these three strands so similar in basic operation is that they are all "based upon the assumption that the problem task they tackle is to select an efficient means of achieving a known and defined end" (Checkland, 1978). The well known, British, systems engineering methodology of G.M. Jenkins (1969) may be taken as a typical example of the hard systems approach.

Jenkins' methodology incorporates four basic phases—systems analysis, systems design, implementation and operation. In systems analysis the real world is taken to consist of systems and is examined in systems terms. The problem is formulated and the system in which it exists is defined and analysed in terms of important subsystems. The interactions between these subsystems are studied. Definition of the wider system and its objectives leads to specification of the objectives of the system being studied. In the second phase (systems design) the future environment of the system is forecast. The system is then represented in a quantitative model which simulates its performance under different operational conditions. The particular design that optimises the performance of the system in pursuit of its objectives is chosen. The model therefore is an aid in the prediction of the consequences that follow from adopting alternative designs. A control system must be incorporated into the design of the optimum system at this point. The implementation and operation phases involve the construction, operation and testing of the system in the real world.

The example of Jenkins' methodology reveals that there are close links between the methods advocated by hard systems thinkers and the methods employed in the natural sciences. The first two phases of Jenkins' methodology correspond to the application of an appropriate coherentist (systems/scientific) method of inquiry. The two controls of coherentism are also in operation. The theoretical control is present in that the methodology always requires a systemic account of the real world and could presumably fail in its attempt to construct one. The implementation and operation phases are consistent with the applicative control outlined by Rescher. The purpose of the systems engineering methodology is very clearly to facilitate prediction and control of the system under surveillance. If this is achieved—if the system performs according to plan—then the systems concepts and tools employed in the earlier phases of the methodology are validated.

In view of this correspondence between hard systems thinking and the scientific method, it is not surprising (given the points made in the previous section) that doubts have been expressed regarding the relevance of the hard approach to social systems. A number of influential books have appeared which criticise the application of hard systems methodologies to social problems. Those of I. Hoos (1972), R. Boguslaw (1965) and R. Lilienfeld (1978) deserve attention. Even among systems thinkers (C.W. Churchman, 1968, 1978; R.L. Ackoff, 1974; P.B. Checkland, 1978) the feeling is growing that while these methodologies may be suitable for dealing with well-structured problems in systems involving non-human components, they are inappropriate for social systems. The next stage of the argument therefore is to examine the criticisms levelled at hard systems methodologies applied to social systems. These criticisms can be divided into two kinds.

The first type of criticism concerns the theory or model of reality implied by these methodologies. These criticisms are closely related to the doubts expressed in the last section about cognitive systems as arbiters of what is acceptable as true in the social sciences and about the nature of the theoretical control. The theory or model implied is invariably functionalist. The methodologies take for granted the existence of systems in the real world. They search for regularities and causal relationships in the interactions between subsystems. They take a deterministic view of human behaviour. It follows that the objectives of the system can be determined by the analyst from outside the system. The problem is simply to design a system which will achieve these objectives. This functionalist orientation is derived naturally from the tradition of engineering from which the hard systems methodologies stem.

The critics argue that this functionalist/engineering model badly misrepresents the nature of social reality. Social systems do not have an objective existence in the real world and it is not easy to discover what objectives they should pursue. A major finding of Checkland's (1981) action research was that "hard systems engineering methodology could not be used in ill-structured problem situations in which the naming of desirable ends was itself problematical." For Checkland one of the major aspects of the problem in dealing with "human activity systems" is the impossibility of defining desirable ends or objectives for such systems. Ackoff (1974) points to the level of apparent conflict that exists in many social systems between the purposes of subsystem, system and suprasystem. Hard systems methodologies tend not to recognise such conflict and lack mechanisms for dealing with it. They seem to believe that the analyst can ascertain the "correct" objective that the system should pursue. Moreover, most hard systems thinkers, as Hoos (1972) has shown, are unwilling to question the functionalist/engineering model they employ even when it seems to others wholly inappropriate to the kind of social problem being tackled. The tendency, rather, is to reduce the problem (and in the process distort it) so that it can be tackled using a methodology based upon the functionalist/engineering model. The "objectives" of criminal justice systems, social welfare systems and management information systems are assumed rather than questioned so that work using a hard systems methodology can proceed (Hoos, 1972). The theoretical control simply fails to operate.

This leads on to the second (related) type of objection to the use of hard systems methodologies to engineer social systems. It may, following M.G. Small (1981), be called the "humanitarian" objection. Hard systems methodologies assume that it is possible to arrive at a clear statement of the objectives of a system from outside the system concerned. But objectives originate from within social systems and different individuals and groups often vary considerably concerning the goals they wish to see pursued. So there would seem to be important practical problems for hard systems thinkers dealing with social systems. In these circumstances hard systems methodologies would not enable better prediction and control to be achieved and would have to be abandoned according to the control employed by hard systems thinkers to validate their procedures. However, in practice, hard systems methodologies do sometimes appear to "work." Logically this success must depend either on there being widespread agreement over objectives among the human beings who make up the system (which is likely to be quite rare) or on there being an autocratic decision-taker who can decide on the objectives of the system. Thus, the Jenkins' methodology, as A.R. Thomas and M. Lockett (1979) point out, "explicitly accepts existing structures of authority and power in its unitary view of management." This is the dangerous authoritarian implication of hard systems thinking when it is applied to many kinds of social system. It risks, according to Habermas (1974), splitting human beings into two classes—"the social engineers and the inmates of closed institutions." The systems theorist as scientist offers "objective" knowledge about how systems should be organised. His science enables him to prescribe the "best" solution irrespective of the values of the individuals in the system. Such an approach finds ready acceptance, according to Lilienfeld (1975), among those

> contemptuous of the untidiness and irrationality of the political process, (who) would prefer to replace the political process by an administrative world, a system which they as philosopher kings would manipulate from on high, from a position outside of and superior to the system they wish to control.

It follows that the "predict and control" criterion (the equivalent of the applicative control) employed by hard systems theorists as a test of their procedures, may not give a fair test of hard systems methodologies when they are applied to social systems. Because of the existence of autocratic decision-makers, the theory or model of social reality advocated by the analyst can be imposed upon other interests in the system—enabling those decision-makers the better to predict and control the workings of the system. The result is that hard systems methodologies do sometimes appear to "work." They are made to work, however, only because of the existence of compulsion. This appearance of "working" is another important reason why the functionalist theories and models employed in hard systems thinking are still accepted by many.

The analysis above suggests that hard systems methodologies will only rarely be applicable for social systems. They can be legitimately employed in that context only where there is agreement over ends and means among the human beings who make up the system. In these circumstances the purposeful character of the components of social systems becomes irrelevant and social systems resemble "hard" systems.

If there was space a similar argument could be pursued against general system theory, cybernetic and socio-technical systems theory as applied to social systems. These versions of systems thinking differ from hard systems methodologies in taking a "structuralist" rather than "positivist" approach to the construction of systems theory; believing that it is possible to uncover certain "structural laws" underpining the viability and effectiveness of systems (see Jackson, 1984). But they depend for their practical effectiveness, just as much as hard systems methodologies, on there being some predetermined goal and also, therefore, for their legitmacy on the individuals and groups within the system agreeing on that goal (see Jackson and Keys, 1984). General system theory has been identified by Checkland (1972) with "utopian engineering"—an approach which rests on the assumption that rational action must be orientated in pursuit of some ultimate goal. Cybernetics, as G. Morgan (1982) has stated, can be treated as a technique for "improving the design, control and performance of systems geared to the achievement of predetermined ends." W. Ulrich (1981) points out, in his critique of Beer's cybernetic work in Chile, that project CYBERSYN did not generate "intrinsic motivation"—distribute the source determining the system's goal state and purpose throughout the system. It was only the top controller—the government—which was in a position to change CYBERSYN's design, according to its political purposes. Socio-technical theory depends on the establishment of a "primary task" for a system (an assumed unitary goal) before joint optimisation of the technical and social-psychological subsystems can proceed. This argument cannot be pursued further here.

SOFT SYSTEMS THINKING APPLIED TO SOCIAL SYSTEMS

"Soft" systems thinking and the justifications used to support this approach to bringing about change in social systems will now be considered. The work of C.W. Churchman, R.L. Ackoff and P.B. Checkland is held to constitute the core of soft systems thinking. This work avoids the functionalism of systems engineering, systems analysis and operational research and is instead "interpretive" in character (Jackson, 1982). Interpretive theorists adopt a more subjectivist approach to social science (see Burrell and Morgan, 1979). They do not seek to study objective "social facts" or to search for regularities and causal relations in social reality. The social world is seen as being the creative construction of human beings. It is necessary therefore to proceed by trying to understand subjectively the point of view and the intentions of the human beings who construct social systems. Hence the importance in soft systems thinking of probing the *"Weltanschauungen"* (Churchman, 1968) or the "appreciative systems" (Vickers, 1970) that individuals employ in understanding and constructing the social world.

The systems approaches advocated by the theorists mentioned are all conditioned by this subjectivist orientation. For Churchman "objectivity" in social systems science is not to be sought by constructing theories and attempting to verify/falsify these by observation of the real world. The social world is perceived (and constructed) by men according to the particular world-views or *Weltanschauungen* (Ws) which they hold. No observation of the world can be free of theoretical and metaphysical underpinning. And no observation or data can ever fatally destroy a *Weltanschauung* (Churchman, 1970). The analyst must therefore respect different points of view concerning the goals to be attained by organisations and society. Thus, "The systems approach begins when first you see the world through the eyes of another" (Churchman, 1968). It follows that social problems are not amenable to technical solution. Room must be made for argument and debate. It is this argument, and the possibility of changing people's Ws, that offers the means for securing change in the social world. If a system is not serving its "clients," the decision-makers in the system must be persuaded to expose their Ws to counter-Ws which represent the "deadly" opponents of their own world-views (Churchman, 1971, 1979). They must confront their most cherished systemic assumptions with plausible counter-assumptions. If they endure this "heroic" trial, then decision-makers and clients may reach agreement concerning the system's goals. This temporary agreement about the nature of the system may be called objective. It is objectivity with a "Hegelian" basis. This whole continuous process of building up and then breaking down again whatever agreement is reached constitutes a "Singerian inquiring system" (Churchman, 1970).

The fundamental differences between this approach, which takes the existence of subjectivity seriously, and hard systems approaches is well brought out in a comparison of the positions of Churchman and H. Simon made by Ulrich (1980). Simon seeks to apply the objective approach of natural science to the human domain. Churchman rests his proposals to improve the purposeful design of whole systems on a full acceptance of subjectivity and the difference this makes to the methods that should be used to study and change social systems.

Ackoff's (1979b) revised operational research (OR) "paradigm" is clearly subjectivist in orientation compared with traditional OR. For Ackoff there are no problems "out-there" to be solved by the OR practitioner. There can be many different definitions of what the problem is in any particular situation. Ackoff's approach is designed to bring about a consensus among the stakeholders concerned with a particular system so that action can be taken. This consensus, arrived at through open debate, is the only kind of objectivity that can be obtained: "Objectivity is the social product of the open interaction of a wide variety of individual subjectivities" (Ackoff, 1974).

Consensus is sought through the process of "interactive" planning (Ackoff, 1981). The stakeholders participate in designing an "idealized future" for the system with which they are concerned. This is a design of the future that begins "from scratch." Ackoff sees this "ends" planning as a way of eliminating petty differences between stakeholders and of concentrating their minds on the broader, long-term interests they share in common.

Checkland's methodology grew out of the frustration experienced by consultants trying to use hard systems methodologies in soft problem situations. Checkland (1981) acknowledges that it has more in common with the tradition of interpretive social science than with functionalism. The emphasis of the methodology, he writes, "is . . . not on any external 'reality' but on people's perceptions of reality, on their mental processes rather than on the objects of those processes."

The various Ws operating in a system (plus any the analyst may wish to introduce) are expressed in "root definitions" of some of the systems which appear relevant to the problem situation. "Conceptual models" of the various systems enshrined in the root definitions are then constructed. These are compared with a "rich picture" of what is perceived to exist in the real world and the comparison used to structure a debate about possible change among the actors concerned with the problem situation. The actors become aware of the implications of their own world-views and of the existence of other, possibly conflicting, Ws. Thus the methodology facilitates a social process in which "appreciative systems" are held up for examination and possibly changed. The analyst and the various actors may then agree upon changes which should be both desirable and feasible.

Soft systems thinkers, as is apparent, proceed in an entirely different way from natural scientists and hard systems researchers. They do not attempt to formulate systemic theories which can be used as cognitive systems to validate other hypotheses about the social world. Their subjectivism reflects a disbelief in the existence of objective features in social reality which could be "captured" by such theories. Thus a book by Churchman (1979) surprises one reviewer (Sica, 1981) because in a book supposedly about social systems we are told remarkably little about what social systems are actually like. Despite Churchman's metaphysical statements about the comprehensiveness and all-embracing character of the systems approach, one's sympathies lie with the reviewer (see Jackson, 1982). Ackoff's interactive planning requires "formulating the mess" in which the corporation finds itself, as a first stage in the planning process. But this does not lead him to take seriously any "objective" constraints there might be on corporate development. He is convinced that the principal obstructions to corporate development are usually self-imposed (Ackoff, 1981) and that system members could have the system they most desire right now, if they really wanted it. Checkland (1981) is clear that the early stages of his methodology should not be conducted in systems terms. The "rich picture" which is built up, and with which the conceptual models are eventually compared, is simply a collection of impressions about the problem situation being confronted.

It is worth considering at this point what criticisms can be levelled at the interpretive theory upon which soft systems approaches are based. Many social scientists argue that though the social world is created by people it is not necessarily created by them in the full awareness of what they are doing. Further, it is created by people who have conflicting aims and intentions and who bring different resources to bear when the social construction is taking place. It follows that the social world can escape the understanding and control of any one person or group of people. It takes on the form of a highly complex and structured external reality which exercises constraint on the individuals who make it up (see Durkheim, 1964). If this account of the construction and nature of social reality is correct, it is clear that soft systems thinking, which ignores the objective aspects of the social world, will be severely limited in terms of its effectiveness in bringing about change in social systems. Soft systems thinkers, because of their subjectivism, tend to work for change at the level of ideas. The impression one gets is that it is relatively easy to bring about change—all one has to do is change people's Ws. But if Ws are linked to other social facts (political and economic) in a constraining social totality, they may not be so easily changed. Changing Ws might depend crucially on first of all changing these other social facts. Some sort of understanding of the nature of the present totality, its laws of transformation and the existing blockages to change, would be required before effective action could be taken. Lacking this understanding, soft systems thinking cannot pose a real threat to the social structures which support the Ws with which it works. It can tinker at the ideological level, but this is likely simply to ensure the continued survival, by adaptation, of existing social elites (see Jackson, 1982). This is not at all what the designers of soft systems methodologies intended. Nevertheless, there is some evidence that it is what is achieved by these approaches. Churchman, Ackoff and Checkland are baffled that their methodologies when applied to the real world tend to lead to conservative or, at best, reformist recommendations for change. It may be that the methods they employ are not appropriate to many of the social systems with which they seek to deal.

Having abandoned the formulation of systemic theories as the starting point of inquiry, it is not open for soft systems thinkers to employ the theoretical control as a check on their methods. Nor do they attempt to employ any version of the applicative control to justify their procedures. Indeed it seems a great strength of soft systems thinkers that they recognise that it is impossible to transfer the "predict and control" criterion of validation to interventions in social systems. Instead, Churchman, Ackoff and Checkland pursue a different kind of validation for their methods. This is a validation based upon respect for the point of view and aims of all the stakeholders affected by the intervention. They believe that the only justification that can be obtained for social system changes is that they are arrived at through open debate in which concerned actors achieve a consensus about the nature of their objectives and the changes they wish to bring about in social systems. This is reflected, for example, in Ackoff's (1983) remark that "a researcher is rational . . . to the extent that his models enable those he tries to serve to improve their performance by their own criteria." Similarly, Checkland's methodology requires improvement to emerge from a generalised and theoretically enhanced debate about feasible and desirable changes as perceived by those involved in the problem-situation. It is this "participative" criterion of validation which must now be examined.

It will be noted that the participative criterion of validation depends upon all the stakeholders of a system being prepared to enter into a free and open discussion about changes to be made. Yet it is surely unrealistic to expect all stakeholders to be willing to enter into such a debate. Privileged stakeholders (in terms of wealth, status or power) are unlikely to risk their dominant position and submit their privileges to the vagaries of idealized design or whatever. So soft systems thinkers, if they take their own criterion of validation seriously, will have to steer clear of the very many social systems where full and effective participation cannot be established.

There is an even more important point. If validation is to depend upon the achievement of a *true* consensus among participating actors, care will have to be taken that the discussions that take place are free and unconstrained. The debates about change will have to conform to something like the model of "communicative competence" proposed by Habermas (1970a, b). It is essential that all actors have an equal say in discussion, have access to all the material available which is relevant to the discussion, and are not hindered by lack of resources from presenting the best possible case for the changes they favour. Finally, the discussion should take place free from a framework of domination. The ability of some participants to impose sanctions on others (because they are more powerful) must not affect the outcome of the discussion. Only if such conditions are met will the consensus at the end of the debate reflect the strength of the arguments and not simply various "constraints" on discussion. Of course in many social systems, in many organisations and societies in which great inequalities exist, the kind of unconstrained debate envisaged here cannot possibly take place. The actors bring to the discussion unequal information resources and are more or less powerful. The result of the unequal information resources is that the ideologies of the privileged are imposed upon other actors who lack the means of recognising their own true interests. The result of the inequalities in power is that the existing social order, from which power is drawn, is reproduced. As Giddens (1976, p. 122) writes:

> The use of power in interaction involves the application of facilities whereby participants are able to generate outcomes through affecting the conduct of others; the facilities are both drawn from an order of domination and at the same time as they are applied, reproduce that order of domination.

Given the participative criterion of validation adopted by soft systems thinkers, it matters considerably that the participation that takes place is "genuine." If, to use Beer's (1983) terminology, the apparent will of the stakeholders is (because of the effect of prevailing power structures) an attenuated version of their true interests, then clearly genuine participation is not taking place. In such circumstances true validation cannot occur either. The attempt to achieve it is nullified by the social environment in which the methodology is working. The soft systems approaches studied here do little to try to redress the effect of prevailing power structures. They are content to work with a manipulated consensus emerging from "distorted communication." For this reason, interventions using soft systems methodologies cannot, on their own terms, be validated.

Churchman, Ackoff and Checkland are therefore rightly criticised (see Jackson, 1982, 1983) for not being "radical" enough when they use their methodologies in social systems where inequalities in the distribution of resources and power exist. Soft systems approaches appear culpable because they seem prepared, in these circumstances, to accept for implementation changes emerging from the "deceptive" consensus produced by distorted communication. They tend merely to facilitate a social process in which the essential elements of the status quo are reproduced. To have any claim to neutrality in these situations, the methodologies would have to incorporate a prior commitment to establishing the conditions for unconstrained discussion. They would have to challenge those social arrangements which produce distorted communication. Committed as they are to subjectivism, they are not in a position to understand let alone challenge these social arrangements. They lack, as was seen, any theory capable of understanding the social structures which produce and support different Ws or capable of indicating where the real levers of change in the social totality might be located.

In many respects soft systems thinking is an advance on the hard systems variety. It recognises the unique character of the subject matter of social systems science—human beings. The methodologies discussed are all based on a respect for the purposeful nature of this subject matter. This is lacking in hard systems thinking. Churchman, Ackoff and Checkland, in producing methodologies more appropriate to social reality, extend the area within which systems thinking can be legitimately used. In those many social systems in which a reasonably full and open discussion can be achieved and in which there is a rough balance of power and resources between different stakeholders, these methodologies can be used successfully. They will provide a mechanism through which learning can take place; facilitating communication between different groups and helping and enhancing debates about social objectives and system change. In this situation, the kind of social system that emerges from the action and interaction of informed participants will be "transparent" to them. It will not take on any "objective" constraining characteristics. There will be no need for a social theory to aid the understanding of its nature and characteristics. If soft systems approaches are to be used wisely, however, there must also be an understanding that there are many social systems for which they are inappropriate. For such social systems there is a need for a more radical and critical approach to producing and verifying social systems theory and practice. This is the concern of the final part of the paper.

THE NEED FOR A CRITICAL APPROACH

In this final part of the paper an alternative approach to validating work in social systems science is considered. This is a "critical" approach derived from the work of Habermas. It is argued that this approach is appropriate to social systems where there are great disparities in power and in resources and which seem to "escape" the control and understanding of the individuals who create and sustain them. This is what Habermas (1974) says about the relationship between theory and practice:

> The mediation of theory and praxis can only be classified if to begin with we distinguish three functions, which are measured in terms of different criteria; the formation and extension of critical theorems, which can stand up to scientific discourse; the organisation of processes of enlightenment, in which such theorems are applied and can be tested in a unique manner by initiation of processes of reflection carried on within certain groups towards which these processes have been directed; and the selection of appropriate strategies, the solution of tactical questions, and the conduct of political struggle.

These three functions will be considered in turn and related to the methodologies already discussed.

The first function involves professional scientists in the formulation of explicit theories about the social world. These theories must be corroborated according to the usual rules of scientific discourse. Theories which do not stand up to such examination must be rejected at this stage. It is interesting to see the form which Habermas' proposed theory takes. He accepts that Karl Marx's critique of political economy is the exemplar for critical social science in the realm of economics. This critique was adequate to the society of Marx's day when the economic base of society clearly determined the nature of the other superstructural instances of the social whole. In the modern era, however, Habermas suggests, the "institutional framework" has become increasingly important. In these circumstances, it is necessary to complement Marx's work with a critique of alienation in the institutional realm of society. Habermas aims to develop an ideology critique; a critique of systematically distorted communication (see Scott, 1978). The theory necessary to ground this critique must begin with a theory of what communication free from distortion would be like—what Habermas (1970b) calls a theory of communicative competence. According to Habermas the very nature of language and the way it is used prefigures an "ideal speech situation." In discourse the participants implicitly accept a number of validity claims which are identified as being present in all speech acts. When these validity claims are respected there is an ideal speech situation and communicative competence is realised. This is only possible, however, when all the participants have an equal opportunity to take part in the discourse and when communication takes place free from constraint. In situations where an unequal distribution of power induces inhibitions in discourse, communication reflects the degree of repressive domination present in society and this, in turn, is closely related to the development of the economic and political spheres of society. It follows that communicative competence depends very much on the establishment of certain social conditions. This is the link back to Marx. Marx analysed the development of society in terms of the forms taken by alienated labour. Habermas wants to reinforce this with an ideology critique of the forms taken by distorted communication. And just as there is anticipated in actual labour an as yet unrealised form of free labour, so there is prefigured in discourse an as yet unrealised ideal speech situation. The two types of critique are closely linked.

The relevance of this brief summary of Habermas' proposed theory to the debates in the earlier parts of the paper will not be lost. Habermas (unlike soft systems thinkers) regards the construction of explicit social theories as an essential part of any social systems science. These theories are unlikely, however, to be constructed according to all of the canons of systematicity outlined by Rescher. They will have to be formulated to cope with aspects of social reality such as conflict, contradiction, power, coercion and change. Whether these will be systems theories at all depends on whether systemic theory can be fashioned in other than the functionalist version in which it is normally found. Buckley (1967) has argued that it is only an unnecessary allegiance to mechanical and biological analogies that has led to systems theory getting "stuck" in the functionalist paradigm. In this case, possibly it can be developed to cope with conflict, contradiction, power, coercion and change. Burrell and Morgan (1979) suggest that systems theory is not intrinsically tied to any specific view of social reality. Systems models can be used to explain conflict and change as well as order and stability. It all depends on the type of system analogy employed; whether it is mechanical, organismic, morphogenic, factional or catastrophic. This would seem to be a sensible idea to develop for systems theorists who wish to follow Habermas.

The second phase of Habermas' mediation of theory and practice, the organisation of enlightenment, involves the authentication of the knowledge produced by the first stage. The theoretical validation by professional scientists in the first stage is not sufficient. It must also be validated by the social actors at which it is aimed in a process of enlightenment. Only if the theory helps these actors to attain self-understanding and they recognise in it an acceptable account of their situation can the theory be said to be authenticated. The method of theory construction is not, therefore, to be subject to the applicative control. Habermas firmly rejects the transference of the "predict and control" criterion of the natural sciences and hard systems thinking to the social realm. Luhmann's functionalist systems theory which encourages such a transference

> represents the advanced form of a technocratic consciousness, which today permits practical questions to be defined from the outset as technical ones, and thereby withholds them from public and unconstrained discussion. (Habermas, 1976)

Instead the method of theory construction and the theory is to be subject to a control which tests its potency in a manner appropriate to the object of concern—thinking and acting human beings.

To explain this second phase Habermas (1974) turns to the psychoanalytic encounter. Psychoanalysis is primarily interpretive. It attempts, like soft systems thinking, to understand what the subject says and to explicate the hidden meaning of what s/he says. But to do this the analyst cannot remain at the interpretive level. The distortions produced by the patient are not accidental. They result from a systematic process through which the patient deceives himself/herself about his/her own condition. The analyst must therefore get below the explanations offered by the subject, to causally explain why they are distorted and conceal material that the subject cannot bring to understanding. S/he must causally explain the patients distorted self-understanding. As L.J. Nicholson (1980) writes,

> In short, what psychoanalysis as opposed to hermeneutics reveals is the need for theory which can ground this process of critique.

If the analyst is successful, s/he liberates the subject from unconscious forces which s/he could not control and increases the area over which the subject has rational mastery. The analyst's success is measured by the extent to which the patient recognises himself/herself in the explanations offered and becomes an equal partner in the dialogue with the analyst. Habermas believes that this psychoanalytic model can, if suitable precautions are taken, be transferred to groups, organisations and society as a whole. The actor in the social world is very often in the same position as the neurotic patient in the psychoanalytic encounter. S/he suffers from false-consciousness and does not truly comprehend his/her situation in that social world. It is incumbent, therefore, on the critical theorist to employ a social theory capable of explaining the alienated words and actions of oppressed groups in society.

> The theory serves primarily (Habermas (1974) writes), to enlighten those to whom it is addressed about the position they occupy in an antagonistic social system and about the interests of which they must become conscious in this situation as being objectively theirs.

This, of course, is the point of the first function outlined by Habermas—the formation and extension of critical theorems. If the social actors involved come to recognise themselves in the interpretations offered, that theory is then authenticated. The social actors previously deprived of self-understanding in the course of distorted communication are able to take up an equal role in the dialogue. The conditions for an ideal speech situation are approximated in respect of this particular enlightened social group.

The achievement of an enlightened social group, in which the conditions for an ideal speech situation are approximated, is a precondition for Habermas' third function—the selection of appropriate strategies. A rational consensus can now be reached over the appropriate strategies to be adopted. As with the soft systems approach, the "clients" of the system have complete autonomy on the matter of what changes to make to the system and its objectives. Now, however, they possess a social theory which enables them fully to comprehend their position in the social world and the possibilities for action that this affords. According to Habermas, the aim of any strategy will be to make progress towards universal enlightenment. The enlightened social group will have to choose, in the case of each new group with which they come into contact, between enlightenment and struggle. They will want, by the communication of theory, to continue authentication and to broaden the process of enlightenment. In the case of certain opponents, however, who are particularly in the grip of ideology, communication may be impossible. It will be necessary temporarily to break off the dialogue and to engage in political struggle against these opponents. This militancy needs to be directed at the institutionalised dominance which is responsible for the distortions in communication preventing effective dialogue. Communication must, of course, eventually be resumed for the social theory to be completely authenticated. Habermas stresses that the decision between continuing and breaking off communication is in each case an empirical question which cannot be prejudged.

> There can be no meaningful theory which *per se*, and regardless of the circumstances, obligates one to militancy. (Habermas, 1974)

It is argued, therefore, that Habermas' suggested approach is more appropriate for a certain class of social system than hard or soft systems methodologies. It seems to take account of the special characteristics of this type of social system. These social systems are characterised by inequalities of power and resources among the participants and by conflict and contradiction. They are the products of thinking and acting human beings but at the same time are not "transparent" to them. They can escape both their understanding and control and take on objective features which constrain them. Habermas' approach seems accurately to reflect the important characteristics of this class of social system.

CONCLUSION

It has been the purpose of this paper to argue the need for a critical approach to social systems theory and practice. The natural scientific method has shown its value in terms of the success of science in explaining, predicting and controlling natural systems. But this method cannot be easily extended to social systems. Hard systems methodologies were very successful in dealing with the engineering type problems for which they were originally designed. They are, however, suitable for application to social systems in only a very restricted range of circumstances—when there is agreement among a system's stakeholders about the goal to be achieved and about the need to find the most efficient way of achieving it. Soft systems methodologies are adapted to many of the special features of social systems and express what any social systems approach must have as its aim—the desire to increase the area of social life where rational peoples' intentions become realised in history. In many situations they can adequately achieve this aim. Ultimately if the social arrangements which produce distorted communication can be abolished, there will be no need for any approach other than soft systems thinking in social systems science. Meanwhile, however, many of our institutions are "sick" in the sense that the people who make them up no longer recognise themselves in their creations. If those people are to be brought to a true understanding of their situation, which will enable them to regain control over their destiny, the more radical therapy of a critical social systems theory and practice is required. A lot of work needs to be done quickly on the detailed working out and development of all three functions outlined by Habermas.

REFERENCES

Ackoff, R.L. (1974). The social responsibility of operational research, *Opl Res. Q.*, **25**, 361–371.

Ackoff, R.L. (1979a). The future of O.R. is past, Chapter 2 in this book.

Ackoff, R.L. (1979b). Resurrecting the future of operational research, *J. Opl Res. Soc.*, **30**, 189–200.

Ackoff, R.L. (1981). *Creating the Corporate Future*, John Wiley, New York.

Ackoff, R.L. (1983). An interactive view of rationality, *J. Opl Res. Soc.*, **34**, 719–722.

Adorno, T.W. (1976). On the logic of the social sciences, in *The Positivist Dispute in German Sociology* (Ed. D. Frisby), pp. 105–122, Heinemann, London.

Bahro, R. (1978). *The Alternative in Eastern Europe*, N.L.B., London.

Bauman, Z. (1977). *Towards a Critical Sociology*, Routledge and Kegan Paul, London.

Beer, S. (1983). The will of the people, *J. Opl Res. Soc.*, **34**, 797–810.

Boguslaw, R. (1965). *The New Utopians: A Study of Systems Design and Social Change*, Prentice Hall, Englewood Cliffs, NJ.

Buckley, W. (1967). *Sociology and Modern Systems Theory*, Prentice Hall, London.

Burrell, G., and Morgan, G. (1979). *Sociological Paradigms and Organisational Analysis*, Heinemann, London.

Churchman, C.W. (1968). *The Systems Approach*, Dell, New York.

Churchman, C.W. (1970). Operations research as a profession, Chapter 1 in this book.

Churchman, C.W. (1971). *The Design of Inquiring Systems*, Basic Books, New York.

Churchman, C.W. (1978). Paradise regained: a hope for the future of systems design education, in *Education in Systems Science* (Eds. B. A. Bayraktar *et al.*), pp. 17–22, Taylor and Francis, London.

Churchman, C.W. (1979). *The Systems Approach and Its Enemies*, Basic Books, New York.

Checkland, P.B. (1972). Towards a systems-based methodology for real-world problem-solving, *J. Syst. Eng.*, **3**, 87–116.

Checkland, P.B. (1978). The origins and nature of "hard" systems thinking, *J. Appl. Syst. Anal.*, **5**, 99–110.

Checkland, P.B. (1981). *Systems Thinking, Systems Practice*, John Wiley, New York.

Durkheim, E. (1964). *The Rules of Sociological Method*, The Free Press, New York.

Giddens, A. (1976). *New Rules of Sociological Method*, Hutchinson, London.

Habermas, J. (1970a). On systematically distorted communication, *Inquiry*, **13**, 205–218.

Habermas, J. (1970). Towards a theory of communicative competence, *Inquiry*, **13**, 360–375.

Habermas, J. (1974). *Theory and Practice*, Heinemann, London.

Habermas, J. (1976). quoted in *The Positivist Dispute in German Sociology* (Ed. D. Frisby), p. xxxii, Heinemann, London.

Hoos, I. (1972). *Systems Analysis in Public Policy: A Critique*, University of California Press, Berkeley.

Jackson, M.C. (1981). Review of Rescher's "Cognitive Systematization", *Int. J. Gen. Syst.*, **7**, 257–259.

Jackson, M.C. (1982). The nature of "soft" systems thinking: the work of Churchman, Ackoff and Checkland, *J. Appl. Syst. Anal.*, **10**, 109–113.

Jackson, M.C. (1984). O.R. in systems: the alternative perspective, *J. Opl Res. Soc.*, **35**, 155–161.

Jackson, M.C. and Keys, P. (1984). Towards a system of systems methodologies, Chapter 7 this volume.

Jenkins, G.M., (1969). The systems approach, in *Systems Behaviour*, 2nd edition (Eds J. Beishon and G. Peters), pp. 78–104, Open University Press, London.

Lilienfeld, R. (1975). Systems theory as ideology, *Social Res.*, **42**, 637–660.

Lilienfeld, R. (1978). *The Rise of Systems Theory*, John Wiley, New York.

Morgan, G. (1982). Cybernetics and organization theory: epistemology or technique, *Hum. Relat.*, **35**, 521–537.

Nicholson, L.J. (1980). Why Habermas?, *Radical Philosophy*, No. 25, Summer.

Popper, K.T. (1972). *Conjectures and Refutations*, 4th edition, Routledge and Kegan Paul, London.

Rescher, N. (1979). *Cognitive Systematization*, Basil Blackwell, Oxford.

Scott, J.P. (1978). Critical social theory: an introduction and critique, *B.J.S.*, **29**, 1–20.

Sica, A. (1981). Review of "The Systems Approach and Its Enemies", *A.J.S.*, **87**, 208–211.

Small, M.G. (1981). What's wrong with systems, *Gen. Syst. Bull.*, **11**, (2).

Thomas, A.R., and Lockett, M. (1979). Marxism and systems research: values in practical action, Chapter 4 this volume.

Ulrich, W. (1980). The metaphysics of design: a Simon–Churchman "debate", *Interfaces*, **10**, 35–40.

Ulrich, W. (1981). A critique of pure cybernetic reason: the Chilean experience with cybernetics, *J. Appl. Syst. Anal.*, **8**, 33–59.

Vickers, G. (1970). *Freedom in a Rocking Boat*, Allen Lane, London.

Chapter 7

Towards a System of Systems Methodologies

MICHAEL C. JACKSON AND PAUL KEYS

INTRODUCTION

Ackoff's papers on the present and future prospects of OR (1979a, b) have provided the stimulus needed for a re-examination of the nature of OR as an activity. These papers, together with the recent contributions of Dando and Bennett (1981) and Rosenhead and Thunhurst (1982), have begun to establish a body of literature which examines OR in a more rigorous way and in terms of a wider range of issues than has previously been the case.

This paper seeks to add to this literature by investigating the relationship between OR and some other problem-solving methodologies. OR is not the only systems-based problem-solving methodology, and the aim of the following is to establish how OR compares to some other methodologies of this general type. A problem solver facing a problem context must address himself to the question of which is the appropriate methodology to use. By considering this issue in detail, it is hoped to provide some valuable insights into the nature, strengths and weaknesses of the methodologies considered.

The first section develops a systematic analysis of *problem contexts*. A problem context is defined to include the individual or group of individuals who are the would-be problem solvers, the system(s) within which the problem lies and the set of relevant decision makers. This set contains all of the elements which can make decisions which may affect the behaviour of the system(s). In particular, the problem solvers may also be decision makers. A classification of problem contexts which is relevant to the issue of which methodology is most appropriate for the problem solvers to use is developed.

In the second section, the *methodologies* most suitable for the different classes of problem context are identified.

These two sections therefore provide a "system of systems methodologies" since the inter-relationship between methodologies is probed, as is the relationship of these methodologies to real-world problem contexts.

In the third section, some ideas which stem from the analysis are presented, and some conclusions are drawn as to the role of OR and its relatonship to other systems-based methodologies. Some practical implications of the analysis are also considered.

A CLASSIFICATION OF PROBLEM CONTEXTS

The choice of suitable criteria to differentiate types of problem context will play a crucial role in determining the success or otherwise of a study relating those problem contexts to different problem-solving methodologies. Good criteria will result in similarities and differences being revealed which are very pertinent to the questions being asked in the study. Poor criteria will not allow much, if any, progress to be made. In this paper, the study is concerned with problem-solving methodologies, and the criteria for classifying problem contexts must therefore identify relevant similarities and differences in problem contexts which are important with respect to problem-solving methodologies. It is the purpose of this section to identify such criteria and to draw up a classification of problem contexts based on these criteria.

The management and improvement of systems requires that attention be paid to two sets of processes—the planning process (broadly defined) and the control process (broadly defined). Problems can occur in relation to either of these processes. A problem in relation to the planning process might concern whether the relevant system(s) are pursuing the correct goals from the decision makers' point of view. A problem in relation to the control process might concern whether the system(s) are pursuing their goal in the most efficient manner. Ackoff (1962) calls problems related to the planning process "development" and problems related to the control process "evaluative". According to Ackoff the minimal necessary and sufficient conditions for the existence of a problem of either type are:

1. an individual;
2. an outcome that is desired by the decision maker (i.e. an objective);
3. at least two unequally efficient courses of action which have some chance of yielding the desired objective;

4. a state of doubt in the decision maker as to which choice is "best";
5. an environment or context of the problem.

Complications do, of course, arise which make problems considerably more complex than is suggested in the above. Ackoff goes on to list the conditions from which these complications arise. When the list is examined, it is found that all these complications arise either from changes in the nature of the decision makers(s) or changes in the nature of the system(s) in which the problem is located. With regard to the decision makers, complications arise when a group of decision makers, rather than one, makes the decision; when some decision maker(s) make the decision but others carry it out; when some decision makers not a party to a particular decision react against it; or when the decision makers' objectives are not consistent or change with time. With regard to the system(s) in which the problem is located, complications arise if the system becomes more complicated and more difficult to understand, because the number of possible courses of action available to the decision makers(s) then becomes very large, even infinite.

It can be seen, therefore, that two aspects of problem contexts (decision makers and systems) seem to have a particularly important effect on the character of the problems found within them. This is so whether the problems are related to the planning process or the control process. A good way to classify problem contexts generally, therefore, would seem to be in terms of the nature of the decision makers and in terms of the nature of the system(s) in which the problem is located. This will yield a very broad classification of problem contexts of particular use in this paper. The concern of the paper is to relate in the most general terms systems-based problem-solving methodologies to the contexts in which problems are found. The emphasis is on the key variables in problem contexts which can, in changing their character, lead to qualitative changes in such contexts, affecting the problems therein and thereby demanding a significant re-orientation in problem-solving approach. Techniques developed to tackle problems relating to specific areas of either the planning process or the control process—for example, cognitive mapping (Eden, Jones and Sims, 1979), or hypergame analysis (Bennett, 1980) to aid strategic planning—will not be considered.

The classification of problem contexts can now be developed. It will clearly be useful to proceed by classifying *systems* and *decision makers* separately. The overall classification of problem contexts will then be a synthesis of these two classification schemes.

The set of all *systems* can be classified in a variety of ways. Boulding (1956) classifies systems into nine categories using the criterion of complexity; while Beer (1967) generates a classification using susceptibility to control as the criterion for differentiation. Jordan (1981) draws up a systems taxonomy consisting of eight cells into which systems can be fitted, according to where they lie along three systems dimensions; while Checkland (1971) identifies five classes of systems which make up a "systems map of the universe." Other classification schemes refer to more specific types of system. Such schemes usually exist within particular areas of study—botany and zoology provide many examples. In the present case a classification of systems will be provided which identifies relevant similarities and differences in systems with respect to problem-solving methodologies.

Problems which are set in systems which are perceived to be simple are often taken to be easier to solve than problems which exist in complex systems. In terms of problem solving, a classification based upon the simple–complex dichotomy will therefore be useful.

There is, of course, a difficulty. The classification of a system as complex or simple will depend upon the observer of the system and upon the purpose he has for considering the system. If his purpose is to solve a problem which is perceived to exist in the system, then the type of problem he is tackling will be a crucial factor in determining the perspective taken. Often the same system may be seen as being simple or complex, depending upon the problem. The labour market, for example, can be treated as a simple supply–demand system and is often so treated in the models of the national economy used by the Treasury, the Cambridge group and the NIESR. In this case the labour market is being treated in a highly aggregate manner because the problems being considered refer to macroeconomic issues such as inflation, interest rate fluctuation, levels of export trade and the like. Alternatively, the labour market may be taken to comprise many individuals, each acting as parts of a highly complex system. This approach is useful if the problem being addressed concerns the individual—issues such as benefit payments, early retirement or redundancy (see, for example, Clarke and Keys, 1982).

Granted the observer-dependent nature of the simple–complex criterion, some points contributing to a distinction between simple and complex systems can still be established. A simple system will be perceived to consist of a small number of elements, and the interactions between these elements will be few, or at least regular. A complex system will, on the other hand, be seen as being composed of a large number of elements, and these will be highly interrelated.

Despite the difficulty, therefore, the simple–complex criterion for classifying systems remains of some use in helping the identification of "easy" problems and "difficult" problems. More, however, is needed in order to understand fully why some systems pose "easy" problems while others pose "difficult" problems. It is possible to identify other points, which, although connected to the simple–complex distinction, are not fully embraced by it. These additional points give us an enhanced version of the simple–complex distinction. In the analysis that follows, it is necessary to refer to simple–etc. systems and complex – etc. systems to make this clear.

The starting point of the analysis is that, in general, problems can be regarded as "easy" if it is relatively straightforward to understand the system(s) in which they are found. Vemuri (1978) identifies four reasons why some systems are more difficult to understand than others. Each of these points contributes to the make-up of a complex – etc. system and has implications for the problem solver.

Firstly, in complex – etc. systems, not all of the attributes of the parts of the system will be directly observable. As a result it is difficult to understand the nature of the system completely. The causes of any problem may be hidden, and this will impede the ability of the problem solver to identify useful solutions. It will also be difficult to establish the effects of any solution to the problem without actually implementing that solution.

Secondly, in complex – etc. systems, even if laws can be established relating the actions of different parts of the system, they will invariably be only probabilistic in nature. Any attempt to use a quantitative approach to aid the solution of a problem can, therefore, only give information about the likely effects rather than the exact effects of a proposed solution.

Thirdly, complex – etc. systems evolve over time. This evolution stems in large part from the fact that such systems are in constant interaction with the environment—they are "open" rather than "closed". Social systems exist in increasingly turbulent environments and this makes it difficult for the problem solver to predict system–environment interactions. Moreover, in social systems, in order for evolution successfully to occur, the parts of the system must have a certain amount of freedom of action. The parts of the system are purposeful, and it is this characteristic which allows the system as a whole to be adaptive to the environment. This autonomy of the parts of the system, of course, poses difficulties for the problem solver. "Solutions" to problems may evoke unpredictable responses.

Fourthly, complex – etc. systems inevitably involve more "behavioural" problems. Decisions made in the system will be affected by political, cultural, ethical, and similar factors. This makes it difficult for the problem solver to fully understand the "rationale" behind decisions made by actors in the system. Changing values are an important internal source of change in such systems.

Complex–etc. systems therefore pose difficult problems because they are often only partially observable, probabilistic, open, have purposeful parts and are subject to behavioural influences. Simple–etc. systems, on the other hand, are likely to pose easy problems because they are fully observable, are governed by well-defined laws of behaviour, are relatively closed to the environment, have subsystems which are passive and do not pursue their own goals, and such systems are not affected by behavioural influences. These characteristics of simple–etc. systems make problem solving easier since such systems are more straightforward to analyse, and it is feasible to establish the likely effect of solutions to problems without actually putting them into practice. The usefulness of the simple–complex criterion for system differentiation is therefore increased when it is extended to include those further factors identified by Vemuri.

Ackoff (1974a) has used the terms "machine-age" and "systems-age" to refer to eras which demonstrated a concern for two different system types. The machine-age was concerned with systems which were closed, had passive parts, were fully observable and could be understood using the reductionism of the traditional scientific method. The systems-age must concern itself with systems which are open, have purposeful parts, are only partially observable and cannot be understood using the methods of reductionism. Applying Ackoff's terminology, reference will be made in what follows to *mechanical problem contexts*, which contain simple–etc. systems manifesting relatively easy problems and *systemic problem contexts*, which contain complex–etc. systems manifesting difficult problems.

The system in which the problem exists is not the only factor which determines the character of the problem context. The nature of the *decision makers* will also greatly affect the type of solution needed to problems and the problem-solving methodology needed to reach that solution. The major factor of interest here concerns the objectives of the decision makers. The criterion to be used in classifying decision makers in particular problem contexts is whether they are a unitary or a pluralist set in respect of their objectives. A set of decision makers is unitary if they all agree on a common set of goals for the whole system and make their decision in accordance with these goals. A set of decision makers is pluralist if they cannot agree on a common set of goals and make decisions which are in accordance with differing objectives. A problem context will therefore be called *unitary* if the set of decision makers is unitary; a problem context is *pluralist* if the set of decision makers is pluralist.

A problem solver acting in a unitary problem context will be acting in a more "stable" environment than if he were acting in a pluralist problem context. The stability is derived from the lack of conflict between the decision makers and the resulting cohesiveness of that group of decision makers. A second feature which characterizes the unitary problem context is the ease with which the behaviour of the system can be understood relative to the situation in the pluralist problem context. The fact that all of the decision makers are acting towards the same overall objectives means that the behaviour of the system will be more unified, and this will ease the understanding of overall systems behaviour. A third benefit of operating in a unitary environment, as far as the problem solver is concerned, is that implementation of the solution to the problem will be acceptable to all parts of the system. Since the objectives are common to all decision makers, a solution which attempts to achieve these objectives will be acceptable to all decision makers. In a pluralist problem context, a solution which is acceptable to some decision makers will not necessarily be acceptable to others. In order to arrive at a "solution" in this case, two approaches can be used, both of which involve difficulties. Either a solution can be arrived at after the various decision makers reach some compromise about overall objectives. Difficulties arise here in trying to achieve a compromise. Or a solution can be imposed if a subset of the decision makers has sufficient power. But the context would not then be pluralist in any meaningful sense. Important ethical problems arise for problem solvers in these circumstances. This point will be taken up in the final section (implication (v)).

Problem contexts, therefore, can be seen as being in one of four categories; *mechanical–unitary, systemic–unitary, mechanical–pluralist* and *systemic–pluralist*. Each problem context differs in a meaningful way from the others. The test of how useful this classification is lies in the insights it provides about what methodology to use in solving problems in each category. In the next section, the type of methodology useful for each type of problem context will be identified.

TYPES OF PROBLEM-SOLVING METHODOLOGY

(The word "methodology" is here used in its broadest sense—to refer to any kind of advice given to analysts about how they should proceed to intervene in the real world.) It is now possible to ask whether there are methodologies available which are capable of helping with problem solving in the four different kinds of problem context identified above. It will be clear that no one problem-solving methodology is likely to be of use in all circumstances—the types of problem and problem context found are too diverse and offer different difficulties to the problem solver. At best there will be a number of different approaches, often developed independently of each other, each being suited to solving problems in only one of the kinds of problem context outlined. Difficulties are almost certain to occur when methodologies suited to particular problem contexts are transferred and adopted for use in problem situations for which they are not designed. All it is possible to do in this section is to see if, for each of the four problem contexts identified, there exists a methodology suitable for problem solving therein.

Problems within a *mechanical–unitary* problem context may be adequately dealt with using the techniques of classical OR. Because of the unitary nature of the context, there will be general agreement about the goals to be achieved. The problem solver will therefore be able to establish without too much difficulty the objectives of the system in which the problem resides. Depending on the relative complexity of the mechanical system involved, the problem solver will employ deterministic or stochastic OR techniques to model the system. If the system is genuinely closed, there are few elements, and these interact little (or in a regular way), then deterministic techniques can be used to arrive at a mathematical representation of the system for use by the problem solver. If the system is more prone to environmental disturbance (but is still "closed" in von Bertalanffy's, 1969, sense), the elements are greater in number and exhibit more interdependence, then the use of simulation and the techniques of stochastic OR may be more appropriate.

The characteristics of the OR methodology reflect its appropriateness for use in dealing with problems in the mechanical–unitary context (Churchman, Ackoff and Arnoff, 1957; Ackoff and Sasieni, 1968). The first step is to formulate the problem in the light of the objectives of the system under study. The system is then represented in a quantitative model (deterministic or stochastic) which will simulate its performance under different operational conditions. The particular design that optimizes the performance of the system in pursuit of its objectives will then be chosen for implementation.

Two "sister disciplines" to classical OR are systems engineering (SE) and systems analysis (SA). These are, like classical OR, probably most appropriate for solving problems in mechanical–unitary contexts.

SE developed in the 1950s from the work of the Bell Telephone Laboratories on the design of engineering systems (see the classical exposition of SE by Hall, 1962). SE has been defined by Jenkins (1969) as "the science of designing complex systems in their totality to ensure that the component subsystems making up the system are designed, fitted together, checked and operated in the most efficient way." Jenkins recognizes close similarities between SE and OR but suggests that, while SE places emphasis on the design of the *total* system, OR tends to be content to tinker at the level of the more mechanical subsystems. For Jenkins, therefore, SE is broader than OR—apparently capable of solving problems in systemic contexts. In Jenkins, too, there is some attempt to take account of the pluralistic nature of some problem contexts. Thus, according to Jenkins, "systems have conflicting objectives". However, it is taken for granted that the systems engineer will be able to conjure up some compromise between those objectives. There are some differences, therefore, between SE and OR, but in the most important aspects Jenkins' SE methodology is very like the OR methodology.

SA (which spawned such variants as planning–programming–budgeting systems) originated, like OR, in wartime military operations planning (see Checkland, 1978). It is designed to appraise the costs and other implications of alternative means of reaching a goal. In the hands of the RAND Corporation, it began to be used in non-military settings. It is said by its proponents to be a broader and more refined methodology than OR. As with SE, there have been attempts from within the SA tradition to enlarge that approach in such a way as to make it appropriate for tackling problems in systemic contexts. Optner (1965) makes use of certain cybernetic notions in his systems analysis; while Krone (1980) presents a systems-analysis/policy-sciences mixture of concepts capable of analysing many areas "where systems analysis faltered on the limitations of its own overly rational methodologies in the past."

Checkland (1978), recognizing the similarities between classical OR, and SE and SA, has labelled the approach they share in common "hard systems thinking". This approach is "based upon the assumption that the problem task they tackle is to select an efficient means of achieving a known and defined end."

It is necessary now to consider whether there is a methodology available which will enable a problem solver to tackle problems arising in *systemic–unitary* contexts. The systems of concern are what Beer (1967) calls exceedingly complex, probabilistic systems. They have many elements in close inter-relationship and exhibit behaviour which is difficult to predict. Furthermore (and this is clear in the above classification but not in Beer's), these systems are open to their environments and include purposeful parts. There is, however, full agreement about the goals of the system(s) (unitary).

Following Beer, it is argued that the tools provided by cybernetics give the problem solver the best chance of dealing with difficulties encountered in this type of problem context. According to Morgan (1982), cybernetics can be treated as a technique for "improving the design, control and performance of systems geared to the achievement of predetermined ends" (as Morgan makes clear, there *is* another side to cybernetics. It can also treat organizations as morphogenic systems, as learning systems and as ecologies). The tools employed by cyberneticians for dealing with systemic–unitary contexts are the black-box technique, variety engineering (based on information theory) and negative feedback. All of these tools receive full articulation in the model of any viable system constructed by Beer in *Brain of the Firm* (1972) and *The Heart of Enterprise* (1979).

Briefly, a system is viable for Beer if it is capable of responding to environmental changes, even if they were not foreseen at the time the system was designed. In order to achieve this capacity for self-regulation, a system needs to achieve "requisite variety" (at a level concordant with its effective performance) with the complex environment with which it is faced. It should reflect possible environmental states in its own organization. Also, because of the great complexity of the environment, if the system is to achieve self-regulation, its goals need to be broken down into sub-goals and these allocated to different subsystems, which are themselves viable systems. These subsystems will have discretion in relation to the achievement of these sub-goals. It is the use of negative feedback which allows both the system as a whole and the subsystems to monitor their performance in relation to their goals. According to Beer, all viable systems need to possess five functions, which may be labelled policy, intelligence, operational control, coordination and implementation (see Espejo, 1977). It is essential that all these functions be adequately catered for in systems and their viable subsystems. Great importance is also given to the design of the information channels which link the different functions and the organization and its environment (the technique of variety engineering is crucial here). The model of any viable system can be used as a diagnostic tool to check for the existence and proper performance of the five functions and the communications channels in any actual system. This should point to the reason for any problems and suggest cures.

The limitations on the applicablity of cybernetics as a problem-solving methodology are brought out in a critique of Beer's work in Chile (project CYBERSYN—the name afforded to the Chilean experiment in the cybernetic regulation of the social economy) developed by Ulrich (1981). Using Ulrich's analysis, it is clear that cybernetics could be employed to solve problems in systemic–pluralist contexts only if it were capable of generating both "intrinsic control" *and* "intrinsic motivation." Project CYBERSYN went some way to generating intrinsic control—spreading the sources of control throughout the system. But it could not generate intrinsic motivation—distribute the source determining the system's goal state and purpose throughout the system. It was only the top controller—the government—which was in a position to change CYBERSYN's design according to its political purposes. There are certainly authoritarian implications in the use of cybernetics for keeping "everything under control" (see Adams, 1973). However, if there is a genuine agreement about goals, cybernetics can be a very effective method for problem solving in systemic–unitary contexts. In Chile, of course, Project CYBERSYN ultimately failed because there was not this agreement about goals. Whether such agreement might have been achieved had not destructive pluralism been "pumped-in" from the outside is a matter for speculation.

It is worth mentioning here that the whole area of work known as socio-technical systems thinking may be regarded as another attempt to come to terms with problems in systemic–unitary contexts. Socio-technical systems theorists believe (see Trist *et al.*, 1965) that the "primary task" of a system (the assumed unitary goal) is best achieved if there is joint-optimization of the technical subsystem and the socio–psychological subsystem. Once the system becomes complex, the sub-tasks which contribute to the primary task are best differentiated and put under the control of semi-autonomous work groups (Rice, 1958). Managers service these work groups by overseeing exchanges across sub-task boundaries. The semi-autonomous work groups are assumed to be better equipped to deal with variances that arise from their tasks and, with the help of the managers, with environmental change—in other words, they are an effective means of coping in systemic contexts.

Mechanical–pluralist problem contexts will now be considered. Because of the nature of the parts of mechanical systems (passive not purposeful) the pluralism must concern differences amongst decision makers outside the system (of whom the problem solver may be one) about the goals to be served by that system. If this disagreement amongst the decision makers can be resolved, then the problems remaining can be solved using the "hard" systems methodologies previously examined.

Perhaps the most sophisticated attempt to develop a methodology designed to bring about a "synthesis" among decision makers so that action can be taken is that of Churchman (1979a). The philosophy underlying the approach is based primarily on the work of Hegel and Singer, as interpreted by Churchman (1971). The notions of thesis, antithesis and synthesis contained in the Hegelian dialectic are employed in a methodology designed to develop the world-views or *Weltanschauungen* of decision makers until a temporary consensus is achieved. Since this process is never-ending and must be endured by the decision makers in an "heroic mood", it can be seen as contributing to a "Singerian inquiring system". Churchman and Schainblatt (1965) have also investigated the important sub-problem of how to bring about an effective relationship between problem solver ("researcher") and the key decision makers ("managers").

Mitroff, Mason *et al.* (1969, 1979, 1981) have helped to develop Churchman's ideas into a rigorous methodology—sometimes referred to as strategic assumption surfacing and testing (SAST). The advocates of this methodology claim that it is appropriate to use it to tackle complex, "wicked" problems in *systemic*–pluralist contexts—and it has indeed been applied to problem areas such as "strategic planning" (Mason, 1969). However, the whole emphasis of the approach is on tackling the pluralist aspects of such contexts and not on the systemic aspects. There seems to be an unwarranted assumption that, once the pluralism has been dissolved, the problems stemming from the systemic nature of the context will disappear as well. Thus, Mason and Mitroff (1981) support Rittle's conclusion that "Every formulation of a wicked problem corresponds to a statement of solution and vice versa. Understanding the problem is synonymous with solving it." The analysis in this paper points to the need to see the systemic characteristics of some problem contexts as presenting peculiar difficulties of their own. Since SAST tends to ignore these difficulties, pretending that all the difficulties stem from pluralism, it is legitimate to see SAST primarily as an aid to solving problems in mechanical–pluralist contexts and to discuss it here.

SAST is a dialectical approach designed to help decision makers understand the different points of view which may exist concerning a problem. Four major stages may be identified. The first stage is "group formation". At least two different groups are formed to be advocates of very different perceptions of the problem and system. These groups may be made up of managers from different functional areas or different organizational levels. The second stage is "assumption surfacing". This consists of various techniques designed to help each group uncover and analyse the key assumptions on which its view of the system and its proposals are based. Each group comes to understand its own key assumptions—its *Weltanschauung* (W). The third stage is "dialectical debate." Each group develops the best possible case for its position. The key assumptions underlying its position are presented and argued for. Each group may be asked to interpret some agreed "data" according to its perspective. Once this stage is complete, and each group begins to understand the assumptions of the others, the fourth "synthesis", stage can begin. The aim is that the different groups should arrive at a synthesis incorporating all their different world-views and going beyond them as well. This synthesis can then become the basis for detailed planning and problem solving.

Finally in this section, the solution of problems in *systemic–pluralist* contexts must be addressed. It is here that the "soft" systems approaches of Ackoff and Checkland seem most appropriate.

According to Ackoff, problem solvers are increasingly faced—in the systems-age—not with separable problems, but with "messes", systems of interdependent problems. The problem-solving orientation of OR should therefore be replaced by one that focuses on planning for and design of systems. Moreover, organizations are purposeful systems which contain purposeful parts and which are themselves parts of larger purposeful systems. Hence organizations have reponsibilities to their own purposes, to the purposes of their parts and to the purposes of the larger systems of which they are parts (Ackoff, 1974b). These responsibilities may often seem to conflict (pluralism). The principal task of the manager and management scientist is to learn how to remove any conflict between these levels of purpose. Ackoff's "interactive planning" is therefore an elaborate attempt to come to terms with problem solving in systemic–pluralist contexts.

Interactive planning has three operating principles (Ackoff, 1981). The first is the participative principle. If possible, all the stakeholders should participate in the various phases of the planning process. Stakeholders here include representatives of the purposeful parts of the system and of the larger system. The second is the principle of continuity. Because values change and because events occur which could not have been foreseen, plans need to be continually revised. The final principle is the holistic principle. A plan should involve simultaneously and interdependently as many parts and levels of the system as possible.

These operating principles are reflected in the five phases of the planning process itself—formulating the mess, ends planning, means planning, resource planning and "implementation and control". The unique feature of the approach is undoubtedly phase two, in which the interactive planner and the stakeholders participate in designing an "idealized future" for the system with which they are concerned. This designing of a desirable future is seen as a way of eliminating petty differences between stakeholders and of concentrating everyone's mind on the broader, long-term interests they all share in common. The idealized future is a design of the future that begins from scratch. It is a statement of the system the planners and stakeholders would create if they were free to create any system they wanted. If pursued positively, interactive planning can lead to the interests of the different parts of the organization, of the organization itself, and of the wider society being reconciled. The problems which contributed to the original mess will be "dissolved" in the new design. They will, of course, be replaced by new problems. Hence the need for continuous planning.

Checkland's methodology (1981) is similarly adept at dealing with systemic–pluralist problem contexts. It grew out of the frustration experienced by consultants trying to use hard systems methodologies in such contexts. A "problem situation" is first analysed and a "rich picture" of the situation is built up. The aim is not to delimit particular problems "out there" in the real world, but to gain an understanding of "a situation in which various actors may perceive various aspects to be problematical."

The various "Ws" operating in the system (plus any the analyst may wish to introduce) are expressed in "root definitions" of systems relevant to the problem situation. "Conceptual models" are then constructed of the various systems enshrined in the root definitions. These are used for comparison with what is perceived to exist in the real world. This comparison helps to structure a debate about possible change among the actors concerned with the problem situation. The analyst and the various actors should now be able to agree on changes which are both "desirable and feasible." The original problem situation is successfully tackled, although a different problem situation simultaneously emerges.

In a sense, the systemic–pluralist problem context embraces the other three types of problem context as special cases. It follows that, in theory, the Ackoff and Checkland methodologies should be able to address problems in all four problem contexts. To use these methodologies in contexts other than the systemic–pluralist would, however, be very inefficient. If they were used in either the mechanical–unitary or systemic–unitary contexts, resources would be wasted in reaffirming an already existing consensus on objectives. If they were used in either the mechanical–unitary or mechanical–pluralist contexts, efforts would be wasted attempting to deal with a complexity that did not exist. Although, therefore, these methodologies are potentially able to address problems in all problem contexts, in practice they are only appropriate for one—the systemic–pluralist context.

IMPLICATIONS OF THE ANALYSIS

The purpose of this section is to consider what benefits of an intellecutal or practical nature can be derived from the analysis pursued up to this point. Because the analysis seems so fruitful in terms of opening up new insights and new avenues of enquiry, it is impossible within the scope of this paper to do more than point to the existence of some of its more important implications. These implications can roughly be considered as being of two kinds: first, theoretical implications which have a bearing on the current debate about the nature of OR as an activity; second, practical implications concerning the conduct of the problem-solving venture.

Theoretical Implications

(i) The analysis presented places a different perspective on the "OR in crisis" debate. Instead of seeing different problem-solving methodologies as competing for the same problem contexts (as Dando and Bennett, 1981, do), different problem-solving methodologies are presented as being appropriate for dealing each with one type of problem context. A "crisis" will not therefore occur if a methodology is only used for its appropriate problem context. A diversity of problem-solving methodologies, each with a defined area of competence, should be encouraged. Classical OR will be one of these with its own unique competence. The way ahead is to work for the establishment of an "avant-garde OR" embracing all the problem-solving approaches discussed above.

(ii) Different problem-solving methodologies, instead of being compared one with another in relation to their ability to solve the generality of problem types, should be evaluated in relation to their success in solving those problems for which they are best suited. This should encourage mutual respect among the proponents of the different approaches. This opens up a much better prospect for further debate and progress than the rather carping criticism of particular problem-solving approaches from other perspectives, which is currently common.

(iii) Once different problem-solving methodologies have been identified, work can begin on establishing the usefulness of each approach and on developing each approach to its natural limits. Methodologies should be evaluated in terms of their success in tackling the problems for which they are suited and in terms of the "size" of the problem domain in which they can be used. Two types of work will be necessary: first, theoretical work which attempts to establish the underlying assumptions about problem contexts which underpin the different approaches—this should help in the identification of those problem contexts for which the different methodologies are appropriate (a start has already been made on this work—see Checkland, 1978, and Jackson, 1982); second, practical work—trying out the different methodologies in cases where you would expect them to be successful *and* cases where you would expect them to fail. Both types of work should see improvements made to the different methodologies which will facilitate their success in their own domains and maybe broaden those domains.

(iv) Raitt (1979) suggests that OR, and therefore all of the complementary methodologies, are technological activities. Raitt's argument is based upon a distinction between models and theories, an overriding concern with the former indicating a technological activity, a dominant concern with the latter indicating a scientific activity. To make such an assertion as this is to simplify the distinction between science and technology. The interactions between science, applied science and technology are complex, and to argue that one can exist in some sort of isolation from the others is to ignore these interactions (see Ihde, 1979). As the analysis makes clear, any problem-solving methodology must take into account the behaviour of the system in which the problem exists. This involves the creation of a model of that system. This model may take one of many forms but it is essentially a representation of the system. In order to create such a model, it is necessary to formulate some ideas concerning the relationships and processes which are embodied in the system. This activity is a theory-building activity, so the model is theory-dependent; it is a representation of the theory which has been built up of the real world.

The question arises, therefore, of where systems methodologies can turn for the theoretical support that seems to be required. One answer might be to turn to the science of systems, general system theory (GST). GST may provide a framework for discussing features common to many problem contexts. As Naughton (1979) and Checkland (1972) have convincingly argued, however, GST is unlikely to be able to provide the theoretical support necessary. As an alternative to GST, it might be better to turn to the particular sciences which are concerned with explaining the nature of the system(s) that exist in the different problem contexts. This, of course, would involve methodologies concerned with systemic–pluralist contexts turning to the social sciences. There are problems. Vickers (1978) has lamented the lack of support the professions which manage human systems derive from the social sciences. But Vickers is probably not being altogether fair here. There is a mass of relevant theory available in the social sciences, although this is certainly in need of being sorted out.

(v) In the analysis, problem contexts of a certain type have been deliberately left out of account. These are problem contexts characterized by contradictions between different political and economic interests. There will be structural conflict between the different groups involved. The way such contexts are structured constrains human development. The systems involved are ripe for radical change. There is a clear difference between this type of problem context and the systemic–pluralist context. In a systemic–pluralist context, it is possible for some compromise solution or some appeal to a desirable future to bring about a *genuine* consensus among the parties involved. In what might be called *systemic–coercive* contexts, any cohesion that does exist will be achieved by the exercise of power and by domination (overt or more or less concealed) of one or more groups over others. Walsh *et al.* (1981) offer a good account of power in organizations and the effect it can have on any "consensus" achieved.

Systemic–coercive contexts have been left out of account, not because it is believed they are rare (it is arguable that the majority of organizations in capitalist societies provide such contexts—see Rosenhead and Thunhurst, 1982), but because it is believed that the drastic problems which exist in such contexts are unlikely to succumb to the remedies of problem-solving methodologies. And it will be remembered that the classification of problem contexts in the earlier section was constructed only with such problem-solving methodologies in mind.

The analysis can, however, help explain why problem-solving methodologies are inappropriate in systemic–coercive contexts. Examples might be offered. Imagine a problem solver with a problem context characterized by structural conflict, contradiction and domination trying to apply a hard-systems methodology. Even if the methodology could be made to work, all the analyst could achieve would be to help the dominant group or groups to strengthen an enforced cohesion. In so doing, he would be contributing to the survival of a situation in which human development was being constrained. Even if he tries to employ a Checkland-type approach, he is likely to do more to buttress the status quo than to challenge it (see Jackson, 1982; Thomas and Lockett, 1977). If the methodology could be made to work, agreement will eventually be reached on feasible and desirable changes. However, as these changes have been agreed by the dominant group or groups in the system, they are likely to be changes which support rather than threaten their authority. Other groups may agree to such changes because of fear of the consequences of opposing them or because they fail to recognize their own true interests (they are subject to the "third dimension of power"—see Lukes, 1974). Again, the problem solver will only tend to contribute to the survival of a situation in which human development is being constrained.

The use of OR/systems methodologies in systemic–coercive contexts can therefore only prolong the existence of systems which benefit some groups at the expense of others. If Rosenhead and Thunhurst's analysis of capitalist society as replete with systemic–coercive contexts is correct, then the use of the methodologies in these contexts only services and legitimates capitalism. To prepare the ground for the abolition of such contexts and the legitimate use of OR/systems methodologies, OR workers and systems researchers must, as Rosenhead and Thunhurst (1982) suggest, "participate in the struggle of labour against capital."

Practical Implications

(vi) If the analysis is taken seriously, it will lead the problem solver to ask, on each occasion he is confronted with a problem, what methodology is appropriate to *this* problem context. It should make it more difficult for him to get away with employing some favourite methodology in all circumstances. There should, for example, be less cause for clients to complain that OR workers always see the world in terms of their favourite problem-solving technique.

(vii) The question of identifying problem contexts correctly obviously becomes crucial. Some work needs to be done to help problem solvers with this difficult task. Problem contexts in the real world rarely announce their character unambiguously. The way any problem context is perceived is going to depend very much on the individual who is observing it (and in the case of a consultant, on the information he can gain from the client—see Eilon, 1982). For example, the wider he draws the system boundaries, the more likely is the problem context to become systemic–pluralist. A problem solver's "W" will very largely determine the way he sees and approaches problem contexts. Problem solvers, of course, may not be aware of the "W" which conditions the way they view problem contexts. Often, the only expression of the "W" will be adherence by the individual to some favourite methodology which acts as the bearer of an unconsciously held "W". It seems necessary, therefore, for the problem solver always to be aware that there are different "Ws" around— different ways of viewing and approaching systems and problem contexts. The problem solver needs to stand back and examine problem contexts in the light of *different* "Ws." Perhaps he can then decide which "W" seems to capture the essence of the particular problem context he is faced with. This whole process needs formalizing if it is to be carried out successfully.

The problem solver needs to be aware of different paradigms in the social sciences, and he must be prepared to view the problem context through each of these paradigms. Burrell and Morgan (1979) provide a framework of sociological paradigms which might be a useful starting point for the work that needs to be done in helping problem solvers identify problem contexts correctly.

(viii) Some problem contexts will, of course, not fit exactly into any one of the above four categories. Faced with such an intransigent problem context, the problem solver may still gain benefits from the analysis. It will be possible, using the analysis, to see how a particular methodology might be extended by making use of aspects of other approaches. For example, a problem solver who is armed with a soft systems methodology appropriate for a systemic–pluralist context may find it possible to "harden up" his/her methodology for a problem context which has some mechanical–pluralist aspects. The resolution of conflict over objectives may be helped by the use of a quantitative approach to aid the decision makers in investigating the effects of their own preferred solutions relative to the solutions of others. A methodology suited to mechanical–unitary problem contexts may be "softened up" in a way which makes it more effective in dealing with problem contexts which exhibit some systemic–unitary features. For example, the use of quantitative methods based on psychological or sociological theory may be used to deal with certain behavioural aspects of a system's behaviour. Some examples of such a "behavioural OR" approach are given in Keys (1982).

(ix) Finally, the analysis aids the understanding of exactly what goes wrong when an inappropriate problem-solving approach is employed in a particular problem context. For example, the attempt by Governor Brown of California to apply systems analysis to social problems in the early 1960s (documented by Hoos, 1972, 1979) can be understood as an attempt to apply a methodology appropriate for problems in a mechanical–unitary context to solve problems in a systemic–pluralist context. More recently, Rosenhead (1978, 1981) has criticized the attempt to apply classical OR to the systemic–pluralist contexts of the health service and urban planning. Churchman (1979b) recounts how he attempted to use his methodology, which can be seen as most appropriate to mechanical–pluralist contexts, to examine the NASA programme to put a man on the moon. This "problem" was conceived by NASA to be set within a mechanical–unitary context. Churchman's analysis received from one NASA group monitoring the work an "F" in relation to NASA's mission and an "A" for interdisciplinarity! Beer's work in Chile can be seen (as previously mentioned) as an attempt to apply a methodology suited to a systemic–unitary context in a situation which was becoming (perhaps artificially) systemic–pluralist. The debate and consensus building which is the hallmark of the soft systems approach would be a waste of time in mechanical–unitary contexts.

CONCLUSION

OR is regarded by many as being in crisis. If OR is taken to be "classical OR," this is indisputable. Classical OR provides the practitioner with an approach suitable for solving problems only in mechanical–unitary contexts. If, however, the definition of OR is widened to embrace other systems-based methodologies for problem solving, then a diversity of approaches may herald, not crisis, but increased competence and effectiveness in a variety of different problem contexts. This paper has suggested that different kinds of problem context exist in the real world. It is essential to develop different methodologies to cope with these. In the diversity of methodologies around can be found attempts to come to terms with each of the different types of problem context discussed. The analysis provided can be used as a starting point for a coordinated research programme designed to deepen our understanding of these different problem contexts and the type of problem-solving methodology appropriate to each.

REFERENCES

Ackoff, R.L. (1962). *Scientific Method*, John Wiley, New York.
Ackoff, R.L. (1974a). The systems revolution, *Long Range Planning* **7**, 2–20.
Ackoff, R.L. (1974b). The social responsibility of O.R., *Opl Res. Q.*, **25**, 361–371.
Ackoff, R.L. (1979a). The future of operational research is past, Chapter 2 in this book.
Ackoff, R.L. (1979b). Resurrecting the future of operational research, *J. Opl Res. Soc.*, **30.**, 189–200.
Ackoff, R.L. (1981). *Creating the Corporate Future*, John Wiley, New York.
Ackoff, R.L., and Sasieni, M.W. (1968). *Fundamentals of O.R.*, John Wiley, New York.
Adams, J.G.U. (1973). Chile: everything under control, *Science for People*, **21**, 4–6.
Beer, S. (1967). *Cybernetics and Management*, English Universities Press, London.
Beer, S. (1972). *Brain of the Firm*, John Wiley, Chichester.
Beer, S. (1979). *The Heart of Enterprise*, John Wiley, Chichester.
Bennett, P.G. (1980). Hypergames: developing a model of conflict, *Futures*, **12**, 489–507.
Boulding, K.E. (1956). General systems theory—the skeleton of science, *Mgmt Sci.*,**2**, 197–208.
Burrell, G., and Morgan, G. (1979). *Sociological Paradigms and Organizational Analysis*, Heinemann, London.
Checkland, P.B. (1971). A systems map of the universe, *J. Syst. Eng.*, **2** (2).
Checkland, P.B. (1972). Towards a systems-based methodology for real-world problem-solving, *J. Syst. Eng.*, **3**, 87–116.
Checkland, P.B. (1978). The origins and nature of "hard" systems thinking, *J. Appl. Syst. Anal.*, **5**, 99–110.
Checkland, P.B. (1981). *Systems Thinking, Systems Practice*, John Wiley, Chichester.
Clarke, M.C., and Keys, P. (1982). What happens when public sector employees are made redundant: some exploratory results using a micro-simulation model, *Working Paper*, **298**, School of Geography, University of Leeds.
Churchman, C.W. (1971). *The Design of Inquiring Systems*, Basic Books, New York.
Churchman, C.W. (1979a). *The Systems Approach*, 2nd edition, Dell, New York.
Churchman, C.W. (1979b). *The Systems Approach and Its Enemies*, Basic Books, New York.
Churchman, C.W., and Schainblatt, A.H. (1965). The researcher and the manager: a dialectic of implementation, *Mgmt Sci.*, **11**, B69–B87.
Churchman C.W., Ackoff, R.L., and Arnoff, E.L. (1957). *Introduction to Operations Research*, John Wiley,New York.
Dando, M.R., and Bennett P.G. (1981). A Kuhnian crisis in management science?, *J. Opl Res. Soc.*, **32**, 91–104.
Eden, C., Jones, S., and Sims, D. (1979). *Thinking in Organizations*, Macmillan, London.
Eilon, S. (1982). Silver Medal address, *J. Opl Res. Soc.*, **33**, 1090–1098.
Espejo, R. (1977). Cybernetics in management and organization, *Working Paper Series*, **76**, University of Aston Management Centre.
Hall, A.D. (1962). *A Methodology for Systems Engineering*, Van Nostrand, New York.
Hoos, I. (1972). *Systems Analysis in Public Policy*, University of California Press, California.
Hoos, I. (1979). Engineers as analysts of social systems: a critical enquiry, *J. Syst. Eng.*, **4**, 81–88.
Ihde, D. (1979). *Technics and Praxis*, D. Reidel, Dordrecht.

Jackson, M.C. (1982). The nature of "soft" systems thinking: the work of Churchman, Ackoff and Checkland, *J. Appl. Syst. Anal.*, **9**, 17–29.

Jenkins, G.M. (1969). The systems approach, in *Systems Behaviour*, 2nd edition (Eds J. Beishon and G. Peters), pp. 78–104, Open University Press, London.

Jordan, N. (1981). Some thinking about "system", in *Systems Thinking*, volume 2 (Ed. F.E. Emery), pp. 15–39, Penguin, Harmondsworth.

Keys, P. (1982). Introducing behaviour into OR models, mimeo, Department of Management Systems and Sciences, University of Hull.

Krone, R.H. (1980). *Systems Analysis and Policy Sciences*, John Wiley, Chichester.

Lukes, S. (1974). *Power: A Radical View*, Macmillan, London.

Mason, R.O. (1969). A dialectical approach to strategic planning, *Mgmt Sci.*, **15**, 403–414.

Mason, R.O., and Mitroff, I.I. (1981). *Challenging Strategic Planning Assumptions*, John Wiley, New York.

Mitroff, I.I. and Emshoff, J.R. (1979). On strategic assumption-making: a dialectical approach to policy and planning. *Acad. Mgmt Rev.*, **4**, 1–12.

Mitroff, I.I., Emshoff, J.R., and Kilmann, R.H. (1979). Assumptional analysis: a methodology for strategic problem solving, *Mgmt Sci*, **25**, 583–593.

Morgan, G. (1982). Cybernetics and organisation theory: epistemology or technique, *Hum. Relat.*, **35**, 521–537.

Naughton, J. (1979). Anti-G.S.T.: an evolutionary manifesto, paper for the Silver Anniversary Meeting of the S.G.S.R.

Optner, S.L. (1965). *Systems Analysis for Business and Industrial Problem Solving*, Prentice-Hall, Englewood Cliffs, NJ.

Raitt, R.A. (1979). Viewpoints, *J. Opl Res. Soc.*, **30**, 835–836.

Rice, A.K. (1958). *Productivity and Social Organisation: The Ahmedabad Experiment*, Tavistock, London.

Rosenhead, J. (1978). Operational research in health services planning, *Eur. J. Opl Res.*, **2**, 75–85.

Rosenhead, J. (1981). OR in urban planning, *Omega*, **9**, 345–364.

Rosenhead, J., and Thunhurst, C. (1982). A materialist analysis of operational research, *J. Opl Res. Soc.*, **33**, 111–122.

Thomas, A.R., and Lockett, M. (1979). Marxism and systems research: values in practical action', Chapter 4 in this book.

Trist, E.L., Higgin, G.W., Murray, H., and Pollock, A.B. (1963). *Organisational Choice*, Tavistock, London.

Ulrich, W. (1981). A critique of pure cybernetic reason: The Chilean experience with cybernetics, *J. Appl. Syst. Anal.*, **8**, 33–59.

Vemuri, V. (1978). *Modeling of Complex Systems*, Academic Press, New York.

Vickers, G. (1978). Practice and research in managing human systems—four problems of relationship, *Policy Sci.*, **9**, 1–8.

Von Bertalanffy, L. (1969). The theory of open systems in physics and biology, in *Systems Thinking* (Ed. F.E. Emery), pp. 70–85, Penguin, Harmondsworth.

Walsh, K., Hinings, B., Greenwood, R., and Ranson, S. (1981). Power and advantage in organisations, *Org. Stud.*, **2**, 131–152.

Chapter 8

Methodological Foundations of Systems Methodologies

JOHN C. OLIGA

INTRODUCTION

For perhaps a number of ideologically compelling reasons, the social sciences sought, right from the outset, to develop in the image of the older, more established and "successful" natural sciences. To a very large extent, that image still remains the exemplar for the overwhelming majority of social scientists, who seem to see no important distinction between the nature of their objects of inquiry and that of the objects of the natural sciences. Even the (relatively) younger systems science (whose domain is unavoidably constituted primarily by social phenomena) did not succeed in escaping this temptation. But more recently (especially since the late 1970s and early 1980s), there has been a growing awareness of, and an open debate about, the inadequacies or inappropriateness of the traditional hard systems thinking and its approach to the study and design of social systems. Parallel with these debates, new systems "methodologies," predominantly at the practical level of real-world problem solving, have been rigorously developed. But the growing mood for methodological criticisms has not spared even these new directions in systems methods.

One thing which seems needed in any serious attempt at clarifying issues of controversy in these debates is a return to the metatheoretical basic assumptions and concerns that underwrite different problem-solving and inquiry methodologies (as, for instance, in the debate between Jackson and Ackoff,

Reprinted by permission from *Systems Practice*, Volume 1, 1988
© 1988 Plenum Press, New York

Churchman, and Checkland on the nature of soft systems thinking (see Jackson, 1982, 1983)). It is the aim of this paper to contribute to the elaboration of such metatheoretical assumptions and concerns.

The paper seeks to make a brief exposition of the methodological foundations that underwrite different approaches to inquiry and problem solving in the domain of social science. The aim of such an exposition is to highlight the nature and (especially) the limits of different methodological claims and aspirations in social theory. In the process, a rationale for a self-reflective choice of specific methodologies (or methods) of inquiry and problem solving should unfold. Following Jackson's (1982, 1985a, b, 1987a), Jackson and Keys' (1984), Checkland's (1983, 1985), Flood and Carson's (1988, Chapter 6) and Banathy's (1984, 1986, 1987) seminal works on (specific) methodological choice, this paper also seeks to relate contemporary systems work on modes of inquiry and problem-solving approaches to their explicit or implicit methodological foundations. The paper concludes by pointing to the need for a critical methodological foundation. Critique does not deny the legitimacy of the human interests underlying empiricist and hermeneutic methodological foundations. Rather, it attempts, in the context of contemporary social formations, to transcend their alterable, historical, and essentially ideological limitations.

The next section seeks to clarify the formal distinction between method and methodology, concepts which, even if employed interchangeably in current usage (as in present systems literature), should be differently understood according to context. It is in that context that while methodological foundations refer to methodology in general, or metatheoretical assumptions and concerns, systems methodologies (or, more properly, methods) refer (logically) to lower-level modes of systems inquiry and problem-solving approaches. The following section is an attempt to elaborate on a metatheoretical framework for methodology in general (or methodological foundations), first in terms of a philosophy of science and a theory of society (Burrell and Morgan, 1979) and then in terms of Habermas' (1972) interest constitution theory. This is followed by a critical examination of empiricism, hermeneutics, and critique as three major methodological foundations corresponding to three forms of human interests: the technical, the practical and the emancipatory interest. The final section relates the foregoing broad philosophic/sociological discussion to contemporary systems work on modes of inquiry and problem-solving approaches.

METHOD OR METHODOLOGY?

Giddens (1976) has described how, throughout the nineteenth and well into the twentieth century, social science developed in the shadow of the triumphs of natural science, whose spectacular, dazzling, and convincing technological accomplishments drew the admiration of the "new" social science and kindled in its practitioners the dream of achieving "the same kind of sensational illumination and explanatory power already yielded by the sciences of nature" (p.13). It was therefore only natural that the process of emulating the natural scientists' approach to the conduct of inquiry (the so-called "scientific method") should proceed with unquestioning and blind faith in its relevance and suitability for the study of human and social phenomena.

Given the nature of the objects of study in the natural sciences, it is perhaps understandable that the basic ontological question regarding the essences of things and phenomena did not seem to arise. In the scientific method (however defined) an ontological unity was assumed in the sense that all objects in the universe, regardless of whether these were inert, living, conscious, or rational beings, were taken to be of fundamentally and qualitatively the same kind. Thus the only meaningful questions of scientific inquiry centred on epistemology and methodology. Since the truth value of any claims to knowledge ultimately depended on the validation process embodying a set of communally controlled, universal rules and impersonal procedures, those rules and procedures not only became identified with the scientific method, but also were seen as exhausting the notion of methodology.

A distinction between methodology and method can be meaningful only where no ontological unity is assumed, with the consequence that the validity of different modes of inquiry and problem-solving approaches (i.e. methods) need to be evaluated against a set of higher-order criteria (i.e. methodology) that lie outside those methods. Despite the long-standing dominance of the scientific method in the social sciences, there has fortunately been a growing awareness that the social world is qualitatively different from the natural world and, in consequence, that the methodological unity assumption cannot be tenable (also see Flood and Carson, 1988; Chapters 5, 6 and 10). It is this view that runs throughout the present paper.

From such an ontological position, methodology, as opposed to method, is viewed as representing a higher-order construct: a method of methods that examines systematically and logically the aptness of all research tools, varying from basic assumptions to special research techniques. A similar distinction is evident in the Parsonian sense of the terms, where methodology relates to the consideration of the general grounds for the validity of scientific procedures, while methods are best identified with research techniques employed in a particular research activity (e.g. case study, interview, questionnaire, statistical methods (see Gould and Kolb, 1964)).

The methodology of a science therefore represents its rationale for evaluating its theories or hypotheses (Christenson, 1983, p.2). In a similar manner, the methodology of research provides the rationale for evaluating what it claims to be a research problem, its theoretical and observational propositions, and the kinds of proposals it suggests or implies. In this sense, methodology is necessarily normative, and for that reason, it is not surprising (as Christenson, 1983, notes) that positivists hold it in low esteem, deriding it as "unscientific" and "meaningless." Quoting Popper (1959, p.51), Christenson adds, "The positivist dislikes the idea that there should be meaningful problems outside the field of 'positivist' empirical science . . . He dislikes the idea that there should be a genuine theory of knowledge, an epistemology or a methodology." But such a positivist dogma, as Christenson argues, does not enable positivists to avoid methodological commitments: it only makes them uncritical and unreflexive about the commitments they make. This may be characteristic of the more established natural sciences with a research tradition of demonstrated fruitfulness. In social sciences, however, the need for being self-conscious about methodology seems to be crucial. Quoting Samuelson (1962, p.21), Christenson adds, "Paradoxically, the soft sciences that are still akin to an art benefit more from an explicit awareness of the canons of scientific method . . . than do the hard sciences, where doing what comes naturally will protect even a fool from gross methodological error."

The view of methodology as a metamethod seems to characterize the thinking of a number of recent writers on the problem of methodology in social science in general, and in systems science in particular. Viewing research as engagement, Morgan (1983) has, for instance, argued for an approach that sees "the research process as involving choice between modes of engagement entailing different relationships between theory and method, concept and object, and researcher and researched, rather than simply a choice about method alone" (p.18). In those terms,

> . . . a much broader self-reflective stance is required. A knowledge of technique needs to be complemented by an appreciation of the nature of research as a distinctly human process through which researchers make knowledge. Such appreciation stands in contrast to the more common view of research as a neutral, technical process through which researchers simply reveal or discover knowledge. Such an appreciation requires that we reframe understanding and debate about research in a way that goes beyond considerations of method alone. (Morgan. 1983, p.7)

Mattessich (1978, p.220) has similarly drawn a useful distinction between general and special methodologies. The former refers to the "sum-total of all rational ways of pursuing knowledge" and can therefore be regarded as a branch of philosophy. Special methodologies, on the other hand, "emerge either out of the needs of specific disciplines or out of a specific attitude towards reality." In systems science, Banathy's classification of "systems methodology" into three categories (cf. Jackson, 1985b) is highly illuminating. The classification represents a logical hierarchy, from practice, to theory to metatheory levels of resolution. While the practical level includes systems methods as approaches to real-world problem solving, the theoretical level includes systems methods as modes of inquiry for knowledge production. It is, however, the third metatheoretical level that constitutes systems methodology (in the formal sense) as the foundation or basis for determining the metacharacteristics of problem-solving and inquiry methods. The next section elaborates a framework for such methodological foundations at the metatheoretical level.

A FRAMEWORK FOR METHODOLOGY IN GENERAL

A Philosophy of Science and a Theory of Society

In a volume describing 21 different approaches to social science research, Morgan (1983) has outlined a framework for analysing their constitutive logics or strategies. Overarching any social research are the constitutive ontological assumptions regarding the researcher's view about the existential nature of the social world and human subjectivity. Such constitutive assumptions define the basic underlying paradigm for a particular inquiry. Concretization of these foundational assumptions in terms of favoured "metaphors," or images, through which the assumptions become meaningful represents a particular epistemological stance, or a particular view of the possibility of knowledge about the social world. Thus, methodology or "puzzle solving" represents a bridging activity that aims at forging a correspondence between paradigmatic ontological assumptions and the particular epistemological positions taken.

In Morgan's (1983) framework, ontology is clearly prior to epistemology. Beyleveld (1975) has noted that substantively the priority between ontology and epistemology may differ from what is posited in a formal structure. Morgan's (1983) framework is in terms of a one-dimensional characterization of the logic of research. This is the cognitive dimension that classifies research methodologies in terms of the subjective–objective dichotomy (Burrell and Morgan, 1979; Morgan, 1980; Morgan and Smircich, 1980). A second dimension, the ethical dimension, brings to the fore the "order–conflict" or "regulation–radical change" dichotomy as an issue separate from the subjective–objective dichotomy (Burrell and Morgan, 1979; Dahrendorf, 1967; Lockwood, 1956; Cohen, 1968). It is in terms of such a two-dimensional perspective that Burrell and Morgan (1979) present a general framework for the analysis of social theory. Figure 8.1 illustrates the framework and its classification of social theories into four paradigms: the "functionalist," "interpretive," "radical–humanist," and "radical–structuralist." The framework reflects the basic philosophical presuppositions or metatheoretical assumptions underlying scientific inquiry. First, it reflects a philosophy of science in terms of four basic assumptions related to ontology, epistemology, human nature, and methodology, along a subjective–objective dimension.

THE SOCIOLOGY OF RADICAL CHANGE

THE SOCIOLOGY OF REGULATION

Figure 8.1 Four paradigms for the analysis of social theory (reproduced by permission from Burrell and Morgan, 1979, p. 22)

Second, it reflects a theory of society in terms of a regulation–radical change dimension. Each of the four resulting paradigms generates theories, perspectives, and methodological approaches which are in fundamental opposition to those generated in other paradigms.

Briefly, the functionalist paradigm is characterized by an objectivist (realist ontology, positivist epistemology, deterministic view of the nature of man, and nomothetic methodology) stance and a regulative ethical commitment that is concerned with providing explanations of the status quo, social order, consensus, social integration, solidarity, need satisfaction, and actuality (Burrell and Morgan, 1979, p.26). The interpretive paradigm, while sharing regulative ethical commitment with the functionalist paradigm, counterposes to it a subjectivist (nominalist ontology, antipositivist epistemology, voluntaristic view of the nature of man, and ideographic methodology) position, with an overriding concern for understanding the social world at the level of subjective experience and seeking "explanation within the realm of individual consciousness and subjectivity" (p.28).

While the functionalist and interpretive paradigms share a common regulative ethical concern, the radical–humanist and the radical structuralist paradigms counterpose an ethical commitment geared to seeking explanations for the radical change, deep-seated structural conflict, modes of domination and alienation, and structural contradictions characterizing modern society. Like the interpretive paradigm, the radical–humanist paradigm is subjectivist but it is committed to a critique of the status quo, seeking at the level of consciousness explanation for radical change, alienation, false consciousness, modes of domination, emancipation, deprivation, and potentiality (Burrell and Morgan, 1979, p.32). The radical–structuralist paradigm, on the other hand, is objectivist but also committed to a critique of the status quo, a critique that emphasizes structural bases of conflict, contradiction, modes of domination, deprivation, radical change, emancipation, and potentiality (p.34).

Table 8.1 Habermas' interest constitution theory—(adapted from Puxty *et al.* (1980) and Giddens (1977))

Knowledge constitutive interest	Basis of human interest	Type of interaction	Underlying paradigm	Methodological approach
Technical (control)	Labour (instrumental action)	Man–nature	Functionalist	Empiricism
Practical (understanding)	Communicative interaction	Man–man	Interpretive	Hermeneutics
Emancipatory (freedom)	Authority (power)	Man–self	Radical/critical	Critique

Habermas' Interest Constitution Theory

Laughlin *et al.* (1981) and Chua *et al* (1981) have sought to critique and extend the Burrell and Morgan (1979) framework by incorporating Habermas' interest constitution theory, in terms of which the concerns of social theories are seen as reflecting either a technical interest for prediction and control (man–nature interaction), a practical interest for understanding (human communicative interaction), or an emancipatory interest (social relations of power, domination, and alienation). The technical interest constitutes empirical knowlege and parallels Burrell and Morgan's functionalist paradigm. The practical interest constitutes historical–hermeneutical knowledge, parallelling the interpretive paradigm. The emancipatory interest constitutes critical knowledge, parelleling the radical–humanist and –structuralist paradigms. These basic ideas in Habermas' interest constitution theory are summarized in Table 8.1.

Laughlin *et al.* (1981) and Chua *et al.* (1981) argue that the two schemes are parallel, but fundamentally different, in that whereas Burrell and Morgan merely explain the different paradigmatic categories, Habermas explains and reconciles the interest categories in terms of their being individually necessary (although insufficient) as human species, universal and invariant (ontological) forms of activity—namely labour, human interaction, and authority relations (Habermas, 1972; Giddens, 1977; Keat, 1981; Puxty *et al.*, 1980). This is an important improvement over the interparadigmatic incommensurability position of Burrell and Morgan (cf. Beyleveld, 1975).

The three different kinds of knowledge imply different methodological approaches—namely, empiricist, hermeneutic, and critical methodologies. It is these methodologies that constitute metatheoretical foundations for lower-order methods in the form of modes of inquiry and problem-solving approaches. The next section is a brief attempt to elaborate on the three methodologies: empiricism (in terms of its positivist and structuralist variants), hermeneutics (in terms of its naturalistic and historical variants), and critique (or critical hermeneutics).

THREE METHODOLOGICAL FOUNDATIONS

In attempting to highlight the three methodological foundations that under-write different modes of inquiry and practice, a focus on two issues is made. These are their underlying interest, and hence their claims about what counts as scientific (valid) knowledge, and the difficulties they face in those claims. It is upon a critical reflection on such claims and difficulties that a rational choice of a particular methodology in general and of specific systems methodologies in particular, can be made.

Empiricism

Underwritten by a functionalist paradigm, the empiricist methodology takes the external social world as being made up of hard, relatively immutable social structures, or immutable deep-level generative mechanisms, whose existence is essentially independent of individual consciousness. Epistemologically, while the positivist position conceives of scientific knowledge as constituted solely by empirical knowledge grounded in the explanation and prediction of observable phenomena, the structuralist position considers empirical knowl-edge as only a special case of a wider knowledge domain comprising the empirical (observed events), the actual (observed and unobserved events), and the real (actual and potential occurrences) (Bhaskar, 1979). Objective knowl-edge is thus defined in terms of theory neutrality (observer independence) and value freedom (ethical neutrality); and thus methodology reduces to merely a question of the appropriate method of validation (typically verifica-tion or falsification), which is seen to guarantee undistorted access to the objective phenomena under study. The overriding concern is order and regulation of social affairs in the interest of maintaining the status quo

Given that positivism is the most powerful and influential variant of empiricism (cf. Beyleveld, 1975), its further elaboration seems warranted.

Positivism is not a unified epistemological/methodological position (Keat, 1981; Beyleveld, 1975; Christenson, 1983). Keat (1981) has identified at least four distinct claims or doctrines that have quite complex logical and historical relationships to one another. These are "scientism," "the positivist conception of science," "scientific politics," and "value-freedom." Briefly, scientism, a doctrine most closely associated with the "logical positivism" of the Vienna Circle, is the claim that science alone represents a genuine form of human knowledge, such that non-science (e.g. religion, metaphysics, ideology, politics, ethics, etc.) represents pseudoknowledge or even cognitive meaninglessness or nonsense (Keat, 1981, p.16). Habermas (1972, p.4) describes scientism as "science's belief in itself: that is the conviction that we can no longer understand science as one form of possible knowledge but rather must identify knowledge with science." Thus, although a logical positivist himself, Popper (1959) rejects this doctrine, arguing that while science could be distinguished from non-science, that did not imply an equivalent distinction between sense and nonsense. More generally, as Keat points out, scientism has been criticized for being self-refuting since it is itself a philosophical, epistemological doctrine, and not, by its own criteria, a scientific one.

The second doctrine, the positivist conception of science, specifies what constitutes scientific knowledge: the explanation and prediction of observable phenomena through the demonstration that such phenomena constitute instances of universal laws that remain invariant in all regions of space and time. This doctrine restricts scientific ontology to the domain of what is observable. Within this doctrine, it is possible to distinguish "realist" from "instrumentalist" positions (Keat, 1981, p.19). Realism holds science as providing statements about some theory-neutral real world and adopts a correspondence theory of truth. Instrumentalism, on the other hand, regards science as a device or instrument that is useful for certain purposes such as technical control or prediction (cf. Friedman, 1953). In this case, the idea of truth is either rejected or pragmatically defined.

Scientific politics is the doctrine that advocates treatment of politics as an applied science (such as engineering or medicine). Fay (1975, pp. 22–23) explains:

> If politics were to become an applied science, it is argued, its conjectural, arbitrary, emotional, and personal elements would drop out, and its arguments and decisions would assume the same neutral characteristics as those of engineering. In political arguments there would be, as there are in scientific arguments, reliable public standards of ascertainable truth, and therefore the possibility of a universally recognizable decisive solution to a particular problem. It is in this way that a social science would be able to eliminate the "anarchy of opinion" which characterizes political thinking.

While scientific politics seeks to "scientize" ends, the doctrine of value freedom opposes this, seeking instead a sharp distinction between means and ends, fact and value, science and politics. Keat (1981) explains how this separation involves two dimensions. First, the truth or falsity of a theory is independent of moral or political commitments or standpoints. Second, political issues or moral judgements cannot be justified solely by means of scientific knowledge.

It should already be evident that the relationships among the four major positivist doctrines are complex and that some are even contradictory. This has, according to Keat (1981), caused confusion and misunderstanding among critics of positivism. For instance, failure to distinguish between the doctrine of value freedom and the doctrine of scientific politics lies at the root of critical theorists' (cf. Horkheimer, 1972; Marcuse, 1964, 1968; Habermas, 1976a, b) mistaken criticism of Weber's (1949) methodological writings as representing both doctrines. Indeed, Keat (1981, p.21) argues and demonstrates that, on the whole, the logical relationships among the four positivist doctrines show that the doctrines do not necessarily entail each other and that, as a result of failure to understand this, "There has too often been a frontal assault on a loosely defined, undifferentiated target called 'positivism,' or at least an assumption that, by successfully criticising one positivist doctrine, the others are thereby shown to fail also" (p.36).

While this may very well be so, it is nonetheless possible to point to certain difficulties in positivism without necessarily implying that it is a unified epistemological/methodological position. For our limited purpose, these difficulties are in relation to the possibility of a positivist methodology for social sciences. The fundamental difficulty in positivism is what Habermas (1972) calls its "false objectivism." The doctrines of value freedom and positivist conception of science jointly entail the notion of objectivism and objective knowledge, notions which have been central to the positivist idea of science and scientific knowledge. Objectivism implies two related beliefs: first, that the objects of scientific knowledge exist independently of the epistemological framework on the basis of which they are investigated (i.e. theory-neutrality (TN) belief); and second, that such knowledge is value-free, meaning that the validation of its claims is independent of the acceptance of normative standpoints (i.e. value-freedom (VF) belief) (Keat, 1981). Objectivism, as a product of TN and VF beliefs, can thus be seen to guarantee two important requirements for a science (conceived positivistically): the need for a consensus of interpretations among its practitioners and the demand that knowledge be given a basis in certainty (Bauman, 1978). Historical hermeneutics addresses these difficulties.

Hermeneutics

Within the hermeneutic or interpretive methodology there exist two variants: the "naturalistic" methodology, also known as "hermeneutics as method"; and the historical–hermeneutic methodology (outlined below). While both represent a distinct ontological break with the empiricist methodology, from a natural world of hard, observable or real objects to a social world of subjective meaning and intention, the first variant, by maintaining objectivist aspirations in the production of knowledge, retains an epistemological unity with empiricism.

The *naturalistic methodology* includes a number of distinct interpretive approaches. Briefly, phenomenological symbolic interactionism seeks to explain how social order, as a real phenomenon, emerges through social action and interaction processes, from which shared meanings in turn emerge. It therefore seeks to understand how particular definitions and interpretations of the social world for ordered joint action are created and sustained within wider social contexts in which interacting individuals use a variety of practices and resources (Blumer, 1969; Denzin, 1970). Ethnomethodology, on the other hand, seeks to explain how actors employ various cognitive resources to order and make sense of their everyday activities and make those activities accountable to others. Order therefore does not exist independently of actors' accounting practices but must depend for its reproduction on actors' capacity to sustain the everyday common-sense suppositions, shared indexical expressions, and reflexive activities that characterize the routines of everyday life, all accomplished as if the social world were objective and factual (Garfinkel, 1967; Zimmerman and Wieder, 1970). Existentialism is preoccupied with a concern for the central lived qualities of individual human existence. Existential phenomenology seeks to understand the "life-world" from the point of view of those involved, using constructs and explanations which are intelligible in terms of the common-sense interpretations of everyday life. The focus is on processes of "typification" through which intersubjective understanding becomes possible (Schutz, 1967). Transcendental phenomenology seeks to produce a form of knowledge free from all presuppositions. This "projection of human imagination" requires silencing experience provisionally, or "bracketing" factual reality, and seeking to penetrate to the level of "ideal essences," "the reality in consciousness" (cf. Burrell and Morgan, 1979).

Although objectivist, the naturalistic methodology nevertheless takes the view that social reality is distinctive in character. Thus, because social phenomena are ultimately acts of men and women and therefore contain a meaningful component which is missing from natural phenomena, they require a mode of analysis different from that of mere explanation. Social science therefore requires an interpretive approach, the analysis of *verstehen* as the method appropriate to "re-experiencing or rethinking of what an author had originally felt or thought" (Bleicher, 1980, p.1). It thus seeks "the retrieval of purpose, of intention, of the unique configuration of thoughts and feelings which preceded a social phenomenon and found its only manifestation, imperfect and incomplete, in the observable consequences of action" (Bauman, 1978, p.12).

Hermeneutics as method is represented especially in the works of Weber (1949), Dilthey (1976), and Betti (1955, 1962). Both Dilthey and Weber were concerned to bridge the gulf between idealism (emphasizing subjectivism) and positivism (emphasizing objectivism) so that the cultural (social) sciences could secure a firm knowledge foundation in terms of "objective" validity. As Burrell and Morgan (1979) observe, Weber's overriding concern was to provide causal explanations of social phenomena through the development of an objective science of sociology, which had to be "adequate at the level of meaning." Weber's notion of *verstehen* was little more than a tool for overcoming the empiricist deficiencies of ignoring the subjective meaning of social action. Similarly, Dilthey's concern was "methodological," devising ways or methods of generating objective knowledge capable of meeting the requirements of positivist science (Burrell and Morgan, 1979, p.256), while giving full recognition to the distinctive subject–object relationship where "life meets life" (Bleicher, 1980). Betti (1955, 1962) developed these objective–idealist approaches further by arguing for "the possibility of *verstehen* as a methodically disciplined form of understanding" (Bleicher, 1980, p.27). Betti's general theory of objective interpretation is geared toward facilitating the reappropriation of objective mind (meaningful forms) by another mind.

Historical hermeneutics or hermeneutic philosophy, as developed by Heidegger (1962, 1966) and Gadamer (1975a, b, 1980), is a rejection of objectivism in both empiricism and hermeneutics as method. As Bleicher (1980) elaborates, hermeneutic philosophy sees the interpreter and object as linked by a context of tradition. This means that as he/she approaches his/her object, the interpreter already has a preunderstanding of it, thereby being unable to start with a neutral mind. There can be no object in itself, or any *factum bructum*. The mere recognition of a fact is theory impregnated and guided by a number of anticipations (Bleicher, 1980, p.102). Thus, meaning becomes not a property of entities but another "existential." Understanding is not the result of interpretation, in the sense of appropriation of meaning intended by another. Historical hermeneutics inverts this process—understanding leads to interpretation, the latter representing merely the working out of possibilities already projected in understanding.

In hermeneutics as method, the issue regarding the possibility of understanding in general is seen in terms of the "hermeneutic circle," "the movement of understanding from the whole to the part and back to the whole . . . (in order) to extend the unity of the understood meaning in concentric circles" (Bleicher, 1980, p.78). The aim here is to avoid possible misunderstanding arising from the historicity (or historical situatedness) of the interpreter. Historical reality is seen in terms of unitary, discrete epochs, each with its own tradition or prejudices that constitute a closed "horizon" of understanding. The task of interpretation becomes the re-creation of the past in order to arrive at objective knowledge.

In contrast, in historical hermeneutics, the hermeneutic circle is regarded as an existential circle or ontological moment of understanding, which proceeds from a commonality that unites us with tradition. Thus, rather than regard the preunderstanding of an object of interpretation as a blemish and the resulting circularity as an inevitable but vicious circle which should be avoided, historical hermeneutics views the hermeneutic circle as a necessary expression of the dialogical process of understanding. Historical reality is characterized by openness of tradition. Through a process of dialogical relationship between the subject and the object (text) and the dialectic between question and answer, the corresponding traditions become integrated. Such a "fusion of horizons" leads not to re-creation of the past but to "a dialogical understanding that transcends both traditions."

Gadamer's notion of "effective history" reflects this "on-going mediation of past and present, which encompasses subject and object and in which tradition asserts itself as a continuing impulse and influence" (Bleicher, 1980, p. 266). Positivism, in its reliance on objectivist methods of interpretation, ignores the force of effective history, but "only that it (the force) will not go away as a result but makes itself felt 'behind the back' of the naive observer" (Bleicher, 1980, p. 111). Historical hermeneutics therefore demands an awareness of effective history, of hermeneutic situation, and that hermeneutic consciousness and experience can never be complete, being limited by our historicality. The fusion of horizons also implies that hermeneutic experience is neither monological nor dialectical (in the Hegelian sense) but discursive or "dialogical." It is in this sense that language as the necessary medium for the fusion of horizons becomes ontologized by Gadamer in his theory of the universality of language. Thus dialogical understanding that emerges from the fusion of horizons represents the full realization of a conversation, the outcome of which is not only the interpreter's or the author's but common to both.

The significance of language or communicative interaction is thus central to historical hermeneutics. In addition, dialogical understanding becomes a necessary methodological feature since the way in which the object of inquiry (an objectivated mind) conceives of his/her own activities is itself a central part of social reality. Historical hermeneutics thus rejects the ontological, the epistemological, and the methodological unity of the sciences (Keat, 1981).

Historical hermeneutics therefore constitutes a fundamental critique of the possibility of objective knowledge, the central claim of empiricism and of the naturalistic methodology, both concerned with methodical procedures to derive truth as the correspondence between fact and proposition, based on the doctrines of theory neutrality and value freedom. Historical hermeneutics' notion of the existential/ontological circle, and hence the universality of hermeneutic experience and practical knowledge, shows the falsity of objectivist claims. In other words, if the subjectivity of the interpreter (social scientist), through the hermeneutic circle or the ontological–epistemological circle (Beyleveld, 1975, p. 211), is inherent in any interpretive activity because of the claim that there can be no direct perception of objects without presuppositions (preunderstanding, prejudices, etc.), objective knowledge is unattainable.

However, historical hermeneutics is in turn confronted with a formidable difficulty: its naturalization of tradition, authority, and language, thereby implying distortion-free communication situations. Critique addresses this difficulty, as discussed below.

Critique

Critique (or critical hermeneutics), as developed, for instance, in the works of Apel (1967, 1971, 1980) and Habermas (1970a, b, 1971, 1972, 1973, 1979) (cf. Bleicher, 1980), is an attempt to mediate the objectivity of historical processes with the motives of those acting within it, the aim being the freeing of emancipatory potential. The approach seeks to remove barriers to understanding that may be operative without the individuals or groups concerned being aware of them.

Bleicher (1980, pp. 148–151) describes this approach as a dialectical mediation of hermeneutic and explanatory approaches in the form of a critique of ideology. The methodological approach is based on a model of psychoanalysis, whereby a neurotic patient is helped to overcome his/her symptomatic behaviour through the combined use of "causal explanation and deepened self-understanding." The task is therefore directed at rendering individual and social processes transparent to the actors concerned so that they can "pursue their further development with consciousness and will—rather than remaining the end product of a causal chain operative behind their backs." By incorporating both the explanatory and the interpretive tasks, critique articulates the critical concerns of both the radical–humanist and the radical–structuralist paradigms. Communicative distortions, false consciousnes, and other ideological distortions are placed in the wider political, social–structural, and material conditions of existence. I now briefly highlight, from the viewpoint of critical hermeneutics, some of the difficulties positivist and hermeneutical methodologies face in their conception of social theory.

Starting with positivism, we have already seen the problem with its doctrine of scientism. We have also seen an historical hermeneutical critique of its objectivism which is central to its doctrines of value freedom and positivist conception of science.

Habermas (1972) has criticized the doctrine of value freedom through his theory of knowledge-constitutive interests. Empirical–analytic sciences are constituted by, and hence presuppose, the "technical" interest, which aims at the instrumental control of natural and social processes and which therefore cannot be considered ethically neutral. More generally, positivism's objectivism, by implying that empirical knowledge is objective, neutral, and rational, misrepresents and mystifies socially created, historically specific phenomena as natural, eternal, and unalterable. Critical theory and historical materialism see these features of positivism as contributing to a false conception of a false reality and therefore working to conceal, if not reinforce, the dominative, repressive, and exploitative nature of an historical system, such as capitalism.

In a similar vein, critique finds the concerns of historical hermeneutics uncritical of the content of its object of inquiry. Gadamer's (1975b, 1980) ontologization of language and naturalization of tradition and authority serve to legitimate the critical components in the understanding of meaning, thereby concealing or mystifying structural features of social control, domination, and power asymmetry (Habermas, 1970a). Thus,

> tradition, as a context that includes the system of work and domination, enables as well as restricts the parameters within which we define our needs and interact in order to satisfy them. That socio-historical processes should occur over the heads and even behind the backs of those carrying them, who may systematically be unable to give an accurate account of their individual actions and the motivations underlying them, points to an approach to social phenomena which transcends the scope of merely meaning-interpretive investigations. (Bleicher, 1980, p.156)

The critique of historical hermeneutics points to its exclusive concern with the self-understanding of social agents. By excluding any consideration of the possibility of self-misunderstanding, ideology, and domination, it legitimates the status quo and precludes the possibility of critical self-reflection.

Thus critique presupposes criteria for distinguishing truth from falsity, without which the very notion of ideology becomes meaningless and at least two types of pernicious consequences follow:

> First, we can no longer hope for a critical understanding of our interests since we lose the ability to distinguish true interests . . . from expressed preferences. Second, in the absence of such distinctions, prevailing power relations become the ultimate arbiters of interests. (Habermas, 1976b)

A critical theory sees ideology as acting to conceal the essential aspects of a sociopolitical reality, such concealment not being accidental (in the sense of errors) but relating systematically to some set of social, psychological, and cognitive interests within a determinate historical context. Hence, because ideologies relate systematically to interests and historical realities, they can be criticized so as to provide knowledge about those interests and realities.

This implies that it is possible and necessary to develop a defensible theory of truth that underwrites both explanation and evaluation of ideologies, as in Freud's "id–ego–superego" construct or in Marx's concept of "mode of production." Related to this is the view that a theory of truth must somehow provide a conception of reason and rational action in terms of which certain forms of consciousness can be said to be ideological and judged to be irrational.

This implication poses a serious difficulty to critique in terms of the problem of truth-claim validation—the problem of how to provide standards to which the critique of ideology can refer in order to legitimize its procedure and justify its claims (Bleicher, 1980). Because critique seeks the true meaning of an ideology in relation to an historical context, it lacks the grounds on which to assert *a priori* criteria of its own truth. It must consider its own truth, in the same way as the inverted truth of ideology, as historically conditioned. The way out of this difficulty is that

> because critique cannot develop formal, *a priori* criteria of what counts as ideology, the strength of a critical theory lies not in a body of theoretical statements from which empirical states of affairs might be inferred, but in a theory-dependent method that guides research into the meaning of a form of consciousness by relating it to its context of interests and realities.

The philosophical implications are that

> in order that critical theory not undermine its own claim to a relative rationality, it must criticise a form of consciousness "immanently." That is, criticism gains its right to impute ideological meanings to a text insofar as the text is irrational with regard to its own criteria of adequacy. (Warren, 1984, p.542)

The implication in programmatic terms for theory and practice is that three functions are necessary for critique (Habermas, 1973): first, the formulation and exposition of critical theories (such as Marx's historical materialism and Habermas's theory of communicative competence); second, the validation of critical theory through processes of critical self-reflection by those (targeted) social actors in need of enlightenment (using, for instance, models based on psychoanalysis); and third, the selection of appropriate strategies aimed ultimately at the progressive realization of universal enlightenment and emancipation (cf. Jackson, 1985a).

SYSTEMS METHODOLOGIES

In this section, the nature of systems methodologies is summarized in relation to their methodological foundations. Criteria for choice of specific systems methodologies are then discussed in terms of Jackson and Keys' (1984) and Banathy's (1987) formulations. The section concludes with a cautionary note in the interest of those who might forget the very contingent nature of some of the methodological implications arising from those formulations and recommendations.

The Nature of Systems Methodologies

In a comprehensive and critical analysis of systems methodological approaches, Jackson (1982, 1983, 1985a, b, 1987a) and Jackson and Keys (1984) have recently classified those methodologies within the Habermasian frame-work. Briefly, the functionalist paradigm and its empiricist methodology underwrite the "hard" systems methodologies, which include (i) the positivist approaches—classical operations research, systems engineering, and systems analysis (e.g. Hall, 1962; Jenkins, 1964); and (ii) the structuralist approaches— organizational cybernetics, general systems theory, sociotechnical systems, and modern contingency theory (e.g. Beer, 1979, 1981; Miller, 1978). The interpretive paradigm and its hermeneutic methodology underwrite the "soft" systems methodologies, which include Churchman's (1971, 1979) dialectical inquiring systems approach and its development into strategic assumption surfacing and testing, Ackoff's (1981) interactive planning, and Checkland's (1981) soft systems methodology. Unfortunately, the radical/critical methodologies have not as yet significantly broken into the intellectual market of systems thinking to establish a distinctive and recognized approach. There are, however, three parallel developments taking place. The first is the emergence of a few writers critical of the present conservative orthodoxy of both hard and soft systems approaches. The second is the emergence of a small but growing number of voices explicitly "crusading" for critical systems thinking. Examples of both these developments include, for instance, the work of Bryer (1979), Hales (1974), Jackson (1982, 1983, 1985a, b, 1987a), Jackson and Keys (1984), Mingers (1980), Oliga (1986a, b, c, 1987a, b), Rosenhead (1982), Rosenhead and Thunhurst (1982), Spear (1987), Thomas (1980), Thomas and Lockett (1979), Tinker and Lowe (1984), Whitley (1974), and Wood and Kelly (1978) and the critical papers presented at the "Interdisciplinary Perspectives on Accounting" conference, University of Manchester, July 1985. The third and perhaps most significant development relates to the emergence of actual attempts to apply critical theory to real-world situations, such as involvement with work on social movements (Touraine, 1981; Melucci, 1985), the Open University's Cooperative Research Unit's involvement with work on worker cooperative organizations and democratic social management (Spear, 1987), the establishment of a Centre for Community Operational Research at the Department of Managment Systems and Sciences, University of Hull (Jackson, 1987b), and critical field research on the problem of organizational control (Oliga, 1986b).

In the foregoing classification, the soft systems methodologies have been shown to be underwritten by the interpretive methodological foundations, but without making the very important distinction between the "naturalistic" methodology and the historical hermeneutic methodology. If we turn to Jayaratna's (1986) detailed analysis in his "NIMSAD" framework, soft systems methodologies appear to involve, at almost every stage of analysis, the joint participation and dialogical processes of understanding between analyst and client. This would point to an historical hermeneutic foundation.

However, there are certain features of soft systems thinking that are equally compelling in seeing them as essentially informed by the assumptions and concerns of the naturalistic (interpretive) methodology. The processes of understanding and interpretation seem to be seen as activities essentially directed at recovering and reconciling the client's multiple diverse and conflicting values, perceptions and definitions of systems problems or "messes."

Thus, as Jackson (1985) notes, Churchman, Ackoff and Checkland all pursue a validation approach for their methods on the basis of "respect for the point of view and aims of all the stakeholders affected by the intervention." No social systems change can be justified except through the process of "open debate in which concerned actors achieve a consensus about the nature of their objectives and the changes they wish to bring about in the social system." Thus, as Jackson elaborates, Ackoff considers a researcher rational if his models bring about improvements in the clients' performance, but "by their own criteria." Checkland's methodology requires that improvements emerge in terms of feasible and desirable changes as perceived "by those involved in the problem-situation." Churchman advocates the need for the analyst to respect different points of view concerning goals to be attained; seeing the world "through the eyes of another" marks the start of a systems approach. Implicit in all these views is the naturalistic assumption that the possibility of an independent observer (analyst) arriving at "objective" knowledge of his/her clients' *Weltanschauungen* or "appreciative systems" is largely unproblematic. It is this possibility that historical hermeneutics denies.

Choice of Systems Methodologies

Although the methodological domain of critique, and arguably of historical hermeneutics, remains at present largely barren in systems science in general, and in managment science in particular, those of empiricism and naturalistic hermeneutics have, since the 1970s, witnessed a vigorous development in the variety of types of specific methodologies. The need to understand the nature of this development has prompted a number of competing interpretations. Was it, as Dando and Bennett (1981) argue, a sign of competing "paradigms" and hence the making of a "Kuhnian crisis"? Or was it, as Checkland (1983, 1985) and Jackson (1987a) have more persuasively argued, more a sign of increasing competence and effectiveness in dealing with different concerns of management science and problem situations. In this sense, while soft systems methodologies take as central the problem of resolving conflicting *Weltan-schauungen* in the interest of achieving a consensus over objectives, the hard systems methodologies presuppose the successful "dissolution" of that problem. As such, hard systems thinking reduces to a special case of the soft systems thinking, appropriate only in those problem situations where the presumption of consensus is unquestionable. It is this complementarist rather than substitutionist view of diverse systems methodologies that has provided a point of departure for the current systems work as well as debate on what criteria might guide methodological choice.

In discussing the choice of such criteria, it becomes understandable that the current work in that area, especially that by Banathy (1987) and Jackson and Keys (1984), should take a contingency approach. In the case of Banathy, the appropriateness of a particular methodology (or its "goodness of fit") is posited as being dependent upon four dimensions of the (design) inquiry: the system type, the nature of the design inquiry, the characteristics of the design problem situation, and the functional context of the design situation. Of these dimensions the system type is perhaps the most important. On the basis of four continua (closed versus open, mechanistic versus systemic, unitary versus pluralist, and restricted versus complex), Banathy constructs a model that displays five major systems types—rigidly controlled (at one end of the continua), deterministic, purposive, heuristic, and purpose seeking (at the other extreme). Corresponding to each system type are specific system methodologies that are judged to display the best fit (see Table 8.2).

Jackson and Keys, however, predicate the appropriateness of different methodologies not on system types as such, but on the nature of different problem contexts. As we see later, there is an important difference between the two criteria of methodological choice. On the basis of differences between types of systems (mechanical versus systemic) *and* (perhaps more crucially) the nature of the relationship between participants (unitary, pluralist, or coercive), Jackson and Keys identify six categories of problem contexts: mechanical–unitary, systemic–unitary, mechanical–pluralist, systemic–pluralist, mechanical–coercive, and systemic–coercive. The six problem contexts imply the need for six types of problem-solving methodologies, as summarized in Table 8.2, where an attempt has been made to superimpose Banathy's schema upon that of Jackson and Keys. As discussed earlier, the emerging picture is that of the glaring poverty of systems thinking in critical methodological terms.

Methodological Choice: A Cautionary Comment

The contingency approach used by both Jackson and Keys (1984) and Banathy (1987) in developing their criteria for methodological choice is highly persuasive. But there is a danger in, for instance, beginning to take Banathy's system types as structurally given, as entities that have an existence and meaning independent of those concerned with solving the problem at hand. Indeed, this impression is likely to be gained from, for instance, Banathy's examples of system types—Are problems of government bureaucracies, small business, and industry typically deterministic in nature? Is it the system type as such or the nature of the problematic issues that is of crucial importance?

It is in that sense that the Jackson and Keys' choice criteria, which focus on problem contexts rather than system types, are less likely to lead to similar dangers. They emphasize that problem contexts are formed from the perceptions and interactions of participants, both actors inside the system and relevant observers outside. Problem contexts are not objective features of the

Table 8.2 Problem contexts and systems methodologies—adapted from Jackson and Keys (1984) and using the schema, in parentheses, of Banathy (1987)

Participants' relationship	Systems type	
	Mechanical	Systemic
Coercive	Mechanical–coercive Methodologies yet to emerge	Systemic–coercive Methodologies yet to emerge
Pluralist	Mechanical–pluralist (heuristic) Methodologies 1. Dialectical inquiring systems, e.g. SAST 2. (Double-loop organizational learning)	Systemic–pluralist (purpose seeking) Methodologies 1. Interactive planning 2. Checkland's soft systems methodology
Unitary	Mechanical–unitary (rigidly controlled) (deterministic) Methodologies 1. Classical OR 2. Systems engineering 3. Systems analysis 4. (Living systems process analysis) 5. (Management cybernetics)	Systemic–unitary (purposive) Methodologies 1. Organizational cybernetics 2. Sociotechnical systems thinking 3. General systems theory 4. Modern contingency theory 5. (Living systems process analysis) 6. (Systems design)

real world (Jackson, 1987a). As such, an overreliance on the analyst's own definition and construction of a model of the problematic situation may be questionable.

The comments so far have focused on the nature of the contingent or explanatory variables. Further issues of interest might be concerned with, for instance, the clarity with which those variables or dimensions have been defined. Flood and Carson (1988) and Ellis and Flood (1987) have, for instance, noted that the perception of a traditional management scientist may be that he/she was working not in a "machine age" but in a "systems age." Also, there is the possibility that there may exist reciprocal interdependencies among contingent dimensions, thus rendering the influence of a specified dimension upon the appropriateness of a particular systems methodology difficult to understand. As Flood and co-workers argue, this is the context in which the soft systems thinkers might question the validity of a problem-context contingency, with its implied idea of "structured" problem situations. Even the die-hard structuralist proponents (hard system thinkers) might find difficulty in discriminating between different problem contexts.

It is not within the scope of this paper to debate these issues further. However, at a more general level, the contingency framework, although very valuable, also needs to be treated with care. Contingency formulations tend to focus almost exclusively upon the contingent relationships, taking, by default, the variables (or dimensions) themselves as unproblematic, in the sense of *not* questioning how they arose and why they came to be what they are. This failure to problematize the origins of posited contingent dimensions can easily lead to the unfortunate tendency to "naturalize" those dimensions as inevitable and unalterable, thereby reducing the inquiry and problem-solving tasks to one of merely correctly pigeonholing unquestioned methodologies to their appropriate (but unquestioned) system types or problem contexts (cf. Flood and Carson, 1988; Ellis and Flood, 1987). If this happened, the insightful, methodological work done by Jackson and Keys, Checkland, Banathy, and others might, especially for practising managers, degenerate into simply a mechanical, non-reflective "do-it-yourself" game of contingency match-making. Thus, the need for a critical, self-reflective approach to the whole question of methodological choice seems inescapable.

CONCLUSION

Current usage, particularly in the literature of systems science, identifies little, if any, difference between method and methodology. An attempt was made here to show that the distinction is epistemologically significant if one does not assume an ontological unity for all the objects of the universe.

Using Habermas' interest constitution theory, the paper elaborates on three methodological foundations (empiricism, hermeneutics, and critique) for social inquiry and problem-solving in general, unfolding in the process a hierarchy of epistemological criticisms. "Naturalistic" hermeneutics finds the empiricist doctrine of ontological unity untenable in relation to the social world. Historical hermeneutics finds the "objectivist" aspirations of naturalistic hermeneutics unattainable. Critique finds the historical naturalization of tradition, authority, and language ideological.

In systems science, it is seen that the basic underwriting assumptions and concerns for the presently established systems methodologies have not "developed" beyond those of empiricism and naturalistic hermeneutics. Such a situation points to the glaring poverty of current systems thinking in relation to both historical hermeneutics and critical methodology. But even leaving this "underdevelopment" aside, the existence of a variety of both "hard" and "soft" systems methodologies poses its own problem—the question of appropriate criteria for methodological choice. Two important contributions, among others, are discussed: one by Jackson and Keys, and their extension of Checkland's complementarist perspective, and the other by Banathy. Both are seen to be informed by a contingency-theory perspective, a valuable framework that provides important insights as well as the basic message that the validity or appropriateness of a specific methodology is crucially dependent on the nature of the problem situation under consideration. However, given the persuasive and potentially influential nature of those contingency formulations, the paper points to the need for a cautious approach. It is important to avoid the temptation to "naturalize" the so-called contingency dimensions into inevitable, unalterable structural features of social life.

REFERENCES

Ackoff, R.L. (1981). *Creating the Corporate Future*, John Wiley, New York.
Apel, K.O. (1967). *Analytic Philosophy of Language and the Geistewissenschaften*, D. Reidel, Dordrecht, The Netherlands.
Apel, K.O. (1971). *Hermeneutik and Ideologiekritik*, Suhrkamp, Frankfurt.
Apel, K.O. (1980). *Towards a Transformation of Philosophy*, Routledge and Kegan Paul, London.
Banathy, B. (1984). *Systems Design in the Context of Human Activity Systems*, International Systems Institute, San Fransisco.
Banathy, B. (1986). The design of design inquiry, in *Mental Images, Values and Reality* (Ed. J.A. Dillon Jr.), Society for General Systems Research, Louisville, Ky.
Banathy, B. (1987). Choosing design methods, in *Proceedings of the 31st Annual Meeting of the International Society for General Systems Research*, pp. 54–63, Budapest, Hungary.
Bauman, Z. (1978). *Hermeneutics and Social Science*, Hutchinson, London.
Beer, S. (1979). *The Heart of the Enterprise*, John Wiley, New York.
Beer, S. (1981). *Brain of the Firm*, John Wiley, New York.
Betti, E. (1955), in *Teoria Generale della Interpretazione* (Ed. D.A. Giuffre), Instituto di Teoria della Interpretazione, Milan. (Translated (1967) as *Allgemeine Auslegungslehre als Methodik der Geistewissenschaften*, Mohr, Tübingen, JCB.)
Betti, E. (1962). *Die Hermeneutik als Allgemeine Methode der Geistewissenschaften*, Mohr, Tubingen, JCB. (Translated (1980) in Bleicher, J. (1980), as *Hermeneutics as the general methodology of the Geistewissenschaften*, pp. 51–94).
Beyleveld, D. (1975). *Epistemological Foundations of Sociological Theory*, Ph.D. dissertation, University of East Anglia.
Bhaskar, R. (1979). *The Possibility of Naturalism*, Humanities, Hassocks, England.
Bleicher, J. (1980). *Contemporary Hermeneutics: Hermeneutics as Method, Philosophy, and Critique*, Routledge and Kegan Paul, London.
Blumer, H. (1969). *Symbolic Interactionism*, Prentice-Hall, Englewood Cliffs, NJ.
Bryer, R.A. (1979). The status of the systems approach, *Omega*, 7, 219–231.
Burrell, G., and Morgan, G. (1979). *Sociological Paradigms and Organizational Analysis*, Heinemann, London.
Checkland, P.B. (1981). *Systems Thinking, Systems Practice*, John Wiley, Chichester.
Checkland, P.B. (1983). OR and the systems movement: mappings and conflicts, *J. Opl Res. Soc.*, 34, 661–675.
Checkland, P.B. (1985). From optimising to learning: a development of systems thinking for the 1990s, Chapter 3 in this book.
Christenson, C. (1983). The methodology of positivist accounting, *Account. Rev.*, 58 1–22.
Chua. W.F., Laughlin, R.C., Lowe, E.A., and Puxty, A.G. (1981). Four perspectives on accounting methodology, paper presented at *The Workshop on Accounting and Methodology*, EIASM, Brussels.

Churchman, C.W. (1971). *The Design of Inquiring Systems*, Basic Books, New York.
Churchman, C.W. (1979). *The Systems Approach and Its Enemies*, Basic Books, New York.
Cohen, P.S. (1968). *Modern Social Theory*, Heinemann, London.
Dahrendorf, R. (1967). *Class and Class Conflict in an Industrial Society*, Routledge and Kegan Paul, London.
Dando, M.R., and Bennett, P.G. (1981). A Kuhnian crisis in managment science?. *J. Opl Res. Soc.*, **32**, 91–102.
Denzin, N.K. (1970). Symbolic interactionism and ethnomethodology, in *Understanding Everyday Life* (Ed. J.D. Douglas), Routledge and Kegan Paul, London.
Dilthey, W. (1976). In Rickman, H.P. (Ed.), *Selected Writings*, Cambridge University Press, London.
Ellis, R.K., and Flood, R.L. (1987). Managing technological change: systems theory or systems technology?, in *Proceedings of the 31st Annual Meeting of the International Society for General Systems Research*, pp. 270–277, Budapest, Hungary.
Fay, B. (1975). *Social Theory and Political Practice*, Allen and Unwin, London.
Flood, R.L., and Carson, E.R. (1988). *Dealing with Complexity: An Introduction to the Theory and Application of Systems Science*, Plenum, New York.
Friedman, M. (1953). *Essays in Positive Economics*, University of Chicago, Chicago.
Gadamer, H.G. (1975a). Hermeneutics and social science, *Cult. Hermeneut.*, **2** (4).
Gadamer, H.G. (1975b). *Truth and Method*, Seabury, New York.
Gadamer, H.G. (1980). The universality of the hermeneutic problem. (Translated (1980) by Linge, D., in Bleicher, J. (1980), pp. 128–140.)
Garfinkel, H. (1967). *Studies in Ethnomethodology*, Prentice-Hall, Englewood Cliffs, NJ.
Giddens, A. (1976). *New Rules of Sociological Method*, Hutchinson, London.
Giddens, A. (1977). *Studies in Social and Political Theory*, Hutchinson, London.
Gould, J., and Kolb, W.F. (Eds) (1964). *A Dictionary of the Social Sciences*, Tavistock, London.
Habermas, J. (1970a) On systematically distorted communication, *Inquiry*, **13**, 205–218.
Habermas, J. (1970b). Towards a theory of communicative competence, *Inquiry*, **13**, 360–375.
Habermas, J. (1971). *Der Universalitatsanspruch der Hermeneutik*. (Translated in Bleicher, J. (1980), as The hermeneutic claim to universality, pp. 181–211.)
Habermas, J. (1972). *Knowledge and Human Interests*, Heinemann, London.
Habermas, J. (1973). *Theory and Practice*, Beacon, Boston.
Habermas, J. (1976a). A positivistically bisected rationalism, in *The Positivist Dispute in German Sociology* (Eds G. Adey and D. Frisby), pp. 198–225, Heinemann, London.
Habermas, J. (1976b). The analytic theory of science and dialectics, in *The Positivist Dispute in German Sociology* (Eds. T.W. Adorno *et al.*), Harper Torchbooks, New York.
Habermas, J. (1979). What is universal pragmatics?, in *Communication and the Evolution of Society* (translated by T. McCarthy), pp. 1–68, Heinemann, London.
Hales, M. (1974). Management science and the "Second Industrial Revolution.", *Radical Sci. J.*, **1**, 5–28.
Hall, A.D. (1962). *A Methodology for Systems Engineering*, Van Nostrand, New York.
Heidegger, M. (1962). *Being and Time*, Harper and Row, New York.
Heidegger, M. (1966). *Discourse on Thinking*, Harper and Row, New York.
Horkheimer, M. (1972). *Critical Theory* (translated by M. O'Connell *et al.*), Herder and Herder, New York.
Jackson, M.C. (1982). The nature of soft systems thinking: the work of Churchman, Ackoff and Checkland, *J. Appl. Syst. Anal.*, **9**, 17–28.

Jackson, M.C. (1983). The nature of soft systems thinking: comment on the three replies, *J. Appl. Syst. Anal.*, **10**, 109–113.

Jackson, M.C. (1985a). Social systems theory and practice: the need for a critical approach, Chapter 6 this volume.

Jackson, M.C. (1985b). Systems inquiring competence and organisational analysis, in *Proceedings of the 1985 Meeting of the Society for General Systems Research*, Louisville, Ky.

Jackson, M.C. (1987a). New directions in management science, in *New Directions in Management Science* (Eds M.C. Jackson and P. Keys), Gower, Aldershot, England.

Jackson, M.C. (1987b). Creating a "Centre for Community Operational Research" at Hull University, UK, in *Proceedings of the 31st Annual Meeting of the International Society for General Systems Research*, pp. 513–519, Budapest, Hungary.

Jackson, M.C., and Keys, P. (1984). Towards a system of systems methodologies, Chapter 7 this volume.

Jayaratna, N. (1986). Normative information model-based systems analysis and design (NIMSAD): a framework for understanding and evaluating methodologies, *J. Appl. Syst. Anal.*, **13**, 73–87.

Jenkins, G.M. (1964). The systems approach, in *Systems Behaviour*, 2nd edition (Eds J. Beishon and G. Peters), pp. 78–104, Open University Press, London.

Keat, R.N. (1981). *The Politics of Social Theory: Habermas, Freud and the Critique of Positivism*, Basil Blackwell, Oxford.

Laughlin, R.C., Lowe, E.A., Puxty, A.G., and Chua, W.F. (1981). The function of subject makers in the epistemology and methodology of accounting, paper presented to the *Annual Conference of the Association of University Teachers in Accounting*, Dundee, Scotland.

Lockwood, D. (1956). Some remarks on the "social system", *B.J.S.*, **7**, 134–143.

Marcuse, H. (1964). *One Dimensional Man: Studies in the Ideology of Advanced Industrial Societies*, Routledge and Kegan Paul, London.

Marcuse, H. (1968). *Negations*, Penguin Press, Harmondsworth.

Mattessich, R. (1978). *Instrumental Reasoning and Systems Methodology: An Epistemology of the Applied and Social Sciences*, D. Reidel, Dordrecht, The Netherlands.

Melucci, A. (1985). The symbolic challenge of contemporary movements, *Soc. Res.*, **52**, 789–816.

Miller J.G. (1978). *Living Systems*, McGraw Hill, New York.

Mingers, J.C. (1980). Towards an appropriate social theory for applied systems thinking: critical theory and soft systems methodology, *J. Appl. Syst. Anal.*, **7**, 41–49.

Morgan, G. (1980). Paradigms, metaphors, and puzzle-solving in organisational theory, *Admin. Sci. Q.*, **25**, 605–622.

Morgan, G. (Ed.) (1983). *Beyond Method: Strategies for Social Research*, Sage, London.

Morgan, G., and Smircich, L. (1980). The case for qualitative research, *Acad. Mgmt Rev.*, **5**, 491–500.

Oliga, J.C. (1986a). Methodology in systems research: the need for a self-reflective commitment, in *Mental Images, Values, and Reality* (Ed. J.A. Dillon, Jr.), Society for General Systems Research, Louisville, Ky.

Oliga, J.C. (1986b). World economic recession: contradictions in the development of societal systems, in *Mental Images, Values, and Reality* (Ed. J.A. Dillon, Jr.), Society for General Systems Research, Louisville, Ky.

Oliga, J.C. (1986c). Accounting and cybernetic control in human activity systems: contradiction or a coherent system of values and images of social order?, in *Mental Images, Values, and Reality* (Ed. J.A. Dillon, Jr.), Society for General Systems Research, Louisville, Ky.

Oliga, J.C. (1987a). Control, systems stability and social change. The architecture of power and ideology, in *Proceedings (Supplement) of the 31st Annual Meeting of the International Society for General Systems Research*, Budapest, Hungary.

Oliga, J.C (1987b). The quantitative vs behavioural aspects of management accounting: wings of dichotomy or dialectic?, in *Proceedings (Supplement) of the 31st Annual Meeting of the International Society for General Systems Research*, Budapest, Hungary.

Popper, K.R. (1959). *The Logic of Scientific Discovery*, Basic Books, New York.

Puxty, A.G., Soo, W.F., Lowe, E.A., and Laughlin, R.C. (1980). Towards a critical–theoretic perspective for an epistemology of managerial theory, in *Proceedings of the Workshop "Towards an Epistemology of Management Research,"* Stockholm School of Economics, Stockholm.

Rosenhead, J. (1982). Why does management need management science?, in *A General Survey of Systems Methodology* (Ed. L. Troncale), Society for General Systems Research, Louisville, Ky.

Rosenhead, J., and Thunhurst C. (1982). A materialist analysis of operational research, *J. Opl Res. Soc.*, **33**, 111–122.

Samuelson, P.A. (1962). Problems of the American Economy, Stamp Memorial Lecture.

Schutz, A. (1967). *The Phenomenology of the Social World* (translated by G. Walsh, and F. Lehnert), Northwestern University Press, Evanston, Ill.

Spear R. (1987). Towards a critical systems approach, in *Proceedings (Supplement) of the 31st Annual Meeting of the International Society for General Systems Research*, Budapest, Hungary.

Thomas, A. (1980). Generating tension for constructive change: the use and abuse of systems models, *Cybernet. Syst.*, **11**, 339–353.

Thomas, A.R., and Lockett, M. (1979). Marxism and systems research: values in practical action, Chapter 4 in this book.

Tinker, A.M., and Lowe, E. A. (1984). One dimensional management science: the making of a technocratic consciousness, *Interfaces*, **14**, 40–49.

Touraine, A. (1981). *The Voice and the Eye: An Analysis of Social Movements*, Cambridge University Press, Cambridge.

Warren, M. (1984). Nietzsche's concept of ideology, *Theory Soc.*, **13**, 541–565.

Weber, M. (1949). *The Methodology of Social Sciences*, Free Press, Glencoe, Ill.

Whitley, R.D. (1974). Management research: the study and improvement of forms of co-operation in changing socio-economic structures, in *Information Sources in the Social Sciences* (Ed. N. Roberts), Butterworths, London.

Wood, S., and Kelly, J. (1978). Towards a critical management science, *J. Mgmt Stud.*, **15**, 1–12.

Zimmerman, D.H., and Wieder, D.L. (1970). Ethnomethodology and the problem of order, in *Understanding Everyday Life* (Ed. J.D. Douglas), Routledge and Kegan Paul, London.

Chapter 9

Testament to Conversations on Critical Systems Thinking Between Two Systems Practitioners[1]

ROBERT L. FLOOD AND WERNER ULRICH

INTRODUCTION

The systems view has often been misunderstood to "embrace all in its outlook." Now it is certainly true that comprehensiveness is in fact an ideal of systems thinking, but from an epistemological point of view this ideal is in need of careful qualification. If epistemology is "reflection on the gaining and disseminating of knowledge and on the validity of that knowledge," then the epistemological ideal of classical comprehensive rationalism would require systems thinkers "to know everything and know it is valid." This is evidently impossible. Such an ideal does not even have a "regulative function" for system thinking because it tells us absolutely nothing about how to deal with our inescapable lack of comprehensive knowledge and understanding.

The call, as will be understood more clearly later, is for a switch in emphasis from "*systems science*" to "*systems rationality*," systems science referring to a conventional understanding of what systems scientists do (explained, among other things, in Flood and Carson's (1988) eclectic work) and systems rational-

---

[1] Conversations were held in Berne and Fribourg, Switzerland, between 30 November and 5 December 1988.

Reprinted by permission from *Systems Practice*, Volume 3, 1990

ity referring to a critical (Kantian) rather than an untenable pre-Kantian understanding of rationality. More specifically, by systems science we mean any effort to employ a systemic outlook in doing basic or applied science according to the conventional ideals of non-reflective positivist empirical–analytical rationality (objective data, testable hypotheses, valid modelling, and so on), whereas by systems rationality we mean an ideal that may orient applied inquiry toward a critically rational social practice *in the face of incomplete knowledge and understanding*.

We propose that an appropriate epistemological ideal for systems thinkers is not the systems–scientific ideal but must be sought *through* the critical idea of systems rationality, *by giving back to the systems idea its originally critical sense* (as forwarded by Immanuel Kant and reconstructed by Ulrich (1983)). Unfortunately, the critical intent of the systems idea has been almost completely lost in contemporary systems science, said to have originated in the 1940s with Bertalanffy's (e.g., 1968) abstract ontological conceptualization of General Systems Theory. This historical reflection today translates into what we would like to designate a *call for a second epistemological break* toward a critical approach in systems thinking (Flood, 1990b). The *first epistemological break* in our understanding is marked by Checkland's (e.g., 1981) moving away from instrumental control of positivist approaches towards a mutual understanding through interpretivist systems thinking and is characterized by a routing attack on modern systems science. Consequences of interpretivism are that systems thinking must free itself from dominance by scientism with its roots in ontological realism.

The second epistemological break, that we support, builds onto the achievements of the first and thus should be seen as an advancement on that line of thinking. Consequences of this critically normative systems thinking are that the two knowledge-constitutive interests in instrumental control (positivism) and in mutual understanding (interpretivism) need to be complemented (and reflected upon) in terms of an emancipatory interest in enlightenment and liberation of people from domination by people or machines, by false consciousness or by whatever conditions which prevent people from truly realizing their potential as individuals.

We will find, therefore, that such a "truly" critical systems thinking cannot "merely" reflect against a backboard of a systems epistemological ideal as sketched out earlier in terms of just systems rationality. Further issues of sociological epistemology are equally important. We believe, in fact, that this is an exceptional point which demands that we find a way of pursuing and somehow bringing these together (i.e. sociological and systems epistemologies) through an epistemological ideal of critical rationality. Witness a first attempt at this below.

We wish to develop an expression of an *adequate epistemological ideal for social inquiry*. This we shall do by linking "our" difficulty with the "problem of metaphysics." We therefore propose to introduce the difficulty in question as one that is "equivalent" to the "classical philosophical problem of (inevitable) metaphysics."

Metaphysics refers to our theories (conceptions or understandings) of social reality, which always go beyond that which the empirical (the phenomenal surface reality that we can observe) apparently tells us. But we need to remind ourselves continually that the difficulty in question not only is (or even primarily) one of theoretical explanation (via concepts and understanding) but is also (or rather) one of taking into account and justifying the normative assumptions flowing into our theories of social reality. These *normative assumptions* concern, for example, "political" issues such as assumptions about the "right" distribution of power but may be complicated by the possibility of "false consciousness' and "effects of material conditions." These are likely to produce genuine conflicts of world views and interests and may lead to coercive conditions.

Ulrich (1983) has suggested that we use the term *social metaphysics* (finding Kant's metaphysics of experience inadequate to social inquiry in terms of social theory and systems practice) in order to help us to appreciate these very relevant concerns. Social metaphysics can be explained as the totality of relative *a priori* judgments that flow into social theories or designs but cannot be validated either empirically or logically.

Now this is helpful because we can clearly see the need for a critical approach, in the precise sense of a politically conscious or self-reflective approach, distinguished by an *openly declared* emancipatory interest in an equal distribution of power and chances to satisfy personal needs and in liberating people from dominance by other people (see Flood (1990a) for a "manifesto" on Liberating Systems Theory in terms of discursive and non-discursive practices). So we now need only one small conceptual step to realize the earlier stated desire that *our* concern with sociological epistemology must also deal with systems rationality. In other words we propose a *dialectical approach* to the problem of practical discourse. This should occur between those claiming the *whole systems rationality* of some design (i.e. of its normative implications) and those bearing witness to the *life-practical irrationality* of the designs in question. Hegelian (or Churchmanian) dialectics, working in an adversarial mode, is complementary to our desire for practical discourse between "a rationality" and "an irrationality." This amounts to our adequate epistemological ideal for social inquiry.

At last we have some regulative and methodologically directive ideas. Let us not be mistaken, however, by concluding that critique should be distinguished from other main areas of social theory (i.e. positivism and interpretivism). Being critical is not a quality of a certain position or approach; rather it is the quality of remaining self-reflective *with respect to* particular and all positions or approaches. This tells us that every conceivable approach to systems thinking *can be dealt with* by a critical handling of its inevitable limitations.

In these systems and sociological terms we conclude over the course of this conversation that:

1. *non-reflective positivist approaches*, by denying the relevance of social metaphysics, inevitably deny subjectivity and the notion of "whole systems rationality" and are *epistemologically untenable* (hence the need for a first epistemological break);

2. *Non-reflective interpretivist approaches*, despite recognizing the inevitability of social metaphysics and in this way *moving toward* an adequate epistemological ideal for social inquiry, sidestep sociological issues of critical significance such as "effects of material conditions" and the possibility of "false consciousness" and therefore have an *impoverished epistemology* (hence the need for a second epistemological break); and

3. critical, or *self-reflective*, ideas amount to an *adequate epistemological ideal* for social inquiry in terms of systems rationality, sociological epistemology, and of course systems practice.

We will therefore consider the legitimacies and limitations of these three contrasting conceptions of rationality in the spirit of Flood (1990b).

CONTRASTING CONCEPTIONS OF RATIONALITY: LEGITIMACIES AND LIMITATIONS

Introduction

Over the years there have been many attempts at reasoning out rational approaches to inquiry. Of particular interest in the social sciences, and somewhat belatedly in systems thinking, are three rationalities: positivist, interpretivist, and emancipatory theories. In one interesting critique of these three types of "science," Fay (1975) reasoned out the limitations of positivist and interpretivist rationalities and suggested why an emancipatory approach might be legitimate where the other two are not.[2] There has been vigourous debate in social theory along these lines. This is a serious matter because it then becomes all too easy to slip into an unwanted adversarial mode of reasoning, such as emancipatory approaches are legitimate while instrumental

---

[2] Brian Fay's account of this debate on types of rationality is useful in that it is relatively short and easily accessible. The reader should note, however, that the book does not (and could not, according to its aims) reach the level of sophistication of Habermas' work and does not attempt to deal with the systems debate herein. Furthermore, there is a real danger in Fay's work of conflating radical with critical. This said, we would still recommend the book as a background read to our debate.

control represents an inferior kind of inquiry. This would merely reintroduce the old prejudices such as the humanities against the natural sciences, with a value continuum marked bad on the right positivist side and good on the left emancipatory side. What we require is an approach to rational systems practice which makes plain the idea that we are dealing with complementary concepts of rationality, each of which has its place and is legitmate so long as we respect its limitations (see Ulrich's, 1988a, research program; Flood, 1989a,b; Jackson, 1990). This is an extremely important point that should stay with us throughout the following discussion lest we slip into a competitive rather than a critical mode of thinking.

We can now look carefully at three sciences/rationalities in order that we may expose some limitations and assess the legitimacies and think about the epistemological breaks which might be proffered with respect to each type. The rationalities are non-reflective positivism, non-reflective interpretivism, and critical (the last defining both a metatheoretical framework through which all rationalities may be dealt with and the fundamental ideas for emancipatory theories as such). Toward the end of this testament we summarize our findings on limitations and legitimacies in tabular form which then broadly explains the contrasting relationship among the three types of science/rationality.

On Positivist Science/Rationality

A positivist approach to science offers a traditional rationality that we can critically examine in various contexts, but in particular in our application domain we can legitimately ask, "Why should we pursue a traditional social science and what would be the consequence of this?"

Brian Fay (1975), somewhat along the lines of Habermas (1971a, b), proposed on behalf of traditional social scientists the following reasoning. The natural sciences have very effectively provided mankind with "knowledge" with which the natural environment can be controlled, making it "more hospitable and productive." This is a power based on knowledge for control. If this is so, then we might be inclined to conclude from Fay's account that it would be a reasonable suggestion to apply the same epistemological (of truth, neutrality, and objective knowledge) and methodological ideas in social contexts, discarding the notion of our needs and values in order to give us the requisite power for objectively based social control, thus making for a more certain and rewarding social environment.

If this idea of a social science sounds appealing (it does not in our or Fay's judgment), then surely we must find out how we can have a social systems science. "How can the ideas of reductionism be translated into those of holism?" The answer is simple. Generally, traditional scientific investigation promotes the identification of causal laws between variables according to *observational* properties. By "building" these into a "system"of causal laws in a clearly specified (holistic) way, we might begin to understand how phenomena are related so that by manipulation of input or internal variables, or by changing structure as defined by model parameters, future scenarios can be generated (along with a whole host of descriptive, predictive, and explanatory investigations). For example, through this, feedforward control can be imposed in order to avoid undesirable future ends by steering toward the more desirable. This would presumably make way for an optimal social environment; i.e. in this strategic means–end fashion it is possible to identify one best way to maximize (or, at worst, satisfice). Thus there would be "universally recognisable decisive solutions to particular problems" (Fay, 1975).

Now the question of theory-neutrality and value-freedom over means and ends must surface here. It is regarded by scientists of the positivist persuasion that objective and neutral decisions can be realized by determining the most efficient means to an end. "But what of ends?" Traditional science cannot inform us of what teleological goals we *ought* to be pursuing since it is fact-based. It is not possible to have neutral social goals. If we are informed of a *should* approach, then we will at least know that it is value-laden. Perhaps, then, the idea of means–end might be considered respectively as fact–value, and so the scientific approach might play an important role in determining an efficient means to a subjectively based end? But, we might ask, "Efficient in terms of what?" "Who is to say that we *should* maximize in terms of money, manpower, time, or happiness or what?" as Fay questioned. We see again that what is required to be neutral is actually value-riddled.

Simply referring the choice of efficiency criteria to the definition of ends and then hoping that, once ends have been selected decisions on means can be value-neutral, will not deal with the difficulties of value judgments.

This is so because the underlying means–end dichotomy is epistemologically untenable. Counter to what the eminent German sociologist Max Weber (1949) assumed in his decisionistic model of the relation of science (theory) to politics (practice), decisions on means cannot be kept free of normative implications by referring all value judgments as the choice of ends; for what matters is not the value judgments that an inquirer consciously makes (or not) but the life-practical consequences of his propositions (regardless of whether they concern "means" or "ends") for those affected.

It is true that Weber's intent originally was a self-critical one: he found it necessary to avow that decisions on the adequacy of ends cannot be justified scientifically but ultimately remain matters of personal faith. Weber was willing to pay this price because he hoped it would make accessible to scientific justification the selection of appropriate means for "given" ends. Once ends are chosen, he argued, decisions on means can be kept value-neutral because they only need to refer to relationships of cause–effect. What Weber apparently did not see is that in a context of applied science, propositions regarding means have not only instrumental but also life-practical consequences; and these cannot be justified *vis-à-vis* those affected by reference to theoreti-cal–instrumental knowledge of cause–effect (relating to the surface) relations, but only by demonstrating their normative acceptability to all concerned citizens. Weber's and his followers' (notably Popper) error was to conceive of (applied) social science in non-life practical terms. The implication of this for our ideal of practical reason (normative acceptability) is that it is reduced to instrumental reason (feasibility). This approach cannot therefore yield what it claims, namely, an immunization of propositions on means against value judgments. Rather, it immunizes such propositions against the critical efforts of practical reason. We must conclude that any social science, and likewise any social systems science, that adopts the means–end scheme is in danger of succumbing to positivism.[3]

A powerful argument against a positivist oriented "hard" approach to systems "problem solving" in social contexts that would be based on such theoretical premises as outlined above has been proposed by Checkland (e.g., 1981). He shows through practical considerations that the "designation of objectives (i.e. ends) is itself problematic." Notably, however, Checkland misses the opportunity to highlight the ideological implications of this positiv-ism.[4] Ideological considerations are important and concern us with issues relating to order and change, a central aspect of our attitude toward problem solving in social situations that must be explicitly addressed.

Positivist oriented traditional science,[5] according to its advocates, can tell us of the laws of social being according only to empirical relationships as derived by scientific *experts*. Once *that* structure has been identified, traditional science will go on to explain *how* it functions, but never will ask *what* value implications it has and how to assess them, for questioning is beyond the traditional scien-tific ideal of objectivity (see again Weber, 1949). But this way of avoiding value judgments often has paradoxical consequences: by not questioning structure and its functions with respect to its value content, traditional science implicitly accepts its being there *as if* it were *necessarily and naturally* that way. Proposals are therefore made in terms of continued existence. Dominant–submissive

---

[3] Checkland (1978) was probably the first systems author to recognize clearly that the means–end scheme is the common defining feature of all variations of "hard" systems thinking. Unfortunately, Checkland has never been similarly clear with respect to the fact that switching from hard to "soft" systems thinking does not automatically buy immunity from positivism. An additional step is required, that is the step from an "interpretivist" to a "critical" (critically normative) understanding of soft systems thinking (Ulrich, 1983, 1988a; the second epistomological break, Flood, 1990a, b).

[4] A neglect that more generally is evident in his work and which has serious consequences in terms of limiting possibilities for change (Flood, 1990a, b), and this is despite his "radical in principle" comments (see Checkland, 1981, p. 283).

[5] Let us here make clear that positivism is not a type or paradigm of science in its own right. No inquirer, regardless of what science is pursued, is ever immune from falling back into positivism (e.g. in the way the means–end distinction is handled). In essence, *positivism is not an approach to inquiry but a sloppy way of dealing with its assumptions and results.*

social relations tend to be accepted by positivist social science as natural and unchallengable. Hence positivism is as a rule conservative, reconciling people to any social order that is being investigated. Systems methodologies that hold a positivist rationality advocate instrumental reason in telling us how to do things, the *ought* having been "sold out" to empirically based scientific findings of *what is* (according only to surface observation or beneath the surface theory).

We proposed at the outset that it is necessary for us to "look through" our systems (scientific) models to uncover normative assumptions that are inherent in them. If this is done, then these assumptions could, *in principle*, be subject to critical reflection. This, of course, cannot be achieved with a non-reflective positivist view of the assumptions.

In summary on non-reflective positivist rationality in social contexts, we note that:

1. it does not lead to objectivity;
2. it is expert driven;
3. the systems epistemological ideal will always be ignored;
4. what is claimed is epistemologically untenable;
5. what is said is ideologically conservative; and
6. therefore what would be achieved is maintenance or strengthening of power relations.

If the non-reflective positivist view of science must be abandoned in social contexts, and we have shown that it must on epistemological grounds and believe that it should on ideological grounds, then the question will arise whether there are alternative views (or rationalities) and, if so, then "What can be determined about them epistemologically and ideologically?" "What is legitimate and what limitations are there?"

In recent systems thinking there have been two alternative views—broadly speaking, the introduction of interpretivism or of critical and emancipatory thinking. These are considered in the next two sections.

On Interpretivist Science/Rationality

In this section we consider (along the same lines as the prior section) interpretivist science and its strengths and weaknesses as a systems and a sociological epistemology and what ideological thinking is inherent in the tenets of the theory. We found Fay's (1975) framework of ideas useful here.

Interpretive social theory is concerned with situations as "defined" through action concepts (hence the need for an interpretive systems language—Flood, 1988). Understanding cannot arise merely from observation and theory (surface and beneath-the-surface material analyses of the traditional scientific approach) since the human actor will have reasons, or intentions, that "lie behind" each action (these are not material). For example, slapping someone on the back might be interpreted as a religious or an inebriated act. Mere observation is not enough to appreciate properly these actions. Deeper understanding is necessary; for example, from the above two situations we could begin by saying, well we need at least intentional and conventional action concepts. "But how can we progress beyond the descriptive/observational (surface) approach to realize an explanation for actions?" Surely it is nonsense to search for material generative mechanisms that lie beneath a material surface?"

The interpretivist moves completely away from issues of materialism and introduces the idea that a specific action concept can be transparent only in the context of a certain set of *social* rules. It is in terms of these that an actor can be said to be doing some particular thing. "Beyond" an observation, we are told, is a *set* of social rules, *a social practice*, that can be drawn upon to explain the action.

There is also a third "non-material deeper layer" that the interpretivist introduces, that of *constitutive meaning* (Table 9.1). This is the least accessible layer to the actors, for as a social practice lies behind an observation, a constitutive meaning lies behind the social practice. It is in terms of these meanings that people speak and act. In order that these meanings can be more fully appreciated, it is necessary for an actor to adopt a contrasting constitutive meaning and thus "take a look" at his/her own world view from "the outside." In this, admittedly difficult, way it is possible to "get a handle" on one's own reality.

An interpretivist social theorist is not, therefore, concerned with privileging views by asking questions such as "What is the correct action in a certain social context (typical of what a scientistic view would be)?" Rather than asking what is appropriate, an interpretivist thinker would pose the question "What makes it appropriate (surely a key question also to ask a systems practitioner about designs)?" A constitutive meaning, then, is equivalent to a world view or *Weltanschauung* that reflects *a culture's* conception of human needs and purposes.

Interpretivist rationality can more easily be seen as systemic in outlook because it helps us to "see" peoples' lives as a whole by uncovering subjectivity and by making dialogue possible where previously only suspicion and distrust "filled the air." Interpretivist rationality does this by "opening up" one's own situation to others (and *vice versa*) and by encouraging mutual understanding about what is being done and why it is being done. "Truth", is approached as communication increases, and in an ideal world, a "valid" systems intervention would require full participation of those involved (Flood and Robinson, 1989a, b).

A penetrating critic might, however, say, "Well these ideas are all 'well and

Table 9.1   Three layers of interpretive analysis: action concepts, social practice, and constitutive meaning

First level: conventional and intentional actions	Second level: social practice	Third level: constitutive meaning
What is done	Set of negotiated rules that explain what is done	Fundamental assumptions that underlie what is done and make it meaningful
Implicit reference to social practice	Implicit reference to constitutive meaning	Fundamental *a priori* assumptions
Example: Family Embracing	Generally understood rules referred to by the concept family which define embracing (e.g. to embrace involves some perceived emotional exchange of love and affection)	The family unit is something that has a particularly important role in our lives and within society[a]
Example: Market place[b] Buying and selling	Generally understood rules referred to by the concept market place which define buying and selling (e.g. to buy involves exchanging my money for someone else's goods)	It is right to exchange goods and services to maximize one's own resources; open competition is fundamentally important[c]

[a] In large sections of Western society two men embracing would come across as natural if they were family and strange if they were friends.
[b] Adapted and tabulated from Fay (1975).
[c] There are other possible constitutive meanings for the concept "market place."

good' as far as they go, but what of *material conditions*? It seems that with your subjective idealism you have forgotten to deal with the 'effects of material conditions'!"

Now we have some sympathy with "this critic" but also have some concern about how such matters might be dealt with. It is tempting to claim that there is a missing fourth layer, i.e. "What material conditions underlie constitutive meanings and what is the history of these?" This argument might continue; material conditions do inevitably affect social life since social structure will adapt to *changes* in the natural and/or technological environment. And so, following on, the social communicative world of the interpretivist is not all; it cannot be independent of the physical stage on which the actions are performed.

Our concern with such a rationality is that it is apt to produce confusion about the nature of the social reality (the "material conditions") in question.

The danger is that such a rationality sets a tightrope to walk, with a substantial danger of toppling into the positivist trap of hypostatizing (relating to an underlying substance as distinct from an interpretation or idea) "material social conditions" as if there were some kind of science that could have access to a social reality of concern. This is in distinction to other types of inquiry that content themselves with considering interpretations and ideas only. It makes no sense to distinguish, say, a "radical" as opposed to less critical kinds of inquiry in terms of ontological realism versus idealism.

The relevant distinction here must be an epistemological one, for the issue of interest is "What are the epistemological requirements that interpretive science does not meet but which are indispensable for adequately dealing with 'material conditions'?" Our answer is that the *crucial difference* is whether or not an inquirer accepts the proposition that rational justification *always* implies claims to *both* theoretical *and* practical rationality. Both a realist and an idealist can adopt a critical stance with respect to this crucial issue. Following Kant, however, critical (or "problematic" as Kant says) idealism is a much better position to depart from because realism tends to hypostatize the "real world" and hence to succumb to a fundamental objectivist illusion. Since we have no direct access to reality, we cannot know reality in all *its* pristine clarity; all reality is real to us only through our minds and all knowledge that we can have is perspective-bound and therefore selective. It is dependent on our world views, values, interests, and so on. Ulrich (1983, p.185), referring to Korzybski, explains that the fundamental and indispensable message of critical idealism is that all our knowledge is in terms of "maps" and we should never confuse the map with "objective" reality.

A critical idealist will know to avoid the danger of hypostatizing social material conditions because it is accepted that *there are no social realities a priori to constitutive meanings*. To the critical idealist it is the other way round: human intentionality is constitutive of the perception and experience of phenomena, such as power, unequal distribution of resources, social stratification, discrimination, and so on, just as it is constitutive of (subjectively) rational action.[6] Critical idealists distinguish themselves from subjectivist idealists by accepting that "out there" are some hard factual conditions that do not exist in the mind only. It is incorrect, however, for interpretivists to make accusations of positivism and hypostatization. Critical theorists depart from the assumption that we might gain some "truly" positivist direct "objective" access to describing those conditions scientifically. We can describe maps of social material reality and, the analogy suggests, a good map will lay open the perspective

---

[6] Ulrich (1983, p.236) therefore argues that "the idea of mental determinism is crucial for understanding the 'facts' of social reality in much the same way that the idea of physical determinism has been crucial for the success of the natural sciences in understanding the 'facts' of nature."

and scale it uses; but we do not distinguish ourselves from "merely interpretive" inquirers by claiming some more direct access to "the" material social world. From a critical point of view, we can claim only to provide adequate maps of "our" (or a defined client's or participant's) social reality.

This type of analysis must involve what Fay (1975) terms quasi-causal accounts of the way "certain" material conditions give rise to "certain" forms of action. "Quasi," we would argue, because the "causes" in question are the subjective acts of human intentionality—human motives, purposes, and so on, including impulses and desires not controlled by the human will—rather than the nomological laws ruling the physical world. In other words, the social communicative world of the interpretivist (of mutual understanding) does of course depend upon "material social conditions" (and should be critically recognized as such), but these conditions have a quasi-causal rather than a strictly causal importance, i.e. they condition our subjective perception of social reality (and of possible improvement) and hence can become obstacles *to mutual understanding* in need of critical reflection. This is the point rather than the fact that (of course) social reality or social practice is never independent of physical reality.

There is also a further metacomplication. Interpretivist rationality assumes that if only we could break out of our world view, our actions could be clearly seen for what they are, perceptions of actions on certain *a priori* constitutive meanings. Yet this ignores the possibility of coercive forces working against the potential for emancipation that an interpretivist view apparently offers, forces which may be designed to "freeze" the dominant constitutive meaning (freeze emancipation) by claiming, through non-transparent false means, that the situation is good or necessarily as it is. This is the case of *false consciousness* built on lies, propaganda, half-truths, and so on.

Perhaps interpretive inquiry does indeed offer hermeneutic scientists the means for uncovering "false consciousness"; for example, with respect to a historian's possibly faulty (nonauthentic) interpretation of historical documents. But it seems to us that the art of hermeneutics, thus understood, still clings to an ideal of objectivity that is unacceptable for us as applied inquirers. Hermeneutic inquiry, to the extent that it succeeds in decoding the authentic message of its subject, might claim to be "objective"; applied inquiry, however, never can. For us, there is no hermeneutic (interpretivist) "royal way" to seizing social reality objectively (much less to redesigning it), simply because there is no such thing as *the* "objective" authentic interpretation of social reality as such. As Ulrich (1983, p.64) has written,

> there is only one way in which we can claim "objectivity"—in the general sense of freedom from hidden presuppositions—for our empirical basis of rational discourse: namely, by acknowledging, in each case, the knowledge-constitutive interests on which the validity and meaning of "facts" depend. To claim objectivity for one's knowledge by referring to the objectivity of one's empirical

basis is an impossible undertaking; but to pursue the ideal of objectivity in the sense of emancipating oneself and others from the objectivist illusion is an indispensable idea.

Our conclusion must be that for the applied sciences, the ideal of objectivity translates into what Habermas (1971a) has called the "emancipatory" interest of the critical sciences.

The translation, basically, reads like this. Mutual understanding (or more generally speaking, as a hermeneutic scientist would probably prefer to say, *authentic* understanding) is a necessary but not a sufficient condition for critical applied science. Authentic understanding of each other's subjective intents is all right in that it allows rationally motivated discourse, but it does not secure by itself the "right" standards of value being applied. Authentic understanding will take the message it believes to have understood authentically as providing the "right" standard, but what about ethically reprehensible implications of the message? Clearly, following the understanding yielded by "authentic" interpretation leaves little room for discrimination, so that every viewpoint must be accepted as equally valid—otherwise, the interpretation is no longer authentic. This poses a major difficulty in terms of ways forward in practical situations since there is no critical means of directing decision making.

This last exact point can be directed at interpretive *oriented* systems practitioners such as P.B. Checkland (1981) and soft systems methodology (SSM) that he largely developed. Throughout the methodological process, as SSM has been defined, we are encouraged to work out ideal system views that are relevant to participants of a problematic situation, but there is no indication as to what might be chosen as most relevant and on what basis this choice should be made; save for the "constraints that must be met" defined by "the unique norms, values and roles of the problematic situation" (i.e. cultural feasibility as Checkland defines it).

Following another line, in an ideological sense interpretive science is implicitly conservative since the only possible way of explaining social tensions is in terms of imperfect communication between involved and affected actors. This accordingly can be corrected only at the communicative level through the promise of enhanced communication, which cannot be promoted merely by "clearing up" misunderstandings with the view that the *natural flow of discourse and order can be re-established*. The point is that a lack of authentic understanding is always involved in situations of coercion but mutual understanding alone cannot secure emancipation; critical reflection on the norms implied in that which is authentically understood can ("critical reflection" meaning to examine the justifications of conflicting norms with respect to their generalizability, thus distinguishing rational from merely factual consensus emanating from practical discourse (see Ulrich, 1983, pp.144–147)).

In summary, on non-reflective interpretive rationality in social contexts we note that:

1. it promotes the notion of subjectivity;
2. there are no explicit directives in the theory that aim to prevent the approach from being expert driven;
3. by recognizing social communicative action it takes one of several necessary steps for "reaching out" toward the systems epistemological ideal;
4. it would be epistemologically tenable in its own sociological terms if full participation was facilitated, however, because false consciousness and the "effects of material conditions" are not dealt with critically, the rationality is clearly epistemologically impoverished;
5. it may well lead to ideological conservatism; and
6. therefore there is nothing in the rationality that helps to prevent the maintenance of power relations.

Presumably, and since earlier we noted that only positive criticisms would emerge that would contribute to the development of the interpretive line of thinking, we can expect there to be an alternative sociological theory that takes on board some of the lessons drawn out above. This is the case, and the theory comes under the broad heading of critique.

On Critical Science/Rationality

We noted earlier that a "truly" critical systems approach must satisfy the two following requirements:

1. it must "reach out" toward the systems epistemological ideal in terms of "systems rationality," and
2. it must be consistent with the sociological emancipatory spirit of critique as such.

We propose that the two requirements, far from being mutually exclusive, ultimately imply each other. Whoever takes seriously the *systems epistemological ideal* cannot help but conclude that beyond the positivist (objectivist) and the interpretive (hermeneutic) ideals of science, the emancipatory force of critical self-reflection is necessary . . . critical self-reflection, that is, on the gap that will always separate the practice of inquiry from those ideals. Similarly, whoever takes seriously the *ideal of critical science*—emancipation from hidden presuppositions—will have to conclude that they cannot easily dispense of what Kant termed the "unavoidable" transcendental idea of a totality of conditions conditioning their knowledge and understanding; i.e. the systems idea.

This becomes apparent if we consider the danger that a one-sided pursuit of either requirement poses to the inquirer. The systems epistemological ideal— a critically motivated quest for comprehensiveness—in practice only too easily lends itself to uncritical claims to comprehensive rationality, neglecting the fact that we never know and understand "the whole system" (the totality of relevant conditions). On the other hand, the ideal of critique just as well lends itself to an uncritical absolutism of one's critical standpoint, for it is an impossible imperative permanently to question all one's presuppositions, including one's standards of critique; but presupposition-free critique is impossible. It seems to us that the two requirements mutually complement each other in a useful way: *"Think systems, but don't ever assume to grasp the whole!"* implies the system's inquirer's need for critical self-reflection, and *"Think critically, but don't ever allow your standards of critique to become absolute!"* implies the critical scientist's need to think beyond any particular standpoint and to look for comprehensiveness in understanding.

Ulrich's (1983) program of critical systems heuristics[7] builds on the assumption that the two requirements are both indispensable and mutually interdependent (neither can be practised without the other) for a "truly" critical systems approach. A wealth of powerful ideas on the notion of a critically understood systems epistemological ideal is contained in this program. Basically, Ulrich suggest that the key to a critical understanding of the systems idea can be found in the works of Immanuel Kant. Ulrich's modern-day reconstruction of Kant's ideas is what Flood (1990b) has termed the second epistemological break for modern systems inquiry. Systems thinking, as understood through Kant's writings, refers to the totality of relevant conditions on which theoretical or practical judgments depend, including basic methaphysical, ethical, political, and ideological *a priori* judgments. For those systems thinkers who argue that the holistic concept is of no practical significance and who are denying Kant's position, we must point out that such a systemic concept offers us a *critical ideal of reason*; i.e. we must reflect heuristically on the *unavoidable incomprehensiveness and selectivity* in every systemic definition. *Reflection*, that is, on the normative content of the *a priori* "whole systems" judgments flowing into our systems designs. And *heuristic* in that it does not attempt to ground critical reflection theoretically, but to provide a method by which presuppositions and their inevitable partiality can be kept constantly under review (Jackson, 1985).

Ulrich's work demands that we carefully reflect upon the epistemological ideal of holistic thinking, but its critical effort is directed at the *practical* goal of *understanding* why "social reality is the way it is" exactly and *"of improving it."* Both goals will require us to deal with the "effects of material conditions" and

---

[7] For brief first introductions to critical heuristics, see Ulrich (1984, 1987). Some of the underlying ideas are also summarized by Ulrich (1977, 1981a, b, 1988a, b, 1989, 1991).

false consciousness that we recognized earlier as additional to the three layers of interpretivism.

Let us now consider some critical objections that may be (and perhaps need to be) raised against such a program. For instance, it has been argued by Jackson (1985) that Ulrich's critical systems heuristics neglects the importance of material conditions because "it is critical in terms of the idealism of Kant, Hegel and Churchman but is not critical in terms of the historical materialism of Marx and the Frankfurt School of sociologists." In terms of our argument above, we must indeed *appreciate* the material conditions that shape our perception of social reality (just as our world views are constitutive of our perceptions of materials conditions). Jackson (1985) noted that Ulrich's style of critical analysis would help to point to such material conditions but could not help in the examination and explanation of the nature and development of those conditions (the possibility of Jackson slipping into hypostatizing "material social conditions" cannot be excluded according to the formulation of his words). Ulrich would reply that critical heuristics and critical theory pursue different, perhaps complementary, ends and that neither can replace the other. Habermas, for example, pursues a different *theoretical* purpose, and Ulrich a likewise difficult *practical* (heuristic) purpose; it makes little sense to dismiss either one by raising the charge of "missing" the other's "problem."

Regarding the charge of idealism, we feel it is important to understand the critical significance of Kantian idealism. Kant conceived of his idealism in terms of "problematic" or "critical" idealism, in distinction to the solipsist's extreme subjective idealism. Kant's point is not of course that the world exists only in the mind, but rather that *all our knowlege of the real world is in terms of maps, and "the map is not the territory"* (after Korzybski). That is to say, all our knowledge is perspective-bound selective, or (in Kant's terms) phenomenal only; not even the most comprehensive systems approach or any kind of "objective" theory will ever be able to change this fact. The critical idealist, unlike the realist, will always be reminded that all knowledge and understanding of the "real world" are in terms of phenomenal maps only and that a good map ought to lay open its perspective and scale, its selectivity and purposes, and should never allow itself to be taken for the territory.

Given this understanding of the basic message of critical idealism, we find it to be an indispensable part of a critical systems approach. Although we are in sympathy with Jackson's critical intentions, we feel it is not possible to identify a "truly" critical or "radical" approach in terms of ontological realism versus idealism, as Jackson's argument implies. Nor can it be identified in terms of ideological "radicalism" versus "idealism," whatever those levels may be taken to mean specifically. The point in trying to be critical is not adopting the one or the other ontological, epistemological, theoretical, or ideological position but rather to keep reflecting on the limitations and value implications of one's position in every specific context of application, *whatever that position may be*.

There also remains the question, raised by Jackson (1985), "Why should the powerful bother to take account of the views and interests of those affected but not involved?" Of course, no methodology, not even a "truly" critical systems approach, can by itself make the powerful less powerful; but this is not different from even the most radically "materialist" social theory. A more relevant point is this. As a rule, the powerful are interested in concealing, rather than laying open, their access to power (strategic action) instead of achieving won consensus (rational communicative action). They seek to conceal their specific private interests behind some facade of common interest, of generally acceptable norms or "objective necessities." A critical approach, although it cannot "force" the powerful to take account of the less powerful, can at least unveil this facade of rationality and objectivity which is so characteristic of the strategic action of powerful vested interests in present-day "interest-group liberalism" (Lowi, 1969). Thus it can deprive the powerful of what Habermas designated "the peculiar force of the better argument"—a "force" on which no individual or interest group, not even the most powerful, will renounce voluntarily.

Critical heuristics, more than any methodology or theory before, specifically addresses this issue with its unique tool of the "polemical employment of boundary judgments" (or whole system judgments); it pays careful and explicit attention not to presuppose that those in control of "decision power" are willing to take account of the views and interests of those affected, but only that they are interested in making their own views and interests appear to be defendable on rational grounds.

Let us now start to summarize our position. A critical theory is (at least partly) rooted in the felt needs and sufferings of groups of people and therefore the interpretive approach of *understanding people from their own view* is fundamentally important. This is not enough, however, since we have already recognized that social action (as expressed through action concepts, etc.) may be shaped by the "effects of material conditions" and by the possibility of false consciousness.

We wish to work toward *both* the systems and the sociological dimensions of a critical theory. It is therefore important for a critical approach to tie its knowledge claims to the ability to satisfy human purposes and desires, and thus "validity" of the theory must be judged primarily in terms of its potential for bringing about practical application and emancipation. We therefore need to build in a facility whereby practical judgments can be constantly reflected upon in transparent non-expert terms, and their partiality revealed by everyday accounts of the nature of social experience in ordinary language. Only in this way can we conceive of a theory that might be translatable into practice so that those involved and those affected can share in the heuristic and critical approach to design and decision making.

Drawing this section to a close, we wish to point out that notions of convergence, or absolutisms, should be avoided in critical studies (Flood, 1990b). For instance, it is anticritical to expect that we can work toward a view with which "we all feel comfortable" (a bounded idea promoted by several eminent "systems thinkers"), be it with the outputs of methodological activities or indeed the methodological approach itself! Contrary to this, we propose that we should remain uncomfortable. A "truly" critical approach must be open to emancipation from itself and even to calls of abolishment, as must the "output" of methodological activities. As we take our theories to the practical world of men and women, we must equally allow these practical people to bring their worlds to our systems intervention.

These ideas, we propose, form the basis of a "truly" critical system thinking of which, in summary, we note that:

1. it promotes subjectivity;
2. it is explicit about preventing the approach from being expert driven;
3. it "reaches out" toward the systems epistemological ideal by accepting the critical idealism of Kant, Hegel, and Churchman and Marx's critical ideas of historical materialism;
4. it is epistemologically tenable in both systemic and sociological terms;
5. it is explicitly ideologically emancipatory; and
6. therefore it promotes emancipation from all repressive conditions.

CONCLUSION

At the outset we called for a switch in emphasis from "systems science"—the use of systems ideas in traditional scientific practice—to "systems rationality"—a critical understanding of rationality. We suggested that a "truly" critical systems thinking cannot "merely" reflect against a background of a systems epistemological ideal in terms of systems rationality. The proposal we made was to integrate sociological and systems epistemologies through an epistemological ideal of critical rationality. This could be achieved only by dealing with the difficulties of social metaphysics—the totality of relevant *a priori* judgments that flow into social theories or systems designs but cannot be validated either empirically or logically—and by addressing normative assumptions that may be complicated by the possibility of "false consciousness" and "effects of material conditions." Three rationalities were considered in the context of these issues and aspirations—positivism, interpretivism, and critique.

Of non-reflective positivist approaches we considered the unappealing (in our view) idea of transferring ideas from the natural sciences to promote objective and neutral power for social control. This was easily shown to be epistemologically untenable because there cannot be theory-neutrality or value-freedom with the notion of means–end; i.e. we must ask what *should* be done and how it *should* be done (normative assumptions flowing into these questions are emphasized by the use of "should").

Also, since positivist approaches adopt traditional scientific rationality, then we expect similar conclusions to arise, like "what is discovered is naturally and inevitably that way"—which highlights the inherent conservative ideology of positivism.

On non-reflective interpretive approaches we found that the empirical (surface) and structuralist (beneath the surface) approaches were replaced with ideas relating to action concepts. Actions are defined surface events, but these are made meaningful only if two non-material deeper layers are introduced. Social rules are the second layer, in terms of which actors can be said to be doing some particular thing. A third, deeper layer is constitutive meaning, that lies behind the social practice and makes the actions and rules meaningful. This does promote mutual understanding but can be shown to be epistemologically impoverished because interpretive science does not adequately deal with effects of, say, material conditions. The critical idealists distinguish themselves from subjectivist idealism (interpretivism) by accepting that "out there" are some hard factual conditions that do not exist in the mind only. The critical idealists, however, do not expect to achieve direct access to those conditions, separating themselves from interpretive inquirers by claiming to provide adequate "maps" of "our" social reality. Interpretivist epistemology is equally impoverished because the notion of freezing constitutive meaning (freezing emancipation) through non-transparent false means (i.e. false consciousness) is not explicitly dealt with.

Also, interpretive science is implicitly conservative since it argues that social tensions arise because of imperfect communication, which can be corrected at the communicative level only through the promise of enhanced communication. We have argued that correction cannot be promoted "merely" by "clearing up" misunderstandings with the view that the natural flow of understanding is always involved in situations of coercion, but mutual understanding alone cannot secure emancipation; critical reflection on the norms implied in that which is authentically understood can. Table 9.2 summarizes the findings of this paper.

In Ulrich's view *a critical solution to the problem of practical reason* is the most urgent of all, for other kinds of inquiry have already developed methodological frameworks that work fairly well in (systems) practice: the experimental or "scientific" method works well for the purpose of securing instrumental rationality (it becomes "scientistic" in a derogative sense if its limitation to instrumental action is forgotten); the humanities have their hermeneutic method for securing communicative rationality and mutual understanding; but the applied disciplines, among them systems practice, have not satisfied the quest for some kind of critically comprehensive rationality and have not

Table 9.2 Summary of findings toward an adequate epistemology for systems practice

	Positivism	Interpretivism	Critique
Assumed view of the nature of social reality	Objective	Subjective	Subjective
Key actor(s) in methodological activities	Expert (élitist)	No explicit directives that prevent expert domination (potentially élitist)	All involved and affected (democratic)
The systems epistemological ideal	Ignored or neglected	It takes one of several steps that can be achieved by recognizing the subjectivity of man and the importance of the social communicative world	It "reaches-out" in terms of critical idealism of Kant, Hegel, and Churchman *and* Marx's historical materialism
Epistemological validity for social inquiry	Untenable	Impoverished	Tenable and adequate
Ideological status	Conservative	Conservative	Emancipatory
Means of dealing with power relations	Maintenance or strengthening	Accepts	Attempts to emancipate, in particular by dealing with effects of material conditions and false consciousness

established an intersubjectively reproducible way of ensuring rational practical discourse on disputed (because of conflict) norms of action.

In Flood's view developing such an emancipatory rationality for systems practice is vital. Equally important, however, is the overarching idea of complementarity among the three sciences, that can be developed in terms of legitimacies and limitations as set out in this conversation. The aim is to ensure that diversity is accepted as a strength, rather than fragmentation as a weakness, in systems-based "problem-solving" by drawing upon approaches of various rationalities. There has been very little space available in this testament for discussion of such pluralist issues, but this important matter is dealt with elsewhere in this book.

The issues of emancipatory and complementarist ideals, above all else, are the concern of Flood (1990b), Flood and Jackson (1991a, b), Jackson (1991), Oliga (1988), and Ulrich (1983, 1988a).

REFERENCES

Bertalanffy, L. von (1968). *General Systems Theory: Foundations, Development and Applications*, Braziller, New York.

Checkland, P.B. (1978). The origins and nature of hard systems thinking, *J. Appl. Syst. Anal.*, **5**, 99–110.

Checkland, P.B. (1981). *Systems Thinking, Systems Practice*, John Wiley, Chichester.

Fay, B. (1975). *Social Theory and Political Practice*, George Allen and Unwin, London.

Flood, R.L. (1988). The need for a substantive soft systems language, *J. Appl. Syst. Anal.*, **15**, 87–91.

Flood, R.L. (1989a). Six scenarios for the future of systems "problem solving", *Syst. Pract.*, **2**, 75–99.

Flood, R.L. (1989b). Archaeology of (systems) inquiry, *Syst. Pract.*, **2**, 117–124.

Flood, R.L. (1990a). Liberating systems theory: Towards critical systems thinking, *Hum. Relat.*, **43**, 49–76.

Flood, R.L. (1990b). *Liberating Systems Theory*, Plenum, New York.

Flood, R.L., and Carson, E.R. (1988). *Dealing with Complexity: An Introduction to the Theory and Application of Systems Science*, Plenum, New York.

Flood, R.L., and Jackson, M.C. (1991a). *Creative Problem Solving: Total Systems Intervention* Wiley, Chichester.

Flood, R.L., and Jackson, M.C. (1991b). *Critical Systems Thinking: Directed Readings*, this volume.

Flood, R.L., and Robinson, S.A. (1989a). Analogy and metaphor and systems and cybernetic methodologies, *Cybernet. Syst.*, **20**, 501–520.

Flood, R.L., and Robinson, S.A. (1989b). Thimbles and hope: an essay on metaphor and systems theory, *Cybernet. Syst.*, **20**, 201–214.

Habermas, J. (1971a). *Knowledge and Human Interests*, Boston, Mass. (German original 1968.)

Habermas, J. (1971b). *Towards a Rational Society*, Beacon, Boston, Mass. (German original 1968.)

Jackson, M.C. (1985). The itinerary of a critical approach . . . "Critical Heuristics of Social Planning": W. Ulrich (book review), *J. Opl Res. Soc.*, **36**, 878–888.

Jackson, M.C. (1990). Beyond a system of systems methodologies, *J. Opl Res. Soc.*, **41**, 657–668.

Jackson, M.C. (1991). *Systems Methodology for the Management Sciences*, Plenum, New York.

Lowi, T.J. (1969). *The End of Liberalism*, Norton, New York.

Oliga, J. (1988). Methodological foundations of systems methodologies, Chapter 8 this volume.

Ulrich, W. (1977). The design of problem-solving systems, *Mgmt Sci.*, **23**, 1099–1108.

Ulrich, W. (1980). The metaphysics of design: a Simon–Churchman "debate", *Interfaces*, **10**, 35–40. Reprinted and slightly expanded in *Decision Making About Decision Making: Metamodels and Metasystems* (Ed. J.P. van Gigch), pp.219–226, Abacus Press, Tunbridge Wells, England, 1987.

Ulrich, W. (1981a). Systemrationalität und praktische Vernunft-Gedanken zum Stand des Systemansatzes. Introduction to Churchman, C.W., *Der Systemansatz und seine "Feinde"*, pp. 7–38, Haupt, Berne, Switzerland.

Ulrich, W. (1981b). A critique of pure cybernetic reason: the Chilean experience with cybernetics, *J. Appl. Syst. Anal.*, **8**, 33–59.

Ulrich, W. (1983). *Critical Heuristics of Social Planning: A New Approach to Practical Philosophy*, Haupt, Berne, Switzerland.

Ulrich, W. (1984). Management oder die Kunst, Entscheidungen zu treffen, die andere betreffen, *Die Unternehmung*, **38**, 326–346.

Ulrich, W. (1987). Critical heuristics of social systems design, *Eur. J. Opl Res.*, **31**, 276–283.

Ulrich, W. (1988a). Systems thinking, systems practice, and practical philosophy: a program of research, Chapter 12 this volume.

Ulrich, W. (1988b). Churchman's "process of unfolding"—its significance for policy analysis and evaluation, *Syst. Pract.*, **1**, 415–428.

Ulrich, W. (1989). Systemtheorie der planung, in *Handwörterbuch der Planung* (Ed. N. Szyperski), columns 1971–1978, Poeschel, Stuttgart, Germany.

Ulrich, W. (1991). Toward emancipatory systems practice, unpublished.

Weber, M. (1949). "Objectivity" in social science and social policy, in *The Methodology of the Social Sciences* (Eds. E.A. Shils and H.A. Finch), pp.72–111, Free Press, New York.

_____ Part Three

Contemporary Critical Systems Theory and Practice

Commentary

In the last section we looked at the main reasons behind the break with soft systems thinking. The soft school had developed a tradition that opposed hard systems thinking as a single superior paradigm. Instead, the soft school proposed, hard systems thinking should be appreciated as a subset of soft systems thinking. Two paradigms had therefore been proposed, with soft as the dominant and hard in support. This is an isolationist interpretation of complementarism. The critical school rejected this idea, arguing that complementarity means reflective use of methodology by analysis of underlying theoretical assumptions and assessing their relevance to the social context at hand. Another crucial weakness of soft systems is its reliance on resolving plurality through the exchange of ideas, neglecting to take into account structural features of society which shape and form power and decision hierarchies and distort the free exchange of ideas. The soft approach was therefore shown to be appropriate only in restricted cases where conflicting views are not resolved through coercive means. For circumstances where coercion does exist explicitly emancipatory methodologies should be used. Critical systems thinking therefore broke away, offering a critically reflective attitude which enables us to assess the special cases in which any particular approach is appropriate.

Achievement of this break with soft systems thinking created conditions in which a whole new area of systemic thought could be developed. This opportunity was quickly seized upon. Critical systems thinking has now branched out to assess critically its own tenets in the face of wider debates such as post-modernism currently being discussed in contemporary social theory. The complementarist idea has also been pragmatised and applied to a multitude of contrasting business, organisational, community and societal problems, followed by reflection and redevelopment. The contributions which make up Part Three enable us to show these continuing and crucial developments in "Contemporary Critical Systems Theory and Practice."

We begin with Schecter's "Critical Systems Thinking in the 1980s: A Connective Summary" (1991). This paper squares with the argument of

Critical Systems Thinking: Directed Readings. Edited by R.L. Flood and M.C. Jackson
© 1991 John Wiley & Sons Ltd

Directed Readings, recognising that three commitments characterise critical systems thinking. These are commitments to critique, to emancipation and to pluralism (we use the term complementarism instead). We concentrate on developing an outline argument in our commentary, but Schecter is able to review each commitment in detail by reflecting on a wider selection of writings. Through this effort, he provides the necessary background, connecting the foundational work of critical systems thinking in the 1980s already discussed with the new challenging ideas that are currently being explored.

Interpretive systemology is one of those challenging ideas. This approach helps to advance the interpretive theory employed in systems thinking from the less-than-adequate accounts given by the soft systems school. Interpretive systemology is a careful construction of the onto-epistemological basis for interpretive thought in the systems sciences. This theory poses a "counter" system of critical thought to the Habermasian perspective that we have emphasised. Heidegger, Husserl and their phenomenological philosophies provide the critical underpinnings. Interpretive systemology can be used to critique critical systems thinking based on Habermas' work, as Fuenmayor shows in his invited contribution "Between Systems Thinking and Systems Practice" (1991). In an argument that demands attention, he claims that a theoretically rooted interpretive systems science is critical in the most authentic sense of that word. A dialectical debate between deeply rooted interpretive thought and critical theory in the systems sciences is clearly called for.

Ulrich argues, in contrast, that contemporary practical philosophy holds the essential foundations necessary for systems thinking to serve the cause of socially rational decision making. In his paper "Systems Thinking, Systems Practice, and Practical Philosophy: A Program of Research" (1988), he builds a bridge between the two traditions of systems thinking and practical philosophy, coming up with a three-level framework of rational systems practice. Level 1 is operational systems management, which is concerned with non-social instrumental action. It is effectively the hard paradigm which includes operational research, systems analysis and systems engineering. Level 2 is strategic systems management. Strategic action shares with instrumental action a utilitarian orientation toward success in maximising output. The focus, however, is toward securing the strategic potentials for the success of complex systems (i.e. self-regulation, resilience and adaption). This avoids the management of conflict (i.e. whose interests are being served). Normative systems management is about deciding on the interests or needs that are to be served by the system in question. This is the problem of practical reason and comes within the scope of practical philosophy. Ulrich concludes by calling for a critical employment of the systems idea and an exploration of the implications of the systems idea for practising practical reason. This directs his program of research toward socially rational systems practice.

Debate on power, ideology and control is opened up by another contributor to critical systems research. That contributor is Oliga and we have included his paper "Power–Ideology Matrix in Social Systems Control" (1990) to represent this strand. He draws attention to power, ideology and social control in sociocultural systems, recognising that preference is usually given to naturalistic accounts of systems behaviour, using either hard or soft systems models. The reason for the very slow appearance of critical thought in systems thinking, Oliga suggests, may be attributable to the ideological dominance of these models (possibly their conservative nature). His main line of argument is that unless an account of systems stability and change is sought in the conscious actions of humans as makers or victims of history, no valid explanation of constancy and change in sociocultural systems is likely to ensue. Indeed, he ends the article by stating that uncritical employment of hard and soft approaches, ignoring the dialectical nature of power and ideology, represent two steps backward from a penetrative understanding of the phenomenon of social control in social systems.

Critical systems thinking in the 1980s rested heavily upon the theoretical work of Habermas and particularly upon his conception of three fundamental human interests—the technical, the practical and the emancipatory. There was a remarkable convergence in the way that three critical systems thinkers— Jackson, Oliga and Ulrich—used Habermas' ideas in developing their own approaches. Habermas has come to be regarded, in modern social theory, as the arch proponent of modernism and his work has come under sustained attack from post-modern writers such as Foucault and Lyotard. It was inevitable, therefore, that critical systems thinking would at some stage have to come to terms with the arguments of the post-modernists. This "coming to terms" is reflected in this volume in the next two contributions from Jackson and Flood.

The first contribution by Jackson, "Modernism, Post-modernism and Contemporary Systems Thinking" (1991), presents an overview of the modernism versus post-modernism debate and considers modern systems thinking in the light of that debate. A critique of contemporary systems approaches and their social effects is launched using the language and ideas developed in the debate. Hard and cybernetic systems approaches are shown to be systemic modernist in orientation, while soft systems approaches represent a very underdeveloped form of critical modernism. Critical systems thinking itself, as it emerged from the 1980s, was modernist to its core—if in a very advanced way. The challenge of post-modernism, therefore, remained to be met by systems thinkers. The next paper makes a first serious attempt at this.

Flood consolidates his argument from *Liberating Systems Theory* (Plenum, New York, 1990), moving a step on from the foundational work discussed in Part Two and on from an uncritical modernism. In "Redefining Management and Systems Sciences" (1990), Flood systematically reconstructs the development of systems thinking, realising that the cybernetic and interpretive approaches are forms of systemic modernism. They are both theoretically isolationist. Critical systems thinking is not theoretically isolationist, having adopted a critically reflective complementary attitude. Nevertheless, it remains firmly in the modernist camp of rationalism. At this point Flood introduces a post-modern critique of the essentially modernist work of the critical systems school. One result of this is the addition of a new methodological element. There is a need to *liberate* knowledges and their logically derived methodologies as well as to critique them. The use of liberation here makes direct reference to Foucault's work. The point being that it is simply no good expecting knowledges and their logical methodological rules to be independently awaiting our critique. There are institutional and other forces invisibly at work at a micro-political level which are suppressing many of them. We therefore need to introduce a methodological element which helps to liberate dominated knowledges and methodologies, which in turn helps to grow a diversity of approaches necessary to tackle the great variety of phenomena we face in contemporary society.

The aim of the last paper is to review "Total Systems Intervention: A Practical Face to Critical Systems Thinking" (1991). TSI is set out in full in *Creative Problem Solving: Total System Intervention* (Robert L. Flood and Michael C. Jackson, John Wiley, Chichester, 1991). In this we see that the critical idea has been employed in a variety of interventions—for example, in the community, in local government, in industry, business and in firms. TSI is also seen to encapsulate and to help us understand the usefulness of a whole range of practical ideas, such as the practice of evaluation and quality management. This final contribution therefore achieves a most significant demand that critical theory makes of itself—that in order to be valid, critical thinking must be shown to have a theory with practical relevance.

In this section we present a number of papers which show new directions in critical systems thinking. These mostly have their roots in the critique of soft systems thinking and the three commitments which arose from that. The foundations that were constructed have now been opened up to critique from the deadliest of enemies. Critical systems thinking is therefore experiencing further rounds of redevelopment.

Chapter 10

Critical Systems Thinking in the 1980s: A Connective Summary

DAVID SCHECTER

INTRODUCTION

In the 1960s, hard systems approaches such as operational research, systems analysis, and systems engineering dominated the field of systems science. In the 1970s, the dominant position of these approaches was challenged by new developments in soft systems thinking and management cybernetics. In the 1980s, the most significant new development was the emergence of critical systems thinking. At the dawn of the 1990s there is a substantial body of work in this area, which has provided much inspiration and provoked a lot of controversy, but so far there has been very little analysis of the critical systems trend as a whole. This paper is an overview of critical systems thinking in the 1980s.

Before proceeding any further it is necessary to define critical systems thinking. My argument is that critical systems thinking is defined by three commitments: to critique, to emancipation and to pluralism. The commitment to critique is a commitment to questioning the methods, practice, theory, normative content and limits of rationality of all schools of thought. It requires a never-ending attempt to uncover hidden assumptions and conceptual traps.

The commitment to emancipation is a commitment to human beings and their potential for full development via free and equal participation in community with others. It is also a commitment to recognizing the barriers to human emancipation—unequal power relations and the conceptual traps

Critical Systems Thinking: Directed Readings. Edited by R.L. Flood and M.C. Jackson

which perpetuate them—and incorporating this understanding into systems thinking.

The commitment to emancipation does not imply that earlier (non-emancipatory) systems approaches should be eliminated. On the contrary, the commitment to pluralism insists that all systems approaches have a contribution to make, and that no single approach (including an emancipatory approach) is adequate to address the full range of problematic situations. The commitment to pluralism is a commitment to develop a broad framework which facilitates productive interaction between the advocates of the different approaches.

The next three sections of the paper will discuss work relating to each of the three commitments in turn. The final section will summarize the major contributions of the critical systems thinking trend as a whole.

THE COMMITMENT TO CRITIQUE

Critical systems thinking began with critiques of earlier systems approaches, examining their theoretical foundations, their history, the assumptions embedded in them, and who they serve. This section discusses critiques of hard systems, structuralist, and soft systems approaches.

Critiques of the Hard Systems Approach

Checkland (1981) has grouped systems analysis, systems engineering, and operations research together under the label of the hard systems approach. Influenced by empiricist philosophy and the functionalist tradition in sociology, this approach is characterized by the search for optimal solutions to clearly defined problems. Checkland and other soft systems thinkers have rightly pointed out that in many real-world situations the definition of problems is extremely problematic in itself. Critical systems thinkers have criticized the hard systems approach as being weak in dealing with three aspects of human systems: complexity, subjectivity and power (Jackson, 1987a; Keys, 1987). They have adopted the soft systems critique of this approach (Ackoff, 1974; Checkland, 1981) in the area of subjectivity, and the cybernetic critique (Beer, 1966, 1979) in the area of complexity. They have developed an original critique of the hard systems approach in the area of power.

Hard systems methods proceed from the assumption of a "given" objective. But whose objective is it? Most likely it will be the objective of whoever has the most power in a situation (including the power to hire a systems consultant). Because of this, critical systems thinkers argue that the hard systems approach is fundamentally oriented toward serving the powerful and neglecting the powerless (Rosenhead, 1982, 1986, 1987; Rosenhead and Thunhurst, 1982).

Jackson (1985) has criticized hard systems thinking for its mechanistic model of social reality and its assumptions of agreement on objectives which supposedly can be determined from outside a given social system. He points out that in human systems the physical scientist's "predict and control" criteria of success can be made to "work" through coercion. This problem cannot be addressed within the framework of hard systems thinking. Oliga (1986b) identifies the hard systems approach with the ideology of economic individualism, and argues that this ideology conceals unequal relations that often exist among so-called "free individuals."

Critiques of the Structuralist Approach

Jackson (1987a) has come up with the useful label "structuralist" to describe the group of systems approaches that include cybernetics, General Systems Theory, and sociotechnical design. The theoretical orientation of these approaches has much in common with that of structuralist social theorists such as Piaget and Levi-Strauss. These approaches differ from hard systems approaches in their focus on generative structures as opposed to empirical events—a difference that has frequently been overlooked by practitioners of hard systems and soft systems schools.

In the critical systems thinking literature, critiques of the structuralist approach have mainly addressed Stafford Beer's management cybernetics (Ulrich, 1981; Jackson, 1988a), focusing on its weaknesses in dealing with human subjectivity and with power relations. Ulrich (1981) argues that cybernetics is ill-suited to work with social systems because it stresses intrinsic control rather than intrinsic motivation, the syntactic level of communication rather than the semantic–pragmatic level, purposiveness rather than purposefulness, and tool design rather than social systems design.

Jackson (1988a) argues that Beer's Viable System Model (VSM) overemphasizes the importance of structural design and underemphasizes the importance of culture, that it ignores self-consciousness of human subjects, and that it is of limited use in facilitating discussion of purposes. He also argues that the VSM has the potential of autocratic misuse, despite Beer's intentions. He notes that there is little in Beer's work about how inequalities of power arise, or how they can be reduced. Finally, he observes that the VSM "provides no mechanisms either for the democratic determination of purposes or for facilitating debate about the nature of the purposes served."

Oliga argues that the structuralist approach is based on the ideology of sociological unitarism, including a consensus view of organizations and a positive or neutral view of power (Oliga, 1989a, b). Yet few organizations are characterized by true (uncoerced) consensus, and power can clearly be used for negative ends.

Critiques of the Soft Systems Approach

Perhaps the first widely read critique of the soft systems approach from the critical systems perspective was Jackson's (1982) path-breaking paper on the work of Churchman, Ackoff and Checkland. Jackson maintains that soft systems thinking is an advance over hard systems thinking because it recognizes the importance of subjectivity. However, he argues that the soft approach is unable to deal with issues of power and social change. While soft systems thinking is able to explore the world views of different actors, it has little to say about how these views are formed and maintained, or why some dominate over others. Soft systems thinking assumes the existence of a free, open and democratic debate among all stakeholders. Yet few such situations exist. Soft systems thinking does not concern itself with studying how distorted communication happens, nor with how to bring about undistorted communication. To Jackson, this stems from its neglect of objective social conditions. Fuenmayor (1990), while agreeing with Jackson that soft systems thinking has been regulative in character, argues that this is not due to a basic flaw in the interpretivist paradigm upon which the soft approach is based, but rather to the lack of interpretive systems theory and to the instrumental and regulative intent of soft systems practice.

Oliga argues that the soft systems approach has made an ontological break with empiricism but not an epistemological break (Oliga, 1988, 1989a, b). While the soft systems approach rejects the "objective world" of empiricism, and advocates an ongoing process of dialogue and learning, it assumes that the possibility of the practitioner attaining "objective" knowledge of the world views of the actors is unproblematic. Oliga also notes that the soft systems approach over-emphasizes the role of world views, thereby neglecting the competing influences of social structural factors and the influence of these factors on the formation and maintenance of world views.

The Critical Kernel

Critique has a positive side as well as a negative one. In addition to identifying the weaknesses of earlier systems approaches, some of the critical systems thinkers have found untapped emancipatory potential in them. Jackson (1989) writes that Beer's Viable System Model and Checkland's Soft Systems Methodology contain a "critical kernel" of emancipatory content. In the case of the Viable System Model, Jackson notes that Beer advocates the decentralization of control, and that the effective functioning of the VSM requires a democratic milieu. Therefore, advocates of the VSM have an interest in working for greater democracy. At a deeper level, the VSM contains the beginning of a cybernetic argument for a truly participatory, democratic society. This aspect of Beer's work has been explored by Robinson (1981).

In the case of Checkland's work, Jackson maintains that the only possible validation criterion for Soft Systems Methodology is open debate leading to democratic consensus among all those involved in a given situation. Therefore, soft systems practitioners have a strong interest in establishing these conditions, and in opposing social arrangements which make this democratic consensus impossible. From a similar perspective, Spear (1987) and Mingers (1980) advocate the adaptation of soft methods to emancipatory use, for example within the Community OR movement.

Jackson (1982) has noted that there are several interpretive systems methods, but no interpretive systems theory. Fuenmayor and his colleagues have taken up the task of developing the critical kernel in interpretive systems approaches by providing a rigorous theoretical foundation for interpretive systems work (Fuenmayor, 1985, 1989). Fuenmayor's work, which he calls interpretive systemology, is focused on the construction of basic theory ("onto-epistemology" in his terms) that is interpretivist, critical and also emancipatory. In his view, there is not a fundamental contradiction between the interpretive view and the critical view. Rather, the reasons for the non-critical nature of current soft systems work are its lack of an interpretive systems theory and the instrumental nature of the way it has been used. Fuenmayor describes the dominant approach to soft systems work as "pragmatic–regulative interpretive management," which uses learning as a tool for managing human organizations. In contrast, interpretive systemology considers learning itself as the key focus. This leads to a much more theoretically grounded, more critical approach.

Oliga, in his critique of underlying assumptions on power and ideology made by different systems approaches, has found emancipatory potential in the ideological foundations of the hard and structuralist systems approaches (Oliga, 1989a, b). He argues that the hard systems approach is based on the ideology of economic individualism. This ideology is based on the concepts of the free individual, utility maximization, and of the free market as the best vehicle for economic allocation. The concept of the "free individual" is often used to obscure the power relations among social actors. Nevertheless, it has emancipatory potential because it is close to what he calls the "rational agency" concept of power. Oliga argues that the structuralist approach is based on the ideology of sociological unitarism. In this ideology there is the recognition that the so-called "power-less" are never completely without power; in fact, the "power-full" depend on them. Also, the kind of power that is emphasized in the structuralist approach, the power that comes from cooperation and synergistic action, can be used in the service of emancipatory ends as well as oppressive ones.

THE COMMITMENT TO EMANCIPATION

The critiques of soft systems thinking discussed above have led to the recognition of what Jackson and Keys (1984) call coercive contexts—those characterized by significant inequalities of power. None of the three strands of systems thinking examined so far have much to say about these situations. Because of this, critical systems thinkers have begun to call for an explicitly emancipatory systems approach that can deal with these issues (Jackson, 1985). This section discusses the second commitment of critical systems thinking, the commitment to emancipation. This commitment has inspired new developments in methods, practice, and theory.

Critical Systems Heuristics

Werner Ulrich's Critical Systems Heuristics is the only explicitly emancipatory method that the systems movement has produced to date (Ulrich 1983, 1989a). It is designed to help people think critically about the system designs that affect them, especially when they are not included in the design process. Ulrich points out that any sort of systems design requires boundary judgements about what is included in the scope of the effort and what is excluded. These judgements cannot be justified by logic, facts, or expertise, but only by democratic consensus. Some systems methods try to eliminate or hide these boundary judgements. Ulrich's method tries to make them explicit, in the light of "what ought to be done" rather than "what is."

To do this, Ulrich has chosen a set of 12 concepts to guide critical reflection on the normative content in systems designs. These concepts are divided into four groups. The first group (client, purpose, measure of success) concerns sources of motivation; the second group (decision taker, resources, and environment), sources of control; the third group (designer, expert, guarantor), sources of expertise; and the fourth group (witnesses, emancipation, world view) sources of legitimation. Each of these is a source of questions about a potential system design. The questions are used by comparing the "ought" and the "is" for each category. For example, someone might ask "What should be the client of this system?" and then "What seems to be the actual client of this system?".

By using these questions, anyone can learn to expose the hidden boundary judgements in system designs, and to defeat the intimidating strategies of technical experts. Critical Systems Heuristics is the first systems method to be explicitly concerned with empowerment, and thus is a major step forward for critical systems thinking.

Community Operational Research

Emancipatory practice in critical systems thinking has centred around the Community Operational Research movement in the United Kingdom (Rosenhead, 1986; Jackson, 1987b). The distinguishing feature of Community OR is its choice of clients. While traditional OR/systems thinking has almost exclusively served the military, business, and government, Community OR serves groups such as trade unions, cooperatives, women's groups, tenant unions, and voluntary agencies (Rosenhead, 1986). Typically, community clients have far fewer available resources than OR's usual clients; they are impatient with technical solutions and suspicious of experts; and they work by democratic debate and consensus decision making. There is usually no autocratic decision maker who can enforce an analyst's recommendations on the rest of the organization (Jackson, 1987b).

The Community OR movement has stimulated discussions of what types of methods are appropriate for community clients. Spear points out that emancipatory practice must demystify the analytical process and constrain the use of expert power by the analyst (Spear, 1987, 1989). While emancipatory methods are important, they are not enough; the analyst/client relationship must become explicitly emancipatory (Rosenhead, 1987).

Rosenhead (1986) has proposed three requirements for an emancipatory OR; re-skilling, decentralization, and liberation. Later he added the following; a satisficing (non-optimizing) approach; the use of analysis to support (not replace) judgement; the treatment of people as active subjects; acceptance of conflict over goals; bottom-up problem formulation; and the acceptance of uncertainty (Rosenhead, 1987). In a previous paper (Schecter, 1989) I have argued that emancipatory methods must: (i) serve the oppressed; (ii) have explicit goals of liberation and social justice; (iii) support those who are directly concerned with problematic situations, not just professional consultants; and (iv) be relevant to the task of transforming oppressive social systems.

Emancipatory Social Theory

To be effective, emancipatory methods and practice must be grounded in emancipatory social theory. In order to provide theoretical support for emancipatory methods and practice, critical systems thinkers have enriched systems thinking by adapting key concepts from radical social theory, especially from the work of Habermas and Foucault.

Jackson (1985) cites Habermas' critique of distorted communication (Habermas, 1970) as a basis for addressing issues of power, and advocates the adoption of Habermas' three stages of work to systems thinking: first, the formation of critical theories of society (including issues such as power, domination, distorted communication and false consciousness); second, the authentication through practice of the knowledge produced by these theories; and third, the selection of appropriate strategies for social action (Habermas, 1974).

Flood (1990) has developed a new perspective by incorporating concepts from Foucault's work. Flood makes use of Foucault's concept of multiple knowledges (Foucault, 1980) which can be suppressed and/or liberated based on power struggles at the micro-level. He suggests that one of the first tasks for critical systems thinkers is to liberate suppressed knowledges in order to launch more penetrating critiques on the dominant ones. Flood has used this powerful strategy of "liberate and critique" to uncover the hidden potential of General Systems Theory, which many systems thinkers believe has been long since refuted. Flood's thesis has been developed under the umbrella term Liberating Systems Theory.

In addition to the adaptations mentioned above, the critical systems movement has produced original work in emancipatory social theory. Oliga has made an important contribution in this area with his critical inquiry into the phenomena of stability and change in social systems (Oliga, 1989a, b, 1990). He points out (Oliga, 1990) that most work on stability and change in the systems movement has expressed a naturalistic orientation—that is, the existing social order is taken as given, and the only problem of interest is the problem of maintaining order. This orientation neglects historical factors which explain the origin of a given social order, it avoids issues of power and ideology, and it excludes problems of social change. Oliga has developed a historically oriented theory of stability and change which deals with these issues explicitly. His thesis is that stability and change are a function of the interaction of power and ideology and he has labelled his work "empower" and "transform."

Oliga points out that hard and soft systems approaches are concerned with how to regulate conflict, not with why conflict occurs. In Oliga's critical approach, the problem of order and conflict is placed in the historical context of the society within which it occurs. The problem of order is the problem of a particular group in a society. As Oliga puts it, "every theory of society defines its own problem of order, and critically, we must ask of that theory, For whom is order a problem?".

Oliga argues that power and ideology play important roles in maintaining stability and in making social change. Therefore an emancipatory systems approach requires a clear understanding of power and ideology. These are very elusive concepts. Oliga (1989a) identifies ten different views of power based on three key issues; Is power positive, negative or contingent? Is power held by one group or many? By agents, structures, or both? He advocates the contingent relational view—that is, the view that power can be positive or negative depending on the situation, and that power is a function of the relationship between different agents and structures. Oliga (1989b) categorizes views of ideology, based on the following questions: Is ideology naturalistic or historical? Is it subjective, objective, or a dialectical combination of both? Is ideology positive, negative, or contingent? He proposes the historical materialist view of ideology (historical, dialectical and negative) for an emancipatory systems approach.

Having explored different views of power and ideology, Oliga (1990) goes on to describe how the interactions between power and ideology affect stability and change in social systems. In Oliga's model, power and ideology affect each other and both affect the possibilities for stability or change. This work is an important step forward in the development of emancipatory systems theory.

Flood and Oliga's ideas come together to form a whole new vision for management and systems sciences, the process "liberate, critique, empower and transform."

THE COMMITMENT TO PLURALISM

Critical systems thinkers have launched strong attacks on hard, structuralist and soft systems thinking. They have advocated the development of emancipatory systems approaches. However, it is very important to emphasize that they do not advocate replacing earlier approaches with emancipatory approaches, or subsuming earlier approaches under a new emancipatory approach. Instead, they are committed to a pluralist path which recognizes the value of all of these approaches for dealing with different dimensions of problematic situations.

Which Method When?

In order to develop a pluralist path for the complementary development of different systems approaches, it is first necessary to create a taxonomy of approaches. Jackson and Keys (1984) proposed a "system of systems methodologies" to guide method selection and to provide insights about the nature of different methods. This framework has been extended by Jackson (1988b). The system of systems methodologies classifies methods in terms of fundamental assumptions built into the methods about the participants in a problematic situation and about the systems they are interested in. In terms of participants, in a unitary context all participants share a common objective; in a pluralist context there are differing views on objectives, but free and open debate is possible; a coercive context is characterized by basic inequalities of power that make open debate impossible. In terms of systems, a mechanical context is characterized by simple, separable problems, while a systemic context contains complex, inseparable "messes." The combination of these two dimensions results in a 3 × 2 grid. As Jackson (1990) points out, it is important to remember that these categories relate to assumptions built into methods, not to types of problems in the world. Keeping this in mind, the system of systems methodologies provides a great deal of insight about the consequences of choosing a particular approach. Flood and Jackson (1991) have developed and expanded it as the basis for a comprehensive multiple-methodology approach to systems work called Total Systems Intervention—a significant new development in applied systems science.

Expanding on Jackson and Keys' work, Oliga (1988) identifies three methodologies (his term is "methodological foundations") on which systems methods are based: empiricism (including positivism and structuralism); hermeneutics (including naturalistic and historical hermeneutics); and critique. These relate to Jackson and Keys' unitary, pluralist, and coercive categories; to Burrell and Morgan's (1979) functionalist, interpretive, and radical humanist/radical structuralist paradigms; and to Habermas' (1972) technical, practical, and emancipatory interests. Oliga notes that the vast majority of systems methods are based on either empiricism or naturalistic hermeneutics, and that there is an urgent need for methods based on historical hermeneutics and critique.

Ulrich (1988) describes three levels of systems practice: operational, strategic, and normative. Operational systems management is concerned with instrumental action, efficiency, and the management of scarcity. Strategic systems management is concerned with strategic action, problem identification and structuring, and the management of complexity and uncertainty. Normative systems management is concerned with communicative action, critical reflection on the normative content in all systems designs, and the free consent of concerned citizens.

The Case for Pluralism

Given multiple approaches based on different theoretical foundations, what possibilities are available for the development of systems thinking as a whole? Jackson (1987a), building on work by Reed (1985), has identified four strategies for the overall development of systems thinking: isolationism (each approach develops independently of the others); imperialism (one approach absorbs the rest); pragmatism (practitioners use any method based on their immediate need, without regard to theory); and pluralism (the complementary development of all approaches). Flood has expanded the four alternatives into six, distinguishing between methodological isolationism (use of one method only) and theoretical isolationism (use of multiple methods, but guided by one paradigm), and also between imperialism by annexation (one approach incorporates the best elements from other approaches) and imperialism by subsumption (one favoured approach provides the "what" and the other approaches provide the "how" according to the needs of the situation) (Flood, 1989a, b). He has provided an in-depth exploration of the implications of Jackson's argument, exploring the consequences of each approach in turn. His conclusion, like Jackson's, is that pluralism is the only adequate option. However, he notes that there are aspects of this argument that cannot be settled at a methodological level. The development of a pluralist framework for methodology requires new thinking in the area of epistemology.

Developing an Adequate Epistemology

Ulrich has done pioneering work in developing epistemology to support critical systems thinking (Ulrich, 1983, 1988, 1989a). His epistemological work demands a re-orientation from "systems science" (using systems approaches in science according to empirical methodology) to "systems rationality" (using systems approaches in social practice in the face of incomplete understanding). He argues that systems thinking must give up its pretense of comprehensiveness, because true comprehensiveness is never attainable. Rather than striving to be comprehensive, Ulrich insists that systems thinking must learn to deal critically with its inevitable lack of comprehensiveness. This requires a shift away from the positivist theory on which most systems work is based. Ulrich (1989b) identifies four strategies for liberating systems theory (cf. Flood, 1990) from its positivist origins: Kant's critical solution, Peirce's pragmatic maxim, Churchman's dialectical pragmatism, and Habermas' communicative rationalization of society. In Ulrich's view, a key problem for a critical systems approach is that of developing a dialectical discourse between those who are involved in a system design and those who are affected but not involved. This is the objective of Ulrich's Critical Systems Heuristics.

Flood and Ulrich (1990) have undertaken a comprehensive epistemological inquiry based on Habermas' (1972) knowledge-constitutive interests and Flood (1990) introduced Foucault's (1980) treatment of subjugated knowledges. This requires a "second epistemological break" in systems thinking (the first such break being the shift from positivist to interpretivist theoretical foundations). The second break involves adding a concern with Habermas' emancipatory interest to the existing (in hard and soft systems thinking) concerns with the technical and practical interests. One requirement for this is to supplement systems epistemology with sociological epistemology. Another requirement is that the critical (overarching) perspective maintains its independence from particular approaches. In their words, "Being critical is not a quality of a certain position or approach, rather it is the quality of remaining self-reflective with respect to . . . all positions or approaches" (Flood and Ulrich, 1990).

CONCLUSION

My aim up to this point has been to summarize and connect the different strands of critical systems thinking in the 1980s. It is now time to point out the contributions that critical systems thinking has made to the field of systems science.

First, critical systems thinking has brought more theoretical depth to systems science. Discussions of meta-theory and social theory in systems science are much more common now than they were at the dawn of the 1980s, partly as a result of this new movement.

Second, critical systems thinking has produced insightful, challenging critiques of earlier forms of systems thinking. These critiques have not only identified the limitations of the earlier approaches, but have also discovered hidden potential in them.

Third, critical systems thinking has put issues of power and human emancipation on the agenda of systems science. This is an urgent necessity if systems thinking is to make a serious contribution to the improvement of the human condition.

Fourth, critical systems thinking has contributed a pluralist framework with powerful potential for the complementary development of all the different systems approaches. This is very important, because no single approach can be sufficient to match the complexity of the problematic situations found in human systems.

Fifth, critical systems thinking has produced some strong original work in meta-theory and social theory.

Sixth, critical systems thinking has put its commitment to emancipation into action with the Community OR movement and with emancipatory methods such as Critical Systems Heuristics.

Finally, critical systems thinking has championed a commitment to careful, critical, self-reflective thinking. In a field that aims at comprehensiveness but is often trapped in a tight conceptual web of its own making, this is perhaps the most important contribution of all.

REFERENCES

Ackoff, R.L. (1974). The systems revolution, *Long Range Planning*, 7, 2–20.
Beer, S. (1966). *Decision and Control*, John Wiley, New York.
Beer, S. (1979). *The Heart of Enterprise*, John Wiley, New York.
Burrell, G., and Morgan, G. (1979). *Sociological Paradigms and Organizational Analysis*, Heinemann, London.
Checkland, P.B. (1981). *Systems Thinking, Systems Practice*, John Wiley, New York.

Flood, R.L. (1989a). Six scenarios for the future of systems "problem solving", *Syst. Pract.*, **2**, 75–99.

Flood, R.L. (1989b). Archaeology of systems inquiry, *Syst. Pract.*, **2**, 117–124.

Flood, R.L. (1990). *Liberating Systems Theory*, Plenum, New York.

Flood, R.L., and Jackson, M.C. (1991). *Creative Problem Solving: Total Systems Intervention*, John Wiley, New York.

Flood, R.L., and Ulrich, W. (1990). Testament to conversations on critical systems theory between two systems practitioners, Chapter 9 in this book.

Foucault, M. (1980). *Power/Knowledge: Selected Interviews and Other Writings 1972–1977* (Ed. C. Gordon), Harvester Press, Brighton.

Fuenmayor, R. (1985). *The Ontology and Epistemology of a Systems Approach: A Fundamental Study and an application to the Phenomenon Development/Underdevelopment*, Ph.D. thesis, Dept. of Systems, University of Lancaster.

Fuenmayor, R. (1989). Interpretive systemology: a critical approach to interpretive systems thinking. Paper presented at the 33rd Annual Meeting of the International Society for Systems Science, Edinburgh.

Fuenmayor, R. (1990). Between systems thinking and systems practice, Chapter 11 in this book.

Habermas, J. (1970). On systematically distorted communication, *Inquiry*, **13**, 360–375.

Habermas, J. (1972). *Knowledge and Human Interests*, Heinemann, London.

Habermas, J. (1974). *Theory and Practice*, Heinemann, London.

Jackson, M.C. (1982). The nature of soft systems thinking: the work of Churchman, Ackoff and Checkland, *J. Appl. Syst. Anal.*, **9**, 17–28.

Jackson, M.C. (1985). Social systems theory and practice: the need for a critical approach, Chapter 6 in this book.

Jackson, M.C. (1987a). New directions in management science, in *New Directions in Management Science* (Eds. M.C. Jackson and P. Keys), pp. 133–159, Gower, Aldershot.

Jackson, M.C. (1987b). Community operational research: purposes, theory, and practice, *Dragon*, **2**, 47–73.

Jackson, M.C. (1988a). An appreciation of Stafford Beer's "viable system" viewpoint on managerial practice, *J. Mgmt. Stud.*, **25**, 557–573.

Jackson, M.C. (1988b). Some methodologies for community operational research, *J. Opl Res. Soc.*, **39**, 715–724.

Jackson, M.C. (1989). The critical kernel in modern systems thinking, *Syst. Pract.*, **3**, 357–364.

Jackson, M.C. (1990). Beyond a system of systems methodologies, *J. Opl Res. Soc.*, **41**, 657–668.

Jackson, M.C., and Keys, P. (1984). Towards a system of systems methodologies, Chapter 7 this volume.

Keys, P. (1987). Traditional management science and the emerging critique, in *New Directions in Management Science* (Eds. M.C. Jackson and P. Keys), pp. 133–159, Gower, Aldershot.

Mingers, J.C. (1980). Toward an appropriate social theory for applied systems thinking: critical theory and soft systems methodology, *J. Appl. Syst. Anal.*, **7**, 41–49.

Oliga, J.C. (1988). Methodological foundations of systems methodologies, Chapter 8 this volume.

Oliga, J.C. (1989a). Power and interest in organizations: a contingent, relational view. Paper presented at the 33rd Annual Meeting of the International Society for Systems Science, Edinburgh.

Oliga, J.C. (1989b). Ideology and systems emancipation. Paper presented at the 33rd Annual Meeting of the International Society for Systems Science, Edinburgh.

Oliga, J.C. (1990). Power–ideology matrix in social systems control, Chapter 13 in this book.

Reed, M. (1985). *Redirections in Organizational Analysis*, Tavistock, London.

Robinson, M. (1981). Management and self management: the objective–subjective dimensions, *Int. J. Man–Machine Stud.*, **14**, 151–167.

Rosenhead, J. (1982). Why does management need management science?, in *A General Survey of Systems Methodology* (Ed. L. Troncale), pp. 834–839, Society for General Systems Research, Louisville.

Rosenhead, J. (1986). Custom and practice, *J. Opl Res. Soc.*, **37**, 335–343.

Rosenhead, J. (1987). From management science to workers' science, in *New Directions in Management Science* (Eds. M.C. Jackson and P. Keys), pp. 109–131, Gower, Aldershot.

Rosenhead, J., and Thunhurst, C. (1982). A materialist analysis of operational research, *J. Opl Res. Soc.*, **33**, 111–122.

Schecter, D.S. (1989). For whom and to do what? Questions for a liberating systems approach. Paper presented at the 33rd Annual Meeting of the International Society for Systems Science, Edinburgh.

Spear, R. (1987). Towards a critical systems approach, in *Proceedings (Supplement) of the 31st Annual Meeting of the International Society for General Systems Research*, Budapest.

Spear, R. (1989). Some issues in a critical systems approach. Paper presented at the 33rd Annual Meeting of the International Society for Systems Science, Edinburgh.

Ulrich, W. (1981). A critique of pure cybernetic reason: the Chilean experience with cybernetics, *J. Appl. Syst. Anal.*, **8**, 33–59.

Ulrich, W. (1983). *Critical Heuristics of Social Planning: A New Approach to Practical Philosophy*, Haupt, Berne.

Ulrich, W, (1988). Systems thinking, systems practice, and practical philosophy: a program of research, Chapter 12 this volume.

Ulrich, W. (1989a). Critical heuristics of social systems design, in *Operational Research and the Social Sciences* (Eds. M.C. Jackson, P. Keys, and S. Cropper), pp. 79–87, Plenum, New York.

Ulrich, W. (1989b). Liberating systems theory: four key strategies. Paper presented at the 33rd Annual Meeting of the International Society for Systems Science, Edinburgh.

Chapter 11

Between Systems Thinking and Systems Practice

RAMSÉS FUENMAYOR

INTRODUCTION

In a very thought-provoking paper published in 1982, M.C. Jackson posed three crucial ideas to the systems community:

1. There is a common conceptual region where the works of three of the most distinguished "soft systems thinkers" can be located; namely "what Burrell and Morgan call the 'interpretive' sociological paradigm" (*ibid.*, p. 17).

2. However, such a location remains theoretically unexplored:

> It is surprising to find that at the moment no genuinely interpretive systems *theory* exists . . . Such a theory would have to probe the systemic nature of the interpretations individuals employ in constructing the social world (*ibid.*, p. 18).

3. Jackson concludes his paper by writing:

> We should recognise however that the degree to which soft systems thinking can bring about change in the real-world is determined by its essentially regulative character. It does not pose a real threat to the social structures which support the *Weltanschauungen* with which it works.

I have tried to meet the challenge posed in the second idea. In 1985 I finished the construction of an onto-epistemology for the interpretive (or

Critical Systems Thinking: Directed Readings. Edited by R.L. Flood and M.C. Jackson
© 1991 John Wiley & Sons Ltd

phenomenological) systems approach (Fuenmayor, 1985). From the stand provided by such a theoretical foundation, the third idea posed by Jackson can be discussed on a more solid ground.[1] I will argue in this paper that the non-critical, regulative character of (instead of "soft systems thinking" I would rather say) "soft systems practice" is tightly chained to its pragmatic[2] character and to the consequent lack of a supporting theory. Jackson's criticism might be sound when applied to the current pragmatic use of soft systems ideas, but not in relation to what could be its theoretical interpretive– phenomenological foundation. Nevertheless, both levels remain ambiguous in Jackson's criticism. I will be claiming that a theoretically rooted interpretive systems science is *critical*, in the most authentic sense of the word. In order to support such a claim I must present an outline of the main principles of this science (Interpretive Systemology), so that its fundamental critical character is properly understood.

THE ILL-DEFINEDNESS OF THE SYSTEMS MOVEMENT

The "systems movement" has been defined as a "diverse and ill-defined intellectual enterprise" (Checkland, 1983, p. 669) whose main common concern is the study and design of systems, which are conceived as interconnected complexes exhibiting *emergent properties* that their parts do not exhibit in isolation. According to Checkland, if the mode of thinking of the systems movement "is stripped to its core ideas, two pairs of concepts remain: emergence and hierarchy, communication and control. The most basic of these concepts is that of emergence" (*ibid.*, p. 669). This most basic concept I would rather take to be that of *wholeness*.[3]

In what follows I hope to show that the *ill-definedness* of the systems movement stems from the lack of an onto-epistemology (developed by and

---

[1] The non-critical character of soft systems thinking has been discussed in other papers apart from Jackson's. For a very interesting discussion on the subject see Flood (1989b). In this article I will not be explicitly participating in the details of that discussion for I am only dealing with the more general aspects of the issue. However, I hope that in a future paper, based on the ideas presented in this one, I will be able to explicitly make a criticism to Jackson's, Key's and Flood's ideas about what they call a "pluralist approach." See Jackson and Keys (1984), Jackson (1987) and Flood (1989a).

[2] The word "pragmatic", as used here, bears the connotation of utility with regard to a non-explicit criterion; hence also that of dogmatism.

[3] I have argued in Fuenmayor (1985, pp. 171–174) that the notion of "emergence" is embedded in an onto-epistemological position which is radically opposed to that of a systems approach. In a recent paper, Checkland seems to accept this point when he writes: ". . . forty years after Bertalanffy's semantic disaster we could begin to undo some of the confusion it has caused. We could improve the clarity of Systems Thinking at a stroke by conceding the word system to everyday language and using holon whenever we refer to the abstract concept of a whole" (Checkland, 1988, p. 238).

continually discussed within the systems community) which explains the very notion of wholeness that is at the core of a systems approach.

Since the time of the ancient Greeks it has been observed that some wholes exhibit properties that are not present in any of their parts (Aristotle, 1943, pp. 161–167). To abide by standard phraseology, it was observed that the *whole is more than the sum of its parts*. This observation, when taken to a more general ground, could be stated as *"the whole transcends the mere collection of its parts"* (which does not necessarily mean that the whole is a functional "emergence" of the interaction of the parts).

The very presence of the intuition of wholeness gives rise to two different strands of meaning and intention: a *pragmatic* meaning/intention and a *cogitative* meaning/intention.

Pragmatic Meaning/Intention of the Intuition of Wholeness

In a pragmatic context, the intuition of wholeness means that changes impinging upon the parts could have an overall effect very different from that which they have on the parts by themselves. Particularly, improvement of the functioning of the parts (according to certain predefined criteria) does not necessarily mean functional improvement of the whole. In Plato's words:

> You ought not to attempt to cure the eyes without the head, or the head without the body, so neither ought you to attempt to cure the body without the soul; and this, he said, is the reason why the cure of many diseases is unknown to the physicians of Hellas, because they are ignorant of the whole, which ought to be studied also; for the part can never be well unless the whole is well. (Plato, 1954, p. 13)

Plato is already claiming a pragmatically intended systems approach in the fourth century BC (!). Here, the intentional substance is a warning for effective action.

Cogitative Meaning/Intention of the Intuition of Wholeness

If the same intuition of wholeness is taken to a reflective and theoretical ground, where one is more concerned about the "why", the "what" and the "how is it possible" than "how to make it work more efficiently", fundamental questions surface: "What is wholeness?", "How is it possible that the whole transcends its parts?", "What is the relation between wholeness and Being?", "Is it possible to have holistic knowledge?", "If so, how should we search for it?" In this cogitative ground we find ourselves in a mood of wonder, amazement, inquiring and questioning. The consequent intention is that of theorising; i.e. offering conceptual constructions that explain (answer the questions) and bring forth new questions.

It might not be possible to find either the pragmatic or the cogitative meaning/intention in absolute purity. The most radical pragmatic meaning/intention would have in it something of a cogitative sense and *vice versa*. However, in each possible situation either one or the other holds sway.

The discussion about the ill-definedness, the lack of theoretical rootedness, and the non-critical character of a systems approach becomes much clearer if we bear in mind the difference between those two meanings/intentions stemming from the notion of wholeness. Let us consider why.

A systems approach restricted within the pragmatic boundaries of a particular time, a particular society and a particular set of interests, would only imply a "clinical" posture and ability to "see" things as wholes. If, on the other hand, a systems approach is to be liberated to the cogitative realms of free inquiry and scientific endeavour, it would need a *systems theory* upon which to be formally based. Obviously, a *systems theory* founded on the idea of wholeness should conceptually develop the "central intuition" of "wholeness." This means that a systems theory requires a *systems philosophy* comprised of both *ontological* and *epistemological* aspects. A systems ontology would present an answer to the question: "*What* is it that makes the whole more than the sum of its parts?" That is, "*What* is this central intuition of *wholeness*?" A systems epistemology would treat the possibility and boundaries of knowledge with regard to wholeness, as well as *how* that knowledge can be methodically sought.

Of course, with a mere pragmatic intention in mind we could dispense with a systems theory and be content with the "clinical" posture to which Plato was referring. This seems to be the case with regard to the systems movement. In Varela's words:

> We feel that little effort has been dedicated to arrive at a precise notion of this central intuition of "wholeness" or of "systemness" (Varela and Goguen, 1978, p. 48)

Indeed, this central *intuition* (as it has remained) has not received much attention within the systems movement. It has only been a sort of ideological tenet which accompanies the general introductory prefacing of a systems approach. It simply constitutes a pragmatic yet vague prescription which is in turn part of the intuitive attitude of the systems thinker but which remains theoretically underdeveloped. In this way the apparently profound meaning of a systems approach is reduced to the *intention* of studying things as if they were wholes which transcend the mere coming together of their parts. And this, in its mere notional condition, as we could see from Plato's quote, is nothing new.

INTERPRETIVE SYSTEMS THINKING:
ITS POSSIBILITIES

There are various ill-defined intellectual sub-enterprises (trends, schools, currents, sub-approaches, etc.) within the ill-defined intellectual enterprise that constitutes the systems movement. One possible classification of these intellectual sub-enterprises is that of Checkland's "hard" and "soft" systems movements (Checkland, 1981). Let me concentrate on the second class, which I prefer to call the *"interpretive systems movement"* (see Jackson, 1982 and Fuenmayor, 1985). I will especially concentrate on its *ill-definedness*.

In my opinion, the interpretive systems movement is driven by two fundamental propellants:

1. *The pragmatic propellant*—the failure (so viewed by soft systems thinkers) of the original pragmatic purpose of hard systems engineering. Hard systems engineering is accused of being ivory-towered, separated from the "real", "tricky", "wicked" and "soft" world of everyday life in organisations where "real" decision-taking occurs.[4] In this way, the models produced within the hard trend are considered as elegant manifestations of mathematical refinement, which seldom are useful for real and effective decision-taking.

2. *The conceptual propellant*—the ideas regarding *cultural* or *Weltanschauungen relativism*, which gradually pervaded an important part of the academic milieu in the second half of the present century. According to the notion of *Weltanschauungen relativism*, different societies, different groups within the same society and even different persons, have different interpretations of facts and, in particular, of human actions. Value systems are not the same for different persons. What is regarded as good or desirable by certain people may be regarded as bad and threatening by another. Hence what a person or group of persons consider a problem, may not be so for other persons. Cultural relativism supports the idea that there are no universal or absolute values. One value is not better than another. To consider it so is just another value. Now, we usually do not have a very clear image of our own way of appreciating or interpreting things and, of course, even less of others' ways of interpreting. Besides we tend to take for granted that our interpretation is the only possible one. The result is that we see neither our interpretation nor that of others.

---

[4] According to Churchman: "During the 1960s in a large variety of departments, [systems engineering] academically became 'modelling'; not really modelling at all, but a study of the delights of algorithms; nuances of game theory; fascinating but irrelevant things that can happen in queues . . ." (Churchman, 1979, "Paradise Regained: A Hope for the Future of Systems Design Education"; (quoted in Checkland, 1983, p. 662). I substituted [systems engineering] for "OR."

Human communication is, therefore, based on very soft grounds. Individuals may have different interpretations of what is believed to be the same thing, without being aware of each other's differences. This is the core of what we shall be calling *interpretive complexity*.

Both the propellant of the pragmatic failure of hard systems engineering and the propellant of *Weltanschauungen relativism* have merged into the argument of the soft systems approach. According to Checkland,

> [the soft systems methodology] as a whole clearly articulates a phenomenological investigation into the meanings which actors in a situation attribute to the reality they perceive . . . .. In contrast to [the] paradigm of *optimising* (or satisficing), soft systems methodology embodies a paradigm of *learning*. The notion of "a solution," whether it optimizes or satisfices, is inappropriate in a methodology which orchestrates a process of learning which, as a process, is never-ending. (Checkland, 1981, pp. 278–279)

If one considers the actual driving intention beneath this "paradigm of learning," bearing in mind our former classification of *pragmatic* and *cogitative* intentions, two different and extreme possibilities come forward: One regards the learning as a means, or rather a tool, for managing human organisations (human activity systems). It is moved by a *pragmatic* intention confined within the boundaries set by managerial decision taking in an industrial–technological social order. This possibility will be called *"pragmatic–regulative interpretive management."* On the opposite extreme, the second possibility considers *learning* itself as the key focus. It is moved by the *scientific* intention of gaining knowledge for its own sake (which does not imply that as such it does not have a social effect that can also be studied). *"Interpretive Systemology,"* as I will be calling this second possibility, is essentially *critical* and hence liberating— not because it is moved by any ideology, but because it is *interpretive*. Yet, some readers might remain puzzled about how a non-pragmatic, scientific and philosophical enterprise could also be critical and liberating. Let us see why by examining both possibilities:

Pragmatic–Regulative Interpretive Management

Here the pragmatic propellant takes into its service the conceptual one. The latter is used as a cognitively useful principle for pragmatic purposes.

Since different actors in an organisation may have different *Weltanschauungen* concerning the ends and the activities of the organisation, in order to find a convenient and feasible organisation of the means it is necessary to have a notion about the plurality of *Weltanschauungen* (and the interpretations derived from them) which may be relevant within a particular situation. Conscious decision-taking is thus based on the knowledge of different interpretations regarding the ends and significations that the organisation of the means may evoke.

Within this perspective, the role of the soft systems practitioner is then to display a dynamic *"map"* of the different possibilities with regard to the ends, the efficient organisation of the means to achieve each of the possible ends (according to the particular values comprised in each end), and again the possible interpretations with regard to those means. This *map* becomes an important tool for those in power ("client," "problem owner") because they can now have two managerial instruments: On the one hand they have the "hard" apparatus provided by OR, control engineering, statistics, etc., devoted to assess the various possibilities with regard to the organisation of the means in terms of financial costs or potential benefits. On the other hand, the *map* provided by the interpretive systems practitioner helps them to assess the organisation of the means in terms of *"cultural feasibility"* inside and outside the organisation. However, there exists the possibility that the "map" could also be used by those which are not "in power."

As announced before, here learning is only a tool. It is a pragmatic tool at the service of something else. *Pragmatic–regulative interpretive management* requires some methodological guidelines, some psychological techniques and a clever "clinical" ability. It does not require a theoretical foundation that goes deeper than the methodological level. To ask for it would be sheer nonsense. Furthermore, and this is crucial for my argument in this article, the question about the inquiry and subsequent modelling of the variety of *Weltanschauungen* goes as far as is *"relevant"* to the pragmatic purposes embedded in the particular problematic situation under consideration. A pragmatic approach does not have to dig into the roots of the considered *Weltanschauungen*. That would mean, from the pragmatic point of view, a waste of time. Of course, that also means that, on the one hand, the *Weltanschauungen* at stake are only superficially explored; and, on the other hand, there might be other possible interpretations of the situation that are not considered at all. This, as I hope to show later, is the reason why a pragmatic approach is always, in one way or another, regulative.

It should be noticed that I have dropped out the word "system" from the title of the possibility under examination. The reason, as already explained, is that *systemness* (or wholeness) is not really an issue within this pragmatic approach. At most it is a secondary "clinical" precept (and maybe an excuse to have a special place in the world of management).

Interpretive Systemology: Outline of its Basic Principles

In order to explain this second possibility I must return to the fundamental principles of an interpretive approach.

When describing the idea of *Weltanschauungen relativism* we came across the notion of *interpretive complexity*. Observe that what is complex in *interpretive complexity* is the difficulty of seeing the variety of interpretations rather than the variety itself. *The source of that difficulty and, at the same time, its most immediate consequence, lie in the difficulty of seeing our own states of mind.* Sir Geoffrey Vickers draws a very dramatic verbal picture in order to depict the idea:

> Lobster pots are designed to catch lobsters. A man entering a man-size lobster pot would become suspicious of the narrowing tunnel, he would shrink form the drop at the end; and if he fell in, he would recognise the entrance as a possible exit and climb out again—even if he were the shape of a lobster. A trap is a trap only for creatures which cannot solve the problems that it sets. Man-traps are dangerous only in relation to the limitations on what men can see and value and do. The nature of the trap is a function of the nature of the trapped. To describe either is to imply the other . . . We the trapped tend to take our own state of mind for granted—which is partly why we are trapped. *With the shape of the trap in our minds, we shall be better able to see the relevance of our limitations and to question those assumptions about ourselves which are most inept to the activity and the experience of being human now.* (Vickers, 1970, p. 15—the emphasis is mine)

But why should it be difficult to "see" our own states of mind? Furthermore, why do I say that the source of interpretive complexity lies in this difficulty to see our own states of mind? In other words, how can we conceptually link together the invisibility of our own states of mind with the rationale of this invisibility and with interpretive complexity. We need to reflect on the concept of *interpretation* in order to gain more insight into the sought link.

The words "interpretation", "meaning" and "sense" are normally used in situations where it is acceptable for something to be understood in different ways (interpretations) according to various contexts (interpretive contexts or contexts of meaning). For example, when we say that the *meaning* of the word "eventual" in the English language is "ultimately resulting," whereas the "same" word (same spelling) means "subject to contingency" in the Spanish language; we are saying that the "same" symbol (set of letters) has different *interpretations* ("ultimately resulting" and "subject to contingency") in different *contexts of meaning*, namely, the English and Spanish languages.

We thus readily accept the relativity of certain objects (for example, symbols). However, there are other things that are normally taken as absolute (independent of the context of meaning) and hence as existing independently of the observer. For example, when we see a watch on somebody's wrist we do not normally think that such an object may be "seen" in different ways according to different contexts of meaning. It is a watch and nothing else. *This simply means that interpretation is taking place according to one single context of meaning which remains implicit and hence we are not aware of it.* We are, to use Vickers' words, "trapped" in it.

The relativity of that which seems absolute can only be brought forward by *contrasting it with another context of meaning* different from that of the everyday one which guides our lives. Such a *contrast* (which is to become the fundamental methodological notion in Interpretive Systemology) also brings forth the everyday invisible context of meaning.[5] The contrasting is itself illuminating and, hence, *liberating* of our deepest trap—that of the giveness and grantedness of everyday life. (Remember that the pragmatic–regulative approach tends to leave under the cover the "non-relevant"—for pragmatic purposes— aspects of the interpretive context under consideration.)

In order to gain more clarity about this central idea of interpretive relativism, I would like to quote an amazing passage from Jonathan Swift's *Gulliver's Travels* (first published in 1726) where a contrast of contexts of meaning takes place. Gulliver is taken to the capital city of Lilliput, where he is searched. A report is given to the king on his possessions. In a fragment of such a report we read:

> There were two pockets which we could not enter: these he called his fobs; they were two large slits cut into the top of his middle cover, but squeezed close by the pressure of his belly. Out of the right fob hung a great silver chain, with a wonderful kind of engine at the bottom. We directed him to draw out whatever was at the end of that chain; which appeared to be a globe, half silver, and half of some transparent metal: for on the transparent side we saw certain strange figures circularly drawn, and thought we could touch them, till we found our fingers stopped with that lucid substance. He put this engine in our ears, which made an incessant noise like that of a watermill. And we conjecture it is either some unknown animal, or the god that he worships: but we are more inclined to the latter opinion, because he assured us (if we understood him right, for he expressed himself very imperfectly), that he seldom did anything without consulting it. He called it his oracle, and said it pointed out the time for every action of his life.

Swift imagines a society (a context of meaning) where its members are of a very small size as compared with Gulliver, and who see things from a different cultural viewpoint—or interpretive context. The new contrasting interpretive context allows us to discover our own interpretive context with regard to what normally looks like an absolute entity, namely a watch. After that, and as long as we think interpretively about it, a watch is not an absolute entity, it is a relative interpretation.

An *interpretation* is a mode of Being whose logical essence lies in its dependence from "that" with regard to which (or "in which") interpretation takes place. "That in which" interpretation occurs is an "interpretive

---

[5] Some classical writers have used this resource of imagining other contexts of meaning in order to discover their own. Good examples are the utopia designers of the Renaissance (Thomas More, Francis Bacon, Campanella). This idea constitutes the source of the core methodological concept of contrasting ideal-type conceptual models, which lies behind the methodological guidelines exposed in Fuenmayor (1985) and Fuenmayor (1988).

context" or "context of meaning." The "interpretive context" is not the "interpretation," but the interpretation cannot *be* without the "interpretive context." Thus an "interpretation" is something which "is-not-in-itself." This "not-being-in-itself" means that it is not identical to itself since it may or may not be, depending on the interpretive context (i.e. it is a *possibility*, a contingency). *The mode of Being of an interpretation is that of a possibility*, since that which it may be depends upon different "interpretive contexts." The very notion of "interpretive context" necessarily implies that there are other "interpretive contexts." Were it not so, the *interpretation* would be only a thing determined in itself. In other words, the singleness or universality of an "interpretive context" makes it invisible (undistinguishable) as a context; the interpretation is only an absolute determination independent of the observer; and we are trapped.

This conception by which phenomena are viewed as *interpretations* is radically different from the onto-epistemological position underlying positivist dualistic science. In the latter a thing is determined in itself. *The purpose of the positivist dualistic scientific enterprise is then to give account of such determination.* This is performed by finding and representing in models the *stable* properties that characterise such phenomena and the relations obtaining among them. These models aim to represent the Laws of Nature. On the other hand, *within an authentic interpretive approach, a phenomenon is not determined in itself; it is an interpretation.*[6]

As a consequence of such an interpretive conception, *the methodical search for knowledge is characterised by the modelling of various contexts of meaning; by explicitly interpreting the phenomenon with regard to such contexts of meaning and by discussing the various interpretations in the light of their respective contexts of meaning.* The deeper the contexts of meaning are theoretically explored, the more critical and liberating the discussion.

We can now recapitulate the conceptual link between interpretive complexity and the invisibility of our own states of mind. By this path we should arrive at the essential character of a cogitative interpretive approach.

When, in everyday life, there is a case of *interpretation*, there is also a case of doubt. Different viewpoints are present in consciousness. Various possibilities with regard to the being of something are allowed. In this case various contexts of meaning, including ours, tend to be present. On the other hand, when, as in the example of the watch on somebody's wrist—not in the case of Gulliver's "oracle"—we have in front of us an absolute independent being, neither our own contexts of meaning nor other possible ones are explicitly offered to our consciousness.

---

[6] "Each interpretation is not reality, but all of them are reality. In other terms, reality is not exhausted in any of its particular interpretations, it is only manifested through them" (Marias, 1968, pp. 193–195—my translation).

This philosophical reflection in which we are now immersed tells us that *"what-ever-is-the-case"* is always an interpretation relative to an *interpretive context* (or *state of mind* as we called it before, following Vickers). However, in everyday life interpretive contexts are normally invisible and we are faced with "absolutely objective beings." Were it not so we would always be doubting everything we see and everyday action would be hindered. In everyday life we can afford to have some moments of doubt but we could not live—at least as we normally see life—if we were constantly to doubt everything. That is, we need to live amidst *absolute objective things* and not amidst *interpretations*. A few cases of variety of interpretations reinforce our valuable determinations; but too many cases of interpretations would make the task of living somewhat difficult.

According to what I have just said, the idea of studying and understanding *interpretive complexity* opposes not only positivist dualistic scientific thinking but also our present everyday thinking and its need for blind determinations. Indeed, the authentic and radical quest of interpretive systems thinking is characterised by being *critical and transcendental* in the Kantian and Husserlian senses of the words. That is, it is a thinking that has to think itself in order to interpretively understand others' actions. Let me explain why. The task of interpretive thinking is the unconcealment of a variety of contexts of meaning in order to understand various possible interpretations of human actions. Nevertheless, as already argued, such an enlightening endeavour requires the unconcealment of the interpretive context of the interpretive thinker. But the interpretive thinker is here understood as *any* interpretive thinker situated in *any* time and place. This is nothing but the abstract idealised notion of interpretive thinking itself. The interpretive context of interpretive thinking so conceived is nothing but the onto-epistemological position on which it stands.

We conclude that *if interpretive systems thinking does not develop for itself an onto-epistemology which accounts for Holism and the possibility of its understanding, and links it with the onto-epistemological foundation of the relativistic approach that is behind the concept of interpretation; if such a philosophical building is not constructed and always reconstructed, then interpretive systems thinking is trapped in a profound conceptual contradiction.* It would fall in its own "trap" (in Vickers' sense). It would be preaching to others the awareness of that which they take for granted without making a serious attempt at being aware of that which it is taking for granted. It would then be essentially self-contradictory. The consequence of such contradiction is that its *thinking* will not go beyond a set of cognitive slogans at the service of a pragmatic intention. Such contradiction is obviously of no harm to the pragmatic–regulative approach.

If, on the other hand, this current of thought (that so far has been called interpretive systems thinking, or the interpretive systems approach) does lay such theoretical foundations and applies them to the understanding of social phenomena, which in turn should allow its enrichment and its never-ending self discovery, then we can speak of a possible new science that could rightly be called Interpretive Systemology.

It is important to stress the idea that when I refer to the *construction* of an onto-epistemological *building*, I do not mean a simple set of propositions and quotations of ontic and epistemic meaning surrounding a methodological guideline.[7] I do mean a theoretical and philosophical construction of a conceptual *system* which accounts for the holistic and interpretive nature of what-ever-is-the-case, together with the possibility of its systematic understanding. It is an interpretive systems philosophy that cannot be expressed in the form of a loose set of predicative judgments typical of natural empirical sciences. Hence, a propositional summary of such a theory *indicates* the conceptual region where it is placed—as when we indicate the place where something is located with our finger. However, such a summary cannot *express* the theory.

Besides the onto-epistemology mentioned so far, an interpretive systems theory requires a social theory and a theory of organisations, both based on the theoretical onto-epistemological foundation. I will be referring to them below.

Now, as I said before, interpretive systems theory is a never-ending construction. It starts with a first iteration—which already is a theoretical building. The first theory is used both to understand phenomena, while sometimes acting on them, and to understand theory itself. This understanding should enrich the theoretical building.

A proposed outline for the development of Interpretive Systemology[8] is represented in Figure 11.1.

A first iteration of a general interpretive systems onto-epistemology has already been constructed.[9] It is a theoretical attempt to deal with the question of Being, of knowledge and of truth from a holistic–interpretive stand. It strives to explain the holistic and interpretive structure (not to be understood in static terms) of *"what-ever-is-the-case"* together with its cognitive possibility. In a very few words, the region where the core of our onto-epistemology is placed can be indicated (not expressed) as follows.

---

[7] Notice that I am making a semantic distinction between the pairs ontic–epistemic and ontological–epistemological. Ontological and epistemological refer to a general theory of Being and to a general theory of the possibility of truthful knowledge respectively. Ontic and epistemic refer to the nature and the possibility of knowing a particular theme; for example organisations, society, etc.

[8] This is how we have understood our task in the research group in Interpretive Systemology of the School of Systems Engineering of the University of Los Andes in Venezuela. For that purpose we have outlined the long-term (life?) research plan represented in Figure 11.1

[9] This was the main outcome of Fuenmayor, 1985. Lopez-Garay (1986) also dealt with the onto-epistemological foundation of an interpretive systems approach by means of a profound investigation on the concept of systems design.

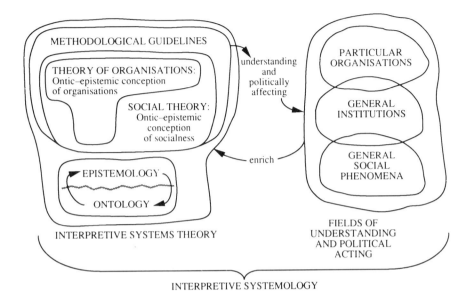

Figure 11.1 Outline of a research programme for interpretive systemology

Whether we see it or not, we are always necessarily in what Vickers calls a "state of mind," or what I called before an "interpretive context." Although most frequently it is invisible to ourselves, a state of mind is indispensable for any awareness about "what-ever-is-the-case." *The case* is always a *distinction* of that which is the case from that which it is *not*. As I have shown elsewhere (Fuenmayor, 1985, pp. 146–174), the very act of *distinction* and the processual structure to which it belongs in any living *situation* is the very core of "what-ever-is-the-case" and the fundamental source of holism. The holistic unity of "what-ever-is-the-case" stems from the transcendental recursive unity of *distinction*. This unity is understood within a non-traditional logical space; namely the logical space of transcendental recursiveness to which the open paradox of Gödel's Proof belongs. *This is why a holistic apprehension requires an interpretive approach.*

The second theoretical brick of our academic enterprise is a social theory which accounts for the nature of that which is social (socialness) and the possibility of its knowledge. This theory is based on the general interpretive systems onto-epistemology mentioned before. Such a theory has not been constructed yet. Sor far, we think that its cornerstone should be the transcendental recursive triad "self–others–objective reality". The work of Dilthey, Husserl, Heidegger, Ortega y Gasset, Schutz, Weber, Berger and Luckmann and others, with regard to socialness should constitute a good starting point for such a purpose.

Our third brick is an interpretive systems theory of organisations also founded in our general onto-epistemology. By linking interpretive diversity within an organisation to the conflicts of power that encompass its dynamics, a general model of an organisation is drawn.[10]

The epistemological aspect of both the social theory and the theory of organisations should contain methodological ideas which can guide the understanding of particular phenomena.

Now that the basic principles and planned outline of interpretive systemology have been presented, I can make a more clear comparison between this scientific enterprise and "pragmatic–regulative interpretive management."

INTERPRETIVE SYSTEMOLOGY: ITS UNCONCEALING INTENTION AND ITS POSSIBLE SOCIAL EFFECT

As explained before, the exploration and modelling of interpretive contexts performed within the boundaries of a pragmatic–regulative interpretive approach are limited (in principle) by the pragmatic intention of the research. Such pragmatic intention is very likely to coincide with the interests of those in power or, in any case, with the interests that are at the base of any pragmatic intention. Hence, certain interpretive contexts are very likely to remain obscure and unexplored. Otherwise managerial action would be hindered.

On the contrary, the driving intention of Interpretive Systemology is to gain a pluralist dialectical understanding of social phenomena (Fuenmayor, 1985, pp. 211–216). This is nothing but the *opening* of interpretive possibilities (interpretations) in terms of their interpretive contexts. This is the unconcealment of that which normally is taken for granted. *Such an unconcealing drive cannot carry with it a pragmatic intention* (which does not preclude the possibility of its practical effect). Were it so, the unconcealing drive would stop and the openness of possibilities would close. In order to clarify this question, we must briefly revise the conception of *truth* comprised by Interpretive Systemology and its relation to human purposive action.

According to our interpretive systems onto-epistemology, *truth is an essentially dynamic process which cannot be finished or stopped because it would turn into the opposite of truth (ibid.,* pp. 195–196). Truth lies in the openness of possibilities. Truth is the never-ending trip towards the horizon in which all possible interpretive contexts are disclosed; a horizon where there are not absolute determinations, only interpretive possibilities. The journey to truth is the journey to mental freedom. The opposite of truth is the closing of possibilities; i.e. the setting of determinations.

---

[10] I have already written about two-thirds of its first iteration. (Fuenmayor, 1988).

Truth so conceived cannot accompany purposive action. We need determinations in order to act intentionally. In order to walk out of this room I need to dogmatically and blindly take for granted that the floor is there. In order to act we need to close possibilities, we need to fall in traps. But intentional action is indispensable to human everyday life.[11] Furthermore, intentional action is indispensable to truthful thought, for everyday life is indispensable to truthful thought. If there is no intentional action, thinking of any kind is frozen to death. Truthful thought stems from everyday life but opposes the determinations required by everyday life. It precisely "parenthesises" everyday life in order to reflectively see it. Truthful thought is then the possibility that everyday life has to see itself. On the other hand, if there is not truthful thinking—or at least its seminal intention—human action "is heard no more; it [becomes] a tale told by an idiot, full of sound and fury, signifying nothing" (Shakespeare, *Macbeth*).

Authentic interpretive systems thinking and intentional action are the opposite parties of a dialectic that cannot dissolve in a non-dialectical synthesis. If interpretive systems thinking intends to serve pragmatic purposes it becomes "technical" or "calculative" thinking[12]; a thinking intended which necessarily relies on one or more dogmatic determinations. This is the negation of liberating interpretive systems thinking.

The former idea does not, by any means, imply that Interpretive Systemology isolates itself from practice, or that practice cannot be oriented by Interpretive Systemology. On the contrary, interpretive systemology is devoted to finding meanings to social practice. Besides, the opening of possibilities brought forth by interpretive discussion should, to use Habermas' words, "be translated into processes of enlightenment which are rich in political consequences." Of course, the political effect depends, as Habermas continues, on "the institutional preconditions for practical discourse among the general public" (Habermas, 1974, p. 3). Both political consequences and the institutional preconditions for practical discourse are, in turn, part of the field of study of Interpretive Systemology. Furthermore, the effect of pragmatic–regulative interpretive management can be a very interesting window

---

[11] I am not referring to life in a dualistic biological sense. I mean by "life" the stream of what we are living.
[12] Heidegger defines "calculative thinking" as a thinking whose "peculiarity consists in the fact that whenever we plan, research, and organize, we always reckon with conditions that are given. We take them into account with the calculated intention of their serving specific purposes. Thus we can count on definite results. This calculation is the mark of all thinking that plans and investigates. Such thinking remains calculation even if it neither works with numbers nor uses an adding machine or computer. Calculative thinking computes. It computes ever new, ever more promising and at the same time more economical possibilities. Calculative thinking races from one prospect to the next. Calculative thinking never stops, never collects itself. Calculative thinking is not meditative thinking, not thinking which contemplates the meaning which reigns in everything that is" (Heidegger, 1966, p. 46).

242 _____ Ramsés Fuenmayor

to observe social action in organisations. However, I must insist, such necessary relation with social practice does not mean that the thinking proper to our endeavour is a *means* for action. The very moment it becomes so, it ceases to be *critical*, and becomes regulative. This is why "pragmatic–regulative interpretive management" cannot, as any other pragmatic oriented thinking, be critical. Its learning is compromised from its very marrow with the rationality (or *Weltanschauung*) that is driving present industrial technological society. It cannot be authentically critical.

Nevertheless, the walk by the path of an authentic critical thinking is not only hindered by its own inner difficulty, but by the overwhelming power of technological rationality. Indeed, the lack of a pragmatic (technical) intention, the lack of usefulness, the radical questioning, the transcendental intention are not popular features for an academic enterprise. It is to be condemned by technological rationality as "ivory towered," "theoretical," "philosophical," "useless," etc. And this, nowadays, is a mortal condemnation—not to be guillotined or put in prison, but to be left aside in indifference, disregard, silence and oblivion. In Mishan's words:

> There may be doubts among philosophers and heart-searching among poets, but to the multitude the kingdom of God is to be realized here, and now, on this earth; and it is to be realized via technological innovation, and at an exponential rate. Its universal appeal exceeds that of the brotherhood of man, indeed it comprehends it. For as we become richer, surely we shall remedy all social evils; heal the sick; comfort the aged and exhilarate the young. One has only to think with sublime credulity of the opportunities to be opened to us by the harvest of the increasing wealth: universal adult education, free art and entertainment, frequent visits to the moon, a domestic robot in every home and, therefore, women forever freed from drudgery; for the common man, a lifetime of leisure to pursue culture and pleasure (or, rather, to absorb them from the TV screen); for the scientists, ample funds to devise increasingly powerful and ingenious computers so that we may have yet more time for culture and pleasure and scientific discovery. . . . Here, then, is the panacea to be held with a fervour, indeed with a piety, that silences thought. (Mishan, 1967, pp. 27–28)

CONCLUSION

I have shown that the third claim of Jackson (mentioned in the "Introduction") with regard to the non-critical character of interpretive systems thinking is a consequence of his second claim (about the theoretical rootlessness of this sort of "thinking"). Indeed, Interpretive Systemology does not need the eclectic addition of other approaches in order to be critical, for it is critical in its very marrow. It is also "imperialist" in the sense of Jackson (1987) and Flood (1989a), for any coherent theory is "imperialist." Were it not so, it would lose its holistic–theoretical character. But I must leave this discussion for a future article.

When Checkland (quoted above) speaks of "a phenomenological investigation into the meanings that actors in a situation attribute to the reality they perceive," I suppose he is referring to a "phenomenological investigation" in Husserl's sense. In my understanding, the hallmark of a phenomenological investigation is the "parenthesising" by which we critically "put out of play all positions taken toward the already given objective world" (Husserl, 1960, p. 20). This is Husserl's "fundamental phenomenological method of transcendental epoché." In it,

> the Delphic motto, "Know thyself" has gained a new signification. Positive science is a science lost in the world. I must lose the world by epoché, in order to regain it by a universal self-examination. (*ibid.*, p. 157)

Under this interpretation of Checkland's words one is left to wonder: What is the meaning of the comma in "Systems thinking, Systems Practice"?

ACKNOWLEDGEMENT

Thanks are due to Professors R.L. Flood and M.C. Jackson for their encouragement to write this article and for their helpful comments and editing of the manuscript. I also want to express my gratitude to the University of Los Andes, the University of Hull and the British Council which have financed my visit to the Department of Management Systems and Sciences of Hull University, where the article was written.

REFERENCES

Aristotle. (1943), *Metafísica*, Espasa-Calpe, Madrid.

Checkland, P.B. (1981). *Systems Thinking, Systems Practice*, John Wiley, Chichester.

Checkland, P.B. (1983). OR and the systems movement: mappings and conflicts, *J. Opl Res. Soc.*, **34**, 661–675.

Checkland, P.B. (1988). A case for "Holon", *Syst. Pract.*, **1**, 235–238.

Flood, R.L. (1989a). Six scenarios for the future of systems "problem solving", *Syst. Pract.*, **2**, 75–99.

Flood, R.L. (1989b). Liberating systems theory: towards critical systems thinking, *Hum. Relat.*, **43**, 49–75.

Fuenmayor, R.L. (1985). *The Ontology and Epistemology of a Systems Approach: A Fundamental Study and an Application to the Phenomenon Development/Underdevelopment*, Ph.D. thesis, Dept. of Systems, University of Lancaster.

Fuenmayor, R.L. (1988). *Resumen de una Teoria Sistemico-interpretativa sobre organizaciones*, Working Paper, Universidad de Los Andes, Merida.

Habermas, J. (1974). *Theory and Practice*, Heinemann, London.

Heidegger, M. (1966). *Discourse on Thinking*, Harper and Row, New York.

Husserl, E. (1960). *Cartesian Meditations*, Martin Nijhoff, The Hague.

Jackson, M.C. (1982). The nature of soft systems thinking: the work of Churchman, Ackoff and Checkland, *J. Appl. Syst. Anal.*, **9**, 17–29.

Jackson, M.C. (1987). Present positions and future prospects in management science, *Omega*, **15**, 455–466.

Jackson, M.C., and Keys, P. (1984). Towards a system of systems methodologies, Chapter 7 this volume.

Lopez–Garay, H. (1986). *A Holistic Interpretive Concept of Systems Design*, Ph.D. thesis, University of Pennsylvania.

Marias, J. (1968). *Introduccion a la Filosofia*, Revista de Occidente, Madrid.

Mishan, E.J. (1967). *The Costs of Economic Growth*, Penguin, Harmondsworth.

Plato. (1954). Charmides, in *The Dialogues of Plato*, volume 1, Clarendon Press, Oxford.

Shakespeare, W. (1623). "Macbeth," in *The Complete Works*, Collins, London.

Swift, J. (1726). *Gulliver's Travels*, Penguin, Harmondsworth.

Varela, F.J., and Goguen, J.A. (1978). The arithmetic of closure, in *Progress in Cybernetics and Systems Research*, volume 3 (Ed. R. Trappl), John Wiley, New York.

Vickers, G. (1970). *Freedom in a Rocking Boat*, Penguin, Harmondsworth.

Systems Thinking, Systems Practice, and Practical Philosophy: A Program of Research

WERNER ULRICH

SYSTEMS PRACTICE: THE NEED FOR A PROGRAM OF RESEARCH

Reason is impelled by a tendency of its nature to venture to the utmost limits of all knowledge, and not to be satisfied save through the completion of its course in a self-subsistent systematic whole. Is this endeavour the outcome merely of the speculative interest of reason? Must we not regard it as having its source exclusively in the practical interests of reason?
Immanuel Kant, *Critique of Pure Reason* (1787, p. 825)

C. West Churchman diagnosed the case several years ago: the systems approach will not serve the cause of socially rational decision making unless it opens itself up to the social life-worlds of the *"enemies"* of systems rationality—the life-worlds of politics, morality, religion, and aesthetics. "What's really happening in the human world is politics, or morality, or religion, or aesthetics" (Churchman, 1979, p. 53).

The systems approach, *because* it strives for comprehensiveness, must learn to live with its own unavoidable incomprehensiveness and must draw the necessary conclusions from this insight. It must bother *to take into account that*

Reproduced by permission from *Systems Practice*, Volume 1, 1988 *which is not systemic in its nature* and hence cannot be rationalized in the terms of systems rationality. Otherwise its quest for comprehensiveness—originally directed critically against the reductionist tendencies of conventional scientific discipline—is bound to lead into new kinds of reductionism; for example, by reducing everything to "nothing but" functional systems aspects.

But of course, what is the use of the most insightful diagnosis if remedies are wanting? Decision makers and planners taking the systems idea seriously enough to consider their decision's (or design's) inevitable *lack* of comprehensive rationality will face a true dilemma: while conventional decision-making tools such as cost-benefit analysis and scientific modelling are clearly too narrow a base for practising the systems idea, they are yet the only tools available that are well defined, and they are apt to offer—within the limits of their range of application—some sort of "objective" basis of argumentation.

It is thus understandable that, for instance, the dialectical debate among systems planners and "enemies" advocated by Churchman has hardly appealed to decision makers as an alternative. Of course Churchman does not sell it as such; he employs it as a tool of philosophical reflection rather than a stringently defined procedure for practical decision making (which is not to say that it could not be "operationalized" in terms of reproducible procedural and institutional arrangements). And of course, the apparent stringency of conventional decision-making tools should not deceive us about their methodological helplessness in dealing with essential issues such as measuring benefits, opportunity costs, or trade-offs between different dimensions of benefits or costs considered. Moreover, it is hardly fair to blame the systems approach for *causing* the difficulty of which it is only the messenger, namely, the inevitable *lack* of comprehensiveness in our knowledge and understanding of whole systems (Ulrich, 1981a). Nevertheless, as justified as these excuses may be, the fact remains that the systems movement has not been able thus far to develop a stringent methodological framwork.

The Methodological Challenge

In view of this situation, we should probably not pretend to be able to do without conventional tools. Rather—and this is my basic presupposition for a research program under the title of "systems practice"—we should develop a *conceptual framework* that would:

1. assign an adequate place to, and yield *proper standards of improvement* for, all kinds of systems methodologies—conventioanl "hard" systems tools as well as newer "soft" and (anticipated) "critical" systems methodologies;[1]

---

[1] Compare, for instance, P.B. Checkland's (1972, 1981) "soft systems methodology" and the recent developments toward a "critical management science" (Jackson and Keys, 1987).

2. help us to deal critically with the theories of social reality, and corresponding *concepts of rational social action*, implied by each type of systems methodology; and

3. finally, embed the application of these tools within well-defined *institutional and procedural arrangements for rational debate* among the various parties involved in, and affected by, a decision.

Such a program of research will require the systems movement to expand considerably its universe of discourse. It will need to open itself up to traditions of thought that promise to offer methodological support for the task of mediating between systems concepts and the life-practical concerns of the "enemies". I propose that one such tradition is *practical philosophy*, which has recently experienced a considerable renaissance, especially in German philosophy (see, e.g., Riedel, 1972–1974; Bubner, 1975; Apel, 1976; Hoffe, 1979; Habermas, 1971a, 1973a, 1981).

In the present essay, I argue that building a bridge between systems philosphy and practical philosophy is not only necessary but also possible, in a systematic and fruitful way. Both traditions are likely to benefit from a systematic link; they share not only a common origin in the critical philosophy of Immanuel Kant, but also the same practical intent—to bring more reason into actual social practice. Historically they have gone separate ways in pursuing this intent and, accordingly, have brought forth different insights and encountered different difficulties. But it seems to me that their respective insights and difficulties are largely complementary; while practical philosophy has failed to take into account Kant's demonstration of the critical significance—and, indeed, unavoidability—of the systems idea, the systems movement has long been neglecting Kant's lesson that practical reason cannot be reduced to (or derived from) "value-neutral" theoretical–instrumental reason but must be grounded in a critically reflected interest. "An interest is that by which reason becomes practical—that is, a cause determining the will" (Kant, 1788, p. 122n). In order to reflect and debate systematically on the normative implications of systems designs, we shall need both the *idea of practical reason* as a critical standard against which to examine the instrumental rationality that our decision-making tools may produce and the *systems idea* as a critical reminder to reflect on those implications of our design which reach beyond the limited context of application that we are able to consider for all practical purposes—i.e. their *whole-systems implications*.

The following attempt to sketch out the framework for a systematic linkage of the two traditions draws mainly on my recent inquiry into the epistemological foundations of a critically normative systems approach, *Critical Heuristics of Social Planning* (Ulrich, 1983), and on Jürgen Habermas' (1981) *Theory of Communicative Action*. First, however, it is necessary to give a short introduction to contemporary practical philosophy and, especially to the major change of its underlying paradigm.

PRACTICAL PHILOSOPHY: TOWARD A "COMMUNICATIVE" PARADIGM OF RATIONAL SOCIAL PRACTICE

Practical philosophy is the philosophical effort to come to terms with the *problem of practical reason*: How can we rationally determine and justify the norms of action contained in recommendations or plans for action?

"Norms regulate legitimate chances for the satisfaction of needs" (Habermas, 1973b, p. 251). Thus we can say that it is the task of practical reason to decide upon the social acceptability of disputed value premises or life-practical consequences of actions with respect to the chances of all those affected to satisfy their needs.

Practical versus Theoretical Reason

It is helpful to contrast the task of practical reason with that of theoretical reason: while theoretical reason is to decide on disputed claims regarding the *empirical validity* of theoretical propositions (hypotheses), practical reason is to decide on disputed claims concerning the *normative validity* of practical propositions (assertions of norms, recommendations for action). In both cases, the decision is to be reached by "the peculiarly unforced force of the better argument" (Habermas, 1973a, p. 240) rather than by resort to power or deception.

Both problems also lead into the same logical difficulty: "How can we ever justify the generalizability of empirical observations or normative assertions to universally valid statements?" Since there is no logical principle allowing us to generalize observational to theoretical statements (nomological "laws"), the *problem of induction* has become the fundamental philosophical problem of empiricism; and since there is likewise no logical principle that would permit us to universalize subjective valuations to generally binding norms of action (moral "laws"), the *problem of practical reason* has become the fundamental concern of practical philosophy.

There are, of course, essential differences between the two basic dimensions of reason. These have to do with the fact that theoretical reason is concerned with producing *"objective" knowledge* about some segment of "the" phenomenal world, whereas practical reason is to secure *ethically justified consensus* about norms regulating interpersonal relationships within "our" world of society (cf. Habermas, 1979, p. 63ff). That is to say, theoretical reason is bound to "observe" (in the double meaning of the word) the "laws" that effectively govern the phenomenal world of experience, while practical reason is free to determine the laws which—according to its own judgment—*ought* to govern our social world of human relationships. This difference explains why "facts"—i.e. empirical statements—cannot be shown to be valid ("true") without reference to some objectified aspects of the phenomenal world, whereas "norms" or practical statements can be established as valid ("right") by their mere intersubjective assertion. As Kant writes in his inimitable terseness: "By 'the practical' I mean everything that is possible through freedom" (1787, p. 828).

The challenge to practical reason consists in using this freedom reasonably, that is, in determining the ends and means of one's actions "with reason". We call this effort of rational deliberation on one's use of freedom, on the ends and means of anticipated social practice, *planning*. Whenever there is freedom to plan, claims to rationality will therefore inevitably involve the problem of practical reason. If such claims are disputed, it will be of no avail for the systems planner to seek refuge in references to theoretical reason; for example, with the common arguments that he "merely" provides tools for those legitimately in control of purposes (cf. Ulrich, 1983, p. 25), or that the critic is not knowledgeable or expert enough with respect to the system in question (Ulrich, 1983, p. 309).

Practical versus Subjective Reason

A second way to introduce the concept of practical reason is by contrasting it with the concept of *subjectively* rational action. This approach is less customary but has the advantage of starting from our daily experience that our personal freedom of choice may conflict with that of others and of taking us from there immediately to the current change of paradigm in practical philosophy.

Subjectively an individual acts rationally if his ends are in agreement with his standards of value *and* if he efficiently utilizes the means at his disposal to achieve these ends. The two conditions mentioned correspond to Max Weber's "ideal types" of rational action, "value-rationality" (*Wertrationalität* = convergence of purposes and values) and "purposive-rationality" (*Zweckrationalität* = adequacy of means in regard to purposes). Together they are constitutive of the *utilitarian concept of rationality*. This type of rationality is oriented toward the success of one's actions, whereby ends are assumed to be given and "success" is measured in terms of cost–benefit analysis. It clearly belongs to the dimension of theoretical reason. Because theoretical reason here serves an instrumental purpose with respect to given ends rather than a theoretical interest in gaining knowledge, Max Horkheimer (1967) has aptly called it *"instrumental" reason*.

In practice, subjectively rational action tends to produce consequences that affect individuals not involved in the underlying decision. Their way of being affected need not correspond to *their* standards of value; the action in question may appear "irrational" or unreasonable to them. Hence any action the consequences of which are not certain to remain limited to those involved—in one word, any action that is *not strictly "private"*—sees itself faced with the question: How can the involved claim rationality for their action even though not all the affected may benefit or agree with the costs imposed upon them, and some may seriously be harmed? How can *conflicts of interests* among the involved and the affected be resolved "with reason"—by argumentative processes of consensus-formation rather than by resort to power and deception?

Rationality that meets the intent of this question is what contemporary practical philosophers call *practical reason*. In addition to the two conditions constitutive of the utilitarian concept of rationality, practical reason requires that the standards of value of all the affected—be they involved or not— converge. And since the group of those actually or potentially affected can never be delimited in advance with certainty, this third condition entails the previously mentioned requirements of the *generalizability* of the standards of value ("norms") underlying the action in question.

Now we have already seen that a logical principle of ethical generalization is not available. Hence another type of "logic" is needed. Kant invented one such logic, his "transcendental logic"; contemporary practical philosophy instead relies on a *pragmatic (or "language-pragmatic") logic of argumentation*. We need only familiarize ourselves with a few basic points in order to be able to understand the major implications of this shift of perspective for systems practice.

The Language-Pragmatic Turn of Practical Philosophy

The change of paradigm distinctive of contemporary philosophy is accurately designated "language-pragmatic":

1. Philosophers no longer conceive of rational action, as did classical philosophy, from the point of view of the subjective consciousness of an abstract and lonely individual but, rather, in terms of specific contexts of *social action*. Social action, in distinction to non-social, is conceived as depending for its success on constructive interpersonal relationships with others and on taking account of their intentions. Hence *language* becomes important as the medium of communicative experience and action.

2. As a consequence, the question arises of what constitutes "the peculiarly unforced force of the better argument" that we have earlier invoked as a rationality criterion. In distinction to the syntactic–semantic approaches to the analysis of language in the tradition of analytical philosophy, practical philos-

ophy cannot reduce the scope of analysis to the syntactic and semantic levels of communication. The force of arguments can be grasped only at a *pragmatic* level, by considering their meaning and significance to human agents in specific contexts of social action. (If it were otherwise, computers could "argue" with each other.) That is, argumentative power is a matter not of deductive–logical modalities such as consistency/contradiction or necessity/impossibility but, rather, of the pragmatic modality of *cogency*.

An argument to the validity of some "fact" or "norm" is *cogent* not if it is logically conclusive (necessary)—as would be the case at the syntactic level—but if it is logically possible (that is, the facts or norms it asserts can be backed by reference to undisputed empirical findings or shared needs and values, rather than being contradicted by them) *and* if the discourse participants can be rationally motivated, by virtue of the backings, to recognize it as valid (cf. Toulmin, 1964; Habermas, 1973b; Ulrich, 1983, p. 137ff). Hence comes the need for a *pragmatic logic of discourse* that would allow us to distinguish rationally motivated ("rational") from merely factual consensus.

As a consequence of the language-pragmatic turn, rationality claims can no longer be established "monologically" but only "dialogically," in a discourse that meets the requirements of the pragmatic logic of argumentation. Whereas rational critical debate about theoretical validity claims has a long tradition in the scientific community, the shift to a communicative paradigm has major implications for the applied disciplines in dealing with normative (especially ethical and political) issues.

Implications for Systems Practice

1. "Systems rationality" thus far has been conceived *one dimensionally* (Marcuse, 1964) in terms of functionalist, utilitarian reason. Just like Max Weber, Karl Popper, Max Horkheimer, and a majority of other scholars, most systems scientists have succumbed to a *fundamental confusion of non-technical rationality with irrationality*.

2. It is probably this confusion which has prevented us from fully realizing the fact that the "objective" instrumental rationality of our tools and the merely "subjective" rationality of ordinary citizens contesting the life-practical consequences that our rationality may impose upon them share a common difficulty: neither meets the standards of practical reason.

3. The only way to meet these standards is by unfolding "one-dimensional" systems rationality into a *two-dimensional understanding of rational systems practice*. The "monological," utilitarian dimension is to be complemented by the communicative dimension of rational practice. (See Table 12.1 for an overview of some defining apsects of the two dimensions.)

Table 12.1 Two concepts of rationality

Aspect	Concept of rationality	
	Utilitarian	Communicative
Concept of action	Non-social action	Social action
Fundamental category of practice (Habermas)	Work	Interaction
Dimensions of rationality considered	*Subjective rationality* 1. Value-rationality (of ends) 2. Purposive-rationality (of means)	*Social rationality* 1. Rationally secured consensus on norms of action 2. Choice of ends conforming to 1 3. Choice of means conforming to 1 *and* purposive (effective and efficient) with regard to 2
Ideal type of rational action (M. Weber)	Purposive-rational action (in regard to given ends)	Socially rational action (with regard to socially acceptable norms)
Perspective of . . .	Those involved	Those involved *and* those affected
Underlying concept of reason (Kant)	*Theoretical reason* (or instrumental)	*Practical reason*
Methodological problem	Theoretical validity ("truth") of nomological hypotheses on causal (means–end) relationships (generalization of empirical observations)	Practical validity ("rightness") of norms of action (generalization of subjective standards of value)
Basic formal theory	Decision theory (theory of rational choice)	Discourse theory (theory of undistorted communication)
Root paradigm of basic theory	Cost–benefit analysis (utilitarian calculus)	Rationally motivated consensus (pragmatic logic of argumentation)
Underlying ethics	Utilitarian ethics	Communicative ethics

4. The *language-pragmatic* turn of contemporary practical philosophy offers us a key to conceiving of this second dimension in well-defined terms of rational discourse. Although the ideal of completely rational discourse will always remain counterfactual, the pragmatic logic of discourse at least gives

us stringent criteria of critical reflection on (and improvement of) the procedural and institutional conditions of decision making.

5. Finally, because in practice the two dimensions of rationality will frequently be in conflict with each other, it is not sufficient to "welcome" the idea of communicative in addition to functional rationalization of systems. It is indispensable to demonstrate exactly how practical reason can be practised *without* presupposing that those affected by a decision are always willing or able to subject themselves to the rationality standards of rational discourse. In this respect, a research program for systems practice must go beyond the actual state of practical philosophy and *develop practicable ways of mediation between the divergent requirements of cogent argumentation* (on the part of the involved) *and democratic participation* (on the part of the affected).

SYSTEMS PRACTICE GROUNDED IN PRACTICAL PHILOSOPHY: A THREE-LEVEL CONCEPT OF RATIONAL SYSTEMS PRACTICE

In his *Theory of Communicative Action*, Habermas (1981, p. 384) has developed a simple but analytically powerful taxonomy of action (Table 12.2). Habermas starts with two basic orientations that correspond to the two concepts of rationality thus far introduced: *"success-oriented action"* refers to the utilitarian paradigm of purposive-rational action; *"consensus-oriented action"* to the communicative paradigm of action based on norms acceptable to those affected. The distinction is akin to his earlier discussion of two fundamental dimensions of practice, the dimensions of "work" and "interaction" (1971b). Rationalization of these two domains implies two entirely different concepts of rationality: rationalization of *'work"* implies an expansion of technical control over objectified processes, while rationalization of *"interaction"* implies an expansion of argumentative means for resolving conflicts of interests and needs through mutual understanding, which amounts to an expansion of control over the domination of men by men (power). The point is not primarily that the interactive dimension of rational practice is different but that it exists: philosophers of science of all schools, from Max Weber to Max Horkheimer as well as Karl Popper, have succumbed to the earlier-mentioned confusion of non-technical rationality with non-rationality.

Habermas now refines this earlier distinction by adding a second distinction, that between situations of action in which interpersonal relationships do and do not play a role (*social* versus *non-social* action). Cross-tabulating the two distinctions yields *three basic types of action*, one referring to non-social action and the remaining two to social action.

Table 12.2   Types of action according to Habermas

	Orientation	
Situation	"Success oriented" (own interest)	"Consensus oriented" (mutual understanding)
Non-social	Instrumental action	–
Social	Strategic action	Communicative action

It seems to me that this taxonomy offers itself as a systematic framework of *three complementary levels of systems practice*, each of which requires its own concept of systems rationality (Table 12.3).[2] The three levels of systems practice thus gained are roughly parallel to the three levels of planning distinguished by Erich Jantsch (1975, p. 209ff) in his *"vertical integration"* approach to planning; operational (or tactical), strategic, and normative planning.[3] Similarly to Jantsch (although with a different purpose in mind), I think that the usual way of presenting systems thinking as an interdisciplinary effort to *"sweep in"* different strands of knowledge and world-views through a process of *"horizontal integration"*, as it were, needs to be differentiated in terms of a multilevel concept of systems rationality.[4] Only thus can we hope to overcome

---

[2] My understanding of the three levels is inspired partly by a similar effort by my brother Peter Ulrich (1988) to explore some implications of Habermas' three types of action for a critically normative theory of business administration. Close parallels are to be expected since management theorists have been similarly blind on their "communicative-theoretical eye," as have systems scientists, in conceiving of rational concepts and tools of business administration.

[3] My own earlier comparison of three major systems paradigms (Ulrich, 1981c, p. 38; 1983, p. 333) might also be useful to characterize the intent of the three levels of systems rationalization. The three systems paradigms in question were defined in terms of their underlying root metaphors ('machine", "organism," or "polis") and of their implied design ideals ("purposiveness," "viability," or "purposefulness"). The original machine paradigm of cybernetics with its focus on regulatory issues is still an effective design ideal at the instrumental level of systems rationalization; the shift of interest to strategic issues of systems management has necessitated a change from the mechanistic to the contemporary "evolutionary" paradigm of cybernetics and systems theory; and the growing interest in more radical approaches to systems management—approaches that would deal critically with the repercussions of functional (instrumental and strategic) systems rationalization on the social life-worlds of those affected—will require a breakthrough to a critically normative paradigm such as the one suggested in *Critical Heuristics*, a paradigm that can deal with the communicative dimension of systems rationalization.

[4] It is unfortunate that "vertical" thinking has become almost exclusively the hallmark of reductionistic systems thinking—e.g. in Herbert A. Simon's (1962, 1969) hierarchy theory of complexity. From a systems point of view, vertical thinking is more of interest because of those emergent systems qualities (including the communicative dimension of social systems) that cannot be grasped and "explained away" in the functional terms of the lower ontological levels. As a counterpart to Simon's brilliantly exposed "Architecture of Complexity," see Feibleman's (1954) "Theory of Integrative Levels," an equally terse statement of the position of non-reductionistic hierarchy theory of complexity. Compare, also, Churchman's counter-

Table 12.3 Three-level concept of rational systems practice

Level or action (type of situation)	Orientation	Core problem	Level of systems rationalization (type of systems rationality)
Social	Critically normative ("consensus")	Social integration of conflicting interests (*management of conflict*)	Communicative rationality
Social	Functional ("success")	Effective steering of complex systems (*management of complexity*)	Strategic rationality
Instrumental (non-social)	Functional ("success")	Efficient use of scarce resources for given ends (*management of scarceness*)	Instrumental rationality

the currently dominant one-dimensional concept of systems rationality and to integrate systematically within our framework of rational systems practice the communicatve dimension opened up by contemporary practical philosophy.

Let us then briefly describe the three levels so as to render clear their respective importance for systems practice—for a systems practice that would really *practise* the systemic idea of comprehensiveness.[5] Owing to space constraints, I limit the discussion to some very general comments on a few key aspects summarised in Table 12.4.

Level 1: Operational Systems Management

One of the most important characteristics of any methodology is its limitation
                                                                    S. P. Nikaranov (1965)

This is the level of non-social, *instrumental* action. It is concerned with the efficient employment of *things* rather than the development of interpersonal relationships. It is the genuine field of application for the problem-solving and planning techniques grown out of Second World War *operational research* efforts; quantitative techniques of systems modelling and optimization which

---

position as summarized in a fictituous debate with Simon (Ulrich, 1987a). In any case it should be clear that in calling for a multilevel concept of systems rationalization, I do not intend ontological reductionism but methodological pluralism.

[5] Compare the quotation from Kant (1787. p. 825) that serves as the motto of this paper.

Table 12.4   The three levels of systems practice

Aspect	Level 1: operational systems management	Level 2: strategic systems management	Level 3: normative systems management
Dominating interpretation of systems idea	"Systematic"	"Systemic"	"Critical idea of reason" (Kant)
Strand of systems thinking (paradigm)	"Hard": mechanistic paradigm	"Soft": evolutionary paradigm	"Soft": critically normative paradigm
Dimension of rationalization	*Instrumental*	*Strategic*	*Communicative*
Main object of rationalization	Resources: means of production	Policies: steering principles	Norms: collective preferences
Crucial task of the expert	*Management of scarceness:* how to allocate resources in view of scarceness	*Management of complexity:* what policies to pursue in the face of uncertainty	*Management of conflict:* whose interests to be served given conflict of needs and values
Type of problem pressure	Costs	Change	Conflict
Basic approach	Building up potentials of productivity (optimizations)	Building up strategic potentials of success (steering capacities)	Building up potentials of mutual understanding (consensus)
Criterion of good solution	"Efficient"	"Effective"	"Ethical"
Characteristic model of theory–practice mediation	Decisionistic: expert adopts ends given by decision maker	Technocratic: expert discloses necessities of the system to the decision maker	Pragmatistic: expert seeks consensus with those affected
Key disciplines: (a) Formal (b) Empirical	Decision theory Economics and engineering	Game theory Ecology and social sciences	Discourse theory Ethics and critical theory
Examples of specific tools	Cost–benefit analysis, linear optimization models	Sensitivity analysis, large-scale simulation models	Purposeful systems assessment, ideal planning
Major trap to be avoided	Suboptimization	Social technology	Ideal standards of rationality excluding the affected

later have been embedded within systematic procedures of *systems analysis* (e.g. Smith, 1966; Quade and Boucher, 1968; Emery, 1969; de Neufville and Stafford, 1971; Quade *et al.*, 1978) and *systems engineering* (e.g. Goode and Machol, 1957; Gosling, 1962; Hall, 1962; Chestnut, 1967; Jenkins, 1969; Optner, 1973; Daenzer, 1976). An excellent historical account of these two strands of the systems movement has been given by Checkland (1978); thus I can be very brief.

The two traditions share an orientation that is better called *systematic* rather than *systemic*: they systematize the problem-solving process within a conventional framework of instrumental reasoning.[6] Ends have to be assumed to be "given" to systems from outside and cannot be questioned within this framework, except with respect to their purely functional implications for higher-level systems. The diversity of the specific modelling techniques developed cannot conceal the fact that they all ultimately rely on the same underlying model of rational choice, *cost–benefit analysis*, whereby costs and benefits arising outside the boundaries of the system to be optimized are disregarded as "external" costs or benefits. The underlying model of theory-practice mediation[7] is *decisionistic*; it adopts Weber's means–end schema which is distinctive of *"hard" systems thinking* (cf. Checkland, 1978, p. 109; Ulrich, 1983, p. 329). In fact not only ends but also problems are assumed to be given; the crucial task of the systems analyst is seen in *problem decomposition* so that complex systems are divided into smaller ones that are easy to control. In sum, the focus is on what Habermas (1971a, p. 309) has designated the *interest in technical control* over objectified processes of feedback-monitored instrumental action.[8]

Even so these techniques may be of considerable value to social planners and decision makers faced with problems of the *management of scarceness*, that is, efficient allocation of scarce resources. These may include intellectual and organizational capacities of project management: NASA's Apollo Moon Project may be cited as an almost ideal example of the power of this kind of systems management. As long as it is employed within its proper field of application and with a clear understanding of its inherent limitations originating in the

---

[6] An exception holds partly true for the RAND and IIASA approaches to systems analysis (Quade and Boucher, 1968; Quade *et al.*, 1978). More than other approaches they emphasize policy considerations and, in this respect, overlap with the methodologies assigned here to the level of strategic systems management.

[7] See Habermas' (1971b, p. 62ff) distinction of three basic models of the relationship between questions of "fact" (theory, science) and questions of "values" (practice, politics), the decisionistic, technocratic, and pragmatistic model. For a discussion of these models in a context of social systems design and, espeically, a critical review of the rise and the implications of decisionism, see Ulrich (1983, p. 67–79, *passim*).

[8] Extensive critical discussion of "hard" systems thinking is given by, for example (apart from the sources already mentioned) Hoos (1972), Checkland (1981), Jackson (1985), and Jackson and Keys (1987; see especially Chapter 1 by Keys and Chapter 8 by Jackson) and is, of course, also implied in the writings of Churchman (e.g. 1968a, b, 1971, 1979, 1981).

underlying concept of rationality, this operational or instrumental level of system rationalization will remain an indispensable part of systems practice. It is in order to take into account the limitations in question that an adequate framework of systems practice must conceptualize at least two additional levels of systems rationalization, the "strategic" and the "normative" levels.

Level 2: Strategic Systems Management

Human systems are different
Sir Geoffrey Vickers (1983)

The strategic dimension of systems practice comes up when the success of an agent's decision is contingent upon the decisions of other agents, each of whom pursues his own interest or, as we have earlier said, his own subjective rationality. As may be seen from Table 12.3, this situation lends itself to two different types of rational action.

Strategic action shares with purely instrumental action a utilitarian orientation toward *success* in maximizing one's own interst. The underlying concept of systems rationality remains functional even where the subjective intentions of human agents are taken into account, for the functioning of the system of interest remains the crucial point of reference. (As far as ethical, political, or other normative concerns are considered, they are typically understood to fall outside the range of "rational" argumentation.)

Communicatiave action, in contrast, is oriented toward *mutual understanding*, and its concept of systems rationalization *includes* the search for rationally motivated consensus on the normative implications of systems design or interventions.

In both cases there may be a conflict of interests between the parties concerned. In both cases, too, there is a conscious attempt to deal rationally with the conflict. The difference lies in the point of reference for determing the rationality of alternative policies: in strategic management, the point of reference is "the system;" in "communicative" management it is the shared (generalizable) interests of all those actually or potentially affected. Thus strategic systems management is concerned with the *management of the complexity and uncertainty* that is distinctive of situations in which the actions of third parties coproduce the system's outcome and hence ought either to be predicted or to be influenced; but only communicative action at the level of normative systems management is oriented toward the *management of conflict* by means of argumentatively secured mutual understanding.

In the case of strategic action, the immediate orientation toward results and efficiency that is distinctive of instrumental action must be replaced by an orientation toward securing "strategic *potentials* of success"—i.e. systems capabilities of self-regulation, resilience, and innovative adaptation in the face of turbulent environments (Emery and Trist, 1965). Strategic management has therefore been understood as "evolutionary management" (e.g. Jantsch, 1975; Malik and Probst, 1982). The focus on problem decomposition and control is replaced by a focus on *problem identification and understanding* with a view to basic policy decisions that will minimize surprise and lost opportunities. To that end, decision-making tools not only need to be capable of processing and condensing a large variety of data about both intrasystemic and environmental interdependencies, but also should help managers to recognize and understand "weak signals" (Ansoff, 1975).

It is with regard to this task of complexity management that systems practice has seen its most impressive development in the past decades. Simulation techniques, cybernetic modelling, the theory of games, the "key factors of success" approach, and portfolio management—to name only a few basic approaches—have considerably expanded our understanding and sensitivity regarding the requirements of complex sociotechnical, socioeconomic, or socioecological systems. Out of these approaches have grown specific tools and concepts that have become widely known and applied: Forrester's "system dynamics" technique for large-scale simulation (1971) has become popular through the Club of Rome's report on the *Limits of Growth* (Meadows *et al.*, 1972). Ashby's (1956) "law of requisite variety" has been of tremendous importance for the cybernetic understanding of complexity management and has found an impressive application in Beer's (e.g. 1972) "managerial cybernetics," which has now been developed into a method for the cybernetic diagnosis of organizations (Beer, 1985). Neumann and Morgenstern's (1944) theory of games has become a core paradigm of strategic thinking, best known as the "prisoner's dilemma" described by Rapoport (1960), and has become influential in the development of ethical theory (Rawls, 1971). As a final example, Frederic Vester's "cybernetic sensitivity model" (Vester and Hesler, 1980) has combined classical sensitivity analysis with bio-cybernetic modelling so as to provide a tool for "systems compatibility assessment," in distinction to conventioanl environmental impact assessment.[9,10]

These tools, and many more that must remain unnamed, burst the narrow

---

[9] A computerized version of the model is presently being developed by NIXDORF Computers Inc., Switzerland, and UNICON Management Systems GmbH, Meersburg, Germany.

[10] The reader will have noticed that I have not mentioned the specific "soft" systems approaches of Churchman, Ackoff, and Checkland. In fact I do not subsume them under the strategic type of rationality. Although in their present form they may not meet all the requirements of communicative rationality established by Habermas' pragmatic logic of discourse, as Jackson (1982, 1985) has argued, they certainly do have a potential for contributing to communicative systems rationalization—no less than Habermas' ideal model of discourse, which in practice cannot secure rational consensus either. In addition, their orientation toward a dialogical, interpretive understanding of systems practice clearly distinguishes them from the decision-theoretical and natural-science orientation of cybernetic modelling, game theory, and other concepts of strategic rationalization. For these reasons, I consider them at the level of normative systems management.

cost–benefit calculation scheme of conventional systems analysis in favour of a truly *systemic* perspective. Strategic systems thinking overcomes the "technological imperative" and the "environmental fallacy" so well described by Churchman (1979, p. 4ff) as the common but inadequate way of dealing with complex social problems.

Fritjof Capra's (1982) widely read book, *The Turning Point*, has made it popular knowledge that the *change of paradigm* from "linear" to systemic thinking pioneered by the systems movement is now gaining ground in almost all fields of knowledge. It seems to me that this change of paradigm, as formulated by Capra, is characterized by the step from the first to the second level of our three-level concept of systems rationality—which is also to say that the social dimension of truly rational systems practice is not yet adequately captured. The social dimension will be adequately grasped only by breaking through the bounds of functional (including ecological) systems rationality and considering the level of communicative systems rationalization. To that end, the still dominating natural-science orientation of Capra's "holistic" systems paradigm will have to be complemented by an orientation toward the cultural and social sciences, as well as toward a grounding in practical philosophy.

Our framework thus suggests that the further development of the systems movement will depend on its readiness to pioneer yet another change of paradigm, the change from today's biologically inspired systems concept (with its root metaphor of the functioning organism or the ecological community) to a systems concept that would be inspired by practical philosophy's *emancipatory utopia* of a community of autonomous and responsible citizens. In view of the steadily increasing gap between the scientifically informed rationality of our systems designs and the practically experienced social *ir*rationality of many of their repercussions upon our daily social life-world, the reproach of "utopianism" is no longer justifiable; the utopia becomes the only means today for maintaining the social and democratic achievements of the past.[11]

Level 3: Normative Systems Management

The capacity for control made possible by the empirical sciences is not to be confused with the capacity for enlightened action . . . The scientific control of natural and social processes—in one word, technology—does not release men from action. Just as before, conflicts must be decided, interests realised, interpretations found—through both action and transaction structured by ordinary language.
Jürgen Habermas (1971b, p. 56)

---

[11] In the ideal of practical reason, systems rationality and social rationality converge. See Ulrich (1983, p. 294ff) for a discussion of the dialectic of systems rationality and social rationality from the point of view of a critically normative systems approach.

While strategic systems thinking takes account of the subjective rationality of other agents coproducing its outcome, it does so with an eye to the effective steering of complex systems (management of complexity) rather than to the ways in which the interests of others may be touched (management of conflict). Its orientation is utilitarian, not communicative. This is not to say that strategic thinking is necessarily ethically reprehensible; management of complexity is a necessary condition of socially rational decision making. But the most sophisticated tools of complexity management will not free us from having to decide upon the interests or needs that are to be served by the systems in question, and that will always mean to decide among *conflicting* needs and interests.

It is at this point that the second, communicative dimension of rationality comes into play. As long as systems thinking remains oriented toward a one-dimensionally functional understanding of rationality and does not *systematically* include the communicative dimension of social action, it will imply not a gain of social rationality but only an expansion of systemic *control* over social processes (*social technology*). Whether or not this enlarged capacity for control will be used for enlightened action toward improvement of the human condition remains (at best) an open question.

Let us briefly consider an example, the concept of *open systems*. When systems are strongly interconnected with their environment, it is advisable from a strategic systems point of view to treat them as open systems that cannot be completely controlled by the decision maker. Now there is a widespread belief that open systems models are more conducive to socially rational decision making than are closed systems models. "Open," in contrast to "closed," systems models consider the social environment of the system; but so long as the system's effectiveness remains the only point of reference, the consideration of environmental factors does nothing to increase the social rationality of a systems design. In fact, if the normative orientation of the system in question is socially irrational, open systems planning will merely add to the socially irrational effects of closed systems planning. For instance, when applied to the planning of private enterprise, the open systems perspective only increases the private (capital-oriented) rationality of the enterprise by expanding its own control over the environmental, societal determinants of its economic success, without regard for the social costs that such control may impose upon third parties.

Generally speaking, a one-dimensional expansion of the reach of functional systems rationality that is not embedded in a simultaneous expansion of communicative rationality threatens to pervert the *critical heuristic purpose of systems thinking*—to avoid the trap of suboptimization and to consider critically the whole-systems implications of any system design—*into a mere heuristics of systems purposes*. This means that it is no longer "the system" and the boundary judgments constitutive of it that are considered as the problem; instead, the problems of the system are now investigated (cf. Ulrich, 1983, p. 299).

It is against this danger that I have been advocating a *critically normative systems approach* (e.g. Ulrich, 1981b, c, 1983, 1984, 1987b, 1988). I suggest that we call a methodology "critically normative" if it offers methodical help not only in formulating and justifying theoretical or practical propositions but also in rendering transparent the normative implications of these propositions in an envisaged context of application.[12] The point is, of course, that *no standpoint, not even the most comprehensive systems approach, is ever sufficient in itself to validate its own implications*. Hence a definition (map, design) of a system can be called "objective" only inasmuch as it makes explicit its own normative content; whether or not it does so cannot be established "monologically," by reference to the expertise of the involved, but only communicatively, by reference to the free consent of those affected (cf. Ulrich, 1983, pp. 306, 308ff). Thus a critically normative systems approach will, of necessity, be a communicatve approach.

Practically speaking, a critically normative approach will have to face at least *three basic challenges*:

1. Simply "adding on" critically normative reflection to instrumental and strategic reasoning will not be enough. *Critically normative reflection must not remain extrinsic to systems thinking and systems practice*, for example in the form of occasional decisionistic appeals to the moral responsibility of systems planners. Rather, it must become an intrinsic part of our understanding of systems rationality. That is to say, it must be conceptualized *in genuinely systemic terms*. To that end, we shall have to go back to the genuinely critical intent of the systems idea in Kant's philosophy. Some philosophical competence *within* the systems community will be indispensable.

2. Habermas' pragmatic logic of discourse implies that not *any* sort of debate will allow the systems planner to claim communicative rationality for his designs. In order to maximize chances for the *free* consent of concerned citizens—or what Habermas calls rationally motivated consensus—it will be imperative to arrange for, and cultivate, processes of maximum *undistorted communication*—i.e. communication in which the force of the better argument gets a chance to prevail over other forces.

Practically speaking, we, nevertheless, shall have to make allowance for the fact that Habermas' model of discourse describes an *ideal*; it cannot make the ideal real. We cannot expect a practicable model of critical debate to secure complete rationality; we can only seek to lay open its inevitable *lack* of complete

---

[12] Recently a growing number of management scientists (especially in Great Britain) appear to be prepared to help develop a critical management science in the sense intended by my definition. See, for example, Jackson (1982, 1985, 1987), Keys (1987), Rosenhead (1982, 1984, 1987), and Tinker and Lowe (1984). Compare, also, the series of debates between Bryer (1979, 1980) and Churchman and Ulrich (1980; also Ulrich, 1981a); Christenson (1981) and Churchman, Cowan and Ulrich (1981); Ulrich (1981b) and Beer (1983); and Jackson (1982, 1983) and Ackoff (1982), Checkland (1982), and Churchman (1982).

rationality. It follows that we should not require systems methodologies to be able to secure the conditions of unconstrained discussion, as Jackson (1982, p. 25) demands in his forceful critique of the "soft" systems methodologies of Churchman, Ackoff and Checkland (cf. also their replies: Churchman (1982), Ackoff (1982) and Checkland (1982). Quite to the contrary, *the systems movement will make a real contribution toward communicative systems rationalization if it puts the systems idea to work on the job of dealing critically with conditions of imperfect rationality.*

There is, for instance, the important task of training ordinary citizens, planners, and decision makers in tracing the normative implications of designs; for example, by explicating the kinds of boundary judgments (or whole-systems judgments) that usually flow into the definition of a system. Under the guise of expertise and rationality, these whole-system judgments (if unchallenged) may provide an unequal distribution of decision power in systems. Or they may make someone other than the declared client the real beneficiary of a plan, etc. Should not systems practitioners be at least as sensitive as, say, practical philosophers, to the unavoidability of such whole-systems judgments and to the fact that no amount of expertise or theoretical competence is ever sufficient to justify all the judgments on which recommendations for action depend? (cf. Ulrich, 1983, p. 306). It seems to me that the soft systems methodologies do indeed have a contribution to make here.

3. Finally, let us not forget that neither systems methodology nor any other kind of methodology can ever supersede the need for democratic legitimation of decisions affecting others than those involved. It is not a sign of insufficient comprehensiveness or rationality to avow that one's procedural arrangements for critical debate remain dependent for their effectiveness on democratically secured *institutional arrangements*. Methodology cannot replace ongoing efforts at institutionalizing, in all domains of socially relevant decision making, democratic participation and majority vote among sovereign and equal (not "equally rational"!) citizens, according to Abraham Lincoln's principle: "government of the people, by the people, for the people." In this respect, *systems practice should not misunderstand itself as a guarantor of socially rational decision making;* it cannot, and need not, "monologically" justify the social acceptability of its designs.

In *Critical Heuristics* (Ulrich, 1983), I sought to lay out the epistemological foundations for a critically normative systems approach that would take due account of such practical limitations on complete rationality. Critical heuristics does not pretend to secure an objective solution to the problem of practical reason; it aims at a merely *critical solution*. A critical solution does not yield any "objective" justification of normative validity claims. It prevents us, rather, from submitting to an objectivist illusion regarding such claims, by helping us to become self-reflective with respect to the normative implications of *any* standard of rationality (cf. Ulrich, 1983, pp. 20, 176, *passim*).

This is not, of course, the place for an adequate introduction to critical heuristics or to any other systems methodology that might conceivably contribute to communicative systems rationalization. As in the case of the previous levels, I must content myself with pointing to a few major concepts and tools that the systems movement has brought forth so far.

In comparison with the instrumental and strategic strands of the systems movement, the critically normative strand has, of course, hardly begun to develop a basic array of well-defined concepts and practical tools. Apart from Kant's original presentation of the systems idea as an "unavoidable" criticial idea of reason (cf. Ulrich, 1983, p. 222ff, *passim*), I would like to mention Churchman's (1968a, p. 4ff; 1979, Chapters 6, 9) "ethics of whole systems," Jantsch's (1975, p. 209ff) earlier-mentioned concept of "vertical integration" (or "vertical centering"), Checkland's (1981, p. 166ff) concept of "root definitions," Mason and Mitroff's (1981) "assumptional analysis," Ackoff's (1974, pp. 26, 29) and Churchman's (1979, pp. 65, 106) concept of "ideal planning," and the related concept of a "process of unfolding" (of whole-systems judgments—Churchman (1979, pp. 80, 82, *passim*); Ulrich (1983, Chapter 5)). Perhaps I may also refer to some key concepts of critical heuristics, apart from the before-mentioned concept of a (merely) "critical solution" to the problem of practical reason; for example, the concept of "*a priori* (versus *a posteriori*) judgments of practical reason" (Ulrich, 1983, pp. 166, 190f, 266, 278), the understanding of "argumentation break-offs" as boundary judgments (Ulrich, 1984, 1987b), and the concept of the "polemical employment of boundary judgments" (or whole-systems judgments—Ulrich (1983, p. 305ff; 1987b)). As a practical tool relying on these concepts, I have sketched out a "purposeful systems assessment" of designs with respect to their normative implications (Ulrich, 1983, p. 334ff). Finally, there is the hardly spelled-out idea of a "critically heuristic training of citizens" on the basis of such concepts (Ulrich, 1983, p. 407).

These, as well as additional concepts and tools, will need much further elaboration and practical testing. It is my firm conviction that in performing this task, we shall considerably benefit from taking up the current state of the art in practical philosophy. We should systematically probe its implications for a *critical* employment of the systems idea, as well as the implications of the systems idea for *practising* the idea of practical reason.

CONCLUDING REMARKS

The three-level framework presented in this paper is meant, first, to give us a general sense of direction for further advancing the systems movement;

second, to provide impetus for debate on a program of research toward socially rational systems practice; and third, to facilitate this task by distinguishing three points of attack for critical systems thinking.

First, at the level of operational systems management, the challenge is to lay open, in each application of systems tools, the limitations and normative implications of instrumental rationality, *without* therefore relaxing our efforts at ever more efficient management of scarceness (a task that is vital as a prerequisite for achieving goals at the other levels of systems rationalization).

Second, at the level of strategic systems management, we must equally recognize the one-dimensionality of strategic social action that is not embedded in consensus-oriented communicative action while, at the same time, continuing to foster the systemic steering capacities that have become indispensable today for the effective management of complexity and uncertainty in our sociotechnical, socioeconomic, and socioecological systems.

Third and finally, at the level of normative systems management, we must seek to procure the heuristic means for systematically tracing the normative implications of systems designs (or steering interventions) and cultivate settings of debate that are conducive to securing argumentative agreement about these implications with those affected by them.

Regarding the last-mentioned task, it is clear that a critically normative systems approach will need to go beyond the actual state of practical philosophy and to develop a *practicable*, although necessarily imperfect, model of practical discourse. On other occasions, I have sought to show that such a model must reconcile the conflicting demands of cogent argumentation (on the part of everybody involved) and democratic participation (of everybody affected). I have argued that the systems idea indeed provides the key to just this requirement. It must suffice here to refer the reader to the main sources (Ulrich, 1983, pp. 301–314; 1984, p. 333ff; 1987b).

I do not say that the task of integrating the communicative dimension of rationality will be easy. But if eventually we succeed, this will considerably ease the quest for rational systems practice, for it will *free the systems approach from the impossible (and élitist) pretension of securing a "monological" justification of rational practice.*

I am well aware of the fact that the program I have sketched out is apt to raise more questions than it can answer. My only excuse is that a research program *is* supposed to formulate questions, not answers. I hope some of the issues raised will prove challenging enough to provoke further discussion.

If this hope is not entirely in vain, perhaps the day is not too far when systems practitioners, asked by young people about how to acquire methodological competence with regard to the pressing social problems of our time, will not have to give the kind of answer that the German satirist Karl Kraus is reported to have given to a student: "You want to study business ethics? Then decide yourself for the one or the other!"

REFERENCES

Ackoff, R.L. (1974). *Redesigning the Future*, John Wiley, New York.

Ackoff, R.L. (1982). On the hard headedness and soft heartedness of M.C. Jackson, *J. Appl. Syst. Anal.*, **9**, 31–33.

Ansoff, H.I. (1975). Managing strategic surprise by response to weak signals, *Calif. Mgmt. Rev.*, **17**, 126.

Apel, K.O. (1976). *Transformation der Philosophie*, Suhrkamp, Frankfurt, Germany.

Ashby, W.R. (1956). *An Introduction to Cybernetics*, Chapman & Hall, London.

Beer, S. (1972), *Brain of the Firm*, Penguin Press, Harmondsworth (2nd edition, John Wiley, Chichester, 1981).

Beer, S. (1983). A reply to Ulrich's "Critique of Pure Cybernetic Reason: the Chilean experience with cybernetics", *J. Appl. Syst. Anal.*, **10**, 115–119.

Beer, S. (1985). *Diagnosing the System for Organisations*, John Wiley, Chichester.

Bryer, R.A. (1979). The status of the systems approach, *Omega*, **7**, 219–231.

Bryer, R.A. (1980). Some comments on Churchman and Ulrich's "Reply" to "The Status of the Systems Approach", *Omega*, **8**, 280.

Bubner, R. (1975). Eine Renaissance der pracktischen Philosophie, *Philos. Rundschau*, **22**, 1–34.

Capra, R. (1982). *The Turning Point*, Simon & Schuster, New York.

Checkland, P.B. (1972). Towards a system-based methodology for real-world problem solving, *J. Syst. Eng.*, **3**, 1–30.

Checkland, P.B. (1978). The origins and nature of "hard" systems thinking, *J. Appl. Syst. Anal.*, **5**, 99–110.

Checkland, P.B. (1981). *Systems Thinking, Systems Practice*, John Wiley, Chichester.

Checkland, P.B. (1982). Soft systems methodology as process: a reply to M.C. Jackson, *J. Appl. Syst. Anal.*, **9**, 34–36.

Chestnut, H. (1967). *Systems Engineering Methods*, John Wiley, New York.

Christenson, C. (1981). The systems approach and its enemies (Book review), *J. Enterprise Mgmt.*, **3**, 197–199.

Churchman, C.W. (1968a). *Challenge to Reason*, McGraw-Hill, New York.

Churchman, C.W. (1968b). *The Systems Approach*, Delacorte and Dell, New York (2nd edition, Dell, 1979).

Churchman, C.W. (1971). *The Design of Inquiring Systems*, Basic Books, New York.

Churchman, C.W. (1979). *The Systems Approach and Its Enemies*, Basic Books, New York.

Churchman, C.W. (1981). *Thought and Wisdom*, Intersystems, Seaside, Calif.

Churchman, C.W. (1982). Reply to M.C. Jackson, *J. Appl. Syst. Anal.*, **9**, 37.

Churchman, C.W., and Ulrich, W. (1980). The status of the systems approach, a reply to R.A. Bryer, *Omega*, **8**, 277–280.

Churchman, C.W., Cowan, T.A., and Ulrich, W. (1981). Counterpoint of Christenson's critique—a dialogue, *J. Enterprise Mgmt.*, **3**, 200–202.

Daenzer, W.F. (Ed.) (1976). *Systems Engineering*, BWI, Zurich, Switzerland, and Hanstein, Cologne, Germany.

de Neufville, R., and Stafford, J.H. (1971). *Systems Analysis for Engineers and Managers*, McGraw-Hill, New York.

Emery, F.E. (Ed.) (1969). *Systems Thinking*, Penguin Books, Harmondsworth.

Emery, F.E., and Trist, E.L. (1965). The casual texture of organisational environments, *Hum. Relat.*, **18**, 21–32 (reprinted in Emery (1969), pp. 241–257).

Feibleman, J.K. (1954). Theory of integrative levels, *Br. J. Philos. Sci.*, **5**, 59–66.

Forrester, J.W. (1971). *World Dynamics*, Wright-Allen, Cambridge, Mass.

Goode, H.H., and Machol, R.E. (1957). *Systems Engineering*, McGraw-Hill, New York.

Gosling, W. (1962). *The Design of Engineering Systems*, Heywood, London.

Habermas, J. (1971a). *Knowledge and Human Interests*, Beacon Press, Boston, Mass.

Habermas, J. (1971b). *Towards a Rational Society*, Beacon Press, Boston, Mass.

Habermas, J. (1973a). *Theory and Practice*, Beacon Press, Boston, Mass.

Habermas, J. (1973b). Wahrheitstheorien, in *Wirklichkeit und Reflexion* (Ed. H. Fahrenbach), pp. 211–265, Neske, Pfullingen, Germany.

Habermas, J. (1979). *Communication and the Evolution of Society*, Beacon Press, Boston, Mass.

Habermas, J. (1981). *Theorie des kommunikativen Handelns*, Suhrkamp, Frankfurt.

Hall, A.D. (1962). *A Methodology for Systems Engineering*, Van Nostrand, Princeton, NJ.

Hoffe, O. (1979) *Ethik and Politik, Grundmodelle und Probleme der Praktischen Philosophie*, Suhrkamp, Frankfurt, Germany.

Hoos, I.R. (1972). *Systems Analysis in Public Policy: A Critique*, University of California Press, Berkeley.

Horkheimer, M. (1967). *Zur Kritik der Instrumentellen Vernunft*, Fischer, Frankfurt, Germany.

Jackson, M.C. (1982). The nature of "soft" systems thinking: the work of Churchman, Ackoff and Checkland, *J. Appl. Syst. Anal.*, **9**, 17–29.

Jackson, M.C. (1983). The nature of "soft" systems thinking: comment on the three replies, *J. Appl. Syst. Anal.*, **10**, 109–113.

Jackson, M.C. (1985). Social systems theory and practice: the need for a critical approach, Chapter 6 this volume.

Jackson, M.C. (1987). New directions in management science, in *New Directions in Management Science* (Eds M.C. Jackson and P. Keys), pp. 133–159, Gower, Aldershot.

Jackson, M.C., and Keys, P. (Eds) (1987). *New Directions in Management Science*, Gower, Aldershot.

Jantsch, E. (1975). *Design for Evolution*, Braziller, New York.

Jenkins, G.M. (1969). The systems approach, *J. Syst. Eng.*, **1**, 3–49.

Kant, I. (1787). *Critique of Pure Reason*, 2nd edition, Macmillan, London (1929).

Kant, I. (1788). *Critique of Practical Reason and Other Writings in Moral Philosophby*, University of Chicago Press, Chicago (1949).

Keys, P. (1987). Traditional management science and the emerging critique, in *New Directions in Management Science* (Eds M.C. Jackson and P. Keys), pp. 1–25, Gower, Aldershot.

Malik, F., and Probst, G.J.B. (1982). Evolutionary management. *Cybernet. Syst.*, **13**, 153–174.

Marcuse, H. (1964). *One-Dimensional Man*, Beacon Press, Boston, Mass.

Mason, R.D., and Mitroff, I.I. (1981). *Challenging Strategic Planning Assumptions*, John Wiley, New York.

Meadows, D.H., Meadows, D.L., Randers, J., and Behrens, W.W., III (1972). *The Limits to Growth: A Report for the Club of Rome's Project on the Predicament of Mankind*, Universe Books, New York.

Neumann, J. von, and Morgenstern, D. (1944). *Theory of Games and Economic Behaviour*, Princeton University Press, Princeton, New Jersey.

Nikaranov, S.P. (1965). Systems analysis: a stage in the development of the methodology of problem solving in the USA, in *Systems Analysis* (Ed. S.L. Optner), pp. 141–169, Penguin Books, Harmondsworth.

Optner, S.L. (Ed.) (1973). *Systems Analysis*, Penguin Books, Harmondsworth.

Quade, E.S., and Boucher, W.I. (1968). *Systems Analysis and Policy Planning: Applications in Defence*, Elsevier, New York.

Quade, E.S., Brown, L., Levien, R., Majone, G., and Rakhmankulov, V. (1978). Systems analysis: an outline for the IIASA international series of monographs, *J. Appl. Syst. Anal.*, **5**, 91–98.

Rapoport, A. (1960). *Fights, Games and Debates*, University of Michigen Press, Ann Arbor.

Rawls, J. (1971). *A Theory of Justice*, Harvard University Press, Cambridge, Mass.

Riedel, M. (Ed.) (1972–1974). *Rehabilitierung der praktischen Philosophy*, Rombach, Freiburg, Germany.

Rosenhead, J. (1982). Why does management need management science?, in *A General Survey of Systems Methodology* (Ed. L. Troncale), pp. 834–839, Soc. Gen. Syst. Res., Washington, DC.

Rosenhead, J. (1984). Debating systems methodology: conflicting ideas about conflict and ideas, *J. Appl. Syst. Anal.*, **11**, 79–84.

Rosenhead, J. (1987). From management science to workers' science, in *New Directions in Management Science* (Eds. M.C. Jackson and P. Keys), pp. 109–131, Gower, Aldershot.

Simon, H.W. (1962). The architecture of complexity, *Proc. Am. Philos. Soc.*, **106**, 467–482.

Simon, H.A. (1969). *The Sciences of the Artificial*, MIT Press, Cambridge, Mass.

Smith, B.L.R. (1966). *The RAND Corporation: Case Study of a Non-profit Advisory Corporation*, Harvard University Press, Boston, Mass.

Tinker, T., and Lowe, T. (1984). One-dimensional management science: the making of a technocratic consciousness, *Interfaces*, **14**, 40–49.

Toulmin, S. (1964). *The Uses of Argument*, Cambridge University Press, Cambridge.

Ulrich, P. (1988). Betriebswirtschaftslehre als praktische Sozialökonomie, in *Betriebswirtschaftslehre als Management und Führungslehre* (Ed. R. Wunderer), 2nd edition, Haupt, Berne, Switzerland.

Ulrich, W. (1981a). On blaming the messenger for the bad news: reply to Bryer's comments, *Omega*, **9**, 7.

Ulrich, W. (1981b). A Critique of pure cybernetic reason: the Chilean experience with cybernetics, *J. Appl. Syst. Anal.*, **8**, 33–59.

Ulrich, W. (1981c). Systemrationalität und praktische Vernunft—Gedonken zum Stand des Systemansatzes. Introduction to the German translation of Churchman (1979), *Der Systemansatz und seine Feinde*, pp. 7–38, Haupt, Berne, Switzerland.

Ulrich, W. (1983). *Critical Heuristics of Social Planning: A New Approach to Practical Philosophy*, Haupt, Berne, Switzerland.

Ulrich, W. (1984). Management oder die Kunst, Entscheidungen zu treffen, die andere betreffen, *Die Unternehmung*, **38**, 326–346.

Ulrich, W. (1987a). The metaphysics of social systems design, in *Decision Making About Decision Making: Metamodels and Metasystems* (Ed. J.W. Van Gigch), pp. 219–226, Abacus Press, Tunbridge Wells, England.

Ulrich, W. (1987b). Critical heuristics of social systems design, *Eur. J. Opl Res.*, **31**, 276–283 (previously circulated as Working Paper No. 10, Department of Management Systems and Sciences, University of Hull, March 1986).

Ulrich, W. (1988). Systemtheorie der Planung, in *Handwörterbuch der Planung* (Ed. N. Szyperski), Poeschel, Stuttgart, Germany.

Vester, F., and Hesler, A. von (1980). *The Sensitivity Model*. Regionale Planungsgemeinschaft Untermain, Frankfurt, Germany.

Vickers, G. (1983). *Human Systems are Different*, Harper & Row, London.

Chapter 13

Power–Ideology Matrix in Social Systems Control

JOHN C. OLIGA

INTRODUCTION

This paper is a critical inquiry into the phenomena of systems stability and social change. It starts by suggesting that while the necessity for critical systems thinking in systems science is undeniable, its very slow appearance may be attributed to ideological reasons. The paper proceeds by arguing that any penetrative account of social systems stability and change must lie in an historical rather than naturalistic explanation. This implies that the concepts of power, ideology, and social control must be confronted and addressed explicitly and not bypassed in silent embarrassment. From a conceptual analysis of power, ideology, and social control, this paper arrives at the justification of its thesis: that systems stability and change tendencies are a consequence of a particular architecture of power and ideology in being. The critical implication is that where the existing social order is founded on coercive systems of exploitation and oppression, then the dissolution of the problem must lie in the radical transformation of that social order.

CRITICAL SYSTEMS THINKING: A VERY SLOW "SLOWCOMER" TO SYSTEMS SCIENCE

An inquiry into the phenomena of systems stability and change cannot proceed in a vacuum. According to Habermas (1972), different kinds of human interests

Reprinted by permission from *Systems Practice*, Volume 3, 1990 motivate different kinds of inquiry and, hence, constitute different forms of knowledge. He identifies three types of constitutive interests arising from two fundamental forms of activity, namely, labour (work) and communicative interaction (language), which, in spatiotemporal terms, are universal and invariant to the human species. The "technical interest" is constitutive of empirical–analytic knowledge aimed at the prediction and control of "things, events and conditions which are, in principle, capable of being manipulated" (Habermas, 1973). The "practical interest" constitutes the historical– hermeneutic knowledge aimed at achieving intersubjective communicative (symbolic) understanding. The "emancipatory interest" constitutes self-reflective knowledge aimed at the realization of autonomy from defective actions and utterances arising from social relations of power, domination and alienation. The three forms of knowledge are underwritten by different paradigms: the "functionalist" (for empirical–analytic sciences), the "interpretive" (for the historical–hermeneutic sciences), and the "radical"/"critical" (for the self-reflective sciences) (Burrell and Morgan, 1979; Giddens, 1977; Jackson, 1982; McCarthy, 1978; Oliga, 1986; Puxty et al., 1980; and in particular, Flood and Ulrich, 1990).

Jackson (1982, 1983, 1985a, b, 1987a) and Jackson and Keys (1984) have classified the present systems methodologies within the Habermasian three-paradigm framework. What clearly emerges from that classification, and their insightful, discursive elaboration of it, is the continuing dominance of the functionalist paradigm, which underwrites all "hard" systems thinking. The "soft" systems methodologies, within the interpretive paradigm, are of more recent origin. However, since they emerged, they have made impressive progress, as exemplified by the classic works of, for instance, Churchman (1971, 1979), Ackoff (1974, 1981a, b), and Checkland (1972, 1981, 1983, 1985). These methodologies have not supplanted the well-entrenched hard systems methodologies; but they have, nonetheless, emerged as real, practicable alternatives. Critical management science, on the other hand, only "emerged as a distinctive tendency in the 1970s" (Jackson, 1987a, p. 143). As I have observed elsewhere (Oliga, 1988a, p. 104) distinctive radical/critical systems methodologies have yet to emerge, although highly significant developments are taking place, at both the theoretical and the practical levels (see Flood, 1990). What is interesting, however, is that while formal reaction against hard systems orthodoxy from both soft and critical systems thinking appeared about the same time in the history of management science, the impact of critical thinking has been, in contrast, very slow to emerge.

Yet, in terms of Habermas' interest constitution theory, it would seem that most institutions and organizations in our present (capitalist) social formations are in dire need of critical inquiry, given that they are generally characterized by power asymmetry, unequal distribution of wealth, structural conflicts, and contradictions (Hales, 1974; Jackson, 1985a; Rosenhead, 1982;

Rosenhead and Thunhurst; 1982; Spear, 1987; Thomas 1980; Thomas and Lockett, 1979; Tinker and Lowe, 1984; Whitley, 1974; Wood and Kelly, 1978). Buckley (1967), for instance, points to the fact that the distinguishing problem foci for sociocultural systems are the structurally induced and maintained conflicts, and social dissensus.

Thus, while it might be quite legitimate and proper, at a general level of systems inquiry, to offer functionalist and interpretive explanations of the phenomena of systems constancy and change, such accounts would not be sufficient where coercive sociocultural systems are involved. Critical systems thinking would clearly be necessary. However, as we have seen, critical systems thinking is a "slowcomer" to systems science, and the reason for this, I guess, is ideological. If this is true, then critical systems thinking is going to be not just a newcomer like soft systems thinking but a very slow slowcomer: the cure it offers (the unmasking of ideological bias) is the very disease dreaded by the patient. It is the aim of this paper to transcend this dread and account for social systems stability and change in critical terms.

SYSTEMS STABILITY AND CHANGE: NATURAL OR HISTORICAL?

When applied to social systems, mainstream systems theories of stability and instability are implicitly or explicitly underwritten by functionalist or interpretive paradigmatic interests. Their overriding concern is to regulate the existing state of affairs, which are seen as natural. Thus, hard systems perspectives are guided either by the morphostatic criteria of equilibrium (minimal organization) and homeostasis (preservation of given structures) or by the morphogenic criteria of adaptiveness and steady state, which allows for structure elaboration and development. In either case the basic form of the existing structure is taken as given, therefore natural, eternal and unalterable. Watt and Craig (1986), for instance, suggest a theory of instability and surprise in terms of signals of impending societal destabilization and how optimal strategies can be designed for quick response and return to stability, stability being defined in terms of "the speed of return of state variables to their equilibrium values or trajectories after a system has experienced a perturbation." Thom's (1975) catastrophe theory is concerned with discontinuities, resulting in the quantum transformation of systems from one equilibrium to another equilibrium. The dissipative structure "paradigm" (Smith, 1986) is ultimately concerned with the viability of the existing structure ("deep structure"), even if dissipative structure processes of transformation and regeneration are seen to allow for improved structural elaboration through systems quantum evolution from one dynamic equilibrium to another.

Similarly, soft systems perspectives are guided by the criteria of consensus, common understanding, and shared meaning, all arising from social processes of interaction in which multiple values, interests, perceptions, and perspectives are seen as the essential resources. These resources are taken as given and natural; the possibility that the particular forms these resources take may be the consequences of power asymmetry, domination, and self-misunderstanding remains outside the interpretive paradigm's agenda.

Both hard and soft systems thinking therefore share a common concern in their view of social control; the problem of maintaining social order in the face of actual or potential conflicts, such conflicts being variously described as (external) environmental disturbances, the problem of shared meanings, deviance, lack of motivation, personal dissatisfaction, goal incongruence or lack of commitment, conflicting political interests, etc. Such perspectives take social order as given and natural, the problem of control reducing to one of containing conflicts whose origins remain unquestioned. It is in these Hobbesian terms that, for instance, the problem of social order has been defined as an abstract problem posed by the antisocial character of human nature (Parsons, 1937). A critical view, however, inverts this conservative formulation. The problem of order becomes not an abstract problem but a concrete historical problem whose terms are defined by the character of the society within which it arises: essentially a problem of resolving the conflicts to which that society gives rise (Clarke, 1982).

Thus the problem of social order presupposes that conflict is an actual or potential problem and so arises only within a theory that defines the problem of conflict. The overriding concern of regulative perspectives is with how conflict is contained and regulated, not why it occurs. The existence of actual or potential conflict, without which there would be no problem of order, implies, however, that the terms on which conflict is resolved and order is reestablished cannot be taken as given, for the imposition of order must resolve that conflict on terms favourable to one or the other party. As a response to the problem of order, every theory of society defines its own problem of order, and critically, we must ask of that theory: For whom is order a problem?

It is in terms of such an inversion of the conservative order problematic that this paper attempts to reconstruct a critical theory of social control and social order (stability). The critical stance taken is one that views particular forms of social life as constituting not a natural order but a particular order in society; and it is that particular (historical) social order that gives rise to conflicts, thereby making control imperative. Such a form of control must inevitably rely on domination for its continued success. Critical to the processes of organizing, maintaining, and transforming such domination are the roles of power and ideology. It is to these two concepts that I now turn.

POWER AND IDEOLOGY

According to Lukes (1974), the view one takes of power is not unproblematic. Indeed, he suggested that his own view of it was "ineradically evaluative and essentially contested." Similarly ideology has been described by Larrain (1979) as perhaps one of the most equivocal and elusive concepts in the social sciences, partly because it is a concept heavily charged with political connotations. And yet both concepts are central to the problem of social order and the very notion of social control. A brief theoretical discussion of the nature of these concepts therefore seems not only desirable but inescapable given the objective of this paper.

For power, Lukes' (1974) contribution provides a good starting point, in terms of which three different views of power can be contrasted, views which represent the first major debate on the nature of power (the so-called "community power debate").

In summary, the first view, the so-called pluralists' "one-dimensional" view of power, defines power in terms of an individual's successful attempt to secure a desired outcome through processes entailing the making of decisions on issues over which there is an observable conflict of subjective interests (Dahl, 1958). The so-called élitists' "two-dimensional" view of power extends the first view by including non-decision-making whereby decisions are prevented from being taken on potential issues over observable conflicts (Bachrach and Baratz, 1963). It is, however, the "three-dimensional" view, Lukes argues, which goes beyond the merely behavioural (individual) focus, by including (i) social forces and institutional practices as sources of bias mobilization, (ii) control over political agenda through ideological processes of preference shaping and selective perception and articulation of what count as social problems and conflicts, and (iii) latent conflicts representing "a contradiction between the interests of those exercising power and the 'real' interests of those they exclude."

However, these conceptions of power and interests have recently been seriously contested. Hindess (1982) has argued against what may be summarized as two broad approaches to power analysis: the "capacity–outcome" view and what might be called the "capacity–conditions–outcome" view of power (p. 498). The first approach parallels the one-dimensional view of power; the second, the two-dimensional and three-dimensional views. Hindess argues that these conceptions unrealistically take the securing of outcomes as unproblematic, instead of predicating it on definite and specifiable conditions or means of action, which not only are not in the hands of "power-full" agents, but invariably confront obstacles and opposition. Thus, he argues, such capacities cease to become capacities to secure, to realize, or to control and, instead, become, at best, capacities to act in pursuit of certain objectives. Even in obvious cases where the means and conditions of action favour one side, the outcomes are rarely the simple products of the initial conditions, but must be seen as produced in the course of struggle itself.

Hindess also argues against the related conception of "interests" as being somehow determined outside of the conditions of particular practices. In particular, in the capacity–outcome view, subjective interests are identified as sets of objectives that are acknowledged by the agents concerned. He sees such a view as inadequate, as it forecloses examination of issues concerning the constitution of arenas of struggle and the contending forces involved. Similarly, the capacity–conditions–outcome conception unwarrantedly gives an ontological privilege to some set of supposed interests rather than any other. As a result, important issues concerning the problems of how contending forces and arenas of struggle are constituted become swept aside in a simplistic manner.

Inevitably, Hindess is led to the conclusion that the concept of power as capacity or attribute belonging to particular agents should cease to be a meaningful object of inquiry. It is the means of action available to agents in specific situations of action that become of theoretical significance. "Arenas of actual or potential struggle would then have to be analysed not in terms of the differential possession of quantities of power but rather in terms of the differential conditions and means of action available to the contending forces, their strategies and objectives, and so on" (Hindess, 1982).

While these critics provide insightful arguments against gross subsumptionist arguments that proceed by transforming general concepts and explanatory principles into "essentialised principles" with immediate consequences for social life (cf. Jessop, 1982), I think there is a tendency in their arguments to err on the opposite extreme: "atheoretical empiricism," which, for instance, Hindess himself partly acknowledges (Hindess, 1982, p. 510)

A similar focus on "micropolitics" of power is evident in Minson's (1980) discussion of Foucault's (1972, 1977, 1980) conception of power. According to Minson, there are three elements in Foucault's conception of power that contest Marxist concepts: "his attack on global conceptions of social relations; his relocation of such categories in the limited field of "social" strategies; and finally, his attack on 'possessive' conceptions of power and concomitantly his emphasis on the determinants and effects of the 'technical' forms of implementing policies and strategic programs" (Minson, 1980).

In Foucault's concept of "pouvior–savoir" (power–knowledge), power (pouvoir) is assumed to be diffused throughout society, at all levels, just as practical, everyday life knowledge, savoir (as opposed to "connaissance," the formal knowledge of science), is. Power is thus a process tied closely to practical knowledge through the general tactic of disciplining human bodies for social purposes. And power and resistance must be seen as dialectical; while discipline seeks to normalize or repress individual differences and autonomy in the interest of domination, resistance to it, far from being an obstacle, is the *sine qua non* of its operation. This means that both the distribution and the exercise of power cross-cut the distinction between the haves and the have-nots. Hence, in relation to ideology, Foucault's pouvoir–savoir challenges the idea of truth or pure knowledge since actual knowledge in society is a political activity, the product of power and its disciplinary techniques. This is the idea in Foucault's concepts of "will-to-truth" or "will-to-knowledge," which explicitly echo Nietzsche's concept of "will-to-power." For both writers, knowledge cannot be divorced from power. This means that the validity of the notions of truth and ideology must be questionable.

Minson sees Foucault and Nietzsche's contribution to the concept of power as being the recognition of the effects of micropolitics in terms of exercise of power rather than in the Marxist notion of its possession in sources located in specific political forces. However, he argues against both possession and exercise notions of power; in fact he rejects the very notion of power, arguing that the concept of power itself lacks any explanatory force or theoretical significance. As he explains:

> Nothing can be explained in terms of power because on any understanding, one thing (be it political subject, economic structure or whatever) must be attributed the unconditional capacity to dominate another . . . To set conditions on a capacity to dominate is to deny that a thing has that capacity.

At best, in Minson's view, "powers" might be conceived as differential advantages (or disadvantages) regarding the possibility of social agents being successful in realizing certain objectives, particularly wherever the compliance and support of other agents are a prerequisite.

Foucault's concept of "micropowers," Nietzsche's "will-to-power," Minson's, "differential advantages," and Hindess' "differential conditions" all share a number of untenable elements in their analyses of power. First, outcomes of struggle are seen as simply dependent on heterogeneous, interdependent, possible tactics and strategies, or on conditions and means of action available in specific situations of action. Second, their alternative explanatory categories are all simply taken as given (springing from nowhere). This naturalistic conception betrays an uncritical view of surface level appearances. The possibility that such parametes of struggle may be ideologically structured is ignored. There is thus a danger of overconcentrating on the tactics and actual "playing out the game," to the exclusion of the ground rules of the game itself, which circumscribe, structure, and bias potential outcomes. For instance, by claiming that interests are a function of discursive processes aimed at reaching decisions and means of acting on them, Hindess forgets that those processes themselves, the ensuing decisions and possible actions are all circumscribed by an initial set of unequal and differential conditions of the capitalist system of domination. Unequal relations of production and the capitalist contradictions, the domination and exploitation and the resulting resistance and struggle, all remain unaddressed. Indeed, one wonders what, in the first place, the social struggles are all about in such uncritical conceptions of power. And is it justifiable to reject the concept of power simply because its scope for definite outcomes is not invariantly determinate in specific instances? Clearly, one may choose not to exercise power over another, and conversely, the other may choose not to obey, regardless of the consequences. There would be no place for power in circumstances of complete determinism. That social struggles are possible and do take place implies the existence of conflicts arising out of domination, and the latter would not be possible without power (Hyman and Brough, 1975). A focus on levels of analysis would point to the possibility of the exercise of power as "pouvoir" being grounded in domination (or "meta-power" as "puissance"), the prior capacity to be able to exercise power at all (cf. Clegg, 1975; Weber, 1968).

A final objection relates more generally to their lack of a concept of truth and, more particularly, to the issue of ideology. Warren (1984) has elaborated on Nietzsche's (1968) concept of ideology, which turns out to be an extremist and wholesale characterization of ideas and cultures as ideological. Nietzsche speaks of culture as "made up of ideals, idols, illusions, and falsehoods" and, in critique of Western culture, as "means to self-deception and masks of essential aspects of existence" (see Warren, 1984, p. 543). Notwithstanding Warren's claim that Neitzsche's concept of ideology as well as his genealogical method of criticizing illusions of consciousness make sense only if understood in terms of his global characterization of the world as will-to-power, critical theorists have argued that the concept of will-to-power sweepingly and irresponsibly postulates a universal motive for power. Not surprisingly, Nietzsche could write of truth in these terms: "What then is truth? A mobile army of metaphors, metonyms, and anthropomorphisms . . . truths are illusions about which one has forgotten that this is what they are" (Warren, 1984, quoting Nietzsche).

Against such a lack of a conception of truth, Habermas (1976) has argued that because Nietzsche reduces intersubjective validity claims to the merely subjective claims of taste and power, he is driven to distinguish between claims genetically. Habermas sees Neitzsche's indiscriminate and uncritical views as destroying the rational ground upon which the critique of ideology is based. Critique presupposes criteria for distinguishing truth from falsity, without which the very notion of ideology becomes meaningless and at least two types of pernicious consequences follow:

> First, we can no longer hope for a critical understanding of our interests since we lose the ability to distinguish true interests . . . from expressed preferences.

Second, in the absence of such distinctions, prevailing power relations become the ultimate arbiters of interests. (Warren, 1984, quoting Habermas).

We saw earlier how Foucault's concept of pouvoir–savoir amounted to a rejection of the concept of ideology and now how Nietzsche conceives of it in the most irrational and uncritical terms which have been attacked by critical theorists. What then is a critical theory of ideology? Warren has summarized the outlines of such a theory (1984, pp. 541–542). First, ideology acts to conceal the essential aspects of sociopolitical reality. Second, such concealment is not accidental (in the sense of errors) but relates systematically to some set of social, psychological, and cognitive interests within a determinate historical context. Third, because ideologies relate systematically to interests and historical realities, they can be criticized so as to provide knowledge about those interests and realities.

Underwriting the first three claims is the claim that it is possible and necessary to develop a defensible theory of truth that underwrites both explanation and evaluation of ideologies, as in Freud's "id–ego–superego" construct or in Marx's concept of mode of production. Related to this is the view that a theory of truth must somehow provide a conception of reason and rational action in terms of which certain forms of consciousness can be said to be ideological and judged to be irrational. In sharp contrast to Hindess' (1982) arguments about "interests," a critical theory seeks to provide agents with the ability to be self-reflective about the content of their interests and the ability to formulate those interests in self-emancipatory terms.

The final claim relates to the problem of truth-claim validation: the problem of how to provide standards which the critique of ideology can refer to in order to legitimize its procedure and justify its claims. Because critique seeks the true meaning of an ideology in relation to an historical context, it lacks the grounds on which to assert a priori criteria of its own truth. It must consider its own truth, in the same way as the inverted truth of ideology, as historically conditioned. This implies that because critique cannot develop formal, a priori criteria of what counts as ideology, its strength lies not in a body of theoretical statements from which empirical states of affairs might be inferred, but in a theory-dependent method that guides research into the meaning of a form of consciousness by relating to its context of interests and realities. The philosophical implications are that for critical theory not to undermine its own claim to a relative rationality, it must criticize a form of consciousness "immanently." That is, "criticism gains its right to impute ideological meanings to a text insofar as the text is irrational with regard to its own criteria of adequacy" (Warren, 1984, p. 542). Thus, if ideology is not conceived of as distorted knowledge which, in the interest of the dominant class, masks contradictions of capitalist social relations, it loses its critical intent (cf. Larrain, 1979; Marx,

1969–1972). It is this critical view of ideology and the dialectical view of power that can be argued to illuminate the problem of social control.

THE POWER–IDEOLOGY MATRIX AND SOCIAL CONTROL

In the previous section, I briefly discussed the concept of ideology. However, it is through an understanding of how it functions that the relationship among social control, power, and ideology can be illuminated. Developing Althusser's (1971) notion of ideological "interpellation–recognition," Therborn (1980) has elaborated on the functioning of ideology in terms of the "subjec- tion–qualification" dialectic. Ideologies operate as discourse, interpellating (addressing) individuals as human subjects. This involves a simultaneous process of subjection and qualification. Subjection refers to the individual's subjugation to a particular force or social order that favours or disfavours certain values and beliefs. Qualification, on the other hand, refers to the enabling of an individual to take up and perform the repertoire of roles given in society (including the role of being a possible agent of social change). This simultaneous process involves three fundamental modes of ideological inter- pellation whereby individuals as human subjects are told and made to recognize (i) what exists and what does not exist (thereby structuring the visibility of the social world in terms of spotlights, shadows and darkness), (ii) what is good, right, just, and its opposites (thereby structuring and normaliz- ing the individual's desires, preferences and values), and (iii) what is possible (thereby patterning and shaping the individual's hopes, ambitions, and fears). These three modes of interpellation form the "is–ought–can" trio.

In a social control context, the success of ideological interpellation results in the ruled accepting the rulers' ideologies as dominant. This means subjecting the ruled to a social order that is in the interest of the ruling class; the ruled thus become qualified to obey. However, the ideological interpellation may not be fully successful, in which case varying degrees of resistance and struggle may ensue; from "covert dissent/reserved consent" to "open dissent/ forced consent." Therborn (1980) has suggested that in addition to the is–ought–can ideological interpellation, a second dimension of the interpella- tion may require an answer to the question: "Does there exist a possible better alternative to the present regime? Yes or No?" (p. 94). The second dimension seeks to highlight the crucial difference between obedience as an intrinsic necessity because no better alternative is conceivable and obedience as a contingent necessity given that a better alternative to the present social order is conceivable.

In the case of intrinsic obedience, three possible types of ideological subjection/domination as well as potential responses by the ruled as "qualified" subjects emerge. The three possibilities correspond to the is–ought–can modes of interpellation. First, obedience may result from a sense of "inevitability," a cognitive belief that it is in the nature of things to be what they are; the existing state of affairs are natural and hence inevitable. Second, there is obedience motivated by a sense of "deference." In this case, the ruled hold normative beliefs in the legitimate domination of the rulers, because the latter are seen as having superior and unique ruling qualities deriving from their descent and breeding (e.g. in Britain and Japan) or their special social/political positions. Third, there is the form of obedience based on a sense of "resignation," a political belief founded on a profoundly pessimistic view of the practical possibilities of social change.

In the case of contingent obedience, there are also three parallel possibilities. First, there is the form of obedience through either "accommodation" or "instrumentalism" (pragmatism). Accommodation results from the cognitive belief by the ruled that, despite their present subordination (e.g. exploitation), which they believe could be alleviated in a better, alternative regime, there exist other features of social life which are perhaps more salient and hence sufficiently compensatory (e.g. job satisfaction, leisure, consumption, sport, the family). A similar belief motivates instrumentalist obedience, where the working/feasibility of present arrangements is more salient than the possibility of a better alternative. Second, there is the form of obedience based on a sense of "representation," a normative belief by the ruled that the domination of the rulers is legitimately founded on accepted, conventional/cultural norms. The rulers may be seen as representing, in the eyes of the ruled, the ideals of that society or as defenders of the needs of the ruled (charismatic representation). "Fear" represents the third source of contingent obedience. Here there are two possibilities: (i) fear of the physical force and violence, and (ii) the moral fear of excommunication/ostracization or the social fear of (for instance) losing one's job or social position.

At this juncture, an important point needs to be borne in mind. In both the intrinsic and the contingent forms of obedience, the specific source of acquiescence (inevitability, deference, etc.) are analytical constructs, rather than empirical, classificatory categories. They are empirically intertwined and coexist in varying degrees of salience. While they may clash, they often reinforce or compensate for one another in ways that work concertedly in the overall interest of conserving the status quo. These mechanisms of ideological subjection and qualification are summarized in Table 13.1.

It is possible to extend the above typology by explicitly introducing the possibilities of open, covert and latent dimensions of obedience/resistance and struggle (Salaman, 1979). Although that is not necessary for our purpose, Table 13.1 is sufficient to demonstrate that the complex possibilities cannot be captured by simple dichotomies of force versus consent, hegemony versus force, or legitimacy versus power. For instance, people do not obey either

Table 13.1 Mechanisms of ideological subjection and qualification

	Alternative regime conceivable?	
Mode of interpellation	Yes	No
What is	Accommodation, or instrumentalism	Sense of inevitability
What is good	Sense of representation	Deference
What is possible	Fear	Resignation

because of consent or because of physical coercion. Both elements of consent and force may be present, as in resigned obedience.

Social control does thus seem to be crucially dependent on power and ideology; but what is the relationship between power and ideology? The processes of ideological interpellation of the ruled result in either their acceptance or their rejection of the (rulers') dominant ideology. This, however, is at the discursive level. Obedience (or resistance and struggle) depends additionally on the power balance, that is, on the matrix of material affirmations and sanctions available to the rulers relative to the ruled. For analytical purposes, power can therefore be related to the non-discursive (i.e. economic and political) dimension of social relations. In these critical terms, power and ideology thus become dialectical notions. The idea of ideology is meaningless except in the context of organizing, maintaining, and reproducing order through "subjection–qualification" processes. This is the sense in which ideology reflects power. Obversely, all ideologies operate only in a material matrix of affirmations and sanctions (power). Thus power in turn reflects ideologies.

The power–ideology matrix has important implications for social systems stability and change tendencies. In terms of our earlier ideological interpellation, whether a possible better alternative regime (social system) is conceivable, Table 13.1 can be extended to yield three possible answers. The first possibility is a negative answer, implying that neither the present regime's dominant ideologies nor the effectiveness of its power is doubted. This is likely to result in obedience through a sense of inevitability, deference, or resignation. The second possibility is a qualified positive answer, where there exist some degrees of doubt on either the power or the dominant ideologies of the rulers. This is likely to result in obedience through a sense of accommodation/ instrumentalism, representation, or fear. The third possibility is an unqualified positive answer, where both power and dominant ideologies are doubted. This is likely to result in some form of organised counterclaims to the legitimacy of the rulers' domination and hence resistance and struggle by the ruled. In this case, the doubts on the regime's right and capacity to rule are a consequence of the breakdown in the effectiveness of the articulation between power and ideology (the power–ideology matrix). Such a breakdown may manifest itself in a number of ways, including (i) legitimation crisis, (ii) a dissensus among the rulers themselves and dissent by the ruled arising from a disarticulation or clash between the forms of their subjection and the forms of their qualification, and (iii) some form of revolutionary class consciousness and possibly transformative action.

The responses that result in obedience, for whatever reason, work toward social conservation, the maintenance of the present regime. They account for the stability tendencies of social systems. Resistance and struggle, on the other hand, account for change tendencies. Of course, in reality there will also be shades of disobedience manifested in what the present regime would call "dysfunctional behaviour" such as social withdrawal, manipulation, protest, and law-breaking; but such unorganized and diffuse "disaffection, scepticism, and cynicism do not amount to a 'crisis of legitimacy'" (Therborn, 1980, p. 108). Figure 13.1 is a schematic summary of the argument that systems stability and change must be seen as a consequence of a particular architecture of power and ideology.

SOME IMPLICATIONS FOR SYSTEMS THEORY

Thematic Consolidation

In a highly influential, seminal work, Jackson and Keys (1984) developed a typology of problem-contexts and systems methodologies, but with a critical intent. Oliga (1988a) sought to consolidate this critical intent by focusing on fundamental philosophical assumptions and concerns that underwrite different types of problem-solving methodology. While the thrust of those two intellectual expeditions centred on design inquiry at both theoretical and metatheoretical levels of critical analysis (see also Banathy, 1987), this paper can be read as an attempt to broaden the inquiry beyond the structural aspects of system control (see also Oliga, 1988b).

The focus here is on processes of organizational power relations and the functioning of ideologies from the point of view of those "under control." Thus, the "powerless" obey, thereby contributing to systems stability tendencies, or resist and struggle, thereby contributing to systems change tendencies, all depending upon their perception of the degree of effectiveness of an organization's power–ideology matrix. This attempt at further thematic consolidation therefore seeks to introduce the "missing" processual aspects of power and ideology as they influence the actual behaviour of organizational members. Such attempts at thematic consolidation in critical management science seek to stimulate more critical explorations of the potentials, the limits, the gaps, the errors, and the implications of diverse critical formulations, all in the

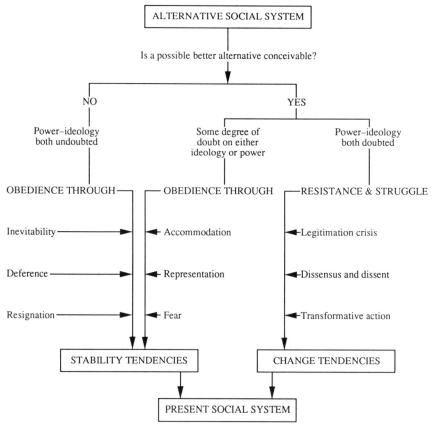

Figure 13.1 Systems stability and change: architecture of power and ideology

interest of fostering a more coherent development of theory and practice in the discipline.

Toward Rereading Constancy and Change

Mainstream literature in political theory has been characterized by what can now be seen as an untenable dichotomization of the grounds for obedience or resistance and struggle: force *versus* consent, force *versus* hegemony, force *versus* legitimacy, or in essence, power *versus* ideology (see Gramsci, 1971; Lukacs, 1971; Weber, 1968). The power–ideology matrix perspective takes the two concepts as essentially dialectical in non-liberated systems. This implies that obedience or revolt is not a consequence solely of either ideology or power. Both phenomena are always implicated, albeit in varying degrees of salience (see Figure 13.1). Given this critical understanding, both hard and soft systems approaches represent a step even further backwards than orthodox political theory. Each approach ignores one or the other end of the power-ideology polarity.

The hard systems approach neglects the ideological dimension in social control, focusing exclusively on the power dimension. The significance of forms of subjective consciousness is all but absent. The approach cannot therefore even begin to develop a penetrative understanding of the problem of constancy and change. For similar reasons, the soft systems approach is trapped in a situation of self-misunderstanding. It is subjectivist, with idealist connotations. The approach is least concerned with issues relating to power and the structures of constraints and contradictions. Of course, as a separate issue, both approaches additionally suffer from the problem of uncritically using power and agents' self-understandings as resources, even in their exclusive focus on one or the other.

CONCLUSION

It has been argued that systems stability and social change are the result of the kind of social control imposed upon a social system. The nature of a particular social control is, in turn, a consequence of the kind of power-ideology motif or architecture in being. And such architecture is not inevitable but, ultimately, the product of conscious actions of human beings as makers or victims of history. Sociocultural systems stability and change cannot therefore be adequately explained in naturalistic accounts rooted either in hard systems functionalist models of physical mechanisms or biological organisms or in soft systems interpretive models. A critical social theory seems necessary. Perhaps the most important implication of this paper is that, insofar as sociocultural systems are concerned, systems theory literature should begin to pay greater attention to the historical processes (such as power relations and exercise of power, and ideological formation of human subjectivities), which ultimately circumscribe individual and social behaviour. In ignoring the dialectical nature of the relationship between power and ideology, and instead uncritically focusing exclusively on one or the other of the two phenomena, both hard and soft systems approaches represent two steps backward from a penetrative understanding of the phenomenon of control in social systems.

REFERENCES

Ackoff, R.L. (1974). *Redesigning the Future*, John Wiley, New York.
Ackoff, R.L. (1981a). *Creating the Corporate Future*, John Wiley, New York.
Ackoff, R.L. (1981b). The art and science of mess management, *Interfaces*, **11**, 20–26.

Althusser, L. (1971). *Lenin and Philosophy and Other Essays*, New Left Books, London.

Bacharach, P.M., and Baratz, S. (1963). Decisions and non-decisions: an analytical framework, *Am. Polit. Sci. Rev.*, **57**, 641–651.

Banathy, B. (1987). Choosing design methods, in *Proceedings of the 31st Annual Meeting of the International Society for General Systems Research*, pp. 54–63, Budapest, Hungary.

Buckley, W. (1967). *Sociology and Modern Systems Theory*, Prentice-Hall, Englewood Cliffs, NJ.

Burrell, G., and Morgan, G. (1979). *Sociological Paradigms and Organisational Analysis*, Heinemann, London.

Checkland, P.B. (1972). Towards a systems-based methodology for real-world problem solving, *J. Syst. Eng.*, **3**, 87–116.

Checkland, P.B. (1981). *Systems Thinking, Systems Practice*, John Wiley, Chichester.

Checkland, P.B. (1983). OR and the systems movement: mappings and conflicts, *J. Opl Res. Soc.*, **34**, 661–675.

Checkland, P.B. (1985). From optimizing to learning: a development of systems thinking for the 1990s, Chapter 3 in this book.

Churchman, C.W. (1971). *The Design of Inquiring Systems*, Basic Books, New York.

Churchman, C.W. (1979). *The Systems Approach and its Enemies*, Basic Books, New York.

Clarke, S. (1982). *Marx, Marginalism and Modern Sociology: From Adam Smith to Max Weber*, Macmillan, London.

Clegg, S. (1975). *Power, Rule and Domination: A Critical and Empirical Understanding of Power in Sociological Theory and Everyday Life*, Routledge and Kegan Paul, London.

Dahl, R.A. (1958). A critique of the ruling élite model, *Am. Polit. Sci. Rev.* **52** 463–469.

Flood, R.L. (1990). *Liberating Systems Theory*, Plenum, New York.

Flood, R.L., and Ulrich, W. (1990). Testament to conversations on critical systems thinking between two systems practitioners, Chapter 9 in this book.

Foucault, M. (1972). *The Archaeology of Knowledge*, Tavistock, London.

Foucault, M. (1977). *Discipline and Punish*, Pantheon, New York.

Foucault, M. (1980). *Power and Knowledge*, Pantheon, New York.

Giddens, A. (1976). *New Rules of Sociological Method*, Hutchinson, London.

Giddens, A. (1977). *Studies in Social and Political Theory*, Hutchinson, London.

Gramsci, A. (1971). *Prison Notebooks* (translated by Q. Hoare), Lawrence and Wishart, London.

Habermas, J. (1972). *Knowledge and Human Interests*, Heinemann, London.

Habermas, J. (1973). *Theory and Practice*, Beacon Press, Boston.

Habermas, J. (1976). The analytic theory of science and dialectics, in *The Positivist Dispute in German Sociology* (Eds. T. W. Adorno *et al.*), Harper Torchbooks, New York.

Hales, M. (1974). Management science and the "Second Industrial Revolution", *Radical Sci. J.*, **1**, 5–28.

Hindess, B. (1982). Power, interests and the outcomes of struggle, *Sociology*, **16**, 498–511.

Hyman, R., and Brough, I. (1975). *Social Values and Industrial Relations: A Study of Fairness and Equality*, Basil Blackwell, Oxford.

Jackson, M.C. (1982). The nature of soft systems thinking: the work of Churchman, Ackoff and Checkland, *J. Appl. Syst. Anal.*, **9**, 17–28.

Jackson, M.C. (1983). The nature of soft systems thinking: comment on the three replies, *J. Appl. Syst. Anal.*, **10**, 109–113.

Jackson, M.C. (1985a). Social systems theory and practice: the need for a critical approach, Chapter 6 in this book.

Jackson, M.C. (1985b). Systems inquiring competence and organisational analysis, in

Proceedings of the 1985 Annual Meeting of the Society for General Systems Research, Louisville, Ky.

Jackson, M.C. (1987a). Present positions and future prospects in management science, *Omega*, **15**, 455–466.

Jackson, M.C. (1987b). New directions in management science, in *New Directions in Management Science* (Eds. M.C. Jackson and P. Keys), Gower, Aldershot.

Jackson, M.C., and Keys, P. (1984). Towards a system of systems methodologies, Chapter 7 this volume.

Jessop, B. (1982). *The Capitalist State: Marxist Theories and Methods*, Martin Robertson, Oxford.

Larrain, J. (1979). *The Concept of Ideology*, Hutchinson, London.

Lukacs, G. (1971). *History and Class Consciousness*, Merlin Press, London.

Lukes, S. (1974). *Power: A Radical View*, Macmillan, London.

Marx, K. (1969–1972). *Theories of Surplus Value, Vols. 1–3*, Lawrence and Wishart, London.

McCarthy, T. (1978). *The Critical Theory of Jurgen Habermas*, Hutchinson, London.

Minson, J. (1980). Strategies for socialists? Foucault's conception of power, *Econ. Soc.*, **9** 1–43.

Nietzsche, F. (1968). *Will-to-Power*, Vintage, New York.

Oliga, J.C. (1986). Methodology in systems research: the need for a self-reflective commitment, in *Mental Images, Values and Reality* (Ed. J.A. Dillon Jr.), International Society for General Systems Research, Louisville, Ky.

Oliga, J.C. (1988a). Methodological foundations of systems methodologies, Chapter 8 this volume.

Oliga, J.C. (1988b). Systems control: managerial perceptions and constructions, in *Systems Prospects* (Eds R.L. Flood, M.C. Jackson and P. Keys), Plenum, New York.

Parsons, T. (1937). *The Structure of Social Action*, Free Press, Chicago.

Puxty, A.G., Soo, W.F., Lowe, E.A., and Laughlin, R.C. (1980). Towards a critical–theoretic perspective for an epistemology of managerial theory, in *Proceedings of the Workshop "Towards an Epistemology of Management Research"*, Stockholm School of Economics, Stockholm.

Rosenhead, J. (1982). Why does management need management science?, in *A General Survey of Systems Methodology* (Ed. L. Troncale), International Society for General Systems Research, Louisville, Ky.

Rosenhead, J., and Thunhurst, C. (1982). A materialist analysis of operational research, *J. Opl Res. Soc.*, **33**, 111–122.

Salaman, G. (1979). *Work Organisations: Resistance and Control*, Longman, London.

Smith, C. (1986). Transformation and regeneration in social systems: a dissipative structure perspective, *Syst. Res.*, **3**, 203–213.

Spear, R. (1987). Towards a critical systems approach, in *Proceedings (Supplement) of the 31st Annual Meeting of the International Society for General Systems Research*, Budapest, Hungary.

Therborn, G, (1980). *The Ideology of Power and the Power of Ideology*, Verso and New Left Books, London.

Thom, R. (1975). *Structured Stability and Morphogenesis*, Benjamin, Reading, Mass.

Thomas, A.R. (1980). Generating tension for constructive change: the use and abuse of systems models, *Cybernet. Syst.*, **11**, 339–353.

Thomas, A.R., and Lockett, M. (1979). Marxism and systems research: values in practical action, Chapter 4 in this book.

Tinker, A.M., and Lowe, E.A. (1984). One dimensional management science: the making of a technocratic consciousness, *Interfaces*, **14**, 40–49.

Warren, M. (1984). Nietzsche's concept of ideology, *Theor. Soc.*, **13**, 541–565.
Watt, K.E.F., and Craig, P.P. (1986). Systems stability principles, *Syst. Res.*, **3**, 191–201.
Weber, M. (1968). *Economy and Society: An Outline of Interpretive Sociology*, Bedminster Press, New York.
Whitley, R.D. (1974). Management research: the study and improvement of forms of co-operation in changing socio-economic structures, in *Information Sources in the Social Sciences* (Ed. N. Roberts), Butterworths, London.
Wood, S., and Kelly, J. (1978). Towards a critical management science, *J. Mgmt Stud.*, **15**, 1–24.

Chapter 14

Modernism, Post-Modernism and Contemporary Systems Thinking

MICHAEL C. JACKSON

INTRODUCTION

The purpose of this paper is to examine contemporary systems thinking in the light of one of the hottest debates currently absorbing time and space in the human sciences—that surrounding the challenge to modernism posed by the post-modernist position. In order to carry out such a review the main aspects of modernism and post-modernism are first described and contrasted. Two different forms of modernism, systemic and critical, are identified and the post-modern assault on each is set out. This section of the paper concludes with a discussion of some of the implications for systems methodologies if what the post-modernists say is correct.

The second half of the paper takes each of the main strands of contemporary systems thinking in turn—hard, cybernetic, soft and critical—and relates it to the debate between modernism and post-modernism. Hard and cybernetic approaches are found to be systemic modernist in orientation, soft systems thinking is revealed as an underdeveloped form of critical modernism and critical systems thinking shown to be a highly advanced form of modernism in which some systemic aspects are subordinated to critical presuppositions. Each form of systems thinking is made the subject of a critique on the basis of its

Critical Systems Thinking: Directed Readings. Edited by R.L. Flood and M.C. Jackson

relationship to modernism. A discussion follows of the consequences that arise for contemporary systems thinking from its lack of attention to post-modernist issues and concerns.

MODERNISM VERSUS POST-MODERNISM

The most important debate in the cultural arena and in the human and social sciences during recent times has been that centred on the attempt to establish a "post-modern" as opposed to "modern" theoretical position. This debate turns crucially on supposed changes in our culture and the way we understand knowledge and "reality", but is usually linked to other developments in society as well. Thus post-modernist culture is variously associated with post-industrial society, with consumer society, media society, knowledge and information-based society, the dominance of multinational companies, a post-Fordist decentralisation of enterprises, and with a new stage in the development of late capitalism in which everything becomes a commodity.

What is not in doubt is that post-modernism has had a significant affect on architecture, the theatre, literature and art, as well as social theory. The systems movement can hardly ignore the post-modernist debate, because if a new social and economic movement is being born, then systems methodologies will certainly have to respond to the "new times" which the post-modernists claim to identify.

I shall concentrate on the debate as it has affected social theory. To begin with some of the main points of schism between modernists and post-modernists are outlined. The key manifestations of modernism as identified by post-modernists are then set out. The post-modernist alternative is described, in so far as this is possible given the movement's dedication to "difference" and indeterminacy. Finally, I consider how acceptance of the post-modernist argument might affect the use and relevance of systems methodologies. For the descriptions of modernism and post-modernism I rely heavily on Lyotard (1984) and Cooper and Burrell (1988), and turn to Burrell (1989) and Jacques (1989) for the relevance of the arguments for systems thinking. The learning gained will be used in the second part of the paper to see if any systems methodologies show signs of being responsive to the "post-modern condition."

Modernism is committed to the achievements of the Enlightenment, upholding reason and believing that rationality can play an increasing role in helping human beings perfect themselves and their societies. The world is seen as logical and orderly so that it can be probed by science to produce "objective" truth. History is seen as having a meaning based upon human purpose or, if not that, upon the rationalisation of social systems. There is progress towards some unitary, predictable end-state which might be the emancipation of humanity or the perfect functioning of the system. Language is "transparent" so that it is capable of conveying truth, and acting as a suitable vehicle for arriving at consensus. It offers security through rational explanations of what is happening, centring on the human subject or the increasing complexity of society. Seriousness and "depth" are characteristics of modernism as it plans and charts the onward march of rationality and progress.

Post-modernism seeks to puncture the certainties of modernism, particularly the belief in rationality, truth and progress; and it delights in doing so. It denies that science has access to objective truth, and rejects the notion of history as the progressive realisation and emancipation of the human subject or as an increase in the complexity and steering capacity of societies. Language is not transparent and it certainly does not offer the possibility of universal consensus. There are many different "language games," obeying different rules, in which speakers take part in order to defeat opponents or for the sheer pleasure of playing. We have, therefore, to be tolerant to differences, to multiple interpretations of the world, and must learn to live with the incommensurable, since there is no meta-theory which could reconcile or decide between different positions. Post-modernism offers no security. Rather, it thrives on instability, disruption, disorder, contingency, paradox and indeterminacy. The image is more significant than "reality" and so post-modernism emphasises superficiality and play instead of seriousness and depth.

Lyotard (1984) recognises two central manifestations of modernism in social theory, and these can be called, following Cooper and Burrell (1988), "systemic modernism" and "critical modernism."

Systemic modernism, as its name suggests, is identified with the systems approach, both as a means of understanding society and programming it for more effective performance. Parsons' work represents an early "optimistic" phase of systemic modernism, reflecting the managed resurgence of capitalist economies after the Second World War and their stabilisation using, particularly, the mechanism of the modern welfare state. The latest phase is found in Luhmann's highly technocratic, all-embracing and despairing version of systems theory. In this, instrumental reason is completely triumphant as everything is subject to the rational requirements of the societal system. It is the system which is the vanguard of history and progress, as it follows its own logic to increase "performativity" (in terms of input–output measures) and handle environmental uncertainty. Humanity is dragged in the wake of the system. Individual hopes and aspirations simply respond to the system's needs and consensus is engineered to improve the system's functioning. Even internal dissension, strikes and conflict represent the system readjusting to increase its viability and effectiveness.

Knowledge under systemic modernism, Lyotard argues, is completely subservient to system imperatives. First, science is privileged over other less malleable forms of learning, and then science and technology are reduced solely to programming the system. Truth gives way to performativity. Only research relevant to the functioning of complex, large-scale systems is financed, and only results which contribute to improving the input–output equation are recognised. The technocrats who subscribe to this knowledge have the power to implement the findings and so to verify their correctness. Thus a vicious circle is set up in which profit, power and proof become indissolubly linked. Further, what is implemented also becomes associated with what is right and just. Power becomes the basis of legitimation. Questions about efficiency and saleability replace those about truth or falsity and justice. Education, too, is turned to the same purpose.

The second form of modernism is "critical modernism." Critical modernism is based upon Kant's programme of enlightenment. It rests upon what Lyotard calls the power of "grand narratives" which seek to explain history in terms of progress. These grand narratives take two forms. First there are philosophical "totalisations" which offer a unified view of all learning. Differences are overcome as previously irreconcilable sciences and knowledges are combined in one language game. A good example is Hegel's universal history of philosophy, celebrating the becoming of the "spirit." Second are those narratives which chart the emancipation of the human subject. History is seen as the progressive liberation of humanity from constraints so that it can assume mastery and take on responsibility for its own destiny. Marxism is, of course, the best example of this kind of grand narrative. The history of all societies can be explained as leading to a communist utopia in which all conflicts and contradictions are overcome.

Not surprisingly, since his work combines elements from both types of grand narrative, Habermas is fingered by Lyotard as being the archetypal representative of critical modernism. Habermas proposes a unified theory of knowledge linked to different human interests, and aims his whole project at human emancipation directed by universal consensus arrived at in the "ideal speech situation", with participants presumably sticking to one language game. More surprising to the reader, perhaps, will be the idea that Luhmann and Habermas can be classified together as "modernists"—even if they are modernists of different varieties. For Habermas regards himself as an implacable opponent of Luhmann's systems theory, and as setting out the grounds on which the imperialism of instrumental reason can be resisted. Lyotard, however, sees more similarities between their two positions than differences. Both Habermas and Luhmann believe that the world is logical and meaningful; that history has a subject—whether this is humanity or "the system"; that discourse can capture the order that exists "out-there" in reality; and that human beings can understand and change, or at least influence, what happens in society.

Looking at the two kinds of modernism, Lyotard is convinced that systemic modernism is much the most powerful. The grand narratives are no longer credible as "more realistic" views of science and knowledge have prevailed. It is obvious, to Lyotard, that the language games people play are too numerous and complicated to be subsumed under any totalising endeavour. Moreover, despite the commitment of critical theories to oppose the status quo, they are in fact easily incorporated into it. In capitalist countries the minor resistances they provoke provide a fertile source of renewal for the system. In those few places where the alternative, communist model of society has not been eliminated, Marxism itself has been transformed into a regulator of society. As Lyotard tellingly argues:

> Everywhere, the critique of political economy (the subtitle of Marx's *Capital*) and its correlate, the critique of alienated society, are used in one way or another as aids in programming the system. (1984, p. 13)

While recognising systemic modernism as the strongest adversary, Lyotard is firm in his opposition to the determinacy of all forms of modernism, whether emphasising the functionality of the system or human emancipation. He wants to construct a post-modern alternative. The certainties encouraged by modernism, the meta-discourses pretending to provide objective understanding of the whole, can exact a high price in terms of a terrorism either of "the system" or of the philosophical and political kind. For this reason it is necessary to "wage war" on totalisations, to emphasise dissension, instability and unpredictability, and to activate "difference." The blindspots of modernism, those things rendered unpresentable and unspeakable in the narratives of modernism, must be brought to the fore.

This task is made easier because, although modernism is powerful, it is becoming clear that it is built upon fragile foundations. Science is seen to be only one kind of language game with limited relevance to social affairs. Even within its sphere of relevance, the modernist account of science is prone to attack. The new physics, as in quantum theory, concerns itself with instabilities and with uncertainty and the undecidable. Put simply, science does not function as modernism would have it. Post-modern science, therefore, rejects performativity and asks questions about purposes. It sees systems not as stable but as subject to discontinuity and catastrophe. They are temporary islands of determinism within a sea of indeterminacy. The quest for precise knowledge about systems is misguided; more precision only reveals greater uncertainty. The attempt to limit individual initiative, according to systemic requirements, destroys exactly the novelty the system needs to adjust to its environment. Our new understanding of science provides no support, therefore, for modernism.

The possibility of developing a meta-language which modernism could employ to legitimate its grand narratives is also open to attack. There is no one social subject that can be addressed using a universal meta-language. And there are many language games of which each of us knows only a few. Nor is it easy to sustain the modernist notion that language is oriented to achieving consensus. Language games are characterised by struggle and dissension and this seems highly necessary in order to promote innovation and to energise and motivate human action and behaviour. Communication should, therefore, be imbued with the capacity for innovation, change and renewal and refusal of conformity encouraged. Consensus can only be possible in localised circumstances and is only desirable if subject to rapid cancellation.

Cooper and Burrell (1988) reference the work of Derrida and Foucault as other prominent post-modernist writers. Derrida's "deconstructive" method seeks to reveal the deceptiveness of language, and the work that has to go into hiding contradictions so that unity and order can be privileged and rationality maintained. Foucault demonstrates how power operates to impose an order on the world so that it fits the categories of modernism. To help us recognise just how extraordinary the ordinary is, he recommends "genealogy"—the search for disparity, difference and indeterminacy and the granting of respect to sudden, spontaneous insight.

For modernists such as Habermas, post-modernism is a philosophy of irrationalism, leading at best to despair because it abandons the hope that humans can improve their lot through their own agency. To Lyotard (1984) and Jacques (1989), however, this is not the case. A post-modernist ethics can be constructed on the basis of the idea of "justice." Giving up on performativity and the grand narratives means we can no longer hide behind "objectivity" to avoid personal responsibility. We have to live in a world of multiple partial truths. But just knowing that you do not know everything can be liberating. It opens up a new world of possibilities in which each of us has to take ethical responsibility for the truths we embrace.

Following Burrell (1989) and Jacques (1989), we can now consider some of the implications for systems methodologies if what the post-modernists say is correct. Some of these derive from the other societal changes said to accompany or give birth to post-modernism itself. Operational research, for example, is a systems methodology which is clearly associated with the post-war consensus. It flourished in the nationalised industries and other large centralised and hierarchical corporations. Classical operational research is modernist and Fordist to its core. No wonder, then, that it is having difficulty adjusting as large organisations are decentralised and even broken up into autonomous units, in a world where consumption rather than production is dominant so that marketing, and the superficialities of packaging and appearance, are all important.

Other lessons stem directly from the cultural change that *is* post-modernism. If history is no longer seen as unilinear and predictable, then there is little point in promulgating forecasts of the future. If there is a decline in belief in rationality and an optimum solution to problems (increase in performativity) then the problem solving techniques will lack legitimation. At a time when the scientific method is being challenged as the sole means of producing knowledge, other forms of learning—from the case study, experience, intuition—may become more acceptable. Deep analysis of systems in search of laws and regularities is unlikely to receive much support. It will be more productive to emphasise the superficial, to concentrate on image, to take note of accidents and to respect arbitrariness and discontinuities. If there are no acceptable grand narratives to guide the idea of progress, then systems methodologies can only hope to bring about temporary and contested improvements. Indeed, in a world of multiple truths competing for prominence, systems practioners will be impotent unless they recognise the social, political and ethical contexts of their work. Finally, the post-modern world does not value "seriousness" very highly—better introduce a bit of humour, lightness, irony, sarcasm and racy language into our systems approaches.

Which, if any, systems methodologies express the spirit of the time as portrayed by post-modernism? This is the subject of the second half of the paper.

CONTEMPORARY SYSTEMS THINKING

All systems approaches make explicit or implicit assumptions about the matters at issue in the modernism versus post-modernism debate; about such things as rationality, truth and progress. It is our concern now to take in turn the four main strands of modern systems thinking—hard, cybernetic, soft and critical—and to analyse and critique them by unearthing their relationship to modernism.

Hard Systems Thinking

Hard systems thinking embraces such methodologies as classical operational research, systems analysis and systems engineering. As Checkland (1978) argues, these are all ". . . based upon the assumption that the problem task they tackle is to select an efficient means of achieving a known and defined end." Once this end has been specified, the problem of concern can be formulated. The system in which the problem is located is then represented in a quantitative model. An attempt is made, using systems ideas, to include all factors of relevance to the problem in the model. Experiments carried out on the model are used to identify an optimal solution which can be implemented in the real world.

Hard systems thinking, it is clear to see, exemplifies the main features of systemic modernism. Its "predict and prepare" paradigm rests upon a belief in an orderly world in which history is unilinear and the future is susceptible to forecast. Hard methodologies seek to employ systemic and rational procedures to optimize the efficient functioning of systems, thus maximising their performance. Knowledge becomes identified with the means of programming the system. Truth is subservient to performativity. The élites which subscribe to this knowledge have the power to implement its conclusions and so validate its correctness. So the vicious circle identified by Lyotard is set up as power becomes the basis of legitimation, and vice versa. Given the power of systemic modernism, the acceptance of multiple perceptions of reality in "soft OR" (see Rosenhead, 1989), and the recommendations for managing participation which ensue, can be seen as no more than a further contribution to smoothing the functioning of the system. This time by engineeering sufficient consensus around the system's purposes.

Most of the common criticisms levelled at the hard systems approach can be reinterpreted according to the post-modernist critique. Thus the argument that hard methodologies require clear objectives and often these are not available, and demand quantification of the unquantifiable, can be seen as a condemnation of an unrealistic search for logic and order in a disorderly world. The argument that hard approaches offer succour to the already powerful relates to the post-modernist notion that in systemic modernism performativity and truth become inextricably linked. The results of hard systems studies set up in the service of the powerful are implemented by that same group of powerful stakeholders, which thereby gives justification to the hard methods employed. Finally, the criticism that hard approaches fail to pay proper attention to the special characteristics of the human component in socio-technical systems is recognisably a lament from the critical modernist position against the excesses of systemic modernism.

Our argument here is essentially that there is much to be gained by thinking about modern systems approaches using ideas from the modernist versus post-modernist debate.

Organisational Cybernetics

Within this category of systems approach can be included those, such as Beer, who explicitly adopt a cybernetic approach, together with many socio-technical, contingency and general system theory thinkers whose work implicitly has a cybernetic basis. The emphasis in all this literature is on the design of organisations to be self-regulating, and even self-organising, systems. Beer's work may be taken as an exemplar.

Beer (1979, 1985) has developed a "viable system model" (VSM) which can be used to "diagnose" the operational effectiveness of any existing or proposed organisational design. A system is viable, for Beer, if it is capable of responding to environmental changes even if those changes could not have been foreseen at the time the system was designed. The main problems for organisations is the extreme complexity and uncertainty exhibited by their environments. In order to become or remain viable, an organisation has to achieve "requisite variety" with the complex environment it faces. It must be able to respond appropriately to the various threats and opportunities presented by the environment. Of course, the potential variety of the environment always threatens to overwhelm that of the system. Complexity, therefore, has to be managed. This is described by Beer as "variety engineering." His VSM sets out the necessary relationships that must obtain between essential organisational elements (Systems 1–5) and information channels, so that the intricate variety equations can be balanced in a satisfactory way. One important recommendation is to make the operational elements of the system (the parts of System 1) autonomous in their own right, so that they can absorb some of the massive environmental variety that would otherwise flood higher management levels (compare the idea of "autonomous work groups" in socio-technical theory).

It would seem obvious that the VSM, and organisational cybernetics generally, is an expression of modernism. The world is perceived as logical and orderly to the extent that it can be probed with a view to discovering the laws of viability of systems. The chief contribution of organisational cybernetics is to the technical interest in prediction and control in the social domain. This, and a lack of self-reflectiveness about the social use to which it is put, demonstrates a "systemic" rather than a "critical" modernist orientation. As Ulrich says (1983), Beer conceives of his task as "tool design" rather than "social system design." Thus, the model lends itself to the increased rationalisation of social systems; its use can assist their "perfect" functioning. There is, however, in Beer's writings, a happy assumption that there is a correspondence between the demands of viability and the requirements of democracy, and Beer would certainly want to see his efforts as assisting human emancipation. Further, it should be mentioned that the VSM is only one part of Beer's contribution to human knowledge. His work as a whole can be seen as a grand cybernetic narrative geared to curing the ills of humankind and putting men and women more in control of their own destiny (e.g. 1983). So critical modernism is also reflected on Beer's agenda.

If we look at the main criticisms of the VSM we can again see how they can be given a post-modernist twist. To its critics the VSM is of dubious value as a source of principles for increasing efficiency and effectiveness because the systemic/structural constraints emphasised in the model are held to be of little determining importance in social systems. To the post-modernist this would simply be an example of a model emphasising logic and orderliness in the face of the reality of organisational and social life which is typified by instability, disruption, disorder, contingency, paradox and indeterminacy. With reference to purposes, the VSM is seen by its critics as paying too little attention to the exercise of power in organisations. In practice, it is argued, the model can easily be turned into an autocratic control device serving powerful interests. It lends itself to this because it provides no mechanisms either for the democratic derivation of purposes or for facilitating debate about the nature of the purposes served. This as it stands is a critical modernist objection to systemic modernism, but it could also be given a post-modernist thrust. Organisational cybernetics is about understanding and programming systems for effective performance. This mobilisation of power on behalf of "who knows what purpose" can exact a high price in terms of a terrorism of "the system."

Soft Systems Thinking

The work of Ackoff (1981), Checkland (1981), Checkland and Scholes (1990) and Churchman (1979) can be taken as representative of soft systems thinking. The points which will now be made generalise about the soft systems trend as a whole, and should be checked for detail against the writings of the representative thinkers.

The emphasis in soft systems thinking is on how to cope with ill-structured problems or messes. Rather than attempting to reduce the complexity of messes so they can be modelled mathematically or cybernetically, soft systems thinkers seek to explore them by working with the different perceptions of them that exist in peoples' minds. Systems are seen as the mental constructs of observers rather than as entities with a real, objective existence in the world. Multiple views of reality are admitted and their implications are examined. Values are included rather than excluded (in theory) from the methodological process. The privileged role of experts is questioned and an attempt made to include problem-owners and other concerned individuals in carrying out the study and finding possible ways forward. The immediate aim is to reach an "accommodation" about action to be taken. This should emerge from a debate involving all those interested in the decision and its implementation. A longer-term objective is to encourage and institutionalise a process of continual learning among the participants of the social system being addressed.

It is probably most accurate to identify soft systems thinking as a rather underdeveloped form of critical modernism, based upon Kant's programme of enlightenment and seeking the progressive liberation of humanity from constraints. Churchman and Ackoff are the most effusive contributors to this tendency in the soft approach. Churchman's Singerian inquirer (1971) is charged with pushing teleology to the ultimate in the heroic mission of increasing or developing purpose in human society, so that "man becomes more and more deeply involved in seeking goals." Ackoff (1974) wants to change the future through the idea of interactive planning. He wants "man" to take over God's work of creating the future. But even Checkland (1981, p. 20) has his moments, seeing SSM as:

. . . a formal means of achieving "communicative competence" in unrestricted discussion which Habermas seeks.

At the same time, because it is so underdeveloped a version of critical modernism, lacking any emancipatory dimension, the soft systems approach is particularly prone to slipping back into becoming no more than an adjunct of systemic modernism; readjusting the ideological status quo by engineering human hopes and aspirations in a manner which responds to the system's needs and so ensuring smoother functioning. Many of the examples we are given (Checkland 1981; Checkland and Scholes 1990) of the use of soft methodologies support the systemic rather than critical modernist interpretation.

The main criticisms levelled at soft systems approaches tend to come from a more advanced critically modernist stance. From an emancipatory perspective the soft systems approach seems to be orientated to regulation rather than to radical change. The concern of soft systems thinkers seems to be to understand and facilitate order and cohesion and to seek to preserve the status quo rather than go beyond it. There is a tendency to accept at face value, and work with, existing perceptions of reality. No attempt is made to unmask ideological frames of reference or to uncover the effects of "false-consciousness." Further, there is a willingness to take as given "compromises" and "accommodations" achieved within the confines of prevailing power structures. Although developed from an advanced modernist position these criticisms could, of course, be given a post-modernist turn. Post-modernists would criticise soft systems thinkers for their belief that language is a suitable vehicle through which to achieve consensus or accommodation, their belief in progressive "learning," and their failure to take account of the realities of power.

Although there are no grounds, currently, for linking soft systems thinking to post-modernism, it is just possible to conceive of Checkland's soft systems methodology (SSM) being developed in a post-modernist direction. This would need to build on SSM's denial of objective truth and acceptance of multiple language games yielding multiple interpretations of the world. Such a move would disarm the critics and put SSM back into the vanguard of fashion in the systems movement. Checkland and Scholes (1990) are tempted by this post-modernist view of SSM, identifying it with a "Mode 2" use of the methodology in which SSM is used not to structure studies but simply to help an observer community make sense of what they are doing by mapping it onto SSM. However, even in its "Mode 2" form SSM carries considerable modernist baggage. Such matters as the commitment to continuous learning, the adherence to open debate and the epistemological commitment to the use of systems ideas to learn about an apparently densely interconnected world, would have to be dropped to make this interpretation plausible. The essential nature of

SSM does not make this possible. Even if it did, such a move would be deeply cynical and deeply despairing, in the way that post-modernism is.

Critical Systems Thinking

Critical systems thinking came to the fore in the 1980s (Ulrich, 1983; Jackson, 1985), and is developing rapidly in the 1990s (Flood, 1990; Jackson, 1991a; Flood and Jackson, 1991). It embraces five major commitments (Jackson, 1991b). The first of these is critical awareness. This comes from closely examining the assumptions and values entering into actually existing systems designs or any proposals for a systems design. It also concerns understanding the strengths and weaknesses and the theoretical underpinnings of available systems methods, techniques and methodologies. The second is social awareness, which involves recognising that there are organisational and societal pressures which lead to certain systems theories and methodologies being popular for guiding interventions at particular times. Social awareness should also make users of systems methodologies contemplate the consequences of use of the approaches they employ. Third is a dedication to human emancipation, seeking to achieve for all individuals the maximum development of their potential. This is to be achieved by raising the quality of work and life in the organisations and societies in which they participate. The fourth commitment is to the complementary and informed use of systems methodologies in practice. The final commitment, which gives bones to the third and fourth, is to the complementary and informed development of all varieties of systems approach. Different strands of the systems movement express different rationalities stemming from alternative theoretical positions. These alternative positions must be respected, and the different theoretical underpinnings, and the methodologies to which they give rise, developed in partnership. This can be achieved by relating different systems epistemologies to the three fundamental human interests unearthed by Habermas—the technical, the practical and the emancipatory interest (Habermas, 1970).

Critical systems thinking was, as it emerged from the 1980s, an advanced form of modernism (embracing systemic aspects of modernism subordinated to a basically critical project) which did not reflect on this fact. In *Liberating Systems Theory* (1990), however, Flood has attempted from a critical systems perspective to come to terms with post-modernism particularly, for his argument, as it is expressed in the works of Foucault. Flood argues that despite their differences, Habermas and Foucault can be seen as contributing to a position in favour of theoretical pluralism. Habermas provides a basis for accepting three types of rationality, for promoting the development of each, and for criticising the limitations of each. However, he is naive in the way he conceptualises power, believing that power can be made to follow knowledge; to issue forth from the force of the better argument. Foucault sees power as immanent in all aspects of social life, and as intimately linked to knowledge so that, for example, it determines what the better argument is. Various localized forces decide which discourses should be dominant and what knowledges subjugated. Flood argues, therefore, that in order to achieve the maximum diversity in systems approaches, so that the fullest support can be provided to Habermas' human interests, it is necessary first to follow Foucault's method to reveal subjugated knowledges. Foucault provides the understanding and the means necessary to "liberate" suppressed knowledges so that a diversity of approaches is achieved. These can then be subject to "critique" according to the principles set out by Habermas for assessing the theoretical and methodological legitimacies and limitations of different knowledges.

Since Flood's contribution, critical systems thinking has the opportunity to be reflectively critically modernist—aware of post-modernist concerns and responding to post-modernist insights, but remaining committed to the project of the enlightenment. There may be little except fashion that might lead it to go any further. Critical systems thinking has always been implicitly aware of many of the issues raised by the post-modernists. Knights (1989) argues that those who criticise OR and aim to reformulate the discipline of management science need to be aware of their own power. Intervention methodologies always involve the exercise of power over human subjects and so critically inclined management scientists especially need to ask themselves what kind of subjects they would feel "morally, politically and socially justified in producing." To this kind of social awareness, of course, critical systems thinking is already heavily committed.

CONCLUSION

The response of systems thinking to the post-modern challenge has so far been, with the exception of Flood's contribution, to largely ignore it. And yet there are at least four issues raised by the post-modernists which emerge from our discussion as having important implications for systems thinking and practice. These concern logic and order, progress, power and language. The search for logic and order and the desire to design well-structured systems seem inherent in hard and cybernetic systems thinking, and yet the feasibility of achieving these has been radically questioned by post-modernism. The pursuit of progress in terms of the performativity of systems (in the case of hard and cybernetic approaches) or the emancipation of the human subject (in the case of the soft and critical variants) seems central to systems thinking, but is regarded as a dangerous myth by post-modernists. Power, which is central to any post-modernist account of social relations, is largely ignored by hard and cybernetic methodologies and is treated simplistically even in modern versions of soft systems thinking. Finally, soft systems thinkers and critical systems thinkers both embrace language as the medium through which understanding, consensus and accommodation become possible. To post-modernists language is deceptive to users and is an unsuitable medium for achieving mutual understanding in groups. It is clear that post-modernism offers little support or security to contemporary systems thinking.

I have introduced contemporary systems thinking in the light of the modernism versus post-modernism debate. How systems thinking, particularly critical systems thinking, responds to the post-modernist critique of modernism remains to be decided.

REFERENCES

Ackoff, R.L. (1974). *Redesigning the Future*, John Wiley, New York.
Ackoff, R.L. (1981). *Creating the Corporate Future*, John Wiley, New York.
Beer, S. (1979). *The Heart of Enterprise*, John Wiley, Chichester.
Beer, S. (1983). The will of the people, *J. Opl Res. Soc.*, **34**, 797–810.
Beer, S. (1985). *Diagnosing the System for Organizations*, John Wiley, Chichester.
Burrell, G. (1989). Post Modernism: threat or opportunity, in *Operational Research and the Social Sciences* (Eds M.C. Jackson, P. Keys and S. Cropper), pp. 59–64, Plenum, New York.
Checkland, P.B. (1978). The origins and nature of "hard" systems thinking, *J. Appl. Syst. Anal.*, **5**, 99–110.
Checkland, P.B. (1981). *Systems Thinking, Systems Practice*, John Wiley, Chichester.
Checkland, P.B., and Scholes, J. (1990). *Soft Systems Methodology in Action*, John Wiley, Chichester.
Churchman, C.W. (1971). *The Design of Inquiring Systems*, Basic Books, New York.
Churchman, C.W. (1979). *The Systems Approach*, 2nd edition, Dell, New York.
Cooper, R., and Burrell, G. (1988). Modernism, post-modernism and organisational analysis: an introduction, *Org. Stud.*, **9**, 91–112.
Flood, R.L. (1990). *Liberating Systems Theory*, Plenum, New York.
Flood, R.L. and Jackson, M.C. (1991). *Creative Problem Solving: Total Systems Intervention*, John Wiley, Chichester.
Habermas, J. (1970). Knowledge and interest, in *Sociological Theory and Philosophical Analysis* (Eds. D. Emmet and A. MacIntyre), pp. 36–54, Macmillan, London.
Jackson, M.C. (1985). Social systems theory and practice: the need for a critical approach, Chapter 6 this volume.
Jackson, M.C. (1991a). *Systems Methodology for the Management Sciences*, Plenum, New York.
Jackson, M.C. (1991b). The origins and nature of critical systems thinking, *Syst. Pract.*, **4**, 131–149.
Jacques, R. (1989). Post-industrialism, post-modernity and OR: towards a "custom and practice" of responsibility and possibility, in *Operational Research and the Social Sciences* (Eds M.C. Jackson, P. Keys and S. Cropper), pp. 703–708, Plenum, New York.
Knights, D. (1989). Intervention and change, in *Operational Research and the Social Sciences* (Eds M.C. Jackson, P. Keys and S. Cropper), pp. 287–292, Plenum, New York.
Lyotard, J-F. (1984). *The Post-modern Condition: A Report on Knowledge*, Manchester University Press, Manchester.

Rosenhead, J. (Ed.) (1989). *Rational Analysis for a Problematic World*, John Wiley, Chichester.

Ulrich, W. (1983). *Critical Heuristics of Social Planning: A New Approach to Practical Philosophy*, Haupt, Bern.

Chapter 15

Redefining Management and Systems Sciences

ROBERT L. FLOOD

INTRODUCTION

Management and systems sciences are currently undergoing redefinition by a growing group of scholars and practitioners. Significant developments have been made in the theoretical domain, by developing a pragmatic version of these ideas and subsequently by their employment in critically reflective technical and social practice. In the following argument, one appreciation of the theoretical redefinition will be developed. Before the details of the redefinition are given, I will first show how the main areas of thought discussed in this paper are understood to relate to each other.

IDEAL TYPE ORGANISATION OF ARGUMENT

The three trends of thought addressed in the argument herein are: systemic modernism in the two forms cybernetic technocratism and systemic interpretivism, critical systemic modernism and post-modernism. Theoretical isolationism and complementarism are rationalist. Post-modernism is indeterminist. Some of these terms used in the argument are taken from the literature of social theory,[1] whilst others have been named and distinguished for the

---

[1] A particularly useful paper drawn upon in parts of this thesis is Cooper and Burrell (1988). This is the forerunner to an interesting series in that journal, which looks in more detail at theorists such as Foucault, Habermas, Derrida and others.

Critical Systems Thinking: Directed Readings. Edited by R.L. Flood and M.C. Jackson

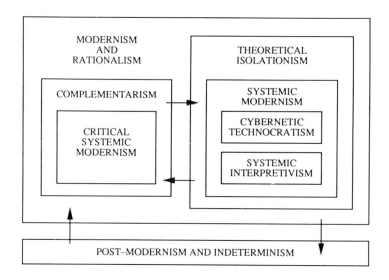

KEY

 CRITIQUE

Figure 15.1 Ideal type organisation of argument

purposes of the current line of work. Figure 15.1 shows how the three trends have been organised in the thesis to follow. Distinction between them will be made later. I will now undertake a first stage redefinition of management and systems sciences.

FIRST-STAGE REDEFINITION: DEALING WITH THEORETICAL ISOLATIONISM

Introduction

This section will develop an understanding of systemic modernism, by presenting details of the two positions cybernetic technocratism and systemic interpretivism. I will outline the nature of society and organisations that each assumes. Epistemological reasoning of each one will be summarised. Then, approaches to "problem solving" that have a logical relationship with those epistemological positions will be linked in. Theoretical isolationism will be shown to be a feature of cybernetic technocratism and systemic interpretivism. Following this, I turn to the relationship between theory and knowledge and, by "reversing" the propositions of theoretical isolationism, work out a complementarist epistemological position called *critical systemic modernism*. I employ the method documented above to analyse critical systemic modernism. The main feature to be found is a working relationship between differing methodological rules that are derived from three fundamental complementary knowledge-constitutive interests. A first-stage redefinition of management and systems sciences will then have been realised.

Cybernetic Technocratism

Society and Organisations

Modern society and organisations are a product of science and technology. Society is organised around scientistic and technocratic knowledge and in this sense it has given itself up to the theory. The theory dictates social control by large-scale technical "systems." This cybernetic monolithism conceives complexity in terms of a system of causal laws, of many interacting variables which are subject to coordination and control in order to achieve set goals. There are correct actions in social contexts. Performance is a key concern. It has its source of legitimation in the "system's" technical capability to reduce complexity and to increase certainty, both internal and external. Control and performance require individuals to redeem self-determination and to adapt their actions, for the benefit that the "system" offers, so that they become compatible with the "system's" goals. This non-reflective position is epistemologically untenable.

Epistemology

Objectivity is assumed in the definition of efficient means and clearly definable ends. Invariant truths are accepted. Positivist cybernetic technocratism, however, cannot inform us of what teleological goals we *ought* to pursue because it is fact-based. It is not possible to have neutral social goals. Any statement of "ends" that *should* be pursued is value-laden and therefore not objective. The same holds for "means" expressed in terms of efficiency. We might ask: "Efficiency, in terms of what—money, manpower, time, happiness . . .?" It is evidently impossible to have means that are neutral in social contexts. Means–ends fundamentals that assume objectivity are epistemologically untenable, but the methodological principles logically derived from this non-reflective positivist position are found to have value within a complementarist scheme.

Methodology

The methodological principles are cybernetic and concentrate on organisation. They reflect parts of a continuum of metaphors rooted in the natural sciences:

mechanical–organic–neurocybernetic. Each metaphor leads to a different interpretation of key concepts; like objectives, communication, control, efficiency, effectiveness and complexity. These wholly different cybernetic conceptions have given rise to a diversity of "problem solving" approaches. Following the continuum we have, for example, systems engineering (e.g. M'Pherson, 1980) and system dynamics (e.g. Roberrts *et al.*, 1983), general systems theory (e.g. Klir, 1985), and viable system diagnosis (e.g. Beer, 1985).

Systemic Interpretivism

Society and Organisations

Modern society and organisations are a product of human interpretations and actions leading to relative truths, and in this sense it has given itself up to the theory. The theory, which assumes subjectivity, dictates social "management" of interpretive actors who perform actions within cultural "systems." This non-reflective interpretive monolithism conceives complexity in terms of interrelations between human interpretations, actions explained by social rules and practices, and constitutive meaning that makes the rules and practices meaningful. Conformance is a key concern. It has an internal source of legitimation in the cultural "system's" power to "manage" complexity of diversity and to increase certainty of action. It has no external source of legitimation. "System manageability" requires individuals to redeem self-determination and adapt their actions so that they become compatible with the rules and practices of the culture. This position is epistemologically impoverished.

Epistemology

The essence of this position is a pluralist conception of relative truths. Each interpretation is equally legitimate. Systemic interpretivism, however, cannot guarantee generation of mutual understanding of what is being done and why it is being done. Each relative "truth" is assumed to be based on ideas only and transmitting its meaning must assume undistorted communication. Such subjective idealism neglects to deal with the social effects of material conditions. Quasi-causal[2] accounts of the way certain material conditions give rise to certain forms of action are not dealt with. Furthermore, relativism ignores forces of coercion. False consciousness, built on lies, half-truths and propaganda, may freeze dominant constitutive meaning by claiming, through non-transparent false means, that a social situation is good, beneficial or necessarily the way it is. Truths may be "forced" into place.

---

[2] "Quasi," because causality refers to the subjective nature of the theory.

It is evident, with systemic interpretivism, that we cannot guarantee a free exchange of ideas. We cannot explain ideas without non-hypostatised reference to material conditions. The epistemology is therefore impoverished but the methodological principles derived from it are found to have value within a complementarist scheme.

Methodology

The methodological principles are interpretive. They are culture-based, but divide into two sets: dialecticism and relativism. *Dialecticism* sets fundamental assumptions against each other, assuming that conflict is inevitable even in the "cohesiveness" of cultures, yet this can have a positive learning side to it. The outcome does not have to be consensus although that is desirable. *Relativism* is about "managing" conflict by encouraging meaningful debate about issues in "peaceful negotiation." All positions are held as equally valid, but conflict between them is reduced in consensus seeking activities where attitudes are assumed to change. Dialecticism is represented by strategic assumption surfacing and testing (e.g. Mason and Mitroff, 1981), and relativism by interactive management (e.g. Ackoff, 1981) and soft systems methodology (e.g. Checkland, 1981). Dialecticism and relativism in systems "problem solving" are ideologically naive because the process of change is not adequately related to issues of power. Hence methodologies are ideologically conservative.

Theoretical Isolationism

Both cybernetic technocratism and systemic interpretivism argue for theoretical isolationism.[3] Knowledge is identified with science and life is placed in theory, so that theory is reflected in the conduct of those who subject themselves to its discipline. The information content of the theories is assumed to produce scientific culture. This is theoretical incommensurability which states that the rationality of one theory is an irrationality to others. All methodological rules are understood and universalised (or denatured if they are brought over from another theoretical position) through a single theory. This is methodological commensurability. Critical systemic modernism is a complementarist approach that stands against theoretical incommensurability (using Habermas', 1971, foundational critical theory).

---

[3] There is a strong argument in support of theoretical, or paradigmatic, incommensurability. A most concise account is given by Carter and Jackson (1990). Other viewpoints are offered by Donaldson (1985) and Hassard (1985). This paper stands as a rebuke to theoretical incommensurability, but unfortunately there is no space to recount the commensurability–incommensurability debate.

Complementarism

Society and Organisations

Modern society and organisations are characterised by two fundamental socio-cultural forms of action—labour and interaction. The production and repro-duction of human lives occurs through the transformation of nature with the aid of technical rules and procedures, and through communication of needs and interests in the context of rule-governed systems. Dialogue is dominated by social constraints and power relations. Complexity is defined by technical (many interacting variables that are subject to coordination and control), practical (interrelations between human interpretations) and emancipatory (power associated with rule-governed "systems") interests. Actions therefore reflect interests. Performance and conformance have their source of legitima-tion in the ideal of human self-determination. Critically self-reflective individ-uals in the ideal situation do not redeem self-determination but may have it removed by the rules and practices of coercive "systems."

Epistemology

Three 'knowledges' can be derived from three human interests. Labour enables human beings to achieve goals and to bring about material well-being. The success of labour depends upon achieving technical mastery. Human beings therefore have a *technical interest* in prediction and control over natural and social processes. Interaction secures and expands possibilities for mutual understanding. This is a *practical interest*, because disagreement between groups can be just as much a threat to achieving technical mastery as it is to the continuation of social processes. Equally, an analysis of the exercise of power helps us to understand past and present social arrangements. It may help to show that there are forces which prevent open and free discussion necessary for securing understanding and then technical mastery. Human beings must therefore have an *emancipatory interest*. The three knowledge-constitutive interests are the epistemological categories of concern to comple-mentarists. The orientation toward technical control, mutual understanding in the conduct of life and emancipation, establish viewpoints from which we may apprehend social reality in any way whatsoever.

Methodology

Complementarist methodological principles are critically self-reflective. They are interest-based and divide into three: technical, practical and emancipatory. In management and systems sciences, *technical interests are served by cybernetic approaches, and practical interests by interpretive approaches.* The first two method-ological categories represent the dichotomy between natural sciences and the humanities that complementarists are struggling to avoid. The third *emancipa-tory category is a new creation represented only by critical systems heuristics* (Ulrich, 1983, 1987). Relieved of positivist and interpretive epistemological positions by critical self-reflection, logical methodological rules are logically related to knowledge-constitutive interests (see Flood and Jackson, 1991).

Summary

Complementarism proposes that sciences are forms of possible knowledge and that human interests constitute necessary theoretical categories. Scientific culture is produced by the formation among theorists of a thoughtful way and enlightened mode of life. Knowledge interests are presuppositions that pro-vide the possibility for a differentiated constitution of meaning of possible objects of experience; hence there is theoretical commensurability. Methodo-logical rules have a logical relationship with knowledge-constitutive interests but have different domains of application; they are "distinct," hence there is methodological incommensurability.

The complementarist position is contrasted with that of theoretical isolation-ism in Table 15.1.

RATIONALISM AGAINST INDETERMINISM

Introduction

The first stage of the argument has dealt with three approaches: the systemic modernism of cybernetic technocratism and systemic interpretivism, and the late late-modernism of complementarism (which treats the last two as special cases). Each of these approaches proposes a form of rationalism. Complemen-tarism is a first-stage redefinition of management and systems sciences.[4] The

---

[4] A comprehensive study of complementarism in the context of metascience can be found in G. Radnitzky, *Contemporary Schools of Metascience—Volume II: Continental Schools of Metascience;* the series is titled "Studies in the Theory of Science," edited by H. Törnebohm. The first volume considers the Anglo-Saxon schools of metascience. From page 59, Radnitzky undertakes a thorough and informative study of complementarism, that precedes Habermas' knowledge-constitutive interests. There is no room in this focused thesis to recount such an analysis. However, a brief insight into Apel's argument is important; see K. O. Apel, "Die Entfaltung der 'sprachanalytischen' Philosophie und das Problem der 'Geisteswissenschaf-ten'," *Phil. Jaharb.*, **72** (1965).

Radnitzky, in preparing us for Apel's key arguments on complementarity between the hermeneutic and naturalistic approaches, underlined the difficulty of moving between traditions. "There is no lazy way, nor short-cut to overcome the ethnocentricity of scientific

15.1 Distinguishing complementarism from theoretical isolationism

Issue	Theoretical isolationism	Complementarism
Knowledge and science	Knowledge is identified with science	Sciences are forms of possible knowledge
Theory and life	Life is placed in theory, theory is reflected in the conduct of those who subject themselves to its discipline	Life interests constitute necessary theoretical categories
Scientific culture	Information content of theories produces scientific culture	Scientific culture is produced by the formation amongst theorists of a thoughtful way and enlightened mode of life
Theoretical (in) commensurability	Theories are contradictory, the rationality of a theory is the irrationality of another—theoretical incommensurability	Knowledge interests are presuppositions for the possibility of a differentiated constitution of meaning of possible objects of experience—theoretical commensurability
Methodological (in) commensurability	All methodological rules are understood and universalised through a single theory—methodological commensurability	Logical methodological rules have a relationship with knowledge constitutive interests and therefore have different domains of application, they are distinct—methodological incommensurability

next stage of the argument is a critique of modern rationalism through post-modern indeterminism. This creates tensions for complementarism which have given rise to a second-stage redefinition. I first consider the critique and then the second-stage redefinition.

---

subcultures expressed and reinforced by the special sublanguages." An understanding depends on ideas of dialectic mediation, polarity and complementary.

Dialectics plays a role in the development of totalities and their parts. Bohr's complementarity thesis is the classical model which inaugurated the application of the dialectic method. Complementarity does not imply presupposition between theories of each other. No single theory can help us catch all aspects of a section of reality; the idea of a complete description is elliptic. Aspects of each theory may complement each other and together give an ever fuller picture. Bohr, for example, argued that the wave and particle theory aspect of elementary particle phenomena complement each other in this way.

Radnitzky continues, that the impression of *polarity* of two theories or of their base explanatory models is typically due to the totalisation of either; that is, the claim for each model that it has a universal application within the sector of reality concerned. Tension

Modernism

Modern rationality assumes an attitude of perfection for humanity through rational thought. This is considered possible because language expresses something other than itself. Such monolithic and universal discourse, even for complementarists, implies that there are already existing answers to questions. Since rational thought "already knows," it is totalising and controlling. This is necessary because the world is seen to hold opportunities and constraints. The world is pro- and anti-human and therefore must be controlled and/or managed. A search for mastery and domination is achieved by destruction of opposition. Consensus therefore compels our attention. (A number of late modern positions, however, show a tendency away from dogmatic rationalism.)

Post-modernism

Post-modern rationality assumes that humanity is determined by "forces" that lie beyond human beings. Language comes in systems that are self-referential. Human beings construct interpretations of the world, in language systems, which have no absolute or universal status. The world is self-referential and is not therefore pro- nor anti-human. Mastery and domination obtain vitality by maintaining difference and provocation, where dissensus compels our attention.

Modern rationality is juxtaposed with post-modern indeterminacy in Table 15.2. Some penetrating criticisms for the late-modernism of complementarism arise from the contrast. One particular position often linked to post-modernism is the interpretive analytics of Foucault. This has been drawn upon to critique complementarism and has led to a second-stage redefinition of management and systems sciences. I will consider Foucault's work and then the second-stage redefinition.

---

between knowledge-systems or theories in polarity is a crisis; it is not merely a dialectical tension such as thesis–antithesis, but a logical contradiction.

Apel's *complementarity* thesis is directed against totalisation, considering knowledge-systems as complementary, and that we can use them to round and fill our picture of man. Apel states that natural science and human science (in the science of man) and quasi-naturalistic and hermeneutic approaches (in human science) are mediating each other, so that in each the developments of knowledge proceed in a continuous tacking between the two approaches or levels. This is a move toward detotalisation.

While Apel provides an appealing notion of complementarity, it is Habermas' knowledge-constitutive interests that turns the argument toward a sound epistemological position, as argued for in this article.

Table 15.2 Distinguishing modernism or rationalism, from post-modernism or indeterminism

Issue	Modernism or rationalism	Post-Modernism or Indeterminism
Humanity	Perfection through rational thought	Determination of humanity lies in forces beyond human beings
Discourse	Language expresses something other than itself	Language is formed in "systems" that are self-referential
World	The world is pro- and anti-human and therefore must be controlled	The world is self-referential and is not therefore pro- nor anti-human
Mastery and domination	Mastery and domination is achieved by destruction of opposition	Mastery and domination obtains its vitality by maintaining difference and provocation
Consensus	Consensus compels our attention	Dissensus compels our attention

Interpretive Analytics

Interpretive analytics[5] proposes an explanation of how and why knowledges come into focus or slip away from dominant positions. It is described as archaeology (Foucault, 1974) and genealogy (Foucault, 1980); analyses of self-referential language systems that constitute knowledges. Emergence of knowledges is a consequence of domination at local discursivity levels, imposed by non-discursive subjugators. There are "forces" holding together discursive formations which give rise to conflict between formations. Some formations rise and others are subjugated. This leads to resistance and relations of power. Historical succession of discursive formations becomes a matter of contests and struggles over systems of rules. Each system of rules is an interpretation and is like a living evolutionary network.

Essentially, Foucault reckoned that power and knowledge are intricately linked and that there are many suppressed knowledges. Critique is an important part of Foucault's work. The aim is to provide the possibility for discursivities that are prevented from being "seen or heard," known or even formed, to be liberated.

Power is rejected in the conceptual form of right, sovereignty and obedience.

---

[5] "Interpretive analytics" is the useful name given to Foucault's archaeology, genealogy and critique by Dreyfus and Rabinow (1982).

Power is not like a commodity. The idea that power is descending and "negative," as would be the sovereign case, is replaced by ascension and "positiveness." Power is constructed and functions on the basis of micropolitical actions and is productive in the way that it produces "reality" (i.e. domains of objects and rituals of thoughts). These are not autonomous nor independent. They are integral with a series of broad historical processes.

Interpretive analytics in action underlines a number of difficulties for complementarists. The contemporary dominant discourse it spotlights is cybernetic technocratism. It holds a command over texts, language and concept articulation. Command is established in the propaganda of school teaching which assumes a modern rationality. This includes the fact-based examination process as a punishment–reward "system," and the characterisation, image building, and immortalisation of the "wise men," and acceptable and confirmatory jokery about non-conformists. Inaccessibility of jargon is also key in fights for discontinuity. And the everyday person experiences trivialising of these disputes. The laity is armed only with an installed rationality in mind and the same in texts on their shelves. The mind is conditioned by the rationality, the body is understood through the rationality and is subject to a social world constituted by that knowledge.

Complementarists must challenge the dominance of cybernetic technocratism if the first redefinition of management and systems sciences is to be realised. Good ideas are not enough. Cybernetic technocratism threatens to prevent any redefinition whatsover. It is held in place by micropolitical forces. Interpretive analytics set out to challenge and to liberate knowledges. It introduces a strategic political element to action. This is dealt with in the second-stage redefinition of the management and systems sciences discussed below.

SECOND-STAGE REDEFINITION: FIRST RESPONSE TO POST–MODERNISM

Introduction

I now work out a second-stage redefinition of management and systems sciences through a unity of interpretive analytics and complementarism, a process that I will call "liberate" and "critique." I then extend that process by introducing another set of ideas which provide two more stages—"empower" and "transform." This redefinition is worked out under the banner of liberating systems theory.

Liberate and Critique

Smart (1983), in his book *Foucault, Marxism and Critique*, notes that reflections on genealogical analysis show commitment to critical analysis by revealing subjugated knowledges that have either been lost or suppressed. Smart points out that Foucault identifies "centralising powers . . . linked to the institution and functioning of organised scientific discourse" (Smart, 1983, p. 84). Throughout this book, Smart wishes to realise a common denominator for Foucault's studies and declares that this factor is "a critical concern with the questions of the relationship between forms of rationality and forms of power" (Smart, 1983, p. 123). He compares this with the works of the Frankfurt School (of which Habermas is second generation) as well as Weber, and in particular notes that "it is the presence of a critique of instrumental rationality at the very foundation of critical theory which has prompted comparison with the work of Foucault" (Smart, 1983, p. 132). A little later, Smart (1983, p. 135) argues a point made by Gordon (1979), that Foucault's conception of power–knowledge relations does not incorporate a relationship between knowledge and ideology. The central notion of Habermas' critical theory and consequently new critical systems "problem solving," however, is the idea that theory and ideology are integrated. If taken as read, there would be a fundamental irreconcilable difference between Foucault's work and that of the Frankfurt School and Habermas (we are mainly interested in knowledge-constitutive interests). Let us consider whether this has to be the case.

Smart (1983, p. 155) argues that the concept of critique can have at least two different meanings. The two meanings reflect two dimensions of power and subjugation. The first, based on this notion of theory–ideology, relates to Habermas' work. The second meaning takes up Foucault's critique as an approach to oppositional thinking, an instrument for fighters and resisters to deny "assumed-as-being" commonplace "truths"—it is of a "liberating rationality."

"Instrumental (scientific) rationality" (as a starting point) is a common general opposition of these two critiques. Science can be linked to control in the human condition. We can extend the idea of power to control the natural world, to the power of science through technology and social structures that control our working and social lives. Domination of instrumental reasoning, of scientific rationality, has also created forces of subjugation over other forms of reasoning.

We need to develop a complementary way of relating knowledge-constitutive interests and interpretive analytics to face up to these different dimensions of instrumental rationality. Foucault's critique can release subjugated knowledges (and hence methodologies). Releasing (systems-based) "knowledge" and methodological principles attacks fragmentation, and reduces weakness and even conflict. Diversity is seen as a strength enabling us to deal with complexity of phenomena. Interpretive analytics can release rationalities, knowledges and methodologies thus helping to grow diversity. Habermas' critical theory also accepts openness and conciliation. It offers the basis of a method to assess the legitimacies and limitations of knowledges and methodologies. Knowledge-constitutive interests therefore can help us to deal critically with the diversity and the tensions between rationalities.

On the one hand, with Foucault, we acknowledge and attempt to deal with forces of isolationism through a liberating rationale. On the other hand, with Habermas, we work against those forces by assessing the legitimacies and limitations of all approaches. This process diversifies in an informed way responses which help us to deal with the complexity of phenomena, that demanded human ingenuity to create a divesity of responses in the first place.

There is, however, a fundamental difficulty that we need to consider. There is apparently a contradiction between the works of Foucault and Habermas. We cannot simply add one unity to the other to achieve a cumulative meta-unity that underpins a new way of (systems) thinking. We must be cautioned by Habermas' (1985) powerful criticism of Foucault's notion of the history of knowledge (also see Honneth, 1985; Fraser, 1981). This debate has been usefully dealt with by Freundlieb (1989). It is drawn upon below as an aid to help to explain how the difficulties might be adequately resolved.

Let us recount certain details of Foucault's argument. Archaeology was conceived as an analysis of the history of discursive formations, explained as the anonymous systems of rules which allegedly form the conceptual and institutional conditions for the possibility of scientific statements. These rules act as historical *a priori ideas* that determine what can be thought and stated within a discourse, what objects can be theorised and what will be accepted as true or valid.

The response of Habermas (and Honneth) was to ask how it might be possible to reconstruct, in an historical analysis, what those historical *a priori ideas* are from within a present discourse which, by definition, must have its own rules of the constitution of objects and of inclusion and exclusion.

This criticism is tackled in the argument of *Liberating Systems Theory* (Flood, 1990a, b). Rules were defined for an adequate epistemology for systems practice. With this, statements of discourse may be said to be true within the rules of a discursive formation, but cannot themselves be given a true or false, valid or invalid, rational or irrational status from an external or objective point. The aim of the adequate epistemology is to ensure that rationality and irrationality of knowledges are critically assessed, although this is not a search for ultimate truth or falseness, validity or invalidity. I do not claim to have achieved the non-ideological approach that Foucault seems to declare that he has achieved with interpretive analytics.

Genealogy was a move away from the archaeological project. It abandoned the idea of autonomy of discursive formations. This new effort accounted for the emergence and disappearance of discourse by an analysis of contingent and external historical circumstances which bring about an interaction of, or a contact between, discursive practices. Discourse now incorporates the idea of apparatuses, these being conceived of as discursive as well as non-discursive practices, but like the discursive formations the apparatus is assumed to play an objective-constitutive role.

On this issue Habermas criticised Foucault's concept of power since it played a dual and irreconcilable role in his work. Power is constitutive, a transcendental condition for the possibility of truth and knowledge, which is contradicted by power as a purely descriptive term in historical analyses.

Broadly speaking, power might be considered to be that which allows a subject to affect objects in successful actions. In Habermas' terms this is dependent on the truth of the judgement that informs the actions. For Foucault it is the other way around since he makes truth dependent on power, which then allows for an uncoupling of power from competences and intentions of individual agents.

This contradiction is extremely difficult to overcome. It is vital that we are successful because our overriding concern is to draw upon both Foucault and Habermas for a foundation to liberate and critique. This can, however, be achieved if we assume that truth is dependent on power. We thus need to liberate discourse. Further, Habermas offers us an ideal by which we can assess the truth of a judgement according to an explicit ideology and through a critical analysis. This is where an adequate epistemology comes in to play.

Finally, Habermas has argued that genealogy is crypto-normative—it cannot say on what grounds its critical rhetoric should be accepted. Decisions have to be made on the basis of certain cognitive and moral values and norms. The choice that has to be made is between a crypto-normativism that refuses to discuss its assumptions and an approach which opens those norms up for critical discussion and assessment.

In *Liberating Systems Theory* a position of openness has been adopted. A statement is made about the rules for discourse and analysis. They are emancipatory and come from an epistemology that declares certain others to be untenable or impoverished. Most important, however, is that this whole effort is indeed up for critical discussion and assessment or, as Connerton (1976) points out, the only unchanging basic thesis of critical thinking is that it is itself changeable (but let me add, "traditionally" within the monolithism of emancipation).

Empower and Transform

We need to extend the process, liberate and critique, to include empower and transform. We can recruit the army of ideas developed in *Systems Practice* by Oliga (1990a, b). He has studied control, power and ideology. The aim of his project is to undertake a critical study of the concepts of control, power and ideology, to uncover the potentially dominating and oppressive nature of these concepts, and to gain a penetrating understanding of the way they contain their own seeds of transcendence. On the one hand there is a need to see these phonomena, not in functional terms for the "system" as a whole, but as systematically working to maintain the interests and advantages of only certain members of the social "system." On the other hand, there is an equal need to tease out those aspects that contradict their oppressive consequences. The aim is to use insights gained to raise the consciousness and spur the will to self-determination of those subjugated and dominated—hence the project can be called "empower" and "transform."

Second-Stage Redefinition: Liberating Systems Theory

Liberating systems theory can be summarised in terms of a process that leads to progressive change in social order. This process "starts" with the need to tackle the difficulty of suppression of knowledges, for without such an attack we begin our scholarly efforts enjoying only diminished intellectual possibilities. *Liberating* knowledges naturally leads to the need for an adequate *critique* of these rationalities, so that their legitimacies and limitations are thoroughly explored. This builds a strong position for *empowerment* of those oppressed leading toward *transformation* of social conditions. Complementarism thus becomes the process "liberate, critique, empower and transform."

A drive to pragmatise (without compromise) the theory recounted in this paper has led to two new sets of methodological ideas for "problem solving." Critical systems heuristics (Ulrich, 1983, 1987) is an emancipatory methodology. Total systems intervention (Flood and Jackson, 1991) is a complementarist meta-methodology. These are reviewed elsewhere in this book.

CONCLUSION

Management and systems sciences remain firmly rooted in positivist cybernetic technocratism. Some new trends that flirt with interpretive rationality seem, at first sight, to have moved the discipline on considerably and have begun to gain much favour in certain quarters. On analysis, however, systemic interpretivism is found to suffer from the same erroneous visions of knowledge and science, theory and life, as cybernetic technocratism and amounts to a second form of positivism. It is non-reflective. These two approaches assume theoretical isolationism and that knowledge is identified with a science. They assume that life is placed in theory, theory being reflected in the conduct of those who subject themselves to its discipline. Such a deeply rooted understanding assumes that theories are contradictory, that the rationality of one is an irrationality to others. Further, all methodological rules are understood and unified through a single theory; hence there is methodological commensurability. The possibilities for management and systems sciences are few with theoretical isolationism, inevitably leading to fragmentation, weakness, non-productive debate and impoverished "problem solving."

A fundamentally different position is that of complementarism, a first-stage redefinition of management and systems sciences. Here, the relationships between knowledge and science, and theory and life are reversed. This leads to remarkable new possibilities. Sciences are considered to be forms of possible knowledge and knowledge interests constitute the necessary theoretical categories. This differentiated constitution of meaning of possible objects from experience assumes theoretical commensurability. Here, logical methodological rules are assumed to hold a relationship with knowledge-constitutive interests and to have their own domains of application; hence there is methodological incommensurability. The possibilities for management and systems sciences are substantial with complementarism, leading to openness and conciliation between approaches, strength, and highly productive debate concerning legitimacies and limitations of "problem solving" methodologies. This leads to relevant coordinated intervention.

This late late-modernism, following Habermas' late modern thought, does come under penetrating attack from post-modern reasoning. In simple terms the clash is between rationalism and indeterminism. Modernism assumes monolithic and universal discourse that assumes already existing answers to questions and hence is totalising and controlling. Language expresses something other than itself. Mastery and domination is achieved by destruction of opposition in the cause of perfection of humanity through rational thought. Post-modernism suggests, however, that language forms systems that are self-referential, that human beings construct interpretations of the world (in language "systems") which have no absolute or universal status. Mastery and domination obtains vitality by maintaining difference and provocation and humanity is determined through forces that lie beyond human beings.

A first critique of complementarism in these terms (and only a first, post-modern thought demanding much more yet) has led to a second-stage redefinition. With Foucaulvian thought we understand that language "systems," each assuming a knowledge, are typically subjugated by dominant discourse. There is a need to "liberate" knowledges, for without such an attack we begin our scholarly efforts with diminished intellectual possibilities. Having grown a diversity we then need to critique that in terms of an adequate epistemology for systems practice. This is the basis of a second-stage redefinition that logically needs to be extended into the process "liberate, critique, empower and transform." This is what I currently term "liberating systems theory," which has two sets of related methodological approaches, one set for theory development and the other for "problem solving."

This refreshing new vision of management and systems sciences sets many new challenges for the discipline. It offers a way out of the hopelessly stagnant mire in which systemic modernists are stuck.

REFERENCES

Ackoff, R.L. (1981). *Creating the Corporate Future*, John Wiley, New York.

Beer, S. (1985). *Diagnosing the System for Organisations*, John Wiley, New York.

Carter, P., and Jackson, N. (1991). In defence of paradigm incommensurability, *Org. Stud.*, **12**, 109–127.

Checkland, P.B. (1981). *Systems Thinking, Systems Practice*, John Wiley, New York.

Connerton, P. (Ed.) (1976). *Critical Sociology*, Penguin, Harmondsworth.

Cooper, R., and Burrell, G. (1988). Modernism, post-modernism and organisational analysis: an introduction, *Org. Stud.*, **9**, 221–235.

Donaldson, L. (1985). *In Defence of Organsiation Theory: A Reply to Critics*, Chapter 4, Cambridge University Press, Cambridge.

Flood, R.L. (1990a). Liberating systems theory: toward critical systems thinking, *Human Relat.*, **43**, 49–75.

Flood, R.L. (1990b). *Liberating Systems Theory*, Plenum, New York.

Flood, R.L., and Jackson, M.C. (1991). *Creative Problem Solving: Total Systems Intervention*, John Wiley, Chichester.

Foucault, M. (1974). *The Archaeology of Knowledge*, Tavistock, London.

Foucault, M. (1980). *Power/Knowledge: Selected Interviews, and Other Writings 1971–1977*, Harvester Press, Brighton.

Fraser, N. (1981). Foucault on modern power: empirical insights and normative confusions, *Praxis Int.*, **1**, 272–287.

Freundlieb, D. (1989). Rationalism *v.* irrationalism? Habermas' response to Foucault, *Inquiry*, **31**, 171–192.

Gordon, C. (1979). Other inquisitions, *Nous*, **6**.

Habermas, J. (1971). *Knowledge and Human Interests*, Beacon Press, Boston.

Habermas, J. (1985). *Der Philosophische Diskurs der Moderne*, Suhrkamp Verlag, Frankfurt.

Hassard, J. (1988). Overcoming hermeticism in organisation theory: an alternative to paradigm incommensurability, *Hum. Relat.*, **41**, 247–260.

Honneth, A. (1985). *Kritik der Macht*, Suhrkamp Verlag, Frankfurt.

Klir, G. (1985). *Architecture of Systems Problem Solving*, Plenum, New York.

M'Pherson, P.K. (1980). Systems engineering: an approach to whole system design, *Radio Electron. Eng.*, **50**, 545–558.

Mason, R.O., and Mitroff, I.I. (1981). *Challenging Strategic Planning Assumptions: Theory, Cases and Techniques*, John Wiley, New York.

Oliga, J.C. (1990a). Power-ideology matrix in social systems control, Chapter 13 in this book.

Oliga, J.C. (1990b). Ideology and systems emancipation. Paper prepared for the 33rd Annual Meeting of the ISSS, Edinburgh, Scotland.

Roberts, N., Anderson, D., Deal, R., Garet, M., and Shaffer, W. (1983). *Computer Simulation: A System Dynamics Approach*, Addison-Wesley, Reading, Mass.

Smart, B. (1983). *Foucault, Marxism and Critique*, Routledge and Kegan Paul, London.

Ulrich, W. (1983). *Critical Heuristics of Social Planning: A New Approach to Practical Philosophy*, Haupt, Berne.

Ulrich, W. (1987). Critical heuristics of social systems design, Chapter 5 in this book.

Chapter 16

Total Systems Intervention: A Practical Face to Critical Systems Thinking

ROBERT L. FLOOD AND MICHAEL C. JACKSON

INTRODUCTION

Total Systems Intervention (TSI) represents a new approach to planning, designing, "problem-solving" and evaluation. It seeks to pragmatise but not to compromise the main principles of critical systems thinking. It has been used by the authors in consultancy practice, on a paid and unpaid basis, in many organisations in the business, public and voluntary sectors. Many of these consultancy engagements, together with an extended account of TSI, can be found described in *Creative Problem Solving: Total Systems Intervention* (Flood and Jackson, 1991).

The purpose of this paper is to provide a brief introduction to TSI, showing how it relates to critical systems thinking, and to set out a couple of examples of its use. The first part of the paper describes the philosophy, principles and methodology of TSI. The second part of the paper shows how TSI can be employed on the one hand to interrogate other management science or consultancy approaches, to see to what extent they are less than "total," and on the other to guide consultancy interventions. For ease of understanding both these examples concern Total Quality Management (TQM).

Reprinted by permission from *Systems Practice*, Volume 4, 1991
© 1991 Plenum Press, New York

TOTAL SYSTEMS INTERVENTION (TSI)

TSI uses a range of systems "metaphors" to encourage creative thinking about organisations and the difficult issues their managers have to confront. These metaphors are linked by a framework (a "system of systems methodologies") to various systems approaches, so that once agreement is reached about which metaphors are most relevant to an organisation's concerns and problems, an appropriate systems-based intervention methodology (or set of methodologies) can be employed. Choice of an appropriate systems methodology will guide problem management in a way that ensures that it addresses what are found to be the main concerns of the particular organisation involved.

TSI itself is a methodology (or perhaps meta-methodology) which advocates combining three building blocks—systems metaphors, "system of systems methodologies," and the individual systems methodologies—in an interactive manner which is deemed to be particularly powerful and fruitful. In this section of the paper, the logic of the combination, and hence the TSI methodology or process itself, is explored theoretically. First the philosophy of TSI is unearthed, then the principles embedded in the approach (seven in this case) are set out, and finally the phases of the methodology (three in TSI) are described. To bring further clarity to this theoretical exposition two examples of the use of TSI are provided in the second part of the paper.

Philosophy of TSI

The philosophy underpinning TSI is critical systems thinking. Briefly, and for our purposes here, critical systems thinking can be seen as making its stand on three positions. These are "complementarism," "sociological awareness" and the promotion of "human well-being and emancipation". The *complementarist* position in systems thinking is best set out in comparison to the prevailing "pragmatist" and "isolationist" arguments (see Jackson, 1987; Flood, 1989).

Pragmatists argue that management scientists should not concern themselves with "airy-fairy" theoretical issues but concentrate on building up a "tool-kit" of techniques which have been shown to work in practice. This is a popular position among, for example, management consultants anxious to get the job done and keep the client happy. It neglects, however, to consider whether better results might be obtained if more theoretically guided interventions were made. It fails to recognise that learning can take place only if practice (successful or otherwise) can be related back to a set of theoretical presuppositions which are being consciously tested through that practice. In elevating "what works in practice" to the position of deciding between "good" and "bad" interventions, the possibility that factors other than "proper" method or methodology choice (e.g. simply serving the powerful) might be the reason behind success is excluded from consideration. Finally, it follows that pragmatism abandons the hope of developing management science as an intellectual discipline, the main tenets of which can be passed on to "apprentices."

Isolationism in its most primitive form implies sticking to one method or methodology only, because the analyst knows and wants to know no other approach. More sophisticated isolationists engage in a kind of "imperialism," adhering stolidly to one well worked out theoretical position and linked methodology, but adapting other methods and methodologies for use under the tutelage of the preferred theoretical position. This has the inevitable effect of distorting the methods or methodologies chosen for incorporation, with a consequent loss of the force they command when properly used in the service of their more appropriate theoretical rationalities. Isolationism divides management science and the systems community into warring factions, each arguing for the primacy of their favoured approach—whether it be hard (approaches based on means–end), soft (approaches based on interpretations and their interrelations) or cybernetic (approaches based on laws of organisation)—and its ability to tackle all (or the great majority) of "problem types."

Complementarism is steadfastly opposed to the "pick and mix" strategy of the pragmatists. Different methodologies express different rationalities stemming from alternative theoretical positions which they reflect. These alternative positions must be respected, and methodologies and their appropriate theoretical underpinnings developed in partnership. Further, the claim of any one theoretical rationality to be the sole legitimate one (isolationism) or to absorb all others (imperialism) must be resisted. This should not lead the management science community to fragment into independent groups. As the discussion of systems metaphors and the "systems of systems methodologies" will show, the existence of a range of systems methodologies, each driven by a different theoretical position, can be seen as a strength rather than as a weakness of the systems movement. All that is required is the guidance offered by complementarism so that each methodology is put to work only on the kinds of issues or "problems" for which it is the most suitable.

The *sociological awareness* of critical systems thinking, which is necessarily incorporated into TSI, recognises that there are organisational and societal pressures which have led to certain systems methodologies being popular for guiding interventions at particular times. For example, it was inconceivable that soft systems thinking could ever have become popular in Eastern European countries dominated by the Stalinist bureaucratic dictates of the one party system. With the move towards free-market capitalism and political pluralism, however, one can expect that the circumstances which allowed "hard" and "cybernetic" approaches to "succeed" will change, and that softer approaches will become more acceptable. From another angle we could point to a dominant or institutionalised view of knowledge, such as the traditional rational scientific approach, dictating which methodologies are legitimate. These are examples which suggest why it is important to enquire into the popularity or otherwise of certain systems approaches in given circumstances, and to "liberate" those which are illegitimately suppressed.

It is the same sociological awareness which should make users of TSI contemplate the social consequences of using particular methodologies. For example, the choice of a "hard" or cybernetic methodology implies that one goal or objective is being privileged at the expense of other possibilities. Is this goal or objective general to all organisational stakeholders, or is it simply that of the most powerful? Similarly, the use of "soft" systems methodologies, which are dependent upon open and free debate for the justification of their results, might have deleterious social consequences if the conditions for such debate were absent.

Critical systems thinking, and the thrust of TSI therefore, is *emancipatory* in that it seeks to achieve for all individuals, working through organisations and in society, the maximum development of their potential. This indeed is the basis on which "complementarism" discussed above can be grounded and guided. As Jurgen Habermas (1972) has argued, there are two fundamental conditions underpinning the socio-cultural form of life in the human species. These he calls "work" and "interaction." "Work" enables human beings to achieve goals and to bring about material well-being through social labour. Its success depends upon achieving technical mastery over natural and social processes. The importance of work leads human beings to have a "technical interest" in the prediction and control of natural and social affairs. This is one of two anthropologically based cognitive interests which Habermas believes the human species possesses. The other is linked to "interaction" and is labelled the "practical interest". Its concern is with securing and expanding the possibilities for mutual understanding among all those involved in social systems. Disagreement between different groups can be just as much a threat to the reproduction of the socio-cultural form of life as a failure to predict and control natural and social processes.

While work and interaction have for Habermas pre-eminent anthropological status, the analysis of "power" and the way it is exercised is equally important, Habermas argues, if we are to understand past and present social arrangements. The exercise of power in the social process can prevent the open and free discussion necessary for the success of interaction. Human beings have, therefore, an "emancipatory interest" in freeing themselves from constraints imposed by power relations and in learning, through a process of genuine participatory democracy, involving discursive will-formation, to control their own destiny.

Now, if we all have a technical, a practical and an emancipatory interest in the functioning of organisations and society, then a management science which can support all these various interests has an important role to play in human well-being and emancipation. But this is exactly what complementarism and sociologically aware systems thinking can provide. It is clear that hard and cybernetic systems approaches can support the technical interest, soft methodologies the practical interest, and critical systems heuristics can aid the emancipatory interest.

So much for the philosophy of TSI, which comes through in the principles and practice, and should be known and respected by all who would use this approach.

Principles of TSI

There are seven principles embedded in the three phases of TSI. These are:

1. Organisations are too complicated to understand using one management "model" and their problems too complex to tackle with the "quick fix."
2. Organisations, their strategies and the difficulties they face should be investigated using a range of systems metaphors.
3. Systems metaphors which seem appropriate for highlighting organisational strategies and problems can be linked to appropriate systems methodologies to guide intervention.
4. Different systems metaphors and methodologies can be used in a complementary way to address different aspects of organisations and their problems.
5. It is possible to appreciate the strengths and weaknesses of different systems methodologies and to relate each to appropriate organisational concerns.
6. TSI sets out a systemic cycle of inquiry with iteration back and forth between the 3 phases.
7. Facilitators, clients and others are engaged at all stages of the TSI process.

TSI Methodology

The three phases of TSI are labelled "creativity," "choice" and "implementation." We shall consider these in turn, looking in each case at the task to be accomplished during that phase, the tools provided by TSI to realise that task, and the outcome or results expected from the phase.

Creativity

The *task* during the creativity phase is to use systems metaphors as organising structures to help managers think creatively about their enterprises. The sort of questions it would be pertinent to ask are:

1. Which metaphors reflect current thinking about organisational strategies, structures, and control and information systems (including past, present and future concerns)?
2. Which alternative metaphors might capture better what more desirably could be achieved with this organisation?
3. Which metaphors make sense of this organisation's difficulties and concerns?

The *tools* provided by TSI to assist this process are "systems metaphors." Different metaphors focus attention on different aspects of an organisation's functioning. Some concentrate on organisational structure, others highlight human and political aspects of an organisation. Some examples are:

1. the organisation as a "machine" (closed system view);
2. the organisation as an "organism" (open system view);
3. the organisation as a "brain" (learning system view);
4. the organisation as a "culture" (emphasis on norms and values);
5. the organisation as a "team" (unitary political system);
6. the organisation as a "coalition" (pluralist political system);
7. the organisation as a "prison" (coercive political system).

The main aspects of organisations highlighted, and those aspects neglected, by each metaphor will be disclosed in order to enhance discussion and debate.

The *outcome* (what is expected to emerge) from the creativity phase is a "dominant" metaphor which highlights the main interests and concerns and can become the basis for a choice of an appropriate intervention methodology. There may be other metaphors which it is also sensible to pursue into the next phase. The relative position of dominant and these "dependent" metaphors may indeed be altered by later work. If all the metaphors reveal serious problems then the organisation is obviously in a crisis state.

Choice

The *task* during the "choice" phase is to choose an appropriate systems-based intervention methodology (or set of methodologies) to suit particular characteristics of the organisation's situation as revealed by the examination conducted in the creativity phase.

The *tools* provided by TSI to help with this stage are the guidelines of the "system of systems methodologies" (as set out in Table 16.1) and, derived from that, knowledge of the underlying metaphors employed by systems methodologies.

Although it would be possible to link systems methodologies and systems metaphors directly, the pattern in the variety of systems methodologies is best

Table 16.1 A system of systems methodologies

	UNITARY	PLURALIST	COERCIVE
SIMPLE	S–U • Operational research • Systems analysis • Systems engineering	S–P • Social systems design • Strategic assumption surfacing and testing	S–C • Critical systems heuristics
COMPLEX	C–U • Cybernetics • GST • Socio-tech • Contingency theory	C–P • Soft systems methodology • Interactive planning	C–C

discerned if the link is made through the "system of systems methodologies." In constructing the "system of systems methodologies" it is necessary to unearth the assumptions underlying different systems approaches. This is done by asking what each assumes about the "system(s)" with which it deals and about the relationship between the "actors" concerned with that system. Systems may be viewed as being relatively simple or complex (according to the metaphors which highlight structure), giving rise to "simple" or "complex" "problem-contexts." Actors can be in a unitary, pluralist or coercive relationship to one another (according to the metaphors which emphasise human and political concerns) and so problem-contexts can be similarly labelled. Putting these points together in a matrix, it is apparent that systems methodologies can be classified according to whether they assume problem-contexts to be simple–unitary, simple–pluralist, complex–unitary, complex–pluralist, simple–coercive or complex–coercive. Some common systems methodologies are classified according to this matrix in Table 16.1.

Combining the information gained about the problem-context during the creativity phase, and the knowledge provided by the "system of systems methodologies" about the assumptions underlying different systems approaches, it is possible to move towards an appropriate choice of systems intervention methodology. For example, if the problem-context is characterised by there being clear and agreed objectives (unitary) and by being transparent enough so that it can be captured in a mathematical model (simple), then a methodology based upon simple–unitary assumptions can be used with every hope of success.

On the basis of the "system of systems methodologies" it is possible to relate

Table 16.2 Example systems methodologies related to systems metaphors

Systems methodology (examples)	Assumptions about problem-contexts	Underlying Metaphors
Operational research	S–U	Machine Team
Cybernetics	C–U	Organism Brain Team
SAST (strategic assumption surfacing and testing)	S–P	Machine Coalition Culture
Soft systems methodology	C–P	Organism Coalition Culture
Critical systems heuristics	S–C	Machine/ Organism Prison

individual methodologies to the systems metaphors previously described, as in Table 16.2. Bearing in mind the metaphors which came out as "dominant" and "dependent" during the "creativity" phase and the conclusions of the "system of systems methodologies", appropriate choice of systems methodology (systems methodologies) to guide intervention and change can now be made.

The most probable *outcome* of the "choice" phase is that there will be a "dominant" methodology chosen, to be tempered in use by the imperatives highlighted by "dependent" methodologies.

Implementation

The *task* during the implementation phase is to employ a particular systems methodology (systems methodologies) to translate the dominant vision of the organisation, its structure, and the general orientation adopted to concerns and problems, into specific proposals for change.

The *tools* provided by TSI are the specific systems methodologies used according to the logic of TSI. The dominant methodology operationalises the vision of the organisation contained in the dominant metaphor. The logic of TSI demands, however, that consideration continues to be given to the imperatives of other methodologies. For example, the key difficulties in an organisation suffering from structural collapse may be best highlighted using the metaphors of "organism" and "brain," but the "cultural" metaphor might also appear illuminating, if in a subordinate way given the immediate crisis. In these circumstances a cybernetic methodology would be chosen to guide the intervention, but perhaps tempered by some ideas from soft systems methodology. Managers in another organisation might wish to redesign their information system but be held back by conflicting views about where the organisation should be going, exacerbated by some political in-fighting. This situation might usefully be understood with the "coalition" metaphor as dominant, but with the "brain" and "prison" metaphors also being illuminating. In this case soft systems methodology might guide the intervention but with aspects of cybernetics and critical systems heuristics also being used.

The *outcome* of the implementation stage is coordinated change brought about in those aspects of the organisation currently most vital for its effective and efficient functioning.

The three-stage methodoology of TSI is set out in Table 16.3. It is important to stress, however, that TSI is a systemic and iterative methodology (see Figure 16.1.) It asks, during each phase, that continual reference be made, back or forth, to the likely conclusions of other phases. So, for example, during phase 1, "creativity," attempts are made to anticipate the likely consequences of particular visions of the organisation's structure, and information and control requirements.

TSI IN ACTION

We are now in a position to consider TSI in action. We shall provide two examples both of which involve, to some degree, TQM and probably demand a little prior knowledge of that area. Those without that knowledge might consult Thorn (1988) or books by the quality "gurus" Crosby, Deming and Juran.

Our first example takes TQM itself as its object of attention. It asks what systems metaphors TQM invokes and which it ignores, and reveals therefore how comprehensive it is as a strategy of intervention. Readers might like to consider the same evidence asking what problem-contexts are addressed by TQM and which are ignored. The logic of our argument is that any intervention approach takes, implicitly, some view of the situations for which it is designed and employs methods and techniques corresponding to that view. TSI tries to take a comprehensive view based around a range of metaphors and to employ a comprehensive set of methods and techniques. It is therefore able to judge other intervention methodologies, such as TQM, as to their comprehensiveness or lack of it.

The second example is of a real-world consultancy engagement in which TSI was used to guide an organisation through the various stages necessary before

Table 16.3 The three phase TSI methodology

CREATIVITY

Task	• to highlight aims, concerns and problems
Tools	• systems metaphors
Outcome	• "dominant" and "dependent" metaphors highlighting the major issues

CHOICE

Task	• to choose an appropriate systems based intervention methodology (methodologies)
Tools	• the "system of systems methodologies", the relationship between metaphors and methodologies
Outcome	• "dominant" and "dependent" methodologies chosen for use

IMPLEMENTATION

Task	• to arrive at and implement specific change proposals
Tools	• systems methodologies employed according to the logic of TSI
Outcome	• highly relevant and coordinated intervention

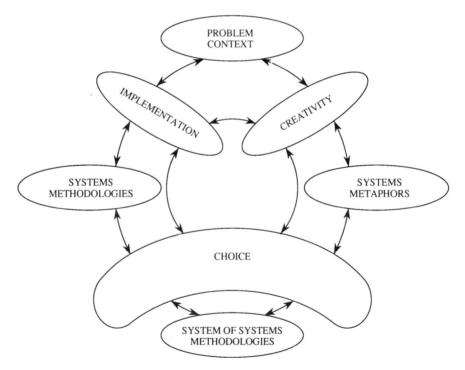

Figure 16.1 The process of TSI

it was ready to accept and implement an appropriate quality management programme.

Systems Metaphors and TQM

We have been involved in specific consultancies working with Total Quality Management, and enhancing our understanding of its philosophy and process through creative use of the systems metaphors has proved to be extremely beneficial. To get the most out of these differing experiences, and to maintain the anonymity of our clients, we present here the general case for TQM. This is done by going through the main points of the philosophy and principles of TQM and suggesting (in parenthesis) what systems metaphor is being invoked by each point. We will then consider the methodology of implementation.

1. There is an emphasis on communication:

   (a) within each part, functional, local homeostasis (a living cell, organic);
   (b) between parts, functional, overall internal homeostasis (an organism, organic); and
   (c) between relevant parts and an environment, open homeostasis, even symbiosis (an organism or perhaps ecological, organic).

2. There is an emphasis on control:
   (a) set clear targets (machine, mechanical);
   (b) drill of team briefing (machine, mechanical);
   (c) consultation for organisation-wide expertise (learning, neuro-cybernetic).

   There are hints, therefore, of mechanical and neurocybernetic thinking in TQM. There are clearer signs of the organic metaphor, drawn from ideas about the cell, the organism and ecology.
   What is even more striking, however, is the emphasis placed on developing cohesion and a common culture. The cultural metaphor is invoked for the possibilities it offers for generating commitment among employees to quality.

3. There is an emphasis on collaboration, and on all employees "owning" quality (culture). TQM encourages:

   (a) greater harmonisation in terms and conditions, thus creating a sense of belonging;
   (b) a collaborative community-like spirit, an emphasis on customer service between departments;
   (c) a collectivity, project teams pursuing a "company-wide policy";

(d) a mutual sense of belonging, all employees are part of the quality culture;

(e) certain practices to be deemed normal and desirable; and

(f) a shared language, the "total quality language."

It is now possible to consider TQM and the metaphors it employs to understand and intervene in organisations, and to ask what possible difficulties might be encountered with TQM. This is done by looking at the limitations of the two major systems metaphors it implicitly uses (the organic and the cultural). In fact we have encountered all these problems in our consultancy practice.

1. An organic view may lead to:

   (a) an emphasis on harmonious relations with no way of dealing with issues of conflict/coercion—we have encountered divergences of opinion among those involved in a TQM programme on matters such as "Who owns and controls quality?"; and

   (b) too little attention being paid to the issue that organisations are socially constructed phenomena and to internally generated change—which in TQM practice are largely overcome by simultaneous use of the cultural perspective.

2. A cultural view may lead to:

   (a) feelings of ideological control, manipulation and mistrust—which, in one large organisation with which we had dealings—did prevail in some localities;

   (b) difficulties with installation—we found that, in some cases, attempts were made to sweep TQM in overnight, but a culture takes time to evolve;

   (c) prevention of instalment if political forces prevail and are ignored; and

   (d) lack of guidance on how to structure an organisation   overcome in the TQM case by simultaneous use of organic thinking.

Turning to the methodology of implementation of TQM, implicit reference to the various metaphors can also be found. The nature of the relationship between participants is assumed to be unitary and this implies no difficulty in setting a clear and generally acceptable mission. This unitary or "team" setting of the political metaphor is usually found accompanying the machine, organism and brain metaphors. The idea of spreading the quality mission by giving each department an "identity" in the quality programme hints at further neurocybernetic thinking. There is much emphasis on control and measurement to be realised through the usual structure of a hierarchical company tree.

This reflects machine thinking based on Taylorist and Weberian organisation theory. Finally, education and training is evidently all about establishing a quality culture in the company.

The account and analysis provided above shows how TQM implicitly draws upon a number of metaphors. The cultural metaphor is dominant, but the organic is also strongly present, and there are elements of machine and neurocybernetic thinking. TQM draws much of its strength from this mixing of metaphors and the consequent range of strategies that it employs. Its weaknesses tend to arise because the "coalition" and "prison" aspects of the political metaphor, and the lessons that could be learnt from using these, are ignored. Obviously it is highly illuminating of TQM to consider it in this creative way using the systemic metaphors, part of the TSI armoury. Hopefully it helps suggest the power of TSI itself, which is able consciously and explicitly to draw on all the metaphors, and a full range of systems methodologies equipped to respond to the lessons learnt from employing any of the metaphors to examine problem situations.

Intervention and Total Quality Management (TQM)

The problem situation initially confronted was a "mess," one that had not been tackled through any rigorous means of inquiry, just being left to take its own course. The organisation, that we will label "Gek Mui Enterprises" (it was a South East Asian company), was suffering from decreasing orders and loss of market share in a buoyant market. The Sales Director detested the Company Secretary. This conflict came to a head when new credit control rulings were introduced which were very strict, and amounted to a drastic change in policy for a company that had traditionally been sales oriented (i.e. customers paid as and when they chose, some debtors frequently running to sixty or even ninety days). The Company Secretary's concern for cash flow seemed understandable, but the poor relationship between him and the Sales Director prevented there being a coherent Board view. The customers, not being used to strict credit control, frequently rang the Sales Director complaining bitterly. This antagonised the Sales Director even more. Accentuating these difficulties, the Managing Director was clearly sales oriented too.

Morale in the Accounting and Finance Department was at an all time low for several reasons. As a consequence of the sales orientation of the company, accountants and finance clerks were seen as the "poor people" doing a low grade job. Members of staff in this service function were consequently subjected to various jibes and were quite prepared to believe them to be true. Even worse, these groups had experienced an unusually high turnover of staff, particularly in management functions, and it was therefore impossible to achieve continuity in relations within or externally to the organisation. A related difficulty concerned the Management Information Systems (MIS). MIS were closely linked to the finance and accounting groupings. The theory was that data would therefore be readily accessible. The MIS group consisted of mathematicians and statisticians, whose job it was to convert the data into specified information. Speed and accuracy were vital but missing, and the feeling was that if Sales were so superior then they undoubtedly could manage as an autonomous function—"let them do their own dirty work." In order to promote access to information, a "hot line" between the MIS manageress and the Managing and Sales Directors was installed. The MIS manageress was expected always to be available and she resented this. She was seen as a stooge for the sales group by her own staff. Another problem with the MIS was that the only information analysed was that which arose naturally within the organisation. External information gathering had never been carried out.

Although these emerged as the main features of the situation, the organisation more generally suffered from poor internal communications and lack of motivation among staff.

Systems metaphors were used in a direct yet *invisible* way to develop an appreciation and understanding of the situation. It was the ideas underpinning the metaphors rather than the metaphors themselves which were exposed to those involved in the intervention. Rather than adopting the straightforward style of asking employees, etc., whether they considered the organisation could or should be considered like a brain, we would look for certain features like volatility of environment, clear organisational mission (i.e. identity) and examine issues relating to control, coordination, commitment, measures of performance, etc. Rather than posing questions such as "Is the organisation like, or ought it be like a machine?", we would consider issues of hierarchy, division of labour, standardised parts, non-adaptability, etc.

The process of creative thinking can be prompted, not only through ideas of "likeness," but also by adopting a dialectical approach; asking when particular metaphors break down in practice and comparing and contrasting the different visions provided by alternative metaphors. The critical process we undertook went as follows:

1. Use metaphors to help enrich perceptions. Ask, When would metaphor "x" be useful in practice? (likeness).
2. Use metaphors to challenge perceptions. Ask, When would metaphor "x" break down in practice? (challenge).
3. Carry out (1) and (2) for other metaphors.
4. Mix and enrich—mix metaphors to seek further likeness and make further challenges.
5. Remix metaphors to further enrich perceptions.
6. By synthesis and resynthesis, move toward appreciation of a dominant and some supporting metaphors.

Using the findings that emerged from the logic and process above, we drew upon the "system of systems methodologies" to guide choice of a relevant "problem solving" approach. This was carried out whilst recognising that TSI emphasises the possibility of a shifting dominance in metaphor and methodology, and the need to continually keep an eye open for this.

Exploring with metaphors led us to believe that there was a desperate need to promote a shared culture in the organisation, particularly because of the fragmentation in the "coalition." In addition, the nature of the business context pointed to the need for substantial evolutionary developments in the firm, the whole situation being characterised by many features of great complexity. With further guidance from the ideals of the "system of systems methodologies," we chose a soft systems methodology, SSM, which assumed that the nature of social and organisational reality was "complex" as well as "cultural" (i.e. SSM was chosen to be dominant at the outset). SSM undeniably can help in pluralistic contexts and would lead to further clarification of what could be done in the future (beyond perhaps any ideas yet conceived) while maintaining some sympathy for organic needs.

The soft systems analysis led us to conclude that there was a need for a "customer satisfaction system," or perhaps more ambitiously a "Total Quality Management" system. This should lead to greater cohesion and help to convince lost customers to place their business with Gek Mui Enterprises once again. That was a good starting point and a coalition genuinely formed and agreed upon the need for quality issues to be addressed. But there was some substantial dispute about the nature of the implementation that would be required.

The Managing Director and a large part of the normal decision making body believed that implementation should be "top down" and that this implied nothing by way of changes in organisation (a major selling point promoted by traditionalist TQM gurus such as Crosby). It was felt that TQM was simply a matter of attitude change and that all efforts should be directed to this end. Some representatives, mainly from "operations," were, however, unhappy about the top-down approach and felt that there were more immediate difficulties to face up to, in terms of organisation in the short term, and that the introduction of TQM *did* imply organisational change as well as attitudinal change.

At this stage strategic assumption surfacing and testing (SAST) was drawn upon to look closely into the assumptions implied by each of the two views. This was certainly logical because the notion of pluralism and culture remained dominant, but now the issues were much more clear-cut. We needed to consider the two interdependent "solutions" and, in particular, to seriously challenge the accepted top-down way of doing TQM. One policy option that diverged considerably from the traditional top-down view had emerged. If we could dialectically resolve these issues by testing strategic assumptions, then we might be ready to change dominant metaphor and methodology again by moving from a "what" methodology (pluralist) to a "how" methodology (unitary). This is consistent with the philosophy of SAST, that once we have dealt with pluralism then we can relatively easily deal with the remaining technical matters through appropriate methods.

At the same time and to enhance the SAST process, systems metaphors were drawn upon to critique TQM (along the lines of the previous example). This effort highlighted the mechanical viewpoint that the Managing Director and other "top-down" supporters assumed. They were considering, as dialectical debate revealed, that Quality Councils should be organised according to the standard bureaucratic organisational tree. This is precisely what TQM gurus suggest. Alternative styles of implementation were brought out by the SAST debate. The principles of TQM were found to be open to metaphorical reinterpretation. It was decided that if quality were to be ensured in this organisation, subject to a volatile environment, then viability would have to become a major consideration.

If we remind ourselves of our previous examination of TQM using systems metaphors, then we will remember that a neurocybernetic view, although present, was not dominant. In this case, however, we decided to use Beer's (1985) cybernetic, "viable system model" to reinterpret some of the ideas of TQM as traditionally conceived. For example, why implement an "identity" down a company hierarchical tree when the VSM has an exceptional contribution to make through recursivity? Also, if we are thinking about continuous learning and improvement then the VSM again shows its strength. This is also the case with auditing of quality and the idea of measures of performance. More generally, can we honestly claim to have a "quality system," or expect to realise the ongoing benefits of one, if we cannot guarantee viability? In short, the principles of TQM and a viable system approach, as we interpreted them, were seen to be highly compatible for Gek Mui Enterprises.

The rest of this diary would amount to technical description and is not included because the purpose of this case study is to examine the logic and process of TSI in action. What we hope has emerged from this account is the highly iterative and systemic nature of TSI, and the realisation by readers that any kind of systematised use of TSI would be unacceptable, and will lack in main emphasis that which we wish to promote—i.e. creativity.

CONCLUSION

We have described the philosophy, principles and methodology of TSI and shown the approach at work in two examples. The reason for including a paper on TSI in this book is that it offers a practical face of critical systems thinking. It will be clear that TSI is complementarist, using a range of systems methodologies chosen according to theoretical consideration of their strengths and weaknesses. TSI is sociologically aware, promoting as many ways of looking at organisations as are readily available in the management and social theory literature, and being conscious of the consequences of taking particular views. TSI also demands that attention be given to human well-being and emancipation by constantly requiring that human issues be brought as much into focus as technical concerns, and by being continuously on the lookout for the existence of coercion (the "prison" metaphor and simple–coercive and complex–coercive contexts).

We hope, therefore, that this paper will assist readers in their own deliberations about how best to apply critical systems ideas in their working and everyday lives.

REFERENCES

Beer, S. (1985). *Diagnosing the System for Organisations*, John Wiley, Chichester.
Flood, R.L. (1989). Six scenarios for the future of systems "problem solving", *Syst. Pract.*, **2**, 75–99.
Flood, R.L., and Jackson, M.C. (1991). *Creative Problem Solving: Total Systems Intervention*, John Wiley, Chichester.
Habermas, J. (1972). *Knowledge and Human Interests*, Heinemann, London.
Jackson, M.C. (1987). Present positions and future prospects in management science, *Omega*, **15**, 455–466.
Thorn, J. (1988). Zeroing in on total quality, *Industrial Society Magazine*, September, pp. 20–21.

Conclusion

In this book we have traced the development of systems thinking as it has unfolded over the last decade or so. First we looked "Beyond Operational Research and Hard Systems Thinking" with the internationally renowned authors Churchman, Ackoff and Checkland. We explained the reasons behind the emergence of a soft systems paradigm to counter the hard one. The main differences between the two are that soft systems reflects interpretive rather than positivist theory, focuses on qualitative rather than quantitative analysis and aims to manage messes adequately rather than to solve problems correctly.

But subjects do not stand still. We showed this to be the case for systems thinking in the section recounting "The Break With Soft Systems Thinking" and the emergence of critical systems thinking. We argued that critical systems thinking has three main lines of development, or commitments as Schecter called them. These are emancipatory practice, adoption of a complementarist style and a critically reflective attitude. Analysis of hard approaches using these commitments shows hard to be conservative in all cases, to reject the idea of complementarism by seeking correct methods for optimisation, and to be critical only in the sense of falsification of theories. Analysis of soft approaches with the three commitments shows soft to be conservative in the face of power inequalities, to have a superficial understanding of complementarism, and to assume a critical attitude which deals only with exposition of ideas. The triple commitment of critical systems thinking is to be emancipatory in all cases, to adopt complementarism with an open and conciliatory style, and therefore to have a critically reflective attitude which is both emancipatory and complementarist.

Given this clear understanding of the new critical school, we were able to press on and to arrive at "Contemporary Critical Systems Theory and Practice." In this section we pointed to key developments and recognised the diverse nature of critical systems thinking. But even with this diversity, it is still possible to construct a meaningful framework through which we can capture and, to some extent, project the future directions of critical systems thinking.

Critical Systems Thinking: Directed Readings. Edited by R.L. Flood and M.C. Jackson
© 1991 John Wiley & Sons Ltd

To achieve this, however, we need to call upon the help of a number of our colleagues.

In February 1990 a group of researchers and practitioners[1] who identify themselves with critical systems thinking, and who wished to clarify its intent and purpose, met up in Merida, Venezuela. After three days of intensive discussion, the group managed to organise research and development in a way that explained critical systems theory and practice. We will conclude this book by describing the framework and identifying how the developments discussed in Parts Two and Three blend with its logic.

The following five "levels" were found to be successful in producing a synthesis of the work in critical systems thinking; meta-theory, theory, practice, politics of science, and the politics of strategy.

The *meta-theory* level encompasses two subdivisions—the meta-paradigmatic and the paradigmatic. The first focuses on issues brought about by the existence of multiple paradigms; the second deals with fundamental issues such as ontology, epistemology, methodology, and ideology.

Whereas the meta-theory level deals with theory about theory, the *theory level* deals with theory about the social world (e.g. anthropological, sociological, economic and political theories).

The *practical level* comprises two subdivisons—social practice and reflective practice. The first works on the development of tools and methods for social practice whilst the second is the application of critique in reflective practice.

Another level is the *politics of science*, which aims to avoid dangers and pitfalls of hidden value biases as they affect scientific work. Examples of relevant critical questions are: "What ideals are we serving?" and "Who are we serving?"

An altogether different level is the *politics of strategy*, which aims to overcome the difficulty that good ideas are usually not enough. Ultimately the success of any project will depend on taking deliberate action to win the support of relevant parties. This level focuses on the need for such action.

Critical systems thinking can be conveniently understood in terms of the five levels described above. The work also can be understood as a process leading to progressive change in social order. This process starts with a critical aim *to liberate* knowledges and logically derived methodologies which have been suppressed by institutional forces. This critique helps to overcome diminished intellectual possibilities from the start. A task closely related to liberating knowledges is *to critique* their rationalities. The result is a clear articulation of their legitimacies and limitations. The "starting" process of liberating knowledges and methodologies, and critiquing their rationality, helps us to build a strong and relevant capability *to empower* those who are oppressed and *to transform* the social structures which are oppressive. The

---

[1] The participants were Robert L. Flood, Ramses Fuenmayor, John C. Oliga, David Schecter, and Werner Ulrich, with contributions from Michael C. Jackson.

Table 1 The programme of research and development for critical systems thinking: Five levels of study and the process of change

	Liberate	Critique	Empower	Transform
Meta-Theory	>	>	>	>
Theory	>	>	>	>
Practice	>	>	>	>
Science—politics of	>	>	>	>
Strategy—politics of	>	>	>	>

whole process is to liberate, to critique, to empower and to transform. It is a never-ending Singerian inquiry of the sort that Churchman was advocating at the outset of the critical endeavour.

The logic of the five levels couples with the process just described to form a framework which organises the research and development programme of critical systems thinking (see the table). The programme recorded in this book will now be explained in these terms. We will present these under the headings of the five levels. The main commitment(s) is (are) recorded in brackets. The process "liberate, critique, empower and transform" is implicit in the explanations.

Meta-theory Level

- The development of critically normative epistemological frameworks (complementarism).
- The study of difficulties of commensurability between paradigms (complementarism).
- The critical examination of meta-theoretical foundations in ideology and in control and in systems methodologies (emancipation).

Theory Level

- The development of emancipatory theories for social action (emancipation).
- The development of critical social theories of control, power and ideology (emancipation).
- The development of emancipatory theories for liberating subjugated knowledges (emancipation and critique).

Practical Level

- The translation and operationalisation of emancipatory theories for critical systems practice (emancipation).

- The translation and operationalisation of epistemological frameworks to develop heuristic tools for critically normative systems practice (complementarism).
- The translation and operationalisation of theories for liberating subjugated knowledges (complementarism and critique).

Level of Politics of Science

- The promotion of dialogical debates for fostering a dialectical milieu (critique).

Level of Politics of Strategy

- The development of research programmes that advance the systems approach and improve academic curricula (emancipation and critique).
- The colonisation of institutions and mechanisms of domination to promote the cause of critical systems thinking (emancipation and critique).

The above records the research and development programme of critical systems thinking as currently understood by a number of the main contributors. It is an historical overview but also clearly suggests where future work might lie. Such a predictive archaeology is a fitting conclusion to a book that is heralding a whole new approach to the management and systems sciences.

It now remains for us to reiterate the challenge set in the "Preface" and "Overview."

Not everyone will agree with our analysis nor indeed the importance that we attach to critical systems thinking. We hope, however, to have convinced *you* of the value of the changes set out in this book, and the necessity for continued efforts to take systems thinking as a powerful force into the new millenium. If so, then take up the challenge with us and contribute to Part Four of this book which has yet to be written.

Appendix

Further Readings

As stated in the "Overview," critical systems thinking has matured rapidly over the last decade and has a number of major texts already available. These are summarised below.

- Two texts deal with emancipatory systems thinking:
Werner Ulrich (1983). *Critical Heuristics of Social Planning*, Haupt, Berne.
John C. Oliga (1992). *Power, Ideology and Control*, Plenum, New York.

- The following texts offer theses on critical systems thinking:
Robert L. Flood (1990). *Liberating Systems Theory*, Plenum, New York.
Michael C. Jackson (1991). *Systems Methodology for the Management Sciences*, Plenum, New York.
And of course this volume, published in 1991.

- The following text provides a comprehensive account of how to apply critical systems thinking:
Robert L. Flood and Michael C. Jackson (1991). *Creative Problem Solving: Total Systems Intervention*, John Wiley, Chichester.

- A commitment to critical systems thinking can be found in the learned journal *Systems Practice*, edited by Robert L. Flood and published since 1988 by Plenum Press from New York.

Index